Hey! You're Reading in the Wrong Direction!

This is the **end** of this graphic novel!

To properly enjoy this VIZ graphic novel, please turn it around and begin reading from **right to left.** Unlike English, Japanese is read right to left, so Japanese comics are read in reverse order from the way English comics are typically read.

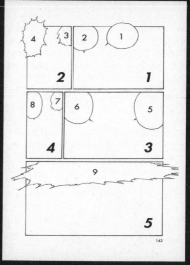

Follow the action this way

This book has been printed in the original Japanese format in order to preserve the orientation of the original artwork. Have fun with it!

TERRA FORMARS

Volume 2
VIZ Signature Edition

Story by YU SASUGA
Art by KENICHI TACHIBANA

TERRA FORMARS © 2011 by Ken-ichi Tachibana,Yu Sasuga/SHUEISHA Inc.
All rights reserved.
First published in Japan in 2011 by SHUEISHA Inc., Tokyo.
English translation rights arranged by SHUEISHA Inc.

Translation & English Adaptation/John Werry
Touch-up Art & Lettering/Annaliese Christman
Design/Izumi Evers
Editor/Mike Montesa

Printed in the U.S.A.

Published by VIZ Media, LLC
P.O. Box 77010
San Francisco, CA 94107

10 9 8 7 6 5 4 3 2 1
First printing, September 2014

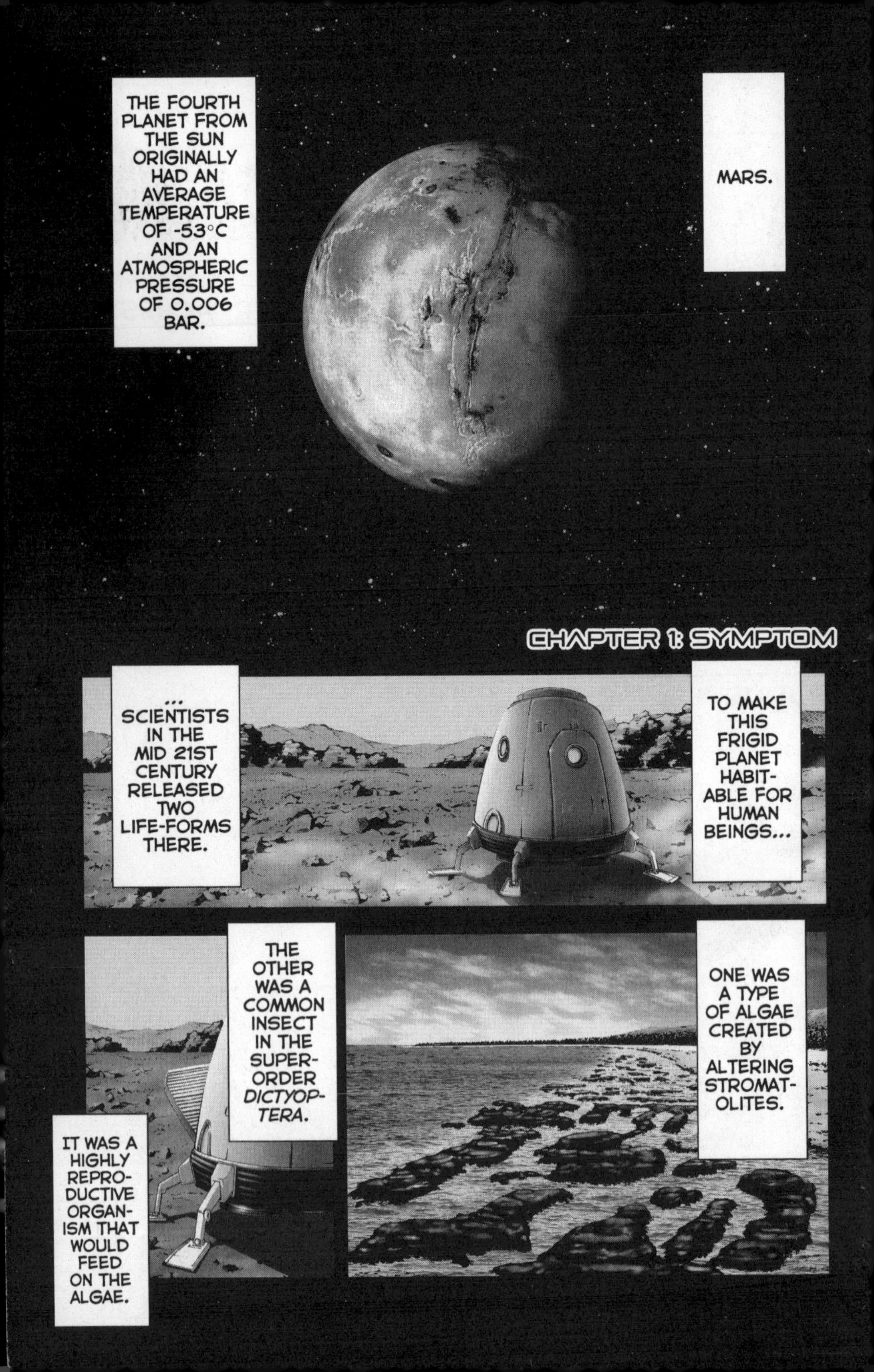
MARS.
THE FOURTH PLANET FROM THE SUN ORIGINALLY HAD AN AVERAGE TEMPERATURE OF -53°C AND AN ATMOSPHERIC PRESSURE OF 0.006 BAR.
CHAPTER 1: SYMPTOM
TO MAKE THIS FRIGID PLANET HABIT-ABLE FOR HUMAN BEINGS...
...SCIENTISTS IN THE MID 21ST CENTURY RELEASED TWO LIFE-FORMS THERE.
ONE WAS A TYPE OF ALGAE CREATED BY ALTERING STROMAT-OLITES.
THE OTHER WAS A COMMON INSECT IN THE SUPER-ORDER *DICTYOP-TERA*.
IT WAS A HIGHLY REPRO-DUCTIVE ORGAN-ISM THAT WOULD FEED ON THE ALGAE.

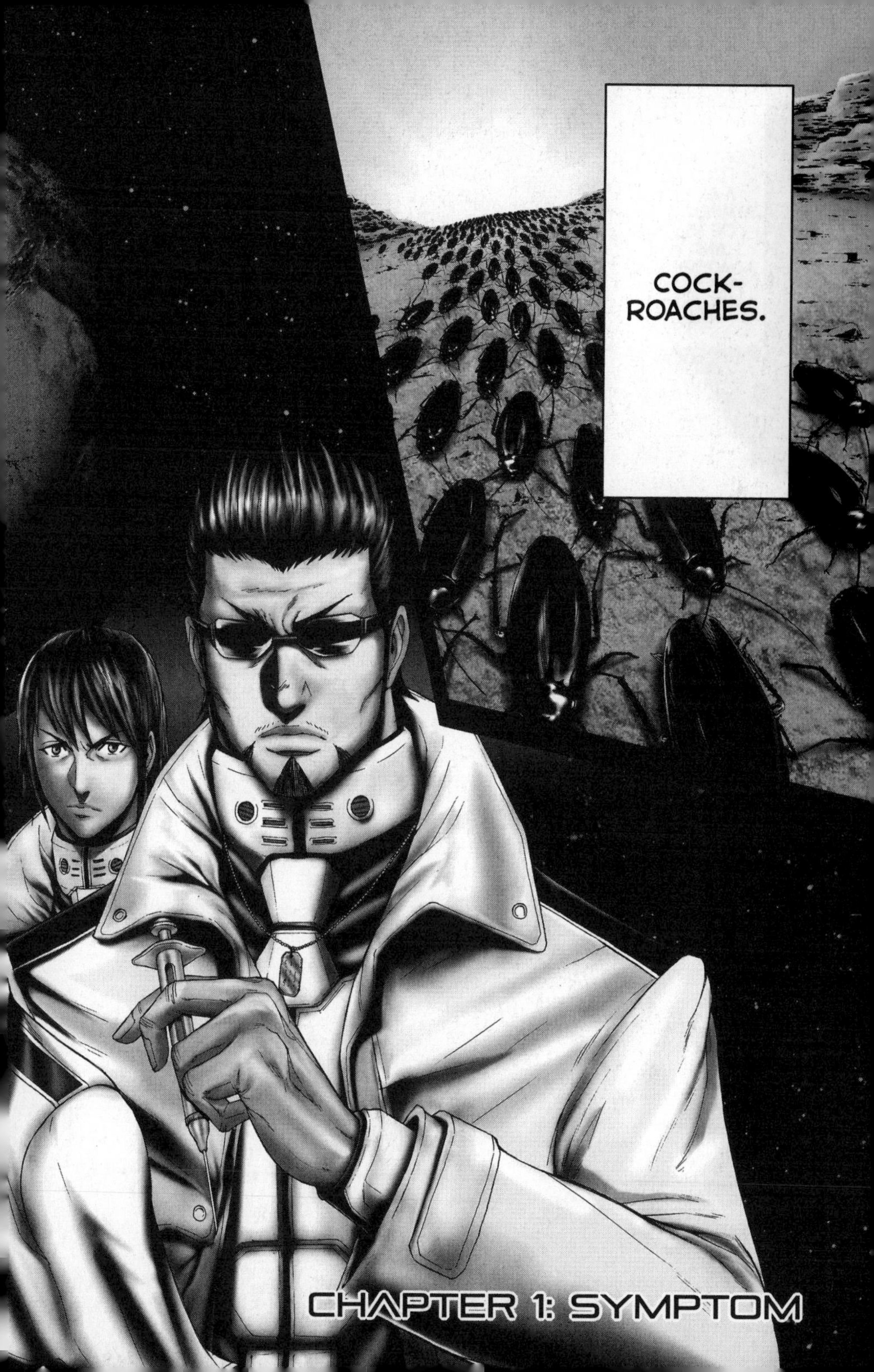
COCK-
ROACHES.
CHAPTER 1: SYMPTOM

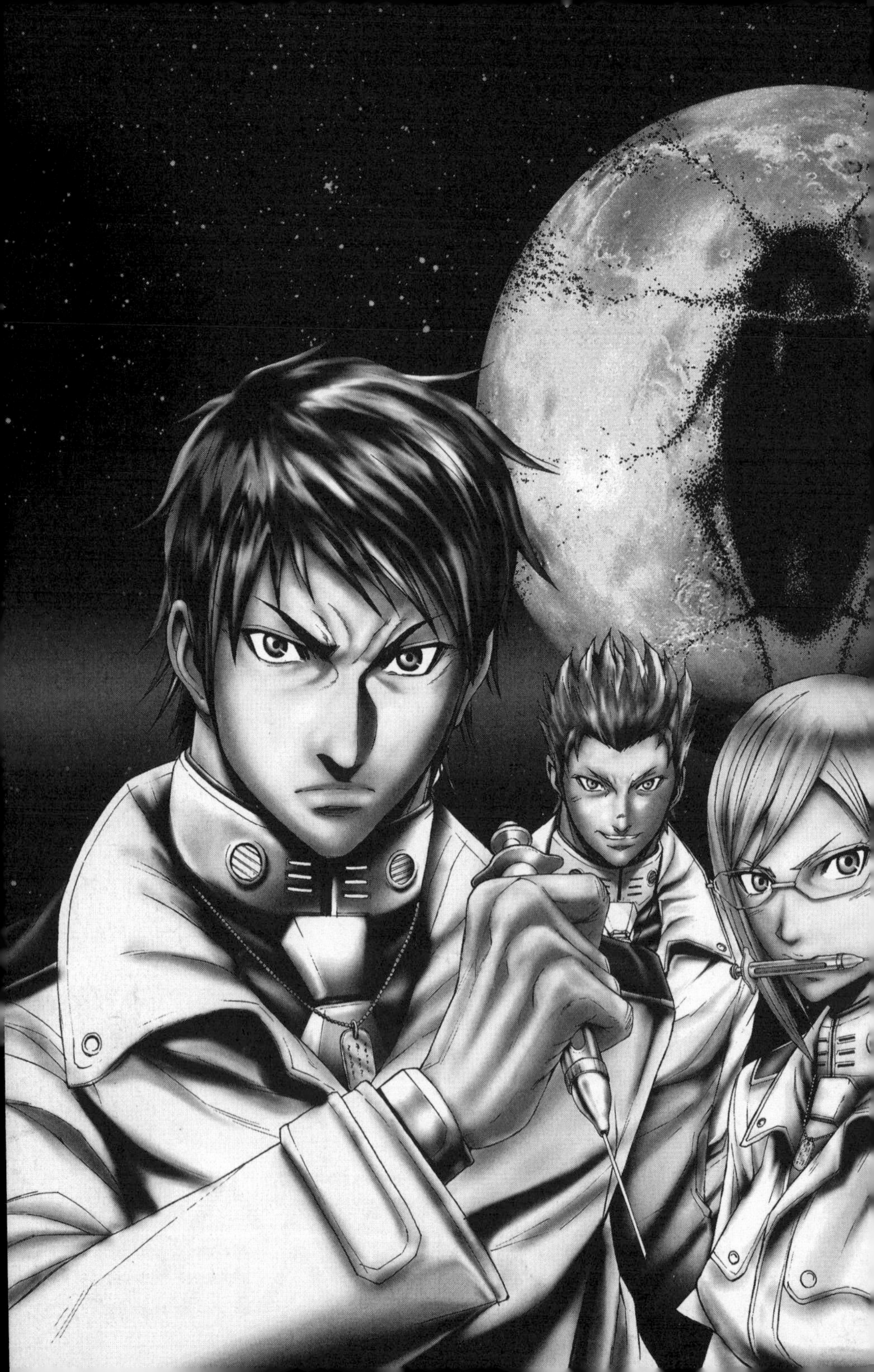

TERRA FORMARS

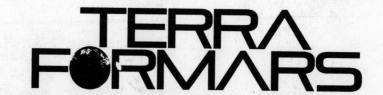

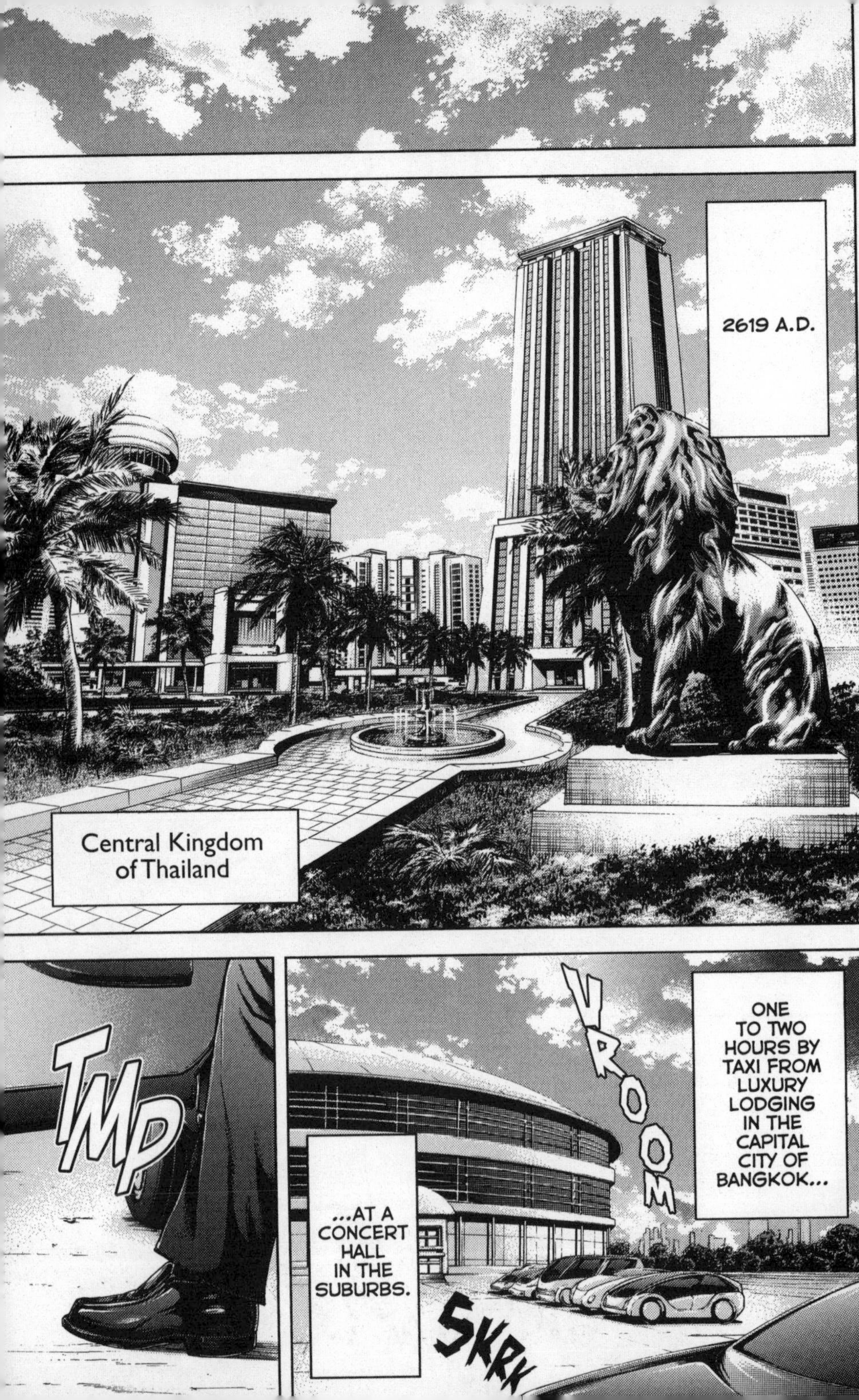
2619 A.D.
Central Kingdom of Thailand
ONE TO TWO HOURS BY TAXI FROM LUXURY LODGING IN THE CAPITAL CITY OF BANGKOK...
VROOM
...AT A CONCERT HALL IN THE SUBURBS.
SKRK
TMP

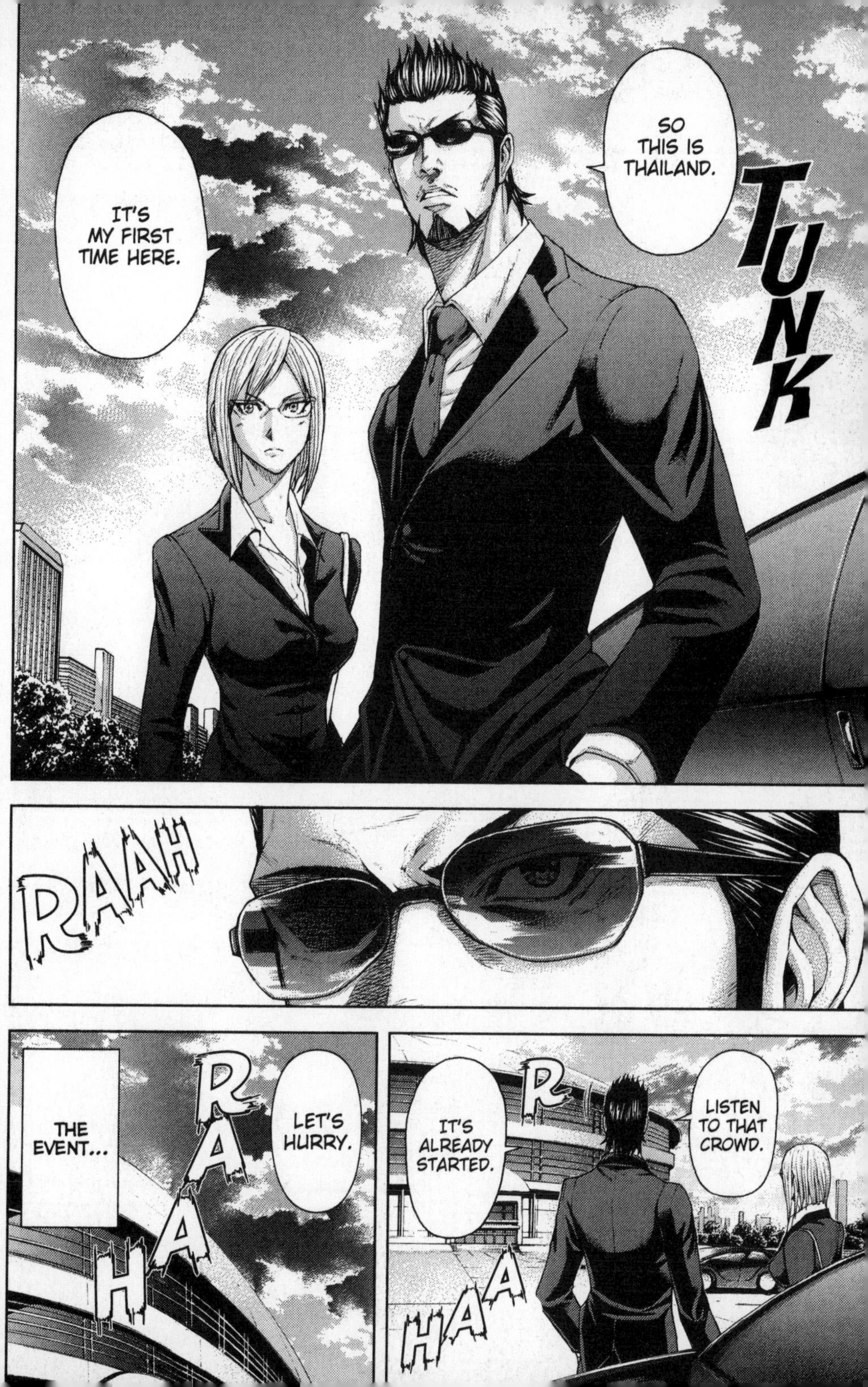
TUNK
SO THIS IS THAILAND.
IT'S MY FIRST TIME HERE.
RAAH
LISTEN TO THAT CROWD.
R
IT'S ALREADY STARTED.
HAA
LET'S HURRY.
RAAHA
THE EVENT...

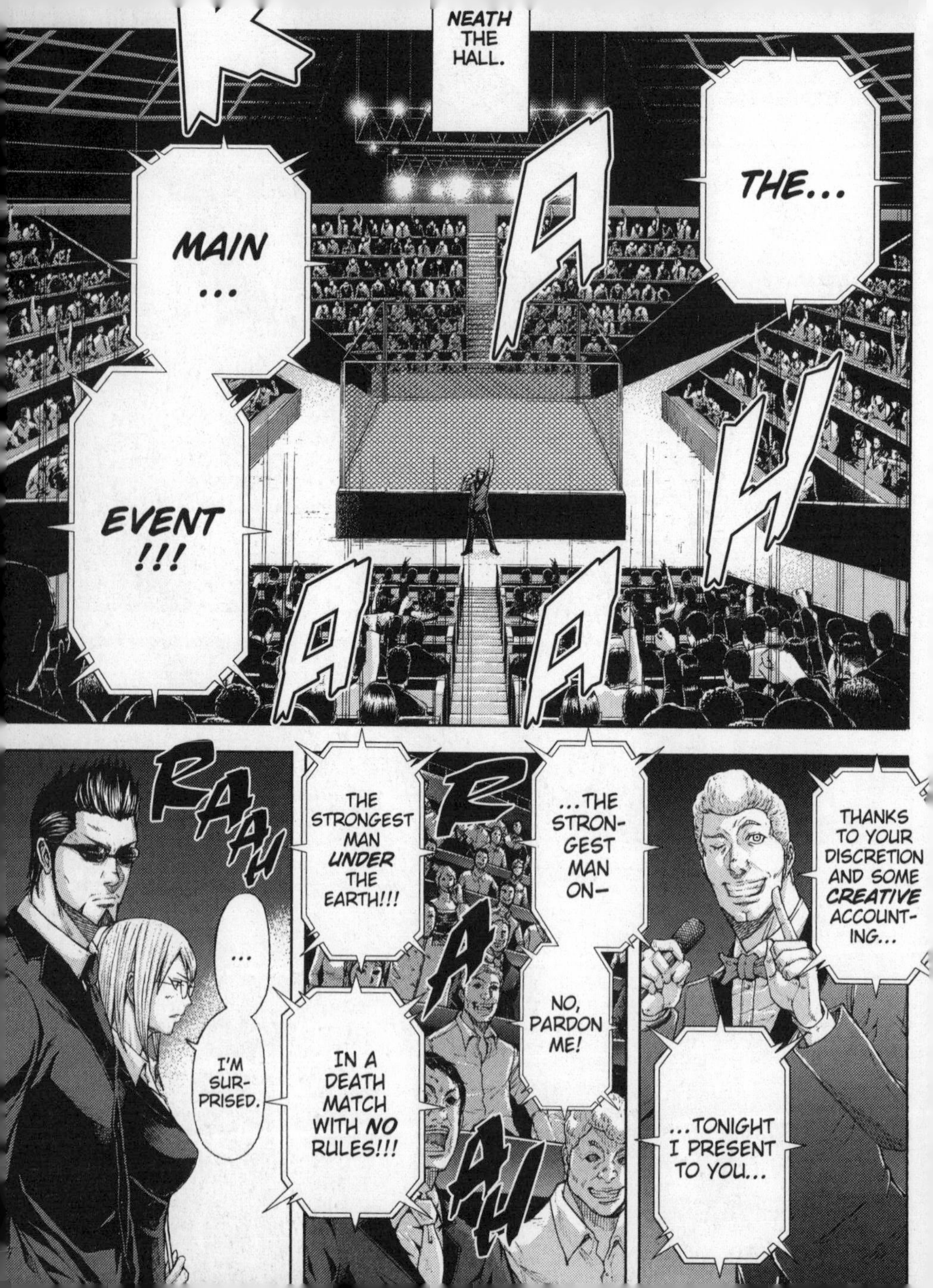
NEATH THE HALL.
THE...
MAIN ...
EVENT !!!
THANKS TO YOUR DISCRETION AND SOME CREATIVE ACCOUNTING...
...TONIGHT I PRESENT TO YOU...
...THE STRONGEST MAN ON—
NO, PARDON ME!
THE STRONGEST MAN UNDER THE EARTH!!!
IN A DEATH MATCH WITH NO RULES!!!
...
I'M SURPRISED.

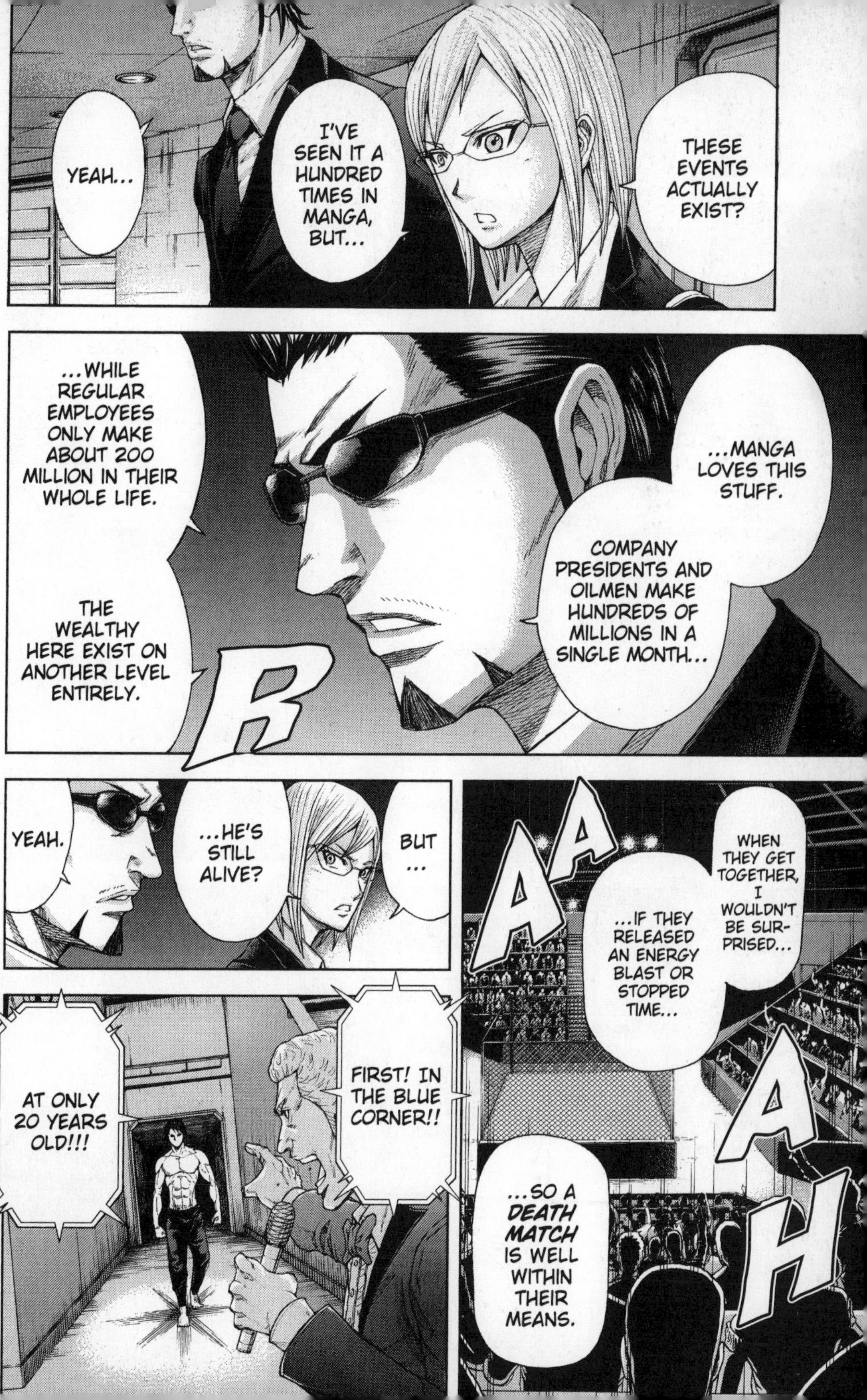
THESE EVENTS ACTUALLY EXIST?
I'VE SEEN IT A HUNDRED TIMES IN MANGA, BUT...
YEAH...
...MANGA LOVES THIS STUFF.
COMPANY PRESIDENTS AND OILMEN MAKE HUNDREDS OF MILLIONS IN A SINGLE MONTH...
...WHILE REGULAR EMPLOYEES ONLY MAKE ABOUT 200 MILLION IN THEIR WHOLE LIFE.
THE WEALTHY HERE EXIST ON ANOTHER LEVEL ENTIRELY.
R
WHEN THEY GET TOGETHER, I WOULDN'T BE SUR-PRISED...
...IF THEY RELEASED AN ENERGY BLAST OR STOPPED TIME...
AAAAH
...SO A *DEATH MATCH* IS WELL WITHIN THEIR MEANS.
BUT...
...HE'S STILL ALIVE?
YEAH.
FIRST! IN THE BLUE CORNER!!
AT ONLY 20 YEARS OLD!!!

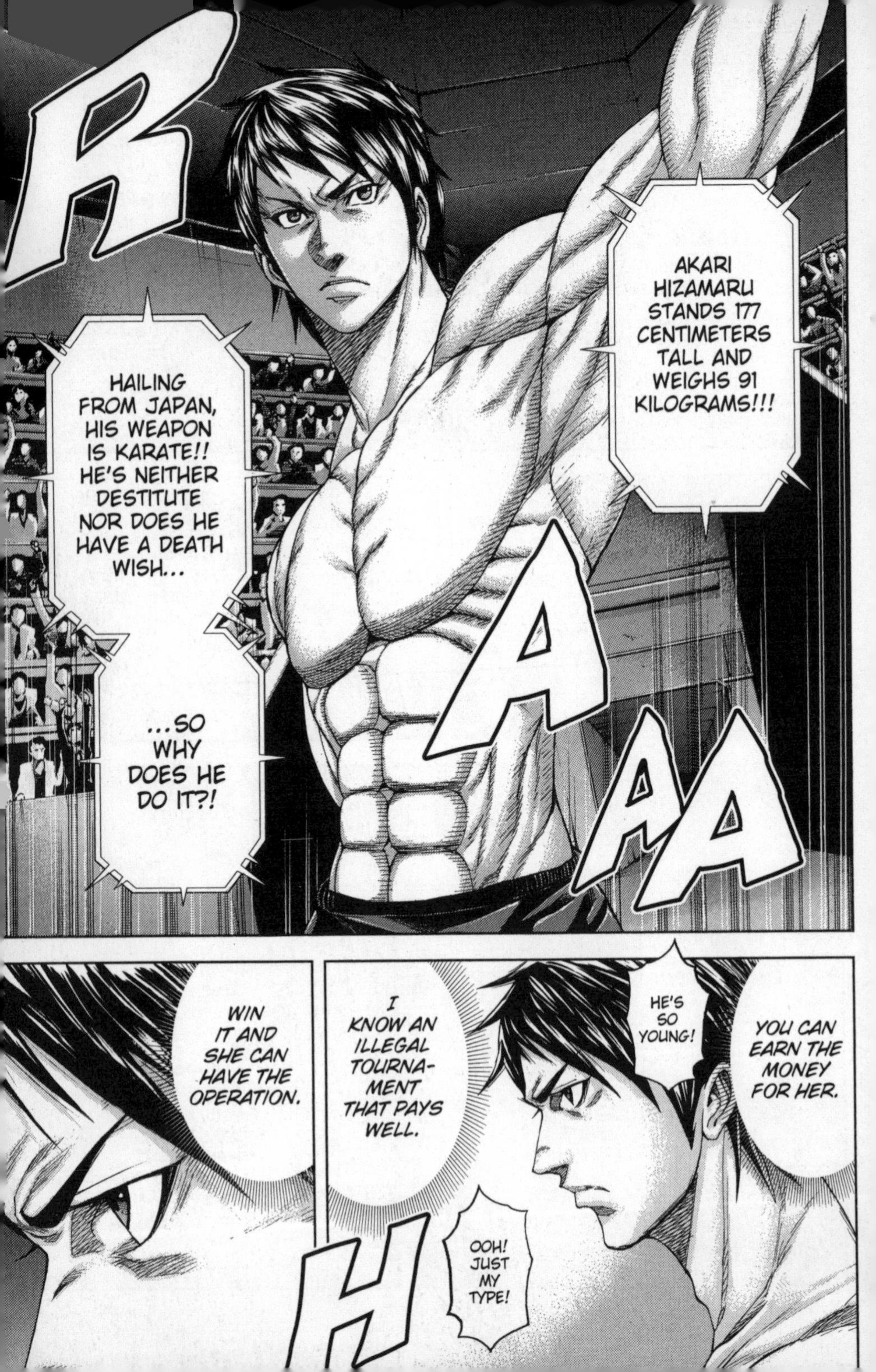
RAAAAH
AKARI HIZAMARU STANDS 177 CENTIMETERS TALL AND WEIGHS 91 KILOGRAMS!!!
HAILING FROM JAPAN, HIS WEAPON IS KARATE!! HE'S NEITHER DESTITUTE NOR DOES HE HAVE A DEATH WISH...
...SO WHY DOES HE DO IT?!
YOU CAN EARN THE MONEY FOR HER.
HE'S SO YOUNG!
I KNOW AN ILLEGAL TOURNA-MENT THAT PAYS WELL.
OOH! JUST MY TYPE!
WIN IT AND SHE CAN HAVE THE OPERATION.

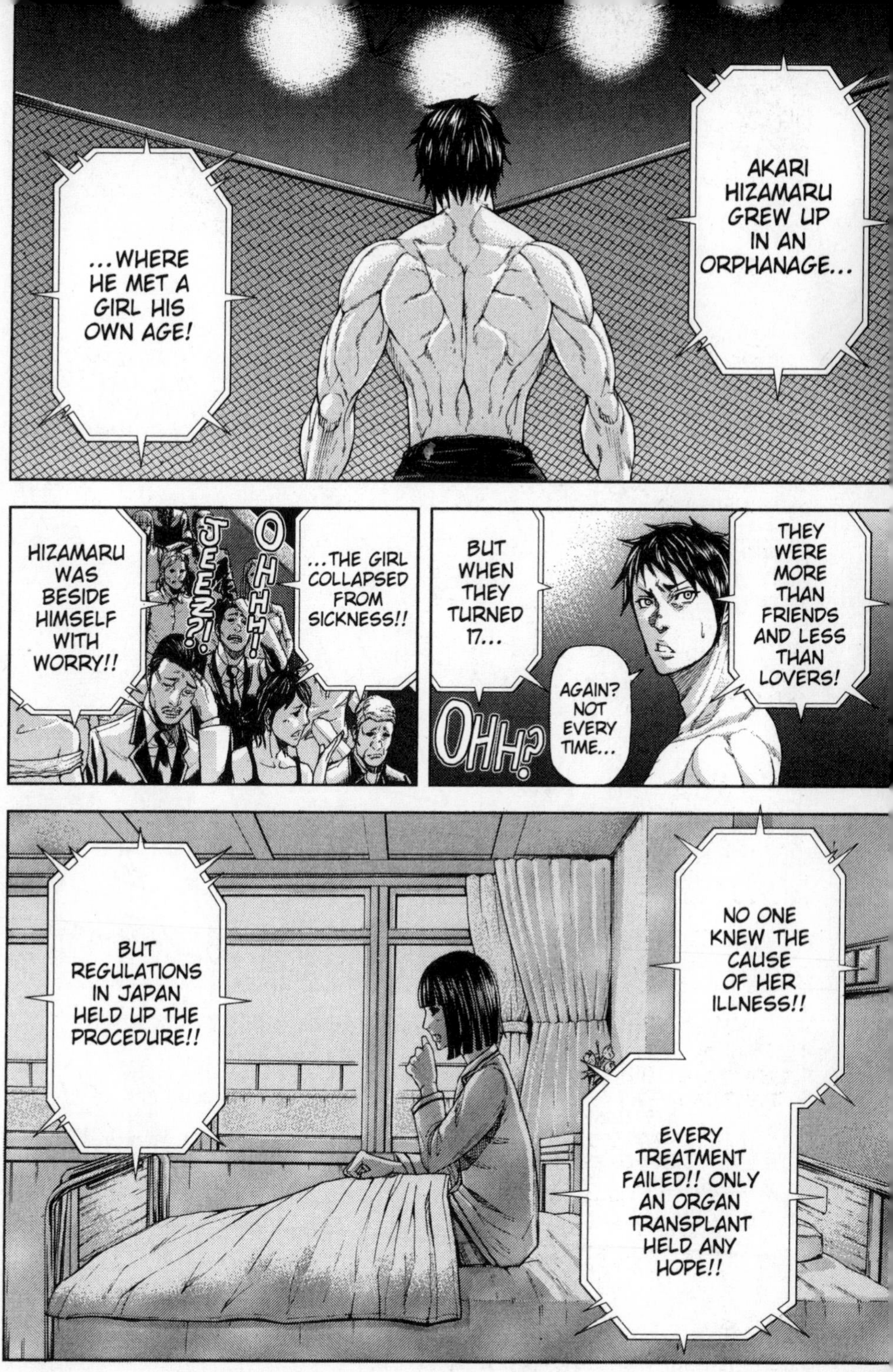
AKARI HIZAMARU GREW UP IN AN ORPHANAGE...
...WHERE HE MET A GIRL HIS OWN AGE!
THEY WERE MORE THAN FRIENDS AND LESS THAN LOVERS!
BUT WHEN THEY TURNED 17...
AGAIN? NOT EVERY TIME...
OHH?
...THE GIRL COLLAPSED FROM SICKNESS!!
OHHHH!
JEEZ?!
HIZAMARU WAS BESIDE HIMSELF WITH WORRY!!
NO ONE KNEW THE CAUSE OF HER ILLNESS!!
EVERY TREATMENT FAILED!! ONLY AN ORGAN TRANSPLANT HELD ANY HOPE!!
BUT REGULATIONS IN JAPAN HELD UP THE PROCEDURE!!

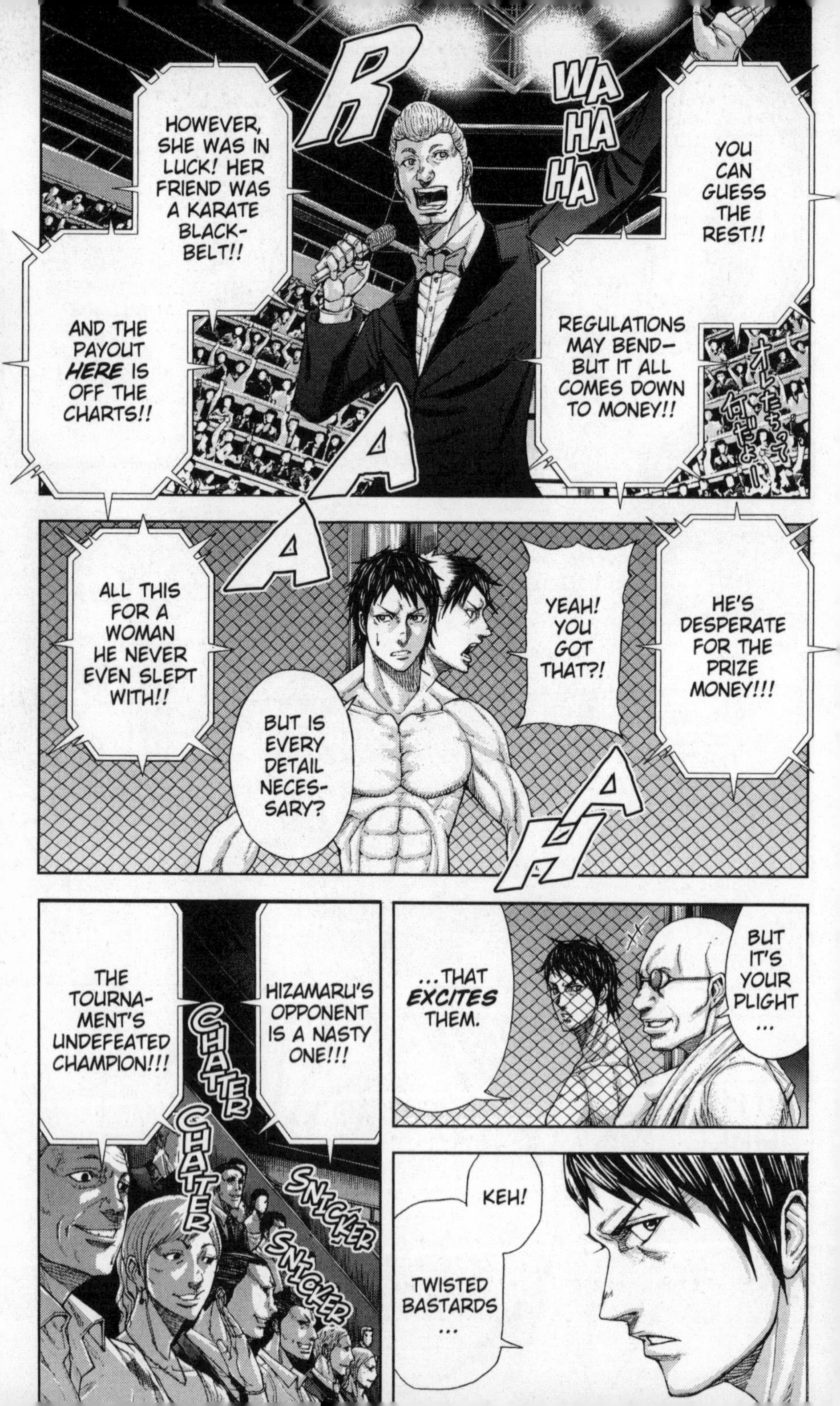
WA HA HA
YOU CAN GUESS THE REST!!
HOWEVER, SHE WAS IN LUCK! HER FRIEND WAS A KARATE BLACK-BELT!!
R
REGULATIONS MAY BEND—BUT IT ALL COMES DOWN TO MONEY!!
オレたちって何だよー!
AND THE PAYOUT **HERE** IS OFF THE CHARTS!!
A
A
HE'S DESPERATE FOR THE PRIZE MONEY!!!
YEAH! YOU GOT THAT?!
ALL THIS FOR A WOMAN HE NEVER EVEN SLEPT WITH!!
BUT IS EVERY DETAIL NECES-SARY?
A
H
BUT IT'S YOUR PLIGHT ...
...THAT **EXCITES** THEM.
KEH!
TWISTED BASTARDS ...
HIZAMARU'S OPPONENT IS A NASTY ONE!!!
THE TOURNA-MENT'S UNDEFEATED CHAMPION!!!
CHATTER
CHATTER
SNICKER
SNICKER

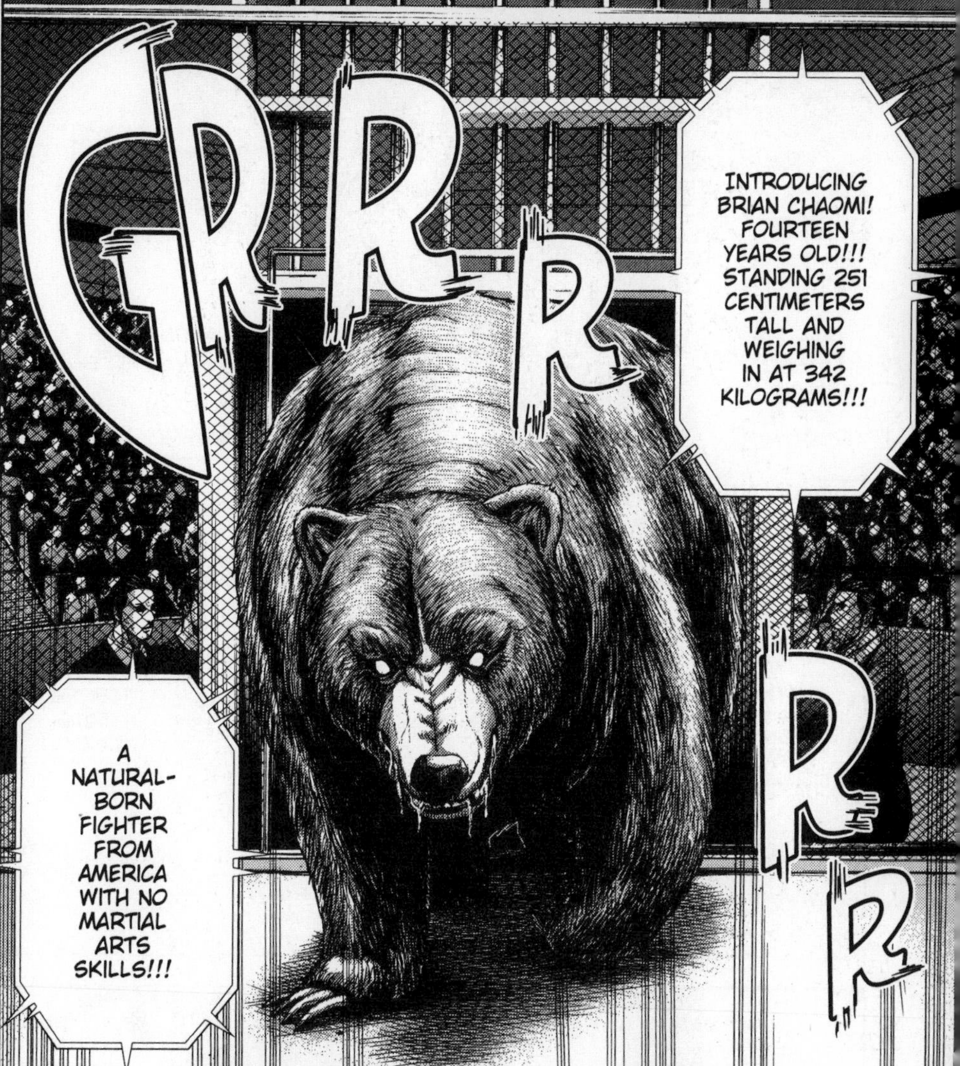
INTRODUCING BRIAN CHAOMI! FOURTEEN YEARS OLD!!! STANDING 251 CENTIMETERS TALL AND WEIGHING IN AT 342 KILOGRAMS!!!
GRRRRR
A NATURAL-BORN FIGHTER FROM AMERICA WITH NO MARTIAL ARTS SKILLS!!!
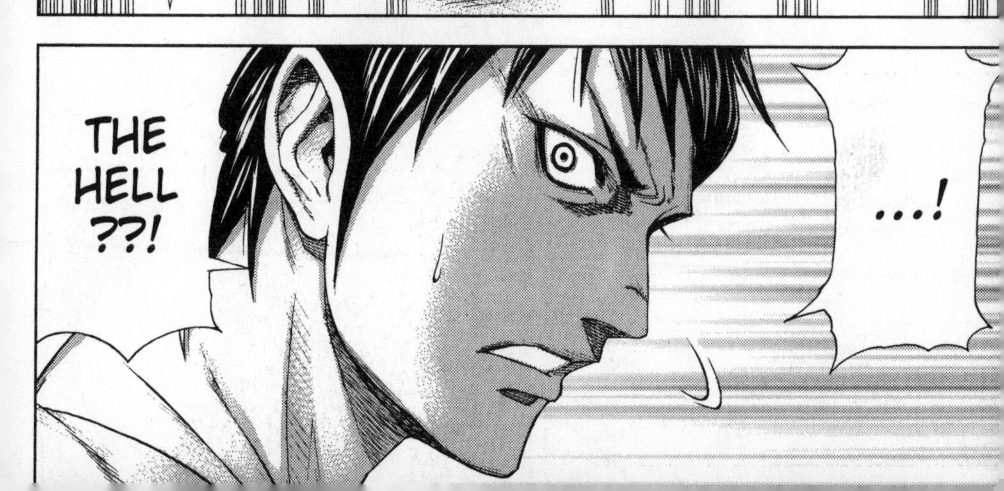
...!
THE HELL ??!

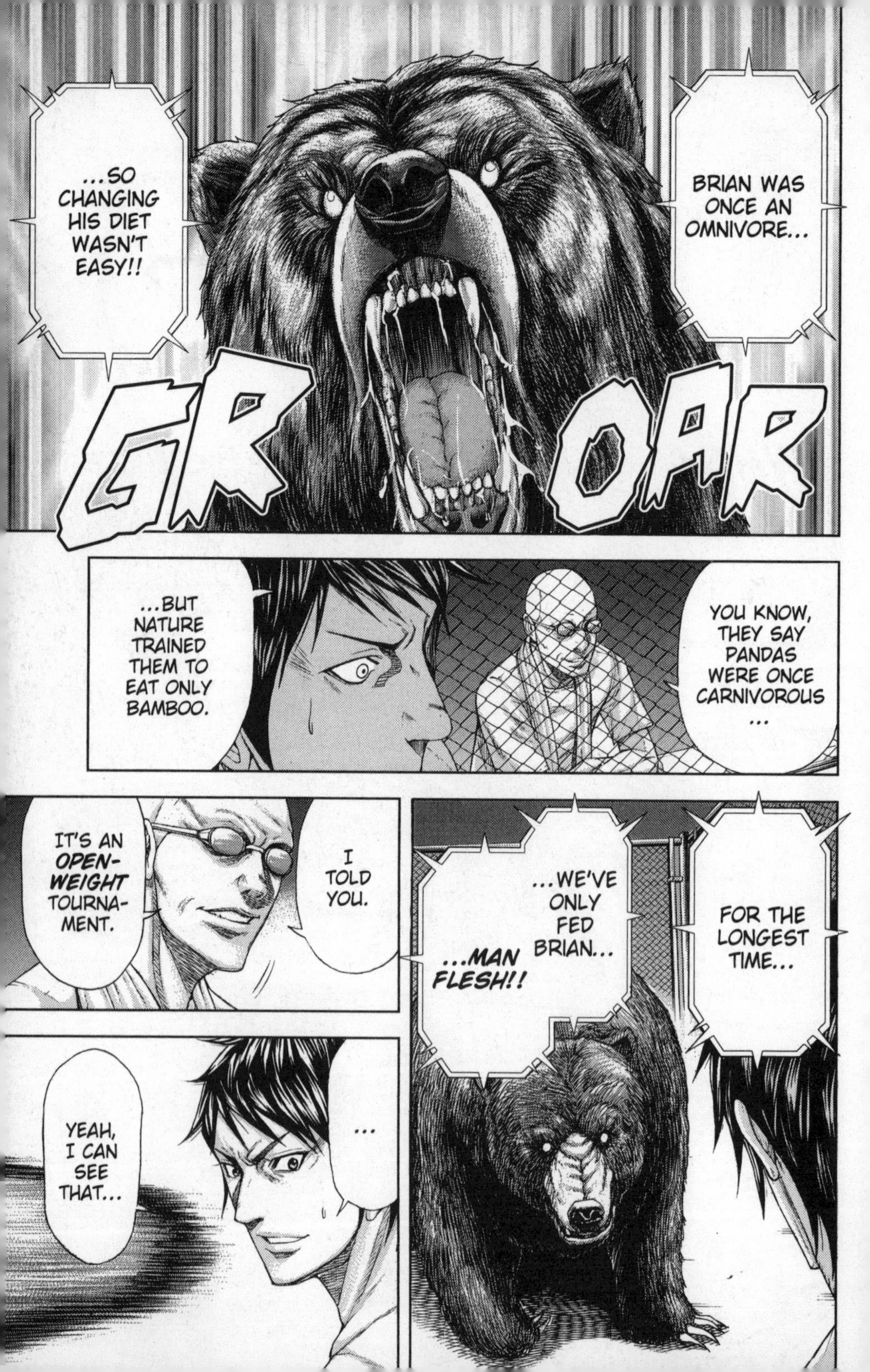
BRIAN WAS ONCE AN OMNIVORE...
...SO CHANGING HIS DIET WASN'T EASY!!
GR OAR
YOU KNOW, THEY SAY PANDAS WERE ONCE CARNIVOROUS ...
...BUT NATURE TRAINED THEM TO EAT ONLY BAMBOO.
FOR THE LONGEST TIME...
...WE'VE ONLY FED BRIAN...
...MAN FLESH!!
I TOLD YOU.
IT'S AN OPEN-WEIGHT TOURNAMENT.
...
YEAH, I CAN SEE THAT...

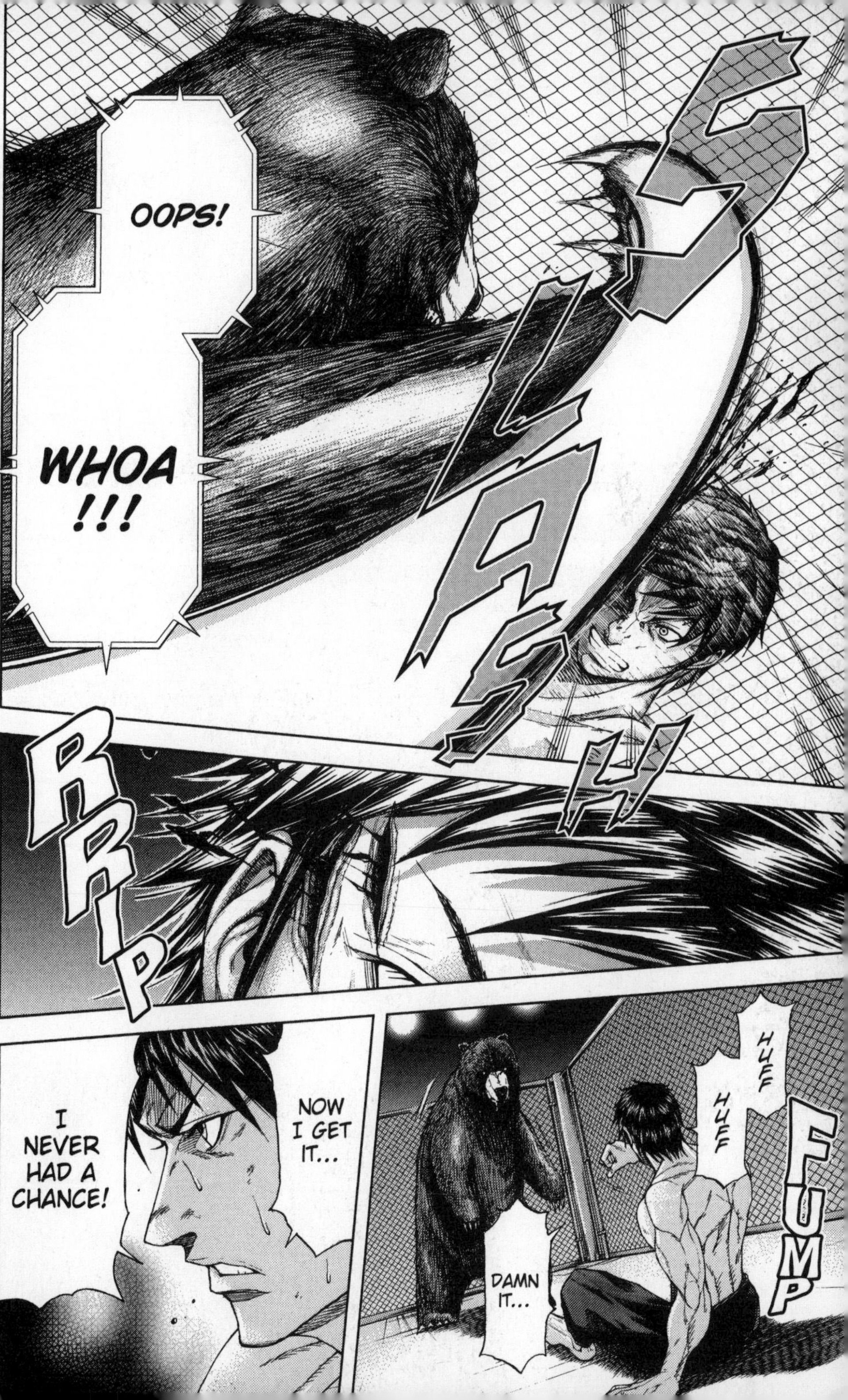
SLASH
OOPS!
WHOA!!!
RRIP
HUFF HUFF
FUMP
DAMN IT...
NOW I GET IT...
I NEVER HAD A CHANCE!

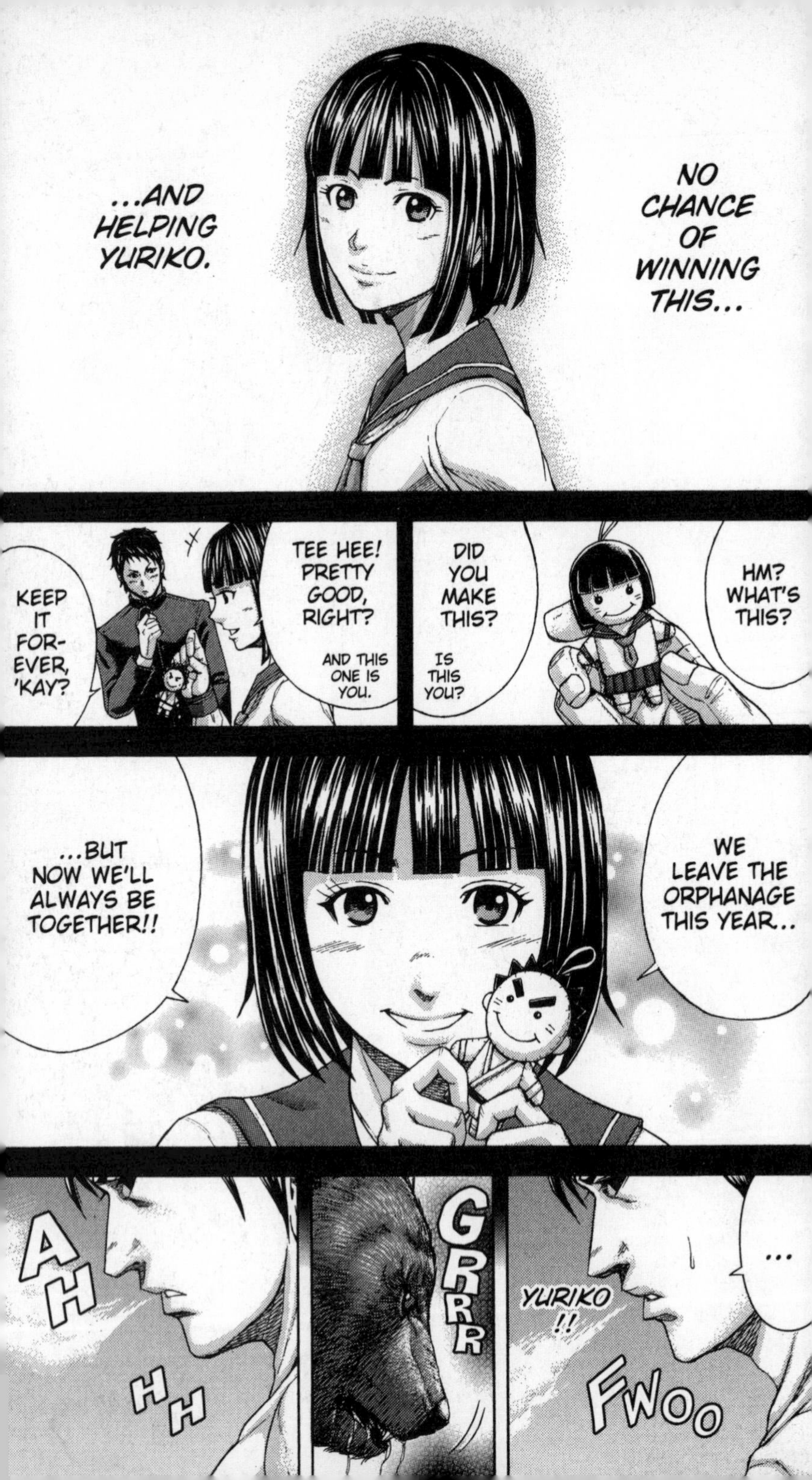
NO CHANCE OF WINNING THIS...
...AND HELPING YURIKO.
HM? WHAT'S THIS?
DID YOU MAKE THIS?
IS THIS YOU?
TEE HEE! PRETTY GOOD, RIGHT?
AND THIS ONE IS YOU.
KEEP IT FOR-EVER, 'KAY?
WE LEAVE THE ORPHANAGE THIS YEAR...
...BUT NOW WE'LL ALWAYS BE TOGETHER!!
...
YURIKO !!
FWOO
GRRR
AHHHH

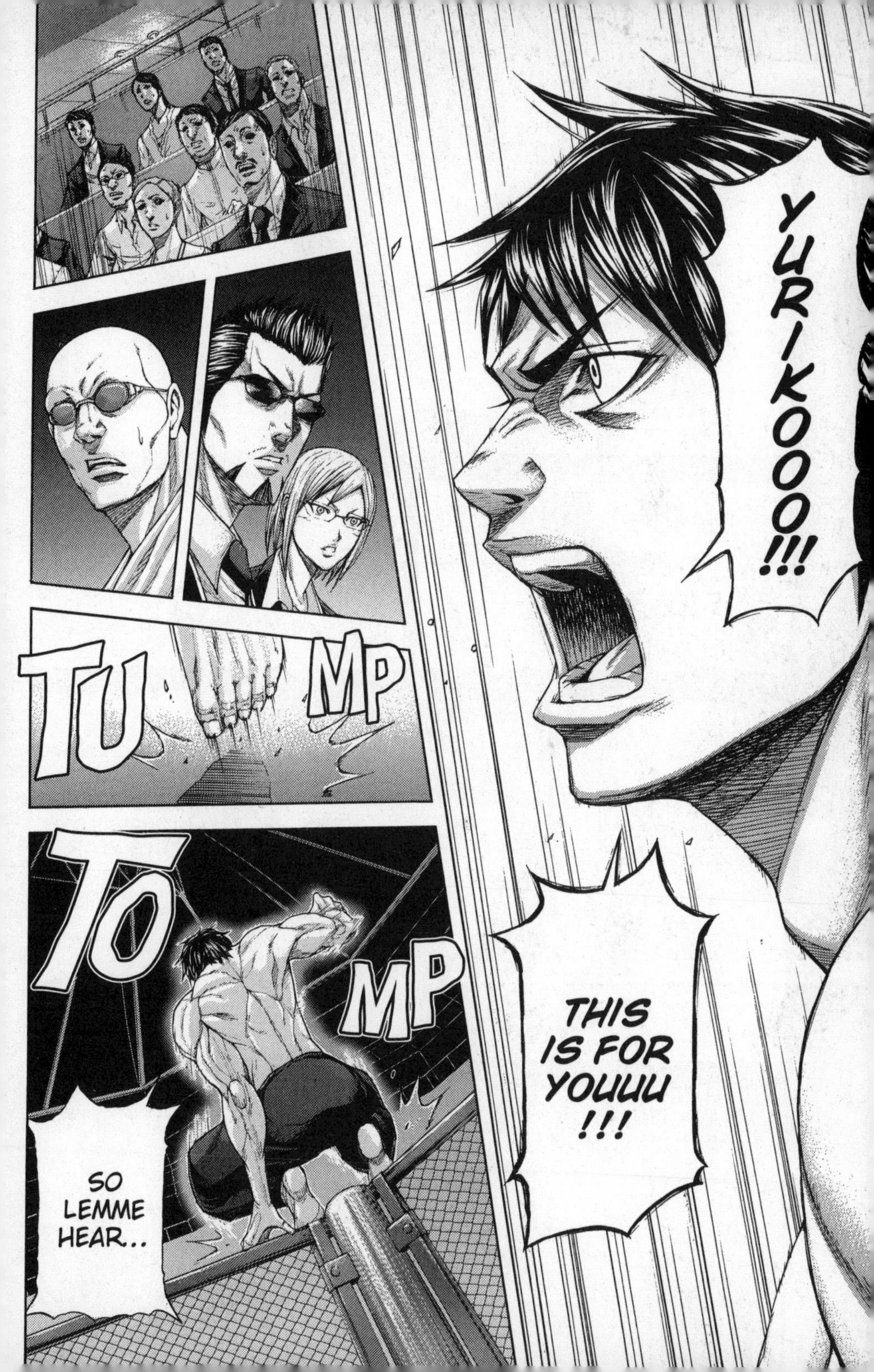
YURIKOOOO!!!
THIS IS FOR YOUUU!!!
TU MP
TO MP
SO LEMME HEAR...

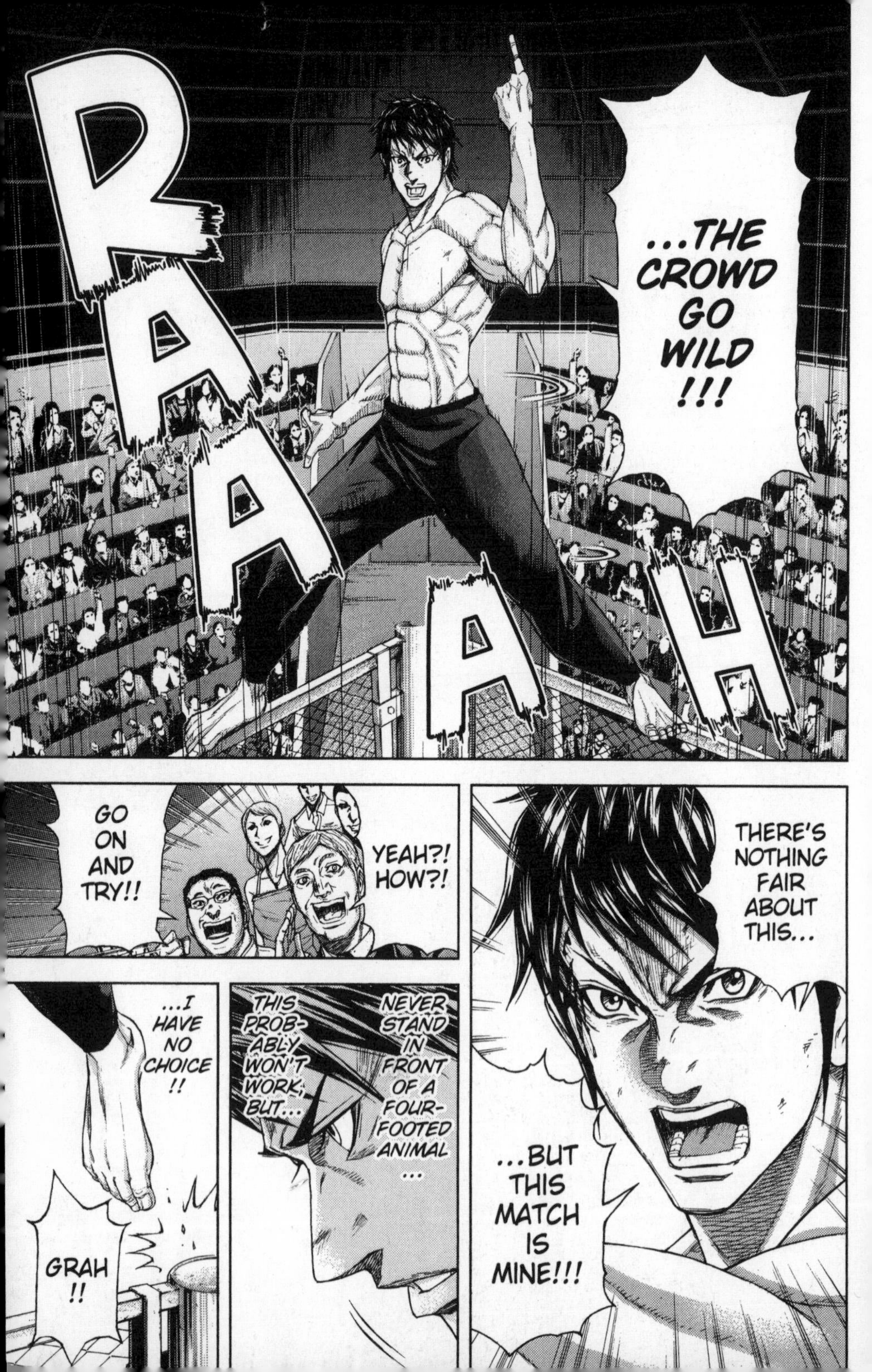
...THE CROWD GO WILD!!!
RAAAH
THERE'S NOTHING FAIR ABOUT THIS...
...BUT THIS MATCH IS MINE!!!
YEAH?! HOW?!
GO ON AND TRY!!
NEVER STAND IN FRONT OF A FOUR-FOOTED ANIMAL...
THIS PROBABLY WON'T WORK, BUT...
...I HAVE NO CHOICE!!
GRAH!!

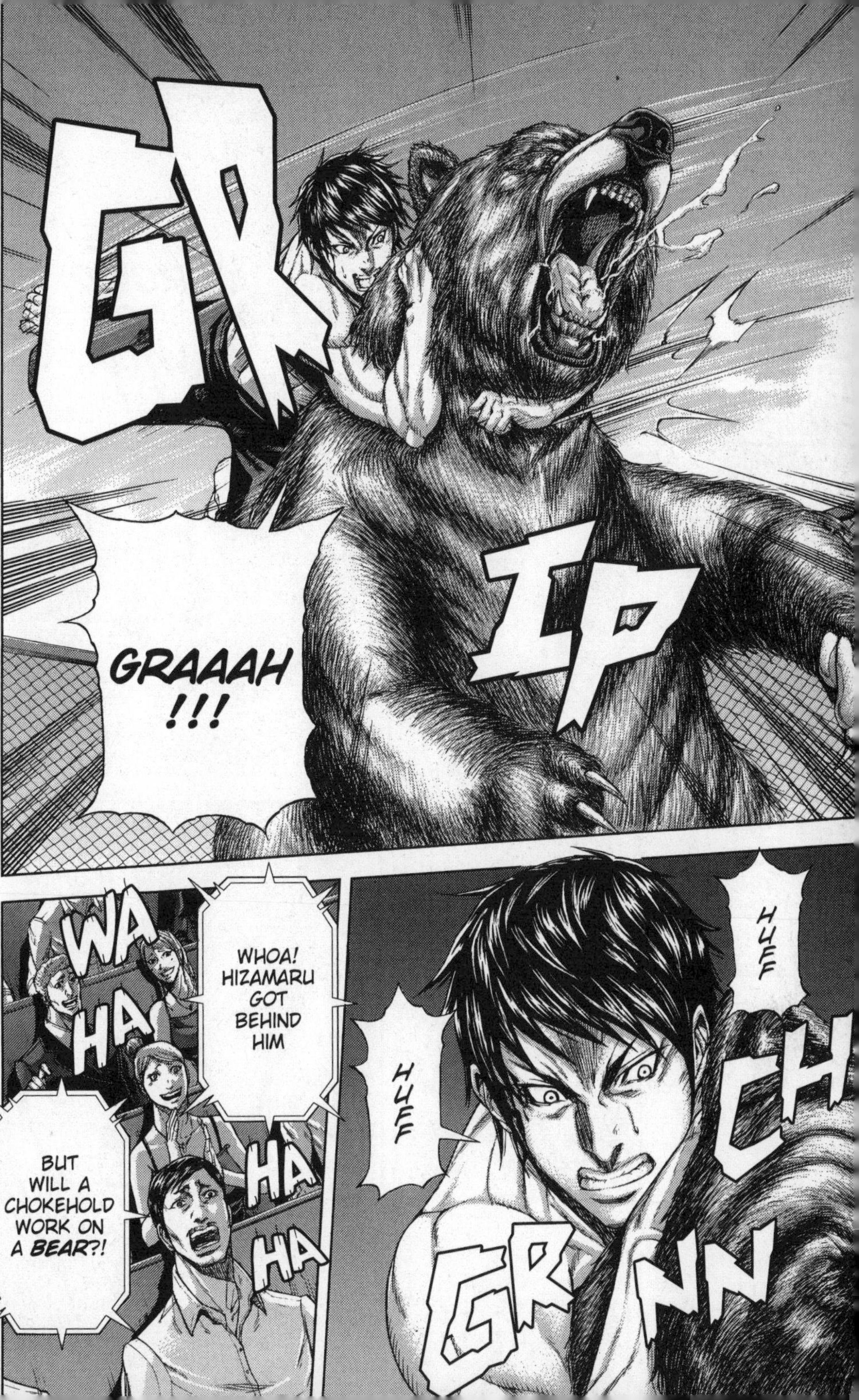
GR
IP
GRAAAH!!!
HUFF
HUFF
CH
GR
NN
WHOA! HIZAMARU GOT BEHIND HIM
WA
HA
HA
HA
BUT WILL A CHOKEHOLD WORK ON A *BEAR*?!

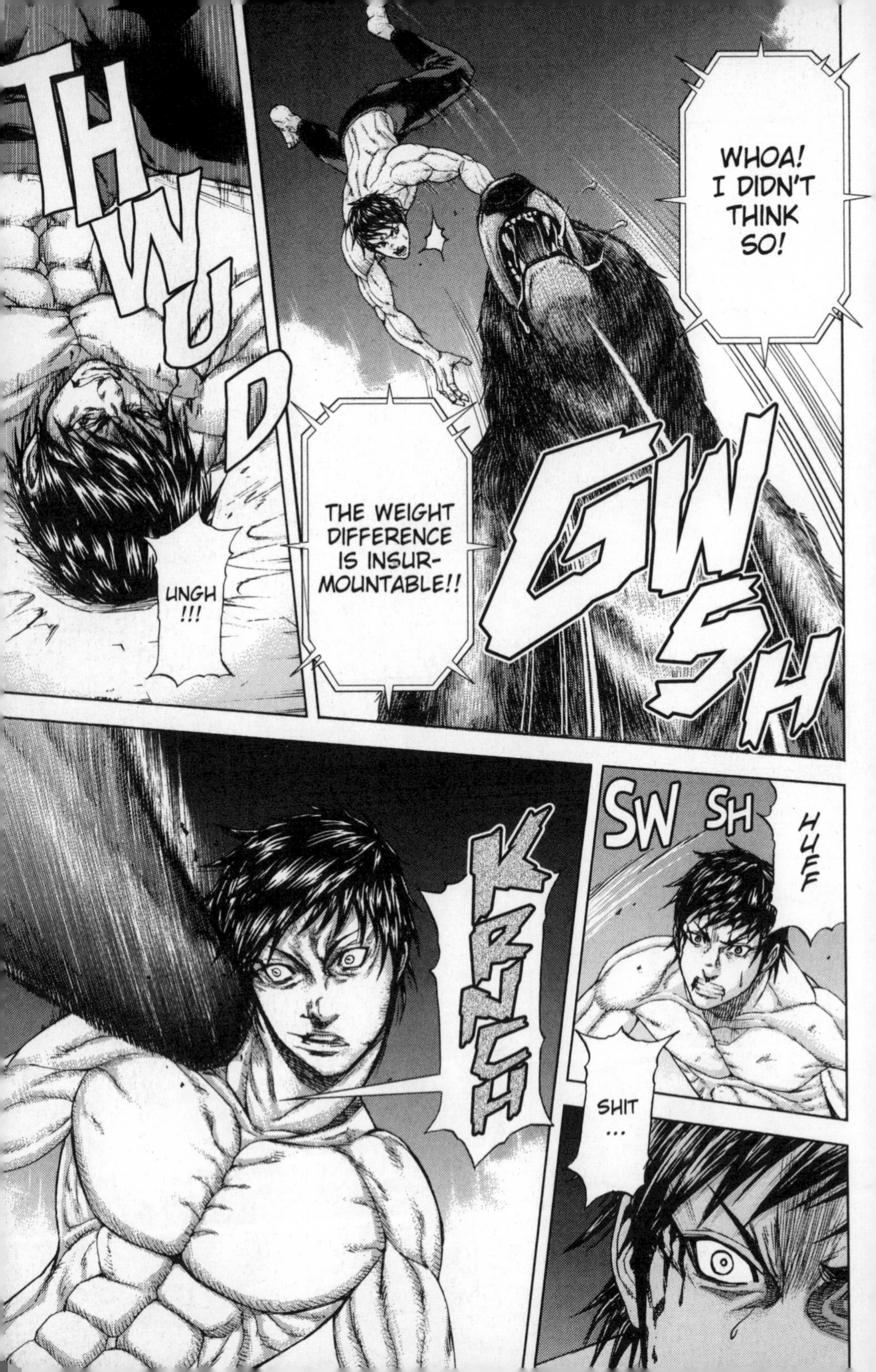
WHOA! I DIDN'T THINK SO!
THE WEIGHT DIFFERENCE IS INSUR-MOUNTABLE!!
GWSH
THWUD
UNGH !!!
SW SH
HUFF
SHIT ...

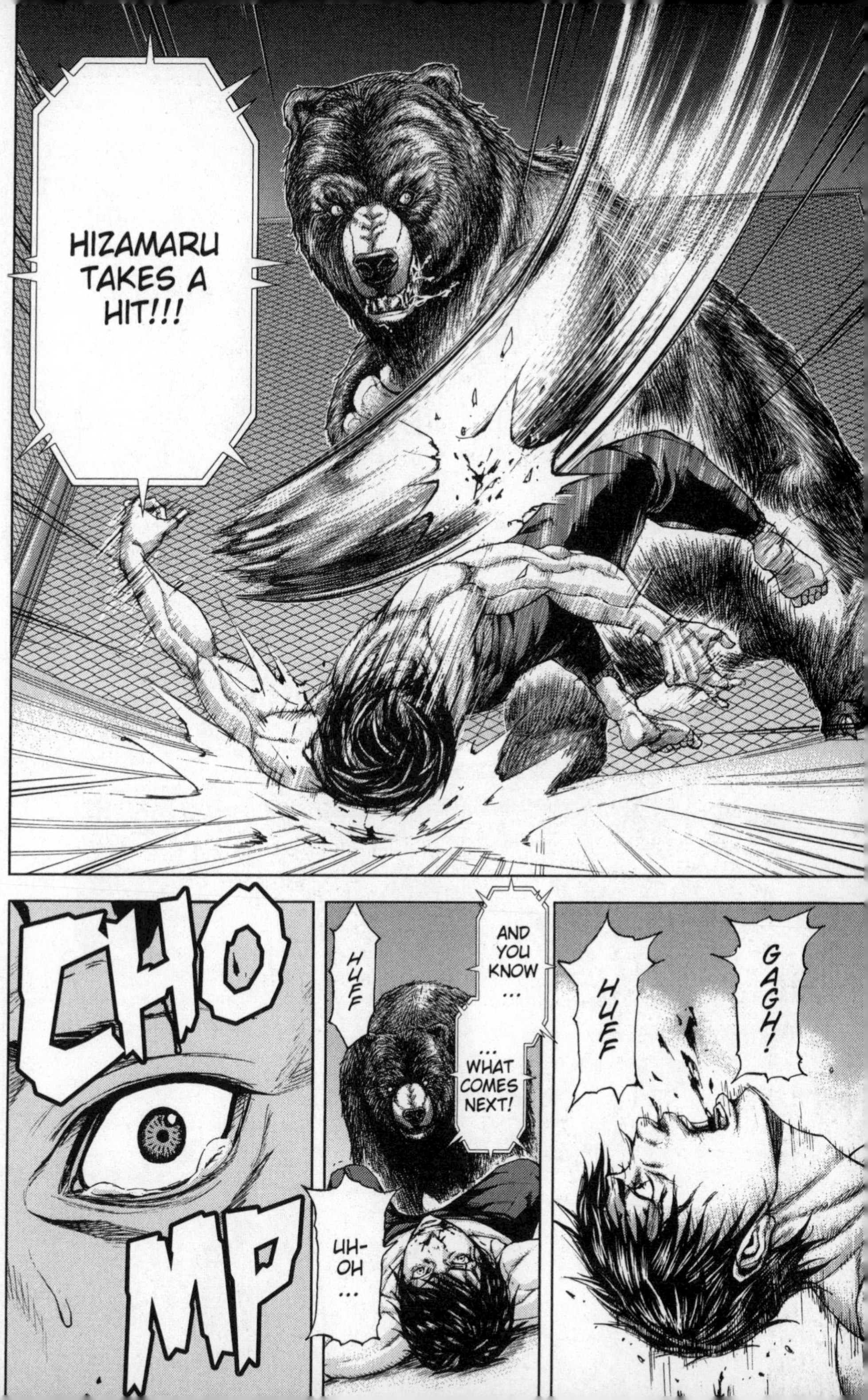
HIZAMARU TAKES A HIT!!!
GAGH!
HUFF
AND YOU KNOW...
HUFF
...WHAT COMES NEXT!
UH-OH...
CHOMP

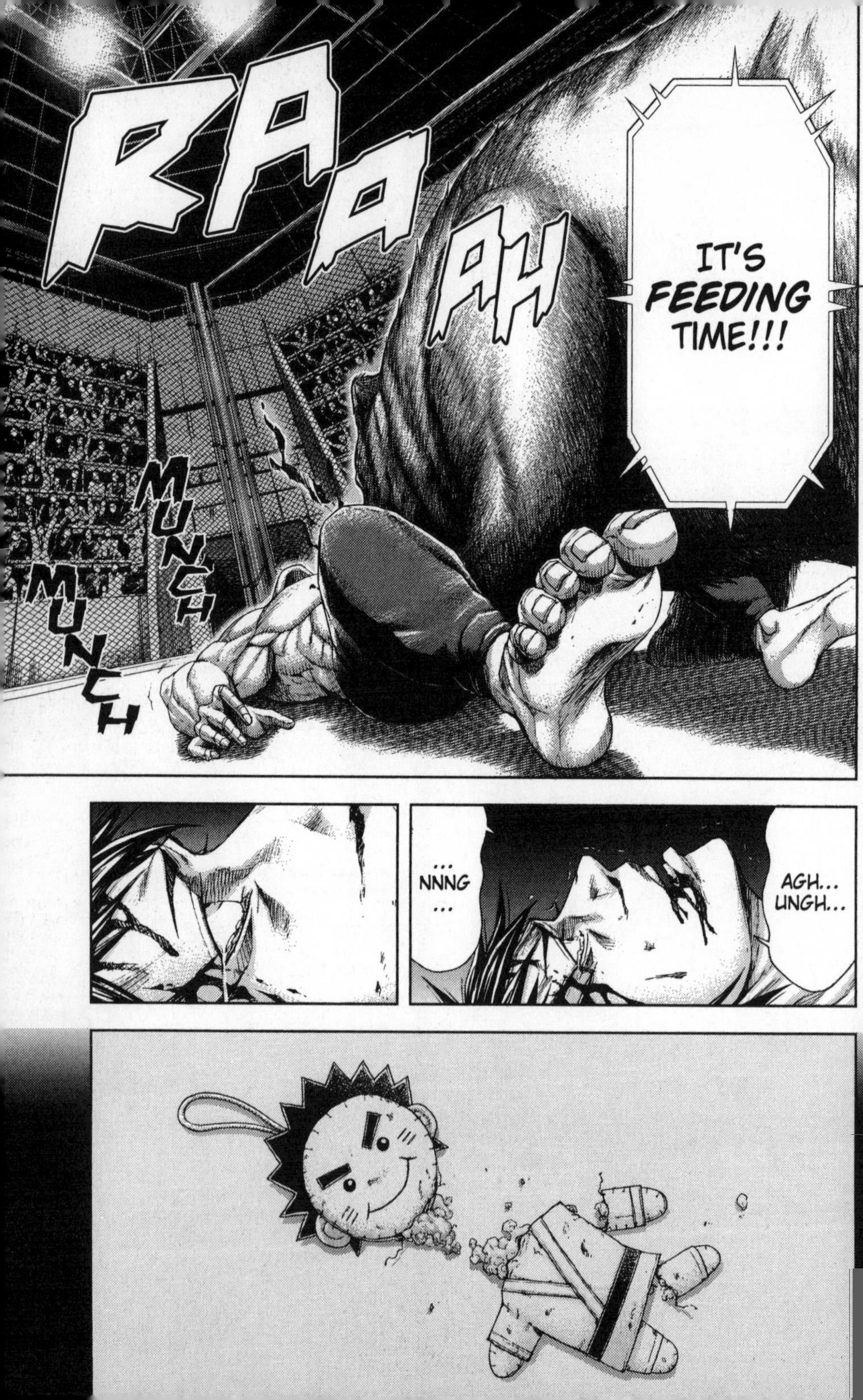
IT'S FEEDING TIME!!!
RAAAH
MUNCH MUNCH
AGH... UNGH...
...NNNG...

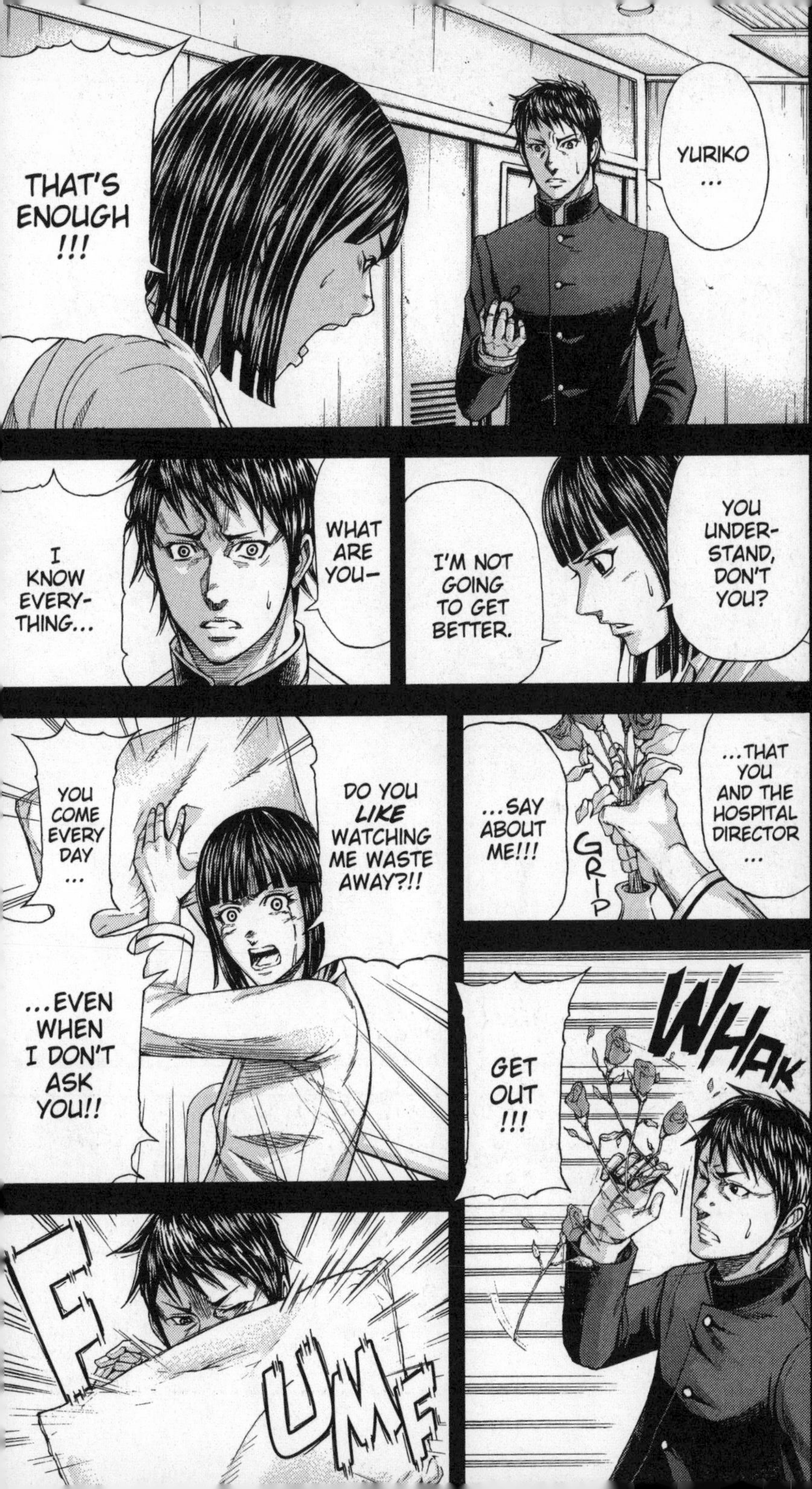
YURIKO ...
THAT'S ENOUGH !!!
YOU UNDER-STAND, DON'T YOU?
I'M NOT GOING TO GET BETTER.
WHAT ARE YOU—
I KNOW EVERY-THING...
...THAT YOU AND THE HOSPITAL DIRECTOR ...
GRIP
...SAY ABOUT ME!!!
WHAK
GET OUT !!!
DO YOU LIKE WATCHING ME WASTE AWAY?!!
YOU COME EVERY DAY ...
...EVEN WHEN I DON'T ASK YOU!!
FUMF

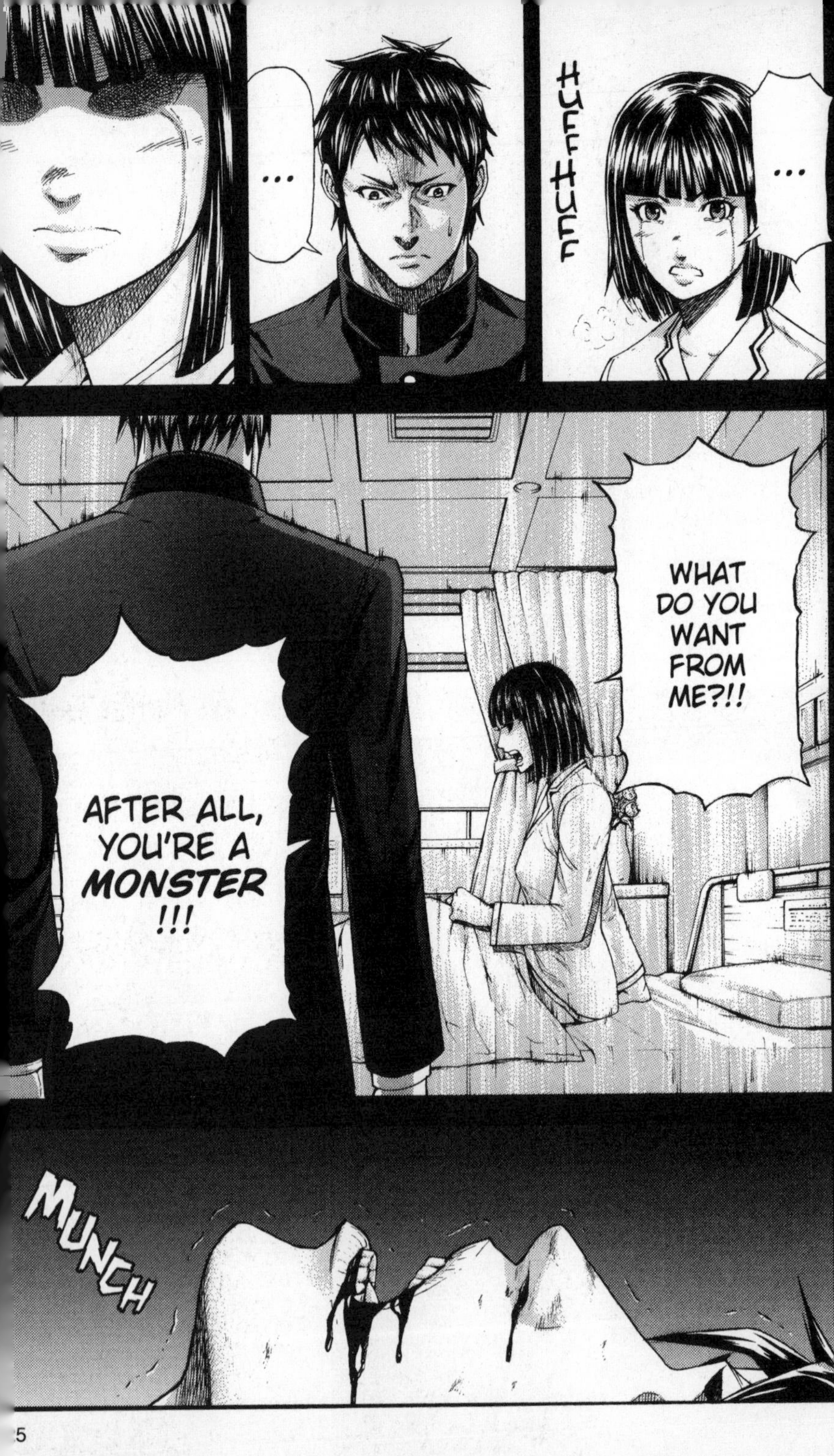
...
HUFF HUFF
...
WHAT DO YOU WANT FROM ME?!!
AFTER ALL, YOU'RE A MONSTER!!!
MUNCH

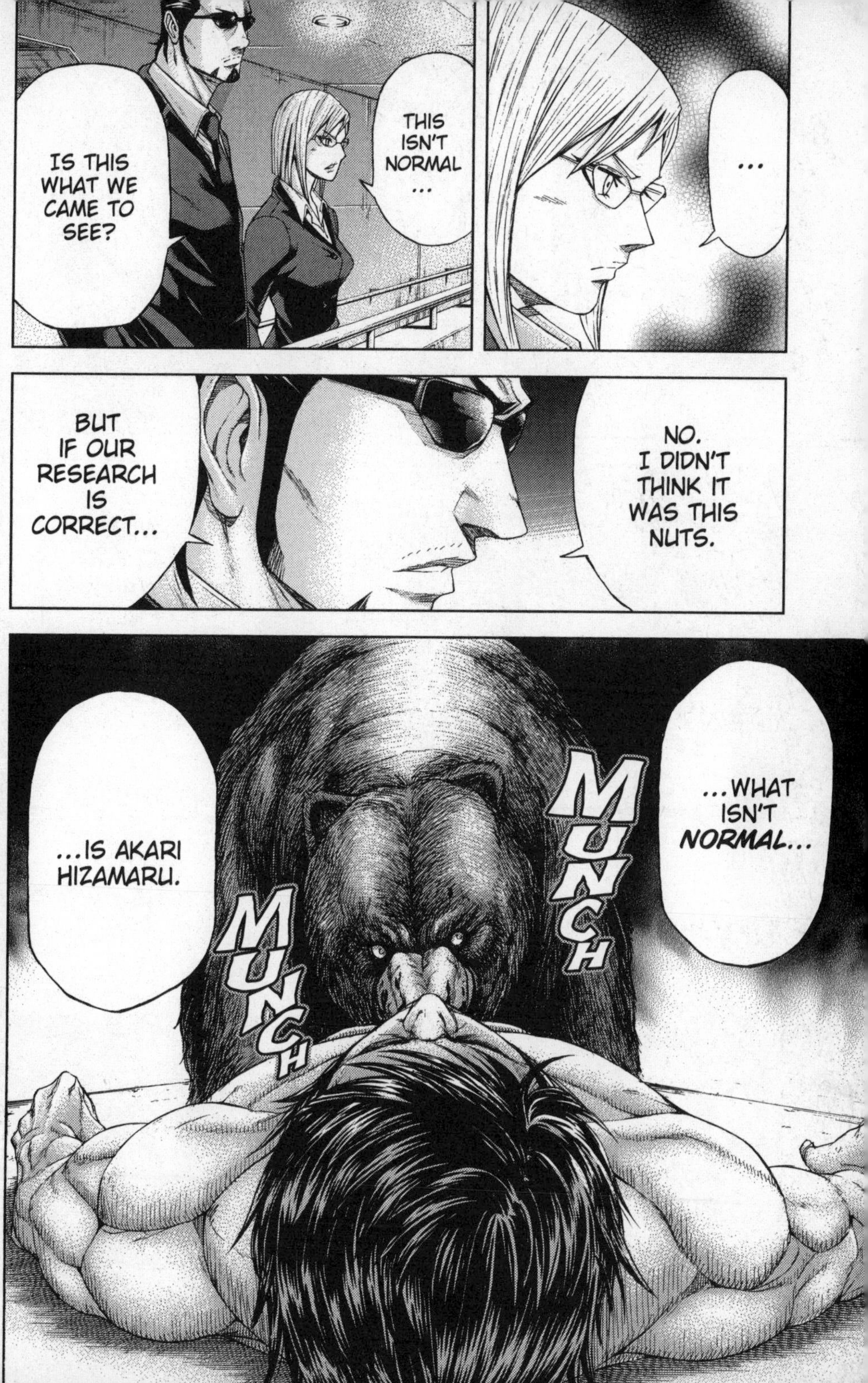
...
THIS ISN'T NORMAL ...
IS THIS WHAT WE CAME TO SEE?
NO. I DIDN'T THINK IT WAS THIS NUTS.
BUT IF OUR RESEARCH IS CORRECT...
...WHAT ISN'T *NORMAL*...
MUNCH
MUNCH
...IS AKARI HIZAMARU.

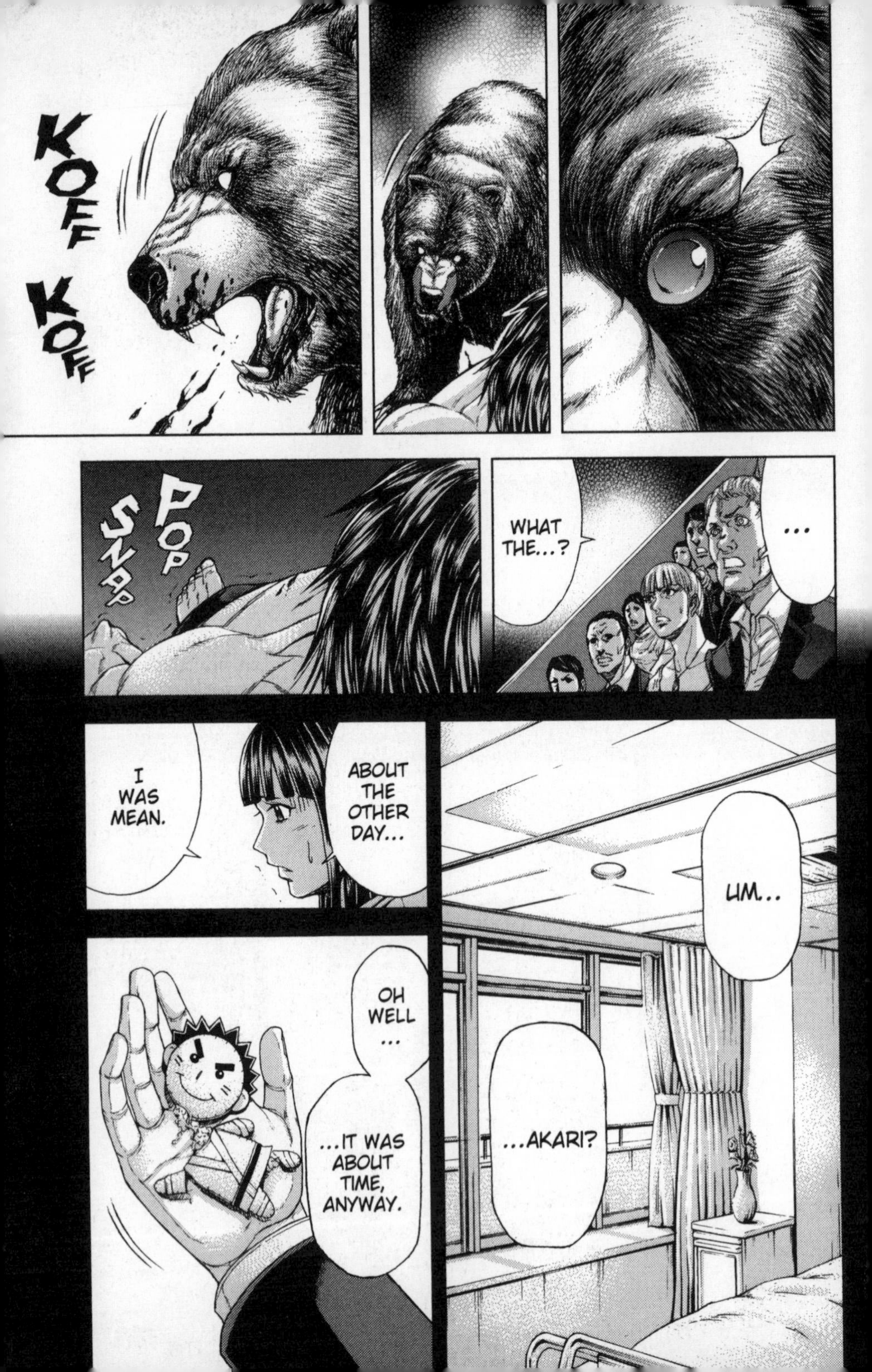
KOFF KOFF
...
WHAT THE...?
POP
SNAP
UM...
...AKARI?
ABOUT THE OTHER DAY...
I WAS MEAN.
OH WELL...
...IT WAS ABOUT TIME, ANYWAY.

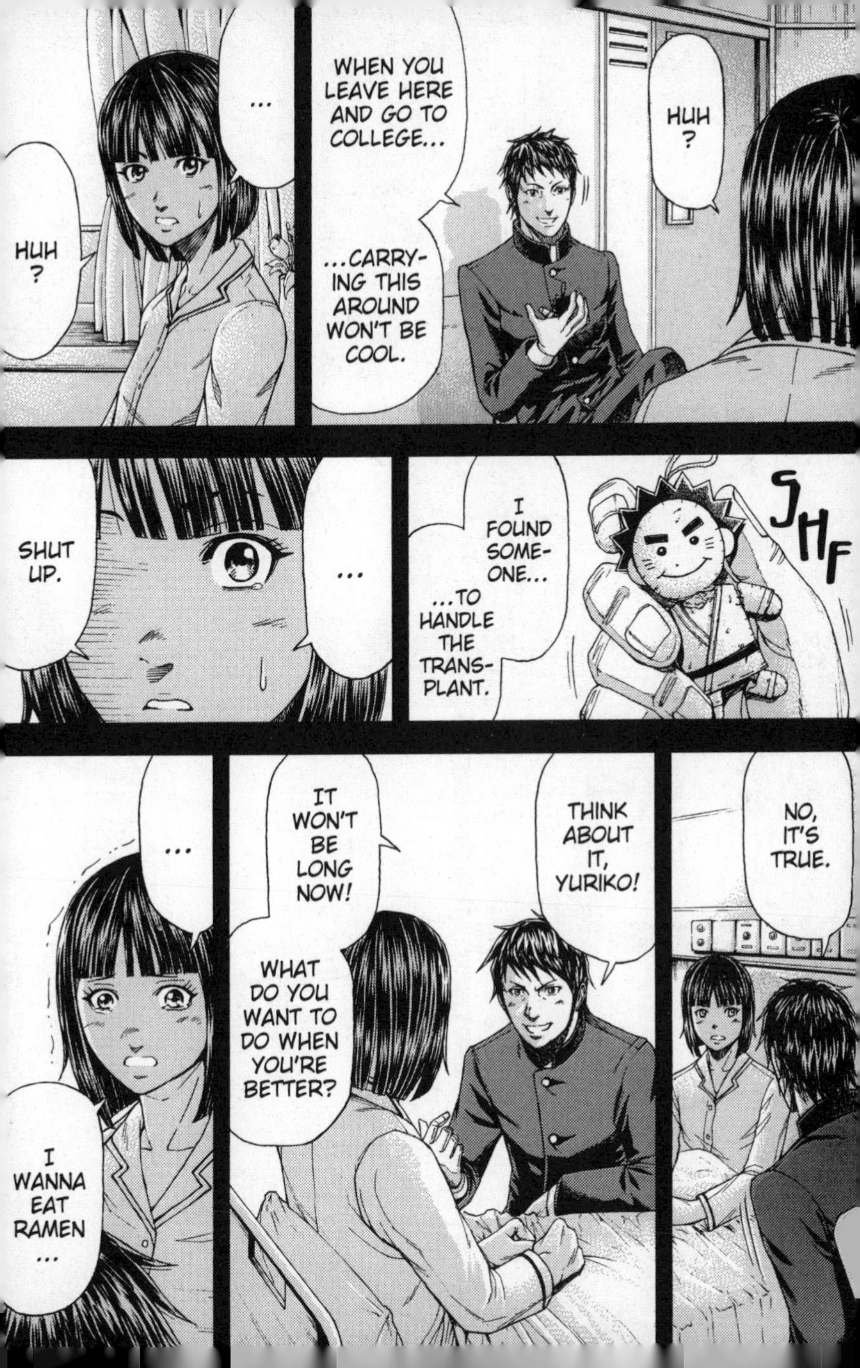
HUH?
WHEN YOU LEAVE HERE AND GO TO COLLEGE...
...CARRYING THIS AROUND WON'T BE COOL.
...
HUH?
SHF
I FOUND SOMEONE...
...TO HANDLE THE TRANSPLANT.
...
SHUT UP.
NO, IT'S TRUE.
THINK ABOUT IT, YURIKO!
IT WON'T BE LONG NOW!
WHAT DO YOU WANT TO DO WHEN YOU'RE BETTER?
...
I WANNA EAT RAMEN...

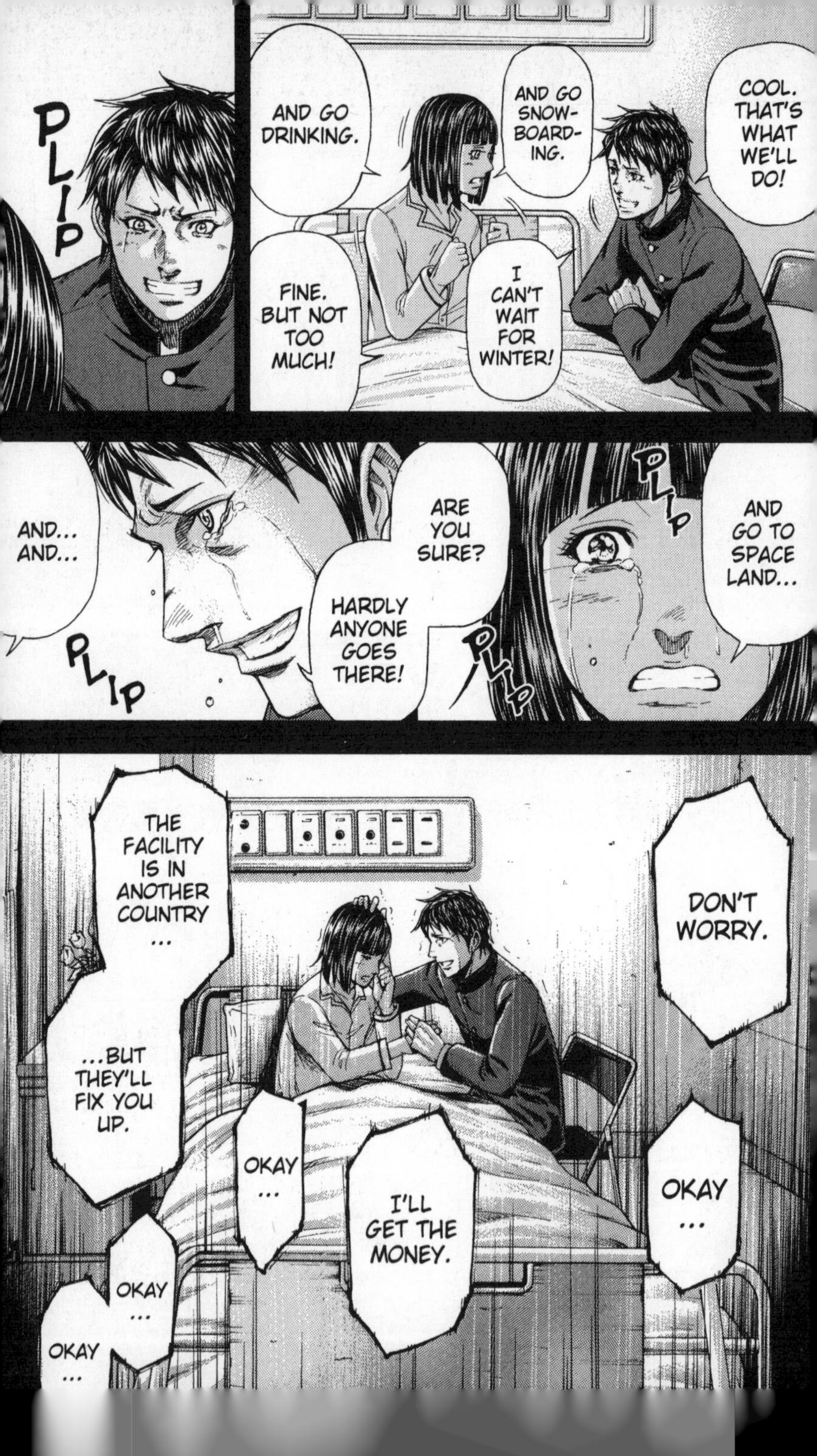
COOL. THAT'S WHAT WE'LL DO!
AND GO SNOWBOARDING.
AND GO DRINKING.
I CAN'T WAIT FOR WINTER!
FINE. BUT NOT TOO MUCH!
PLIP
AND GO TO SPACE LAND...
PLIP
PLIP
ARE YOU SURE?
HARDLY ANYONE GOES THERE!
AND... AND...
PLIP
DON'T WORRY.
THE FACILITY IS IN ANOTHER COUNTRY...
...BUT THEY'LL FIX YOU UP.
OKAY...
I'LL GET THE MONEY.
OKAY...
OKAY...
OKAY...

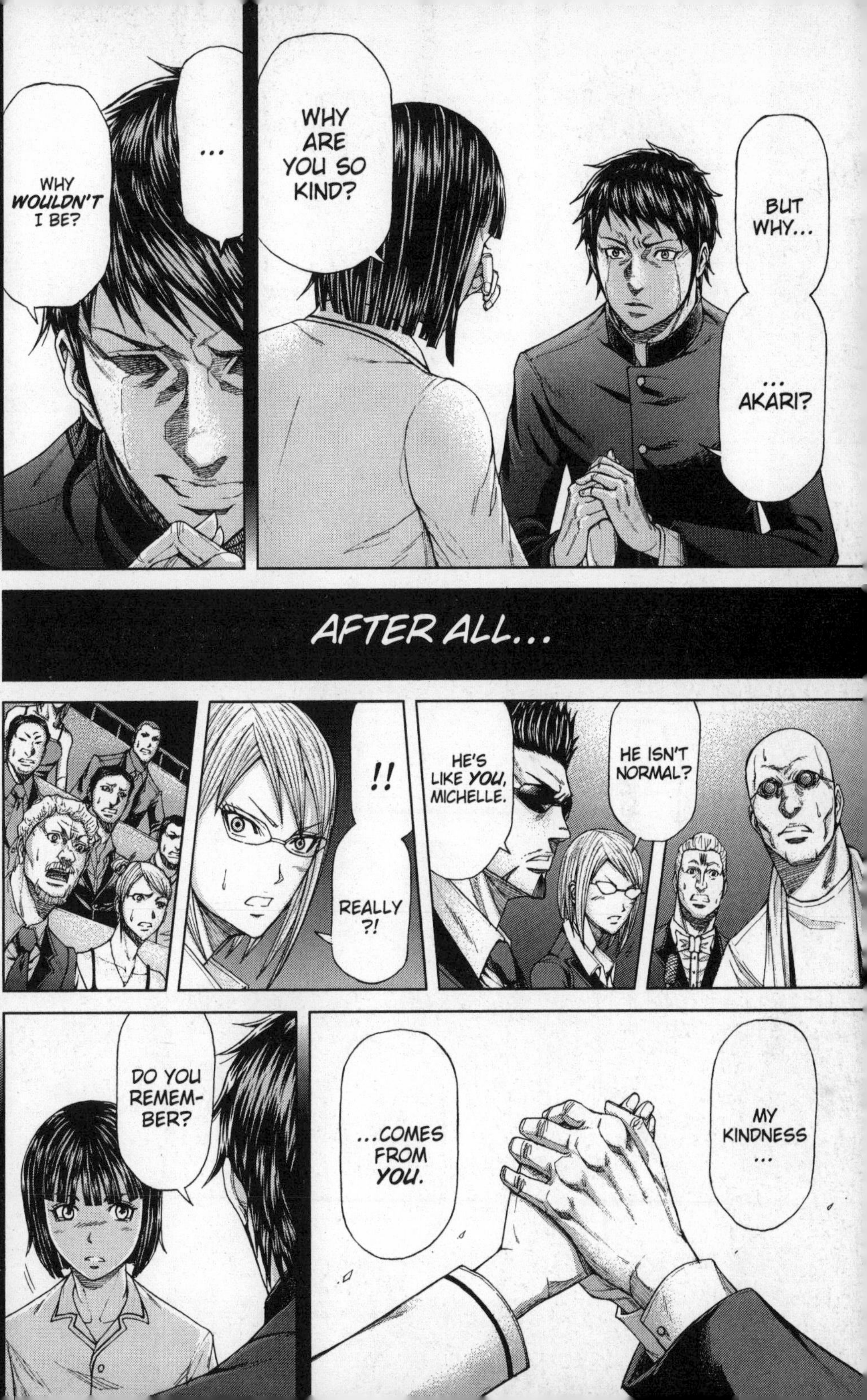
BUT WHY...
... AKARI?
WHY ARE YOU SO KIND?
...
WHY WOULDN'T I BE?
AFTER ALL...
HE ISN'T NORMAL?
HE'S LIKE YOU, MICHELLE.
!!
REALLY?!
MY KINDNESS...
...COMES FROM YOU.
DO YOU REMEM-BER?

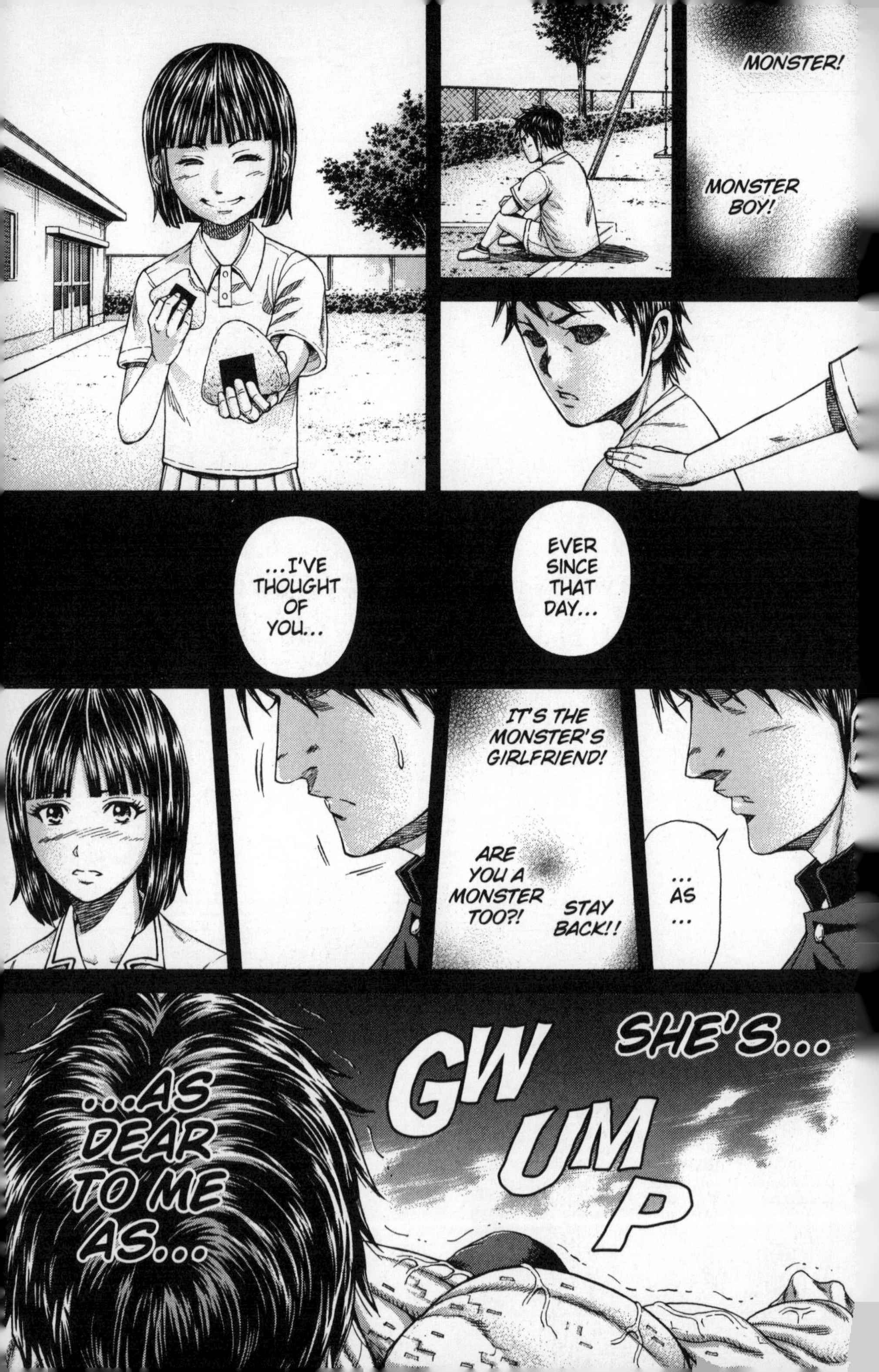

MONSTER!
MONSTER BOY!
EVER SINCE THAT DAY...
...I'VE THOUGHT OF YOU...
... AS ...
IT'S THE MONSTER'S GIRLFRIEND!
STAY BACK!!
ARE YOU A MONSTER TOO?!
SHE'S...
GWUMP
...AS DEAR TO ME AS...

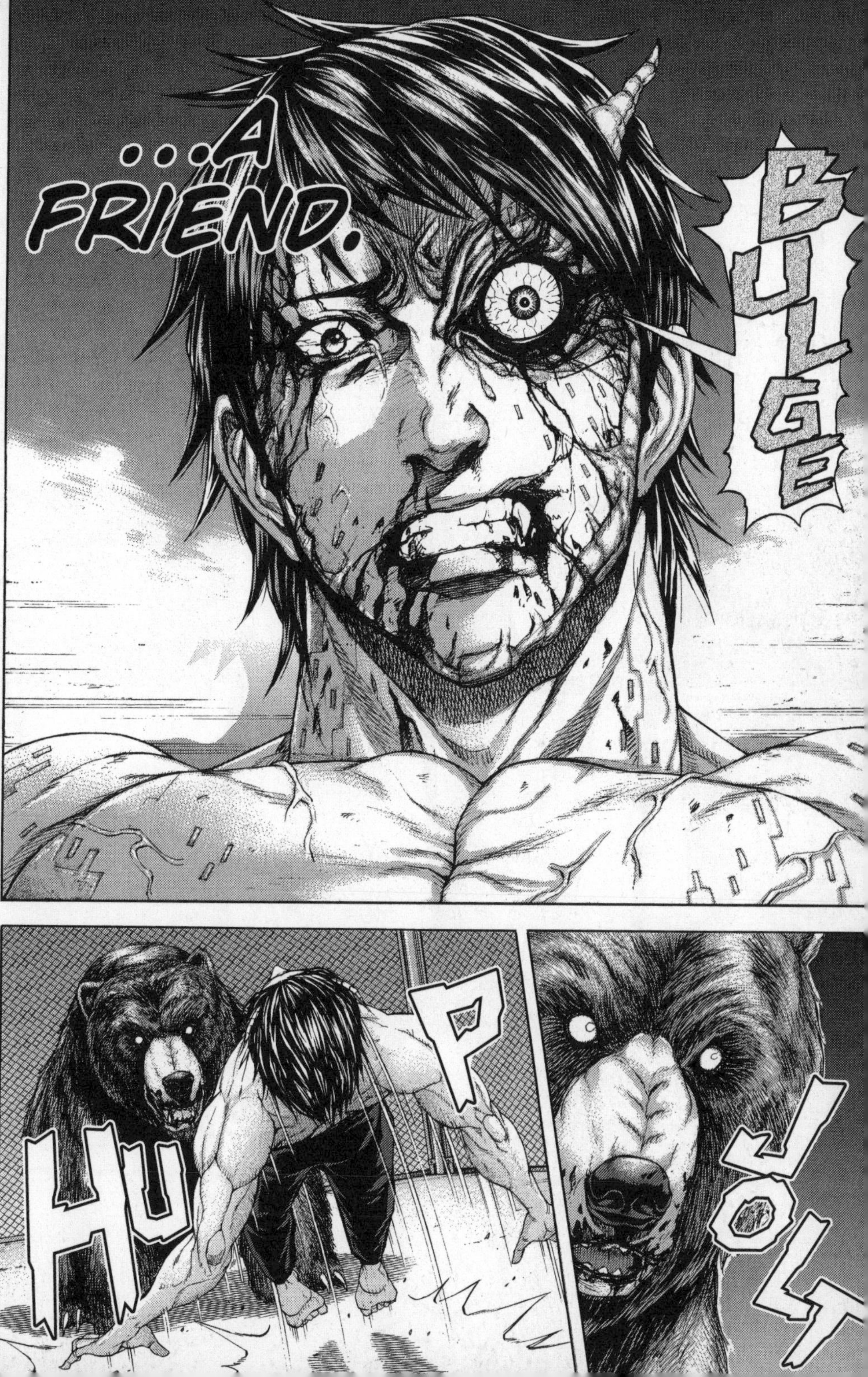
BULGE
...A FRIEND.
JOLT
HUP

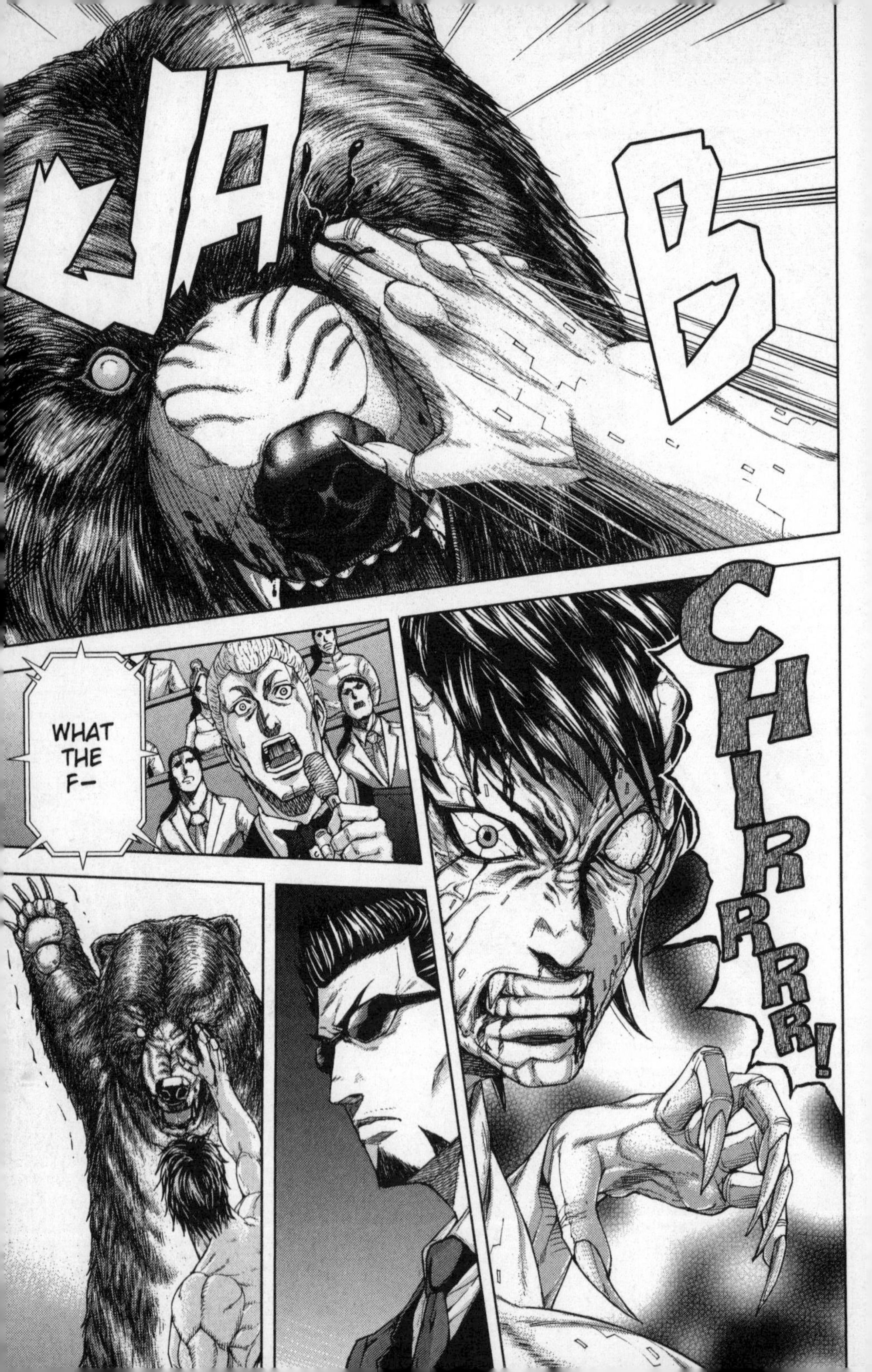
JAB
CHIRRRRR!
WHAT THE F–

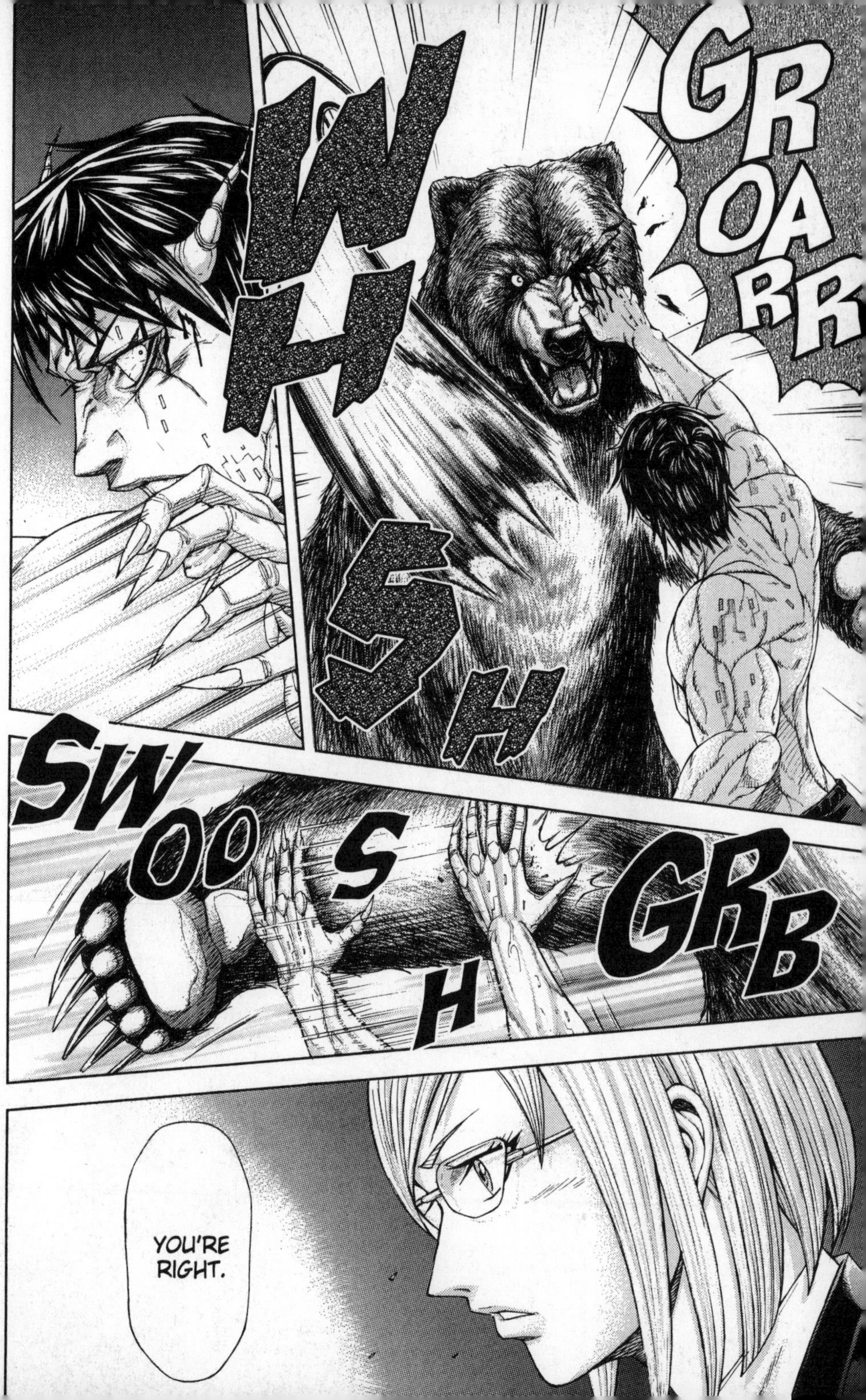
GROAARR
WHSH
GRB
SWOOSH
YOU'RE RIGHT.

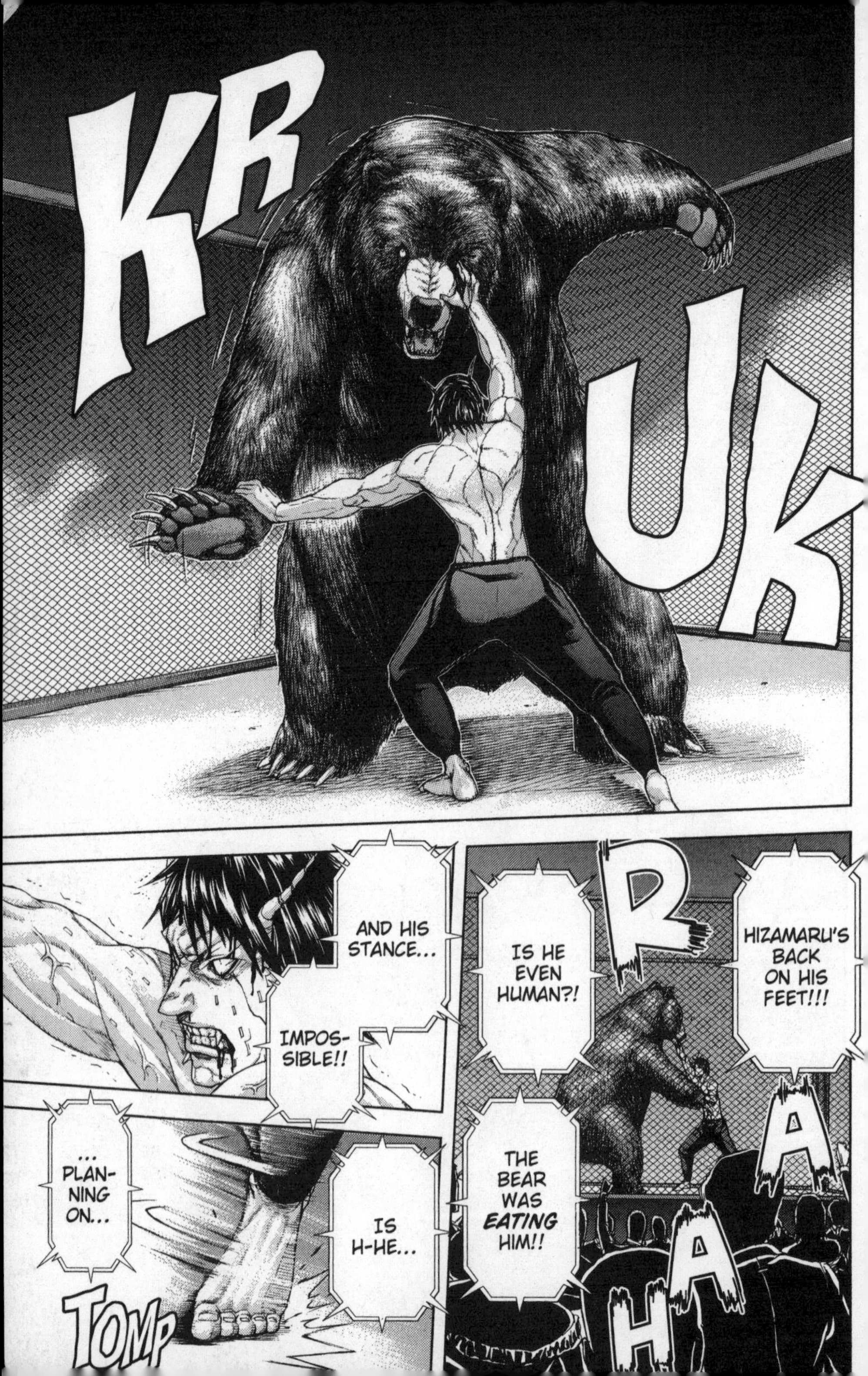
KRUK
HIZAMARU'S BACK ON HIS FEET!!!
R
IS HE EVEN HUMAN?!
THE BEAR WAS *EATING* HIM!!
A
A
HA
H
AND HIS STANCE...
IMPOSSIBLE!!
IS H-HE...
...PLAN-NING ON...
TOMP

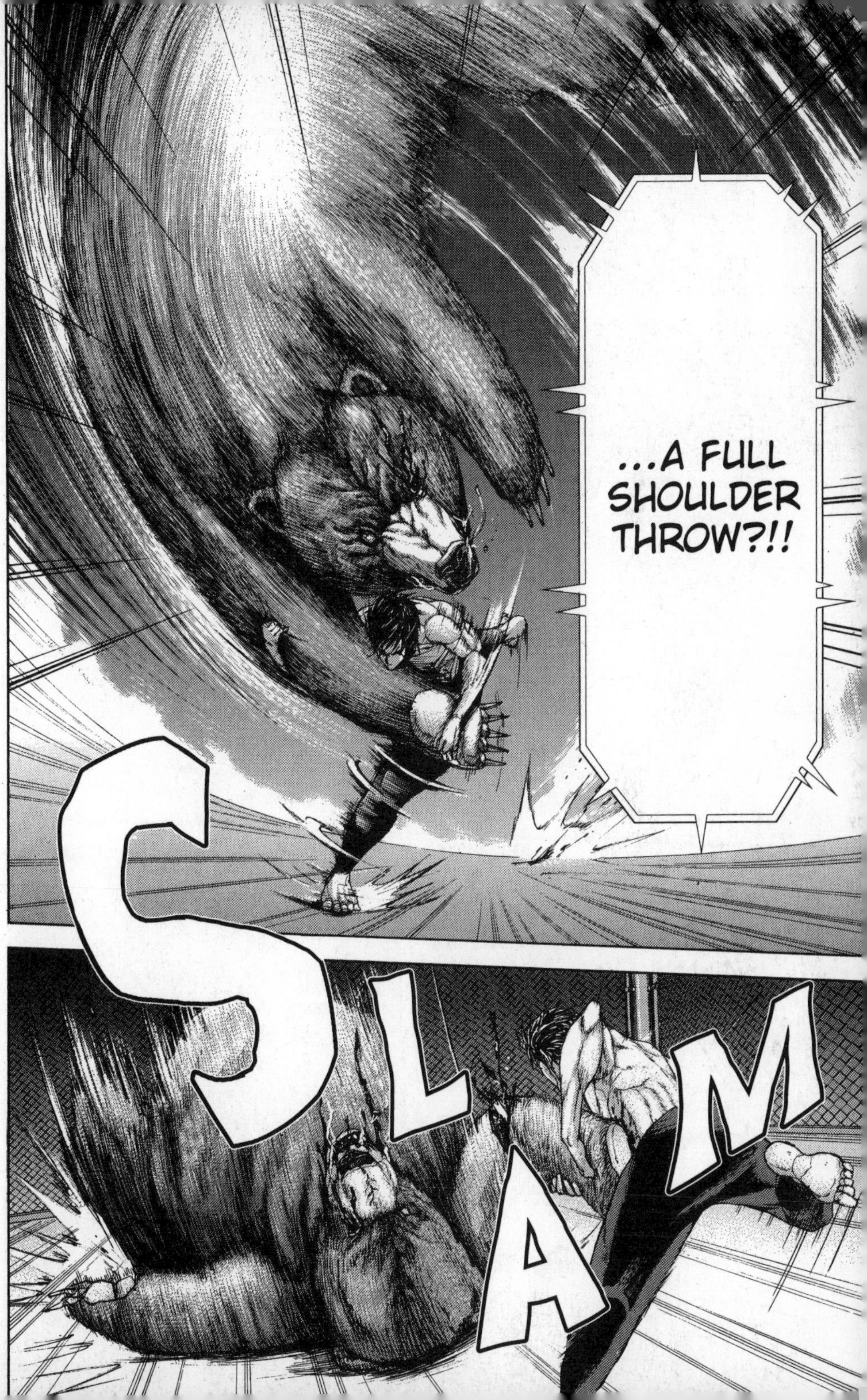
...A FULL SHOULDER THROW?!!
SLAM

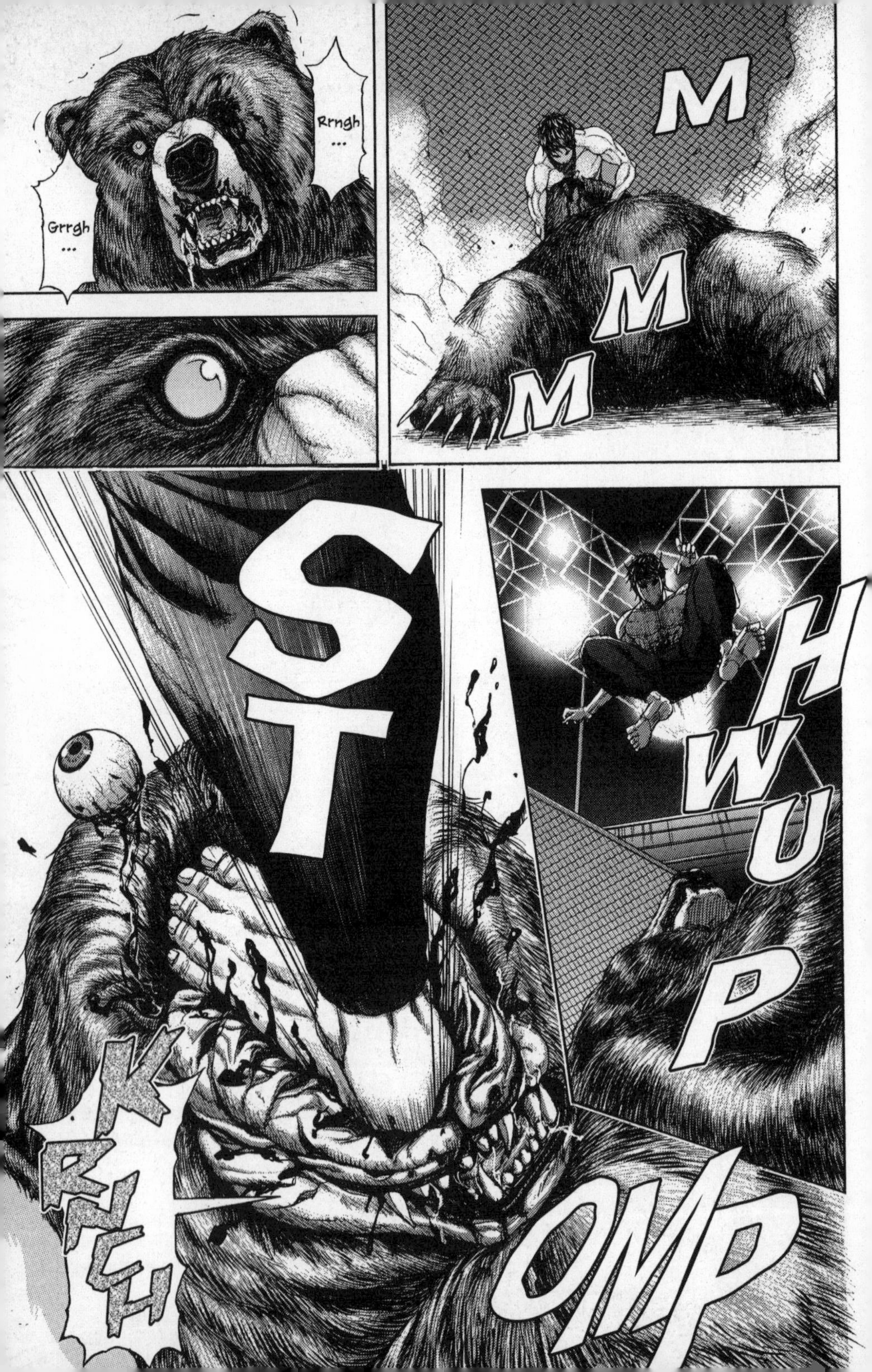
MMM
Rrngh ...
Grrgh ...
HWUP
ST
OMP
KRNCH

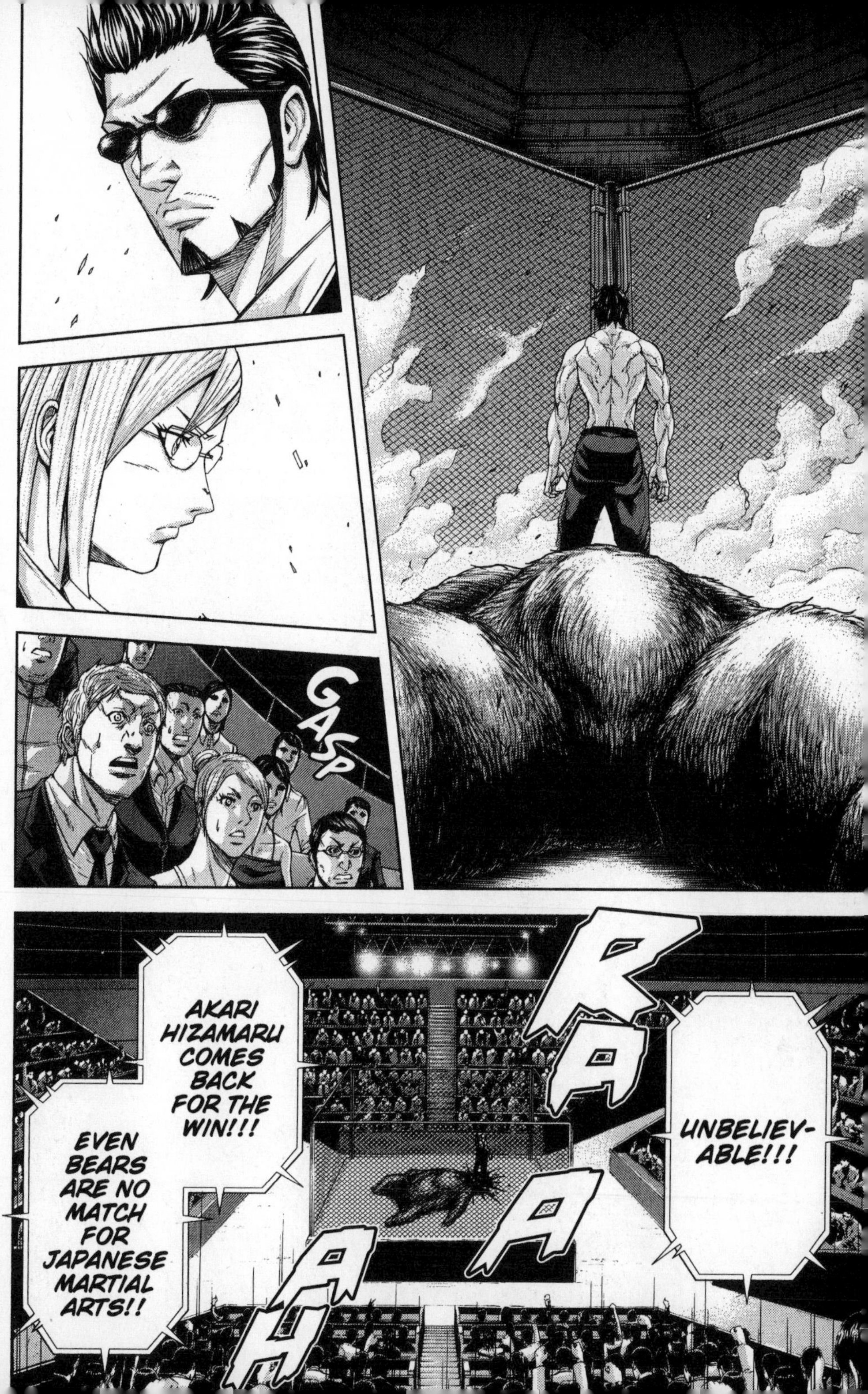
GASP
UNBELIEV-ABLE!!!
RAAAH
AKARI HIZAMARU COMES BACK FOR THE WIN!!!
EVEN BEARS ARE NO MATCH FOR JAPANESE MARTIAL ARTS!!

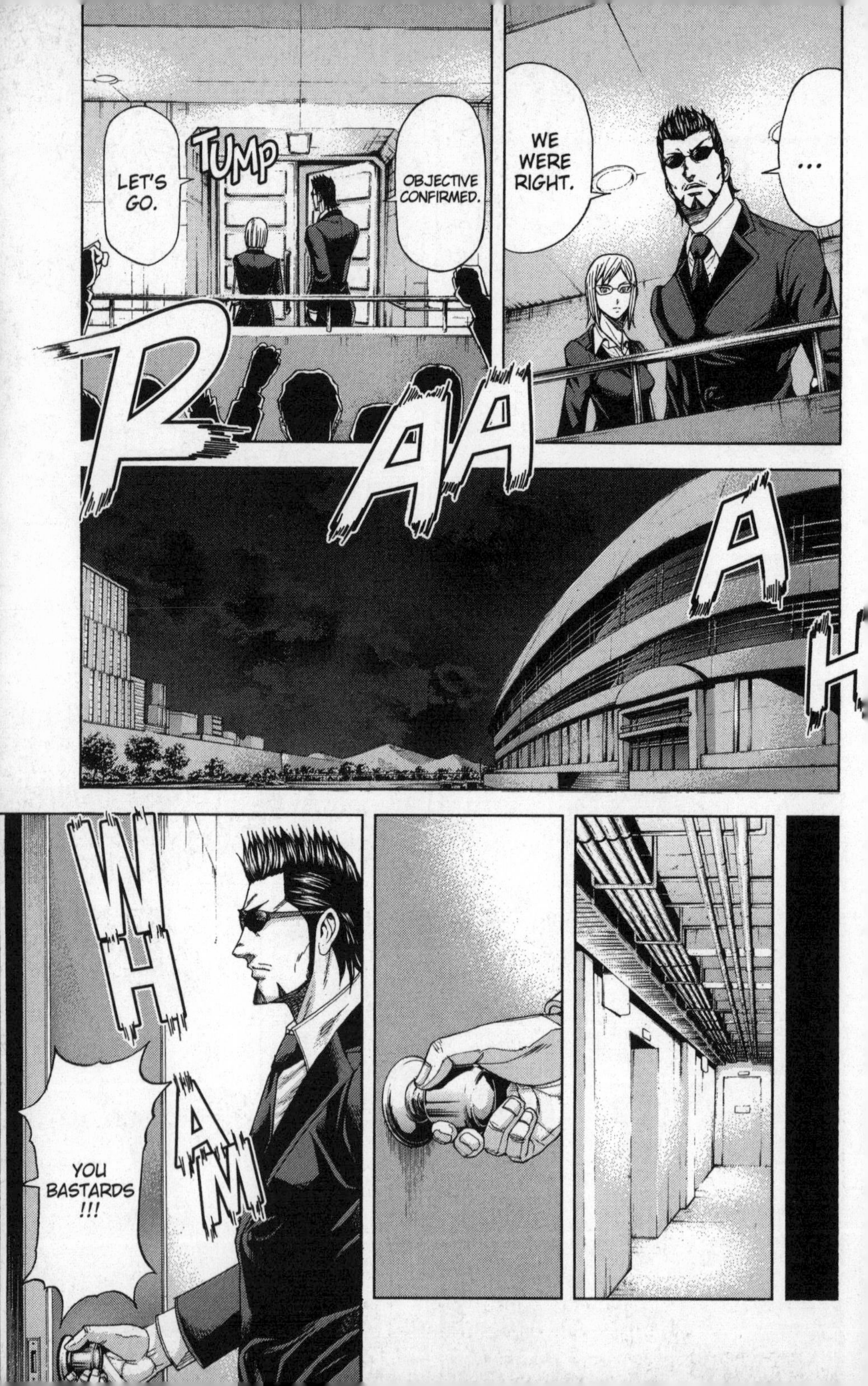
...
WE WERE RIGHT.
OBJECTIVE CONFIRMED.
TUMP
LET'S GO.
RAAAAH
WHAM
YOU BASTARDS!!!

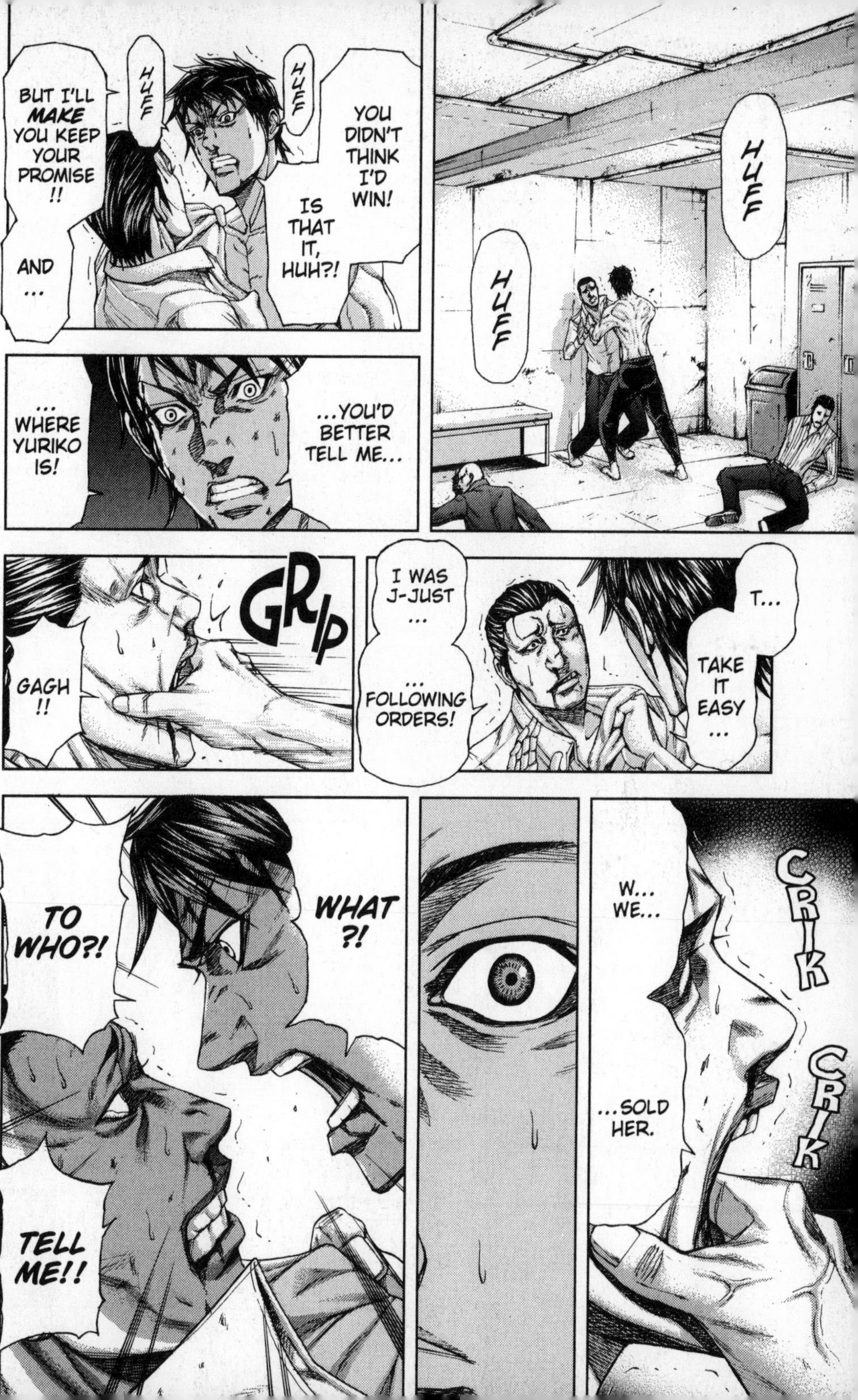
HUFF
HUFF
YOU DIDN'T THINK I'D WIN!
IS THAT IT, HUH?!
HUFF
HUFF
BUT I'LL MAKE YOU KEEP YOUR PROMISE !!
AND ...
...YOU'D BETTER TELL ME...
... WHERE YURIKO IS!
T...
TAKE IT EASY ...
I WAS J-JUST ...
... FOLLOWING ORDERS!
GRIP
GAGH !!
CRIK
W... WE...
CRIK
...SOLD HER.
WHAT ?!
TO WHO?!
TELL ME!!

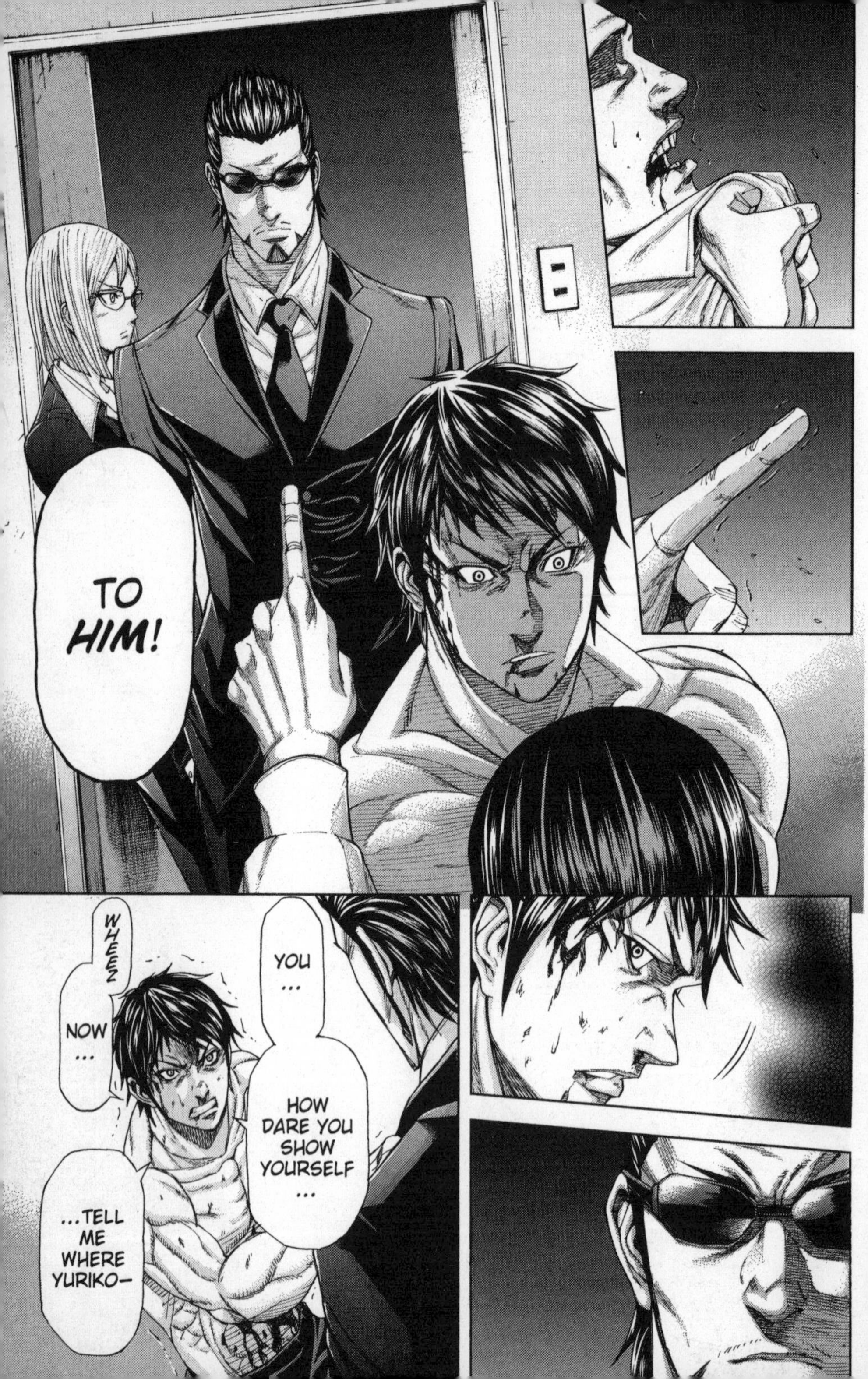
TO HIM!
YOU ...
HOW DARE YOU SHOW YOURSELF ...
WHEEZ
NOW ...
...TELL ME WHERE YURIKO—

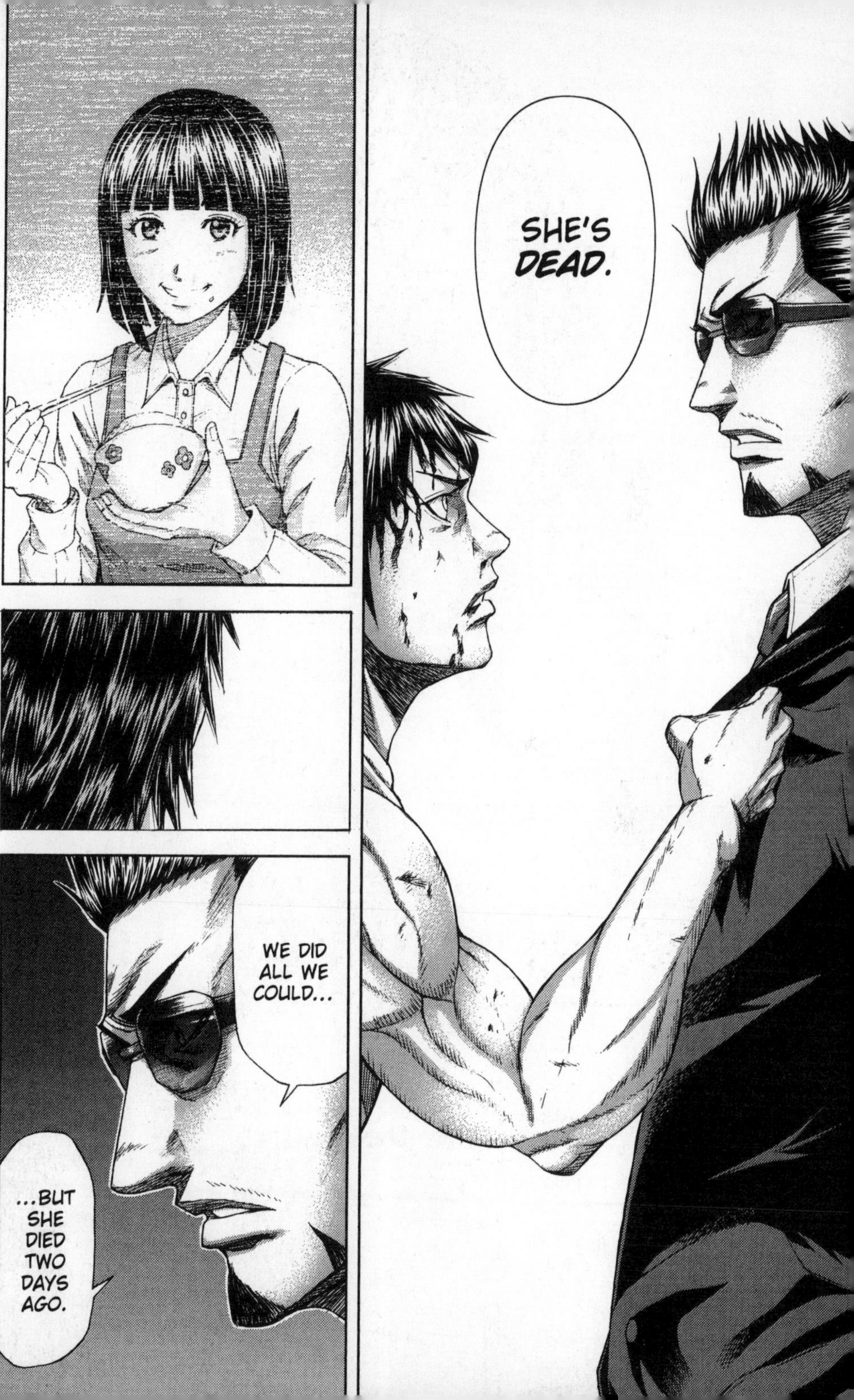
SHE'S *DEAD.*
WE DID ALL WE COULD...
...BUT SHE DIED TWO DAYS AGO.

GO AHEAD.

TMP

NGH
...

WE WERE TOO LATE.

SO IF YOU'RE GONNA HIT ME, DO IT.

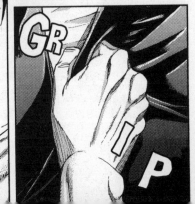

GR

IP

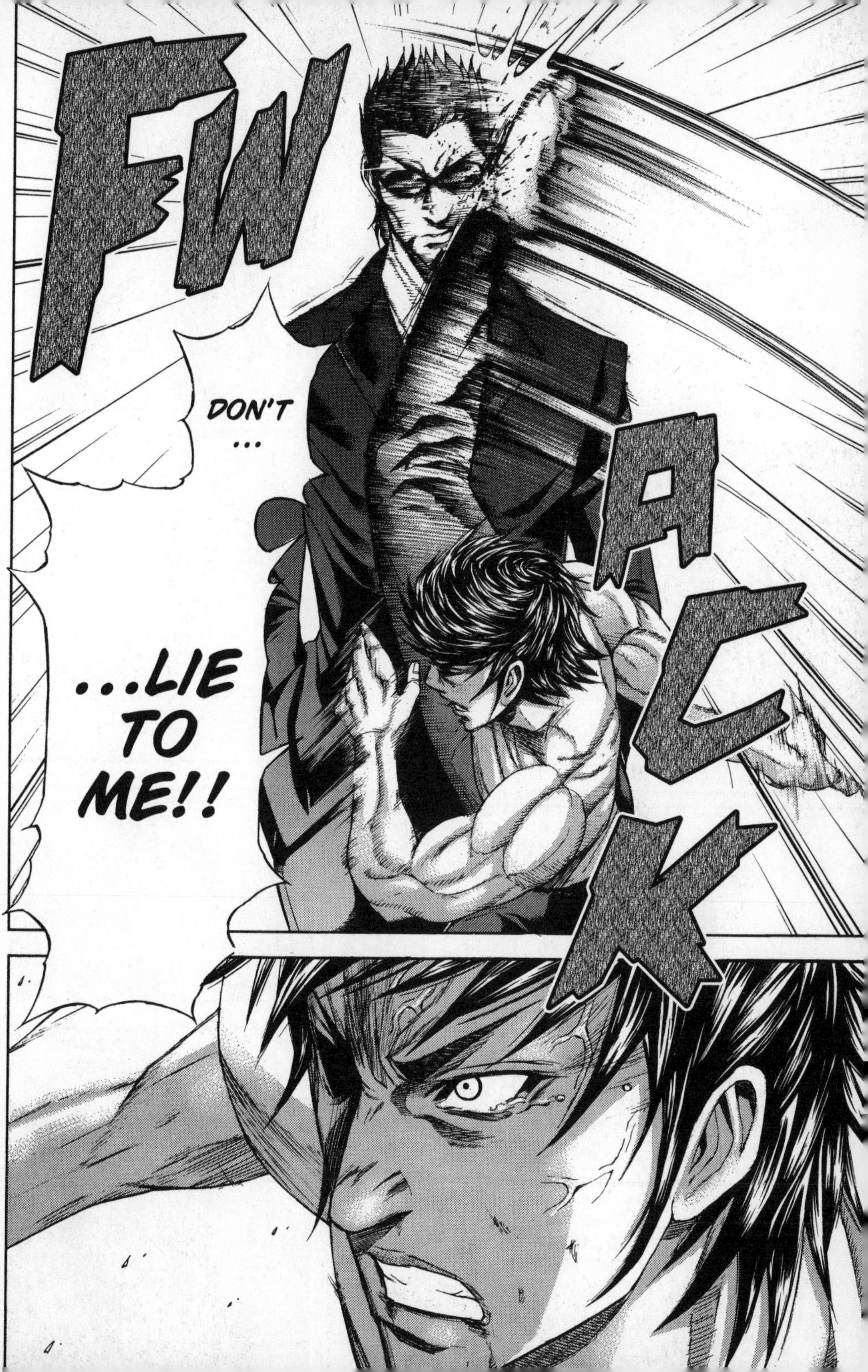
FWACK
DON'T ...
...LIE TO ME!!

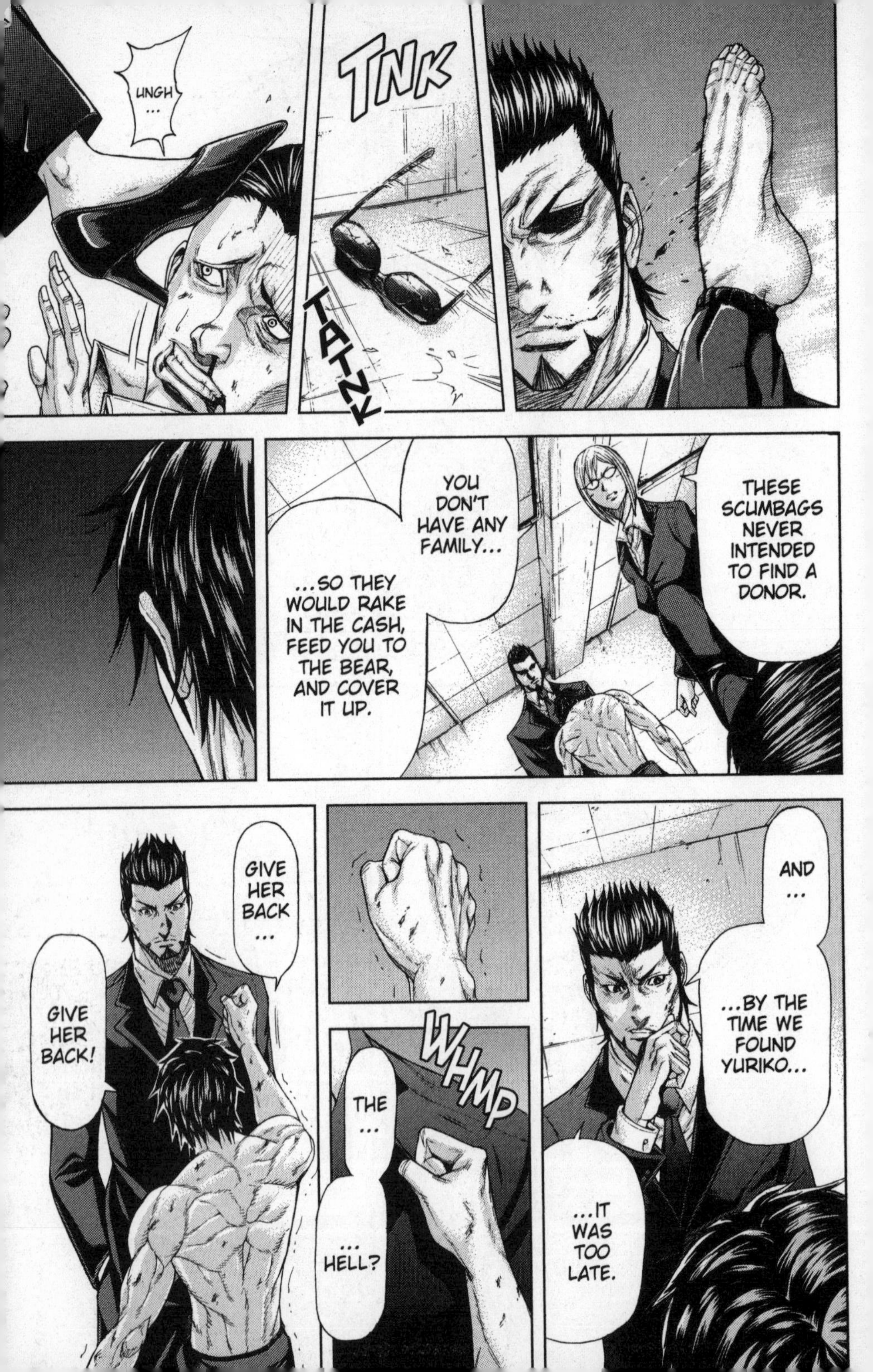
TNK
TATNK
UNGH...
THESE SCUMBAGS NEVER INTENDED TO FIND A DONOR.
YOU DON'T HAVE ANY FAMILY...
...SO THEY WOULD RAKE IN THE CASH, FEED YOU TO THE BEAR, AND COVER IT UP.
AND...
...BY THE TIME WE FOUND YURIKO...
...IT WAS TOO LATE.
WHMP
THE...
...HELL?
GIVE HER BACK...
GIVE HER BACK!

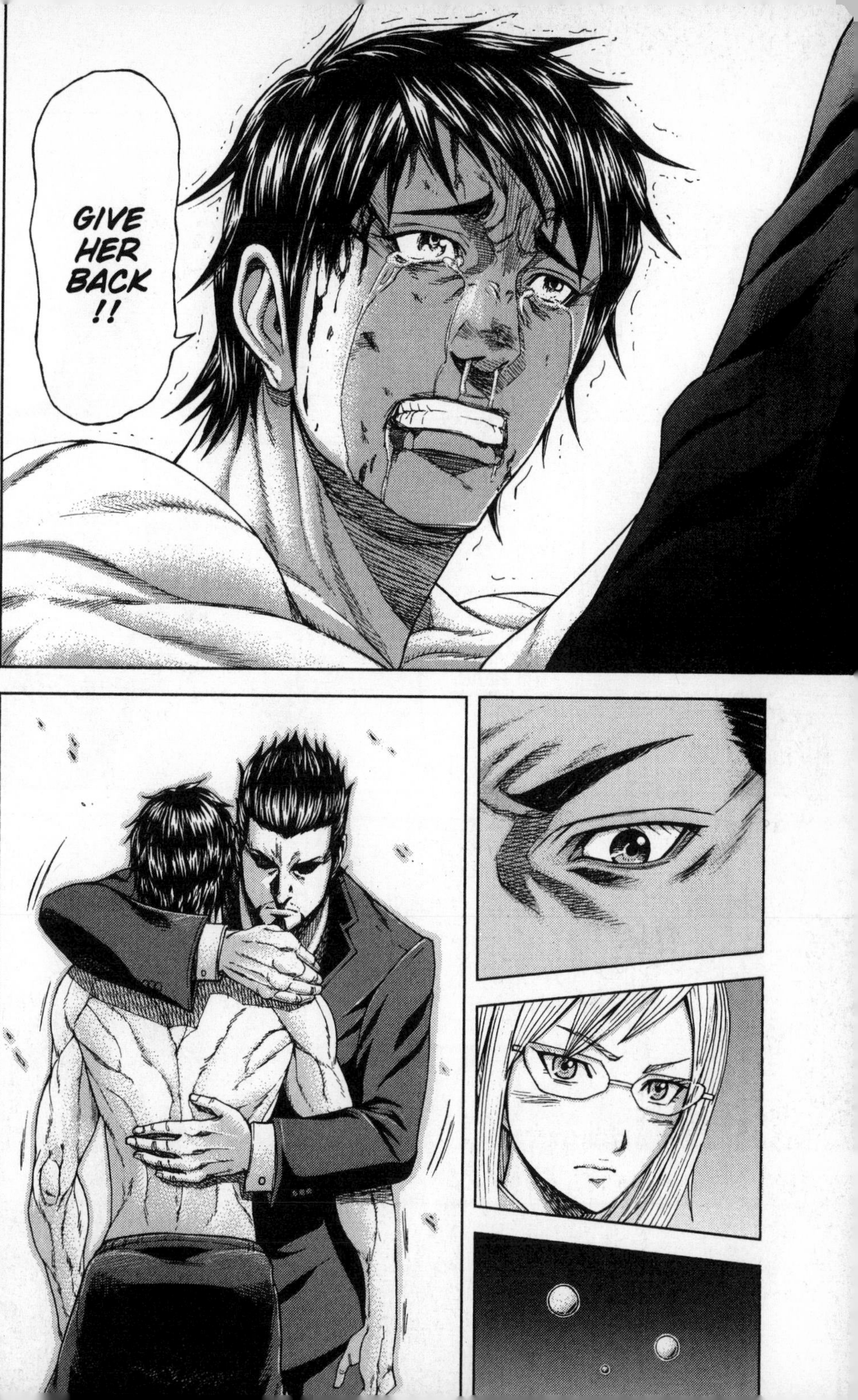
GIVE HER BACK !!

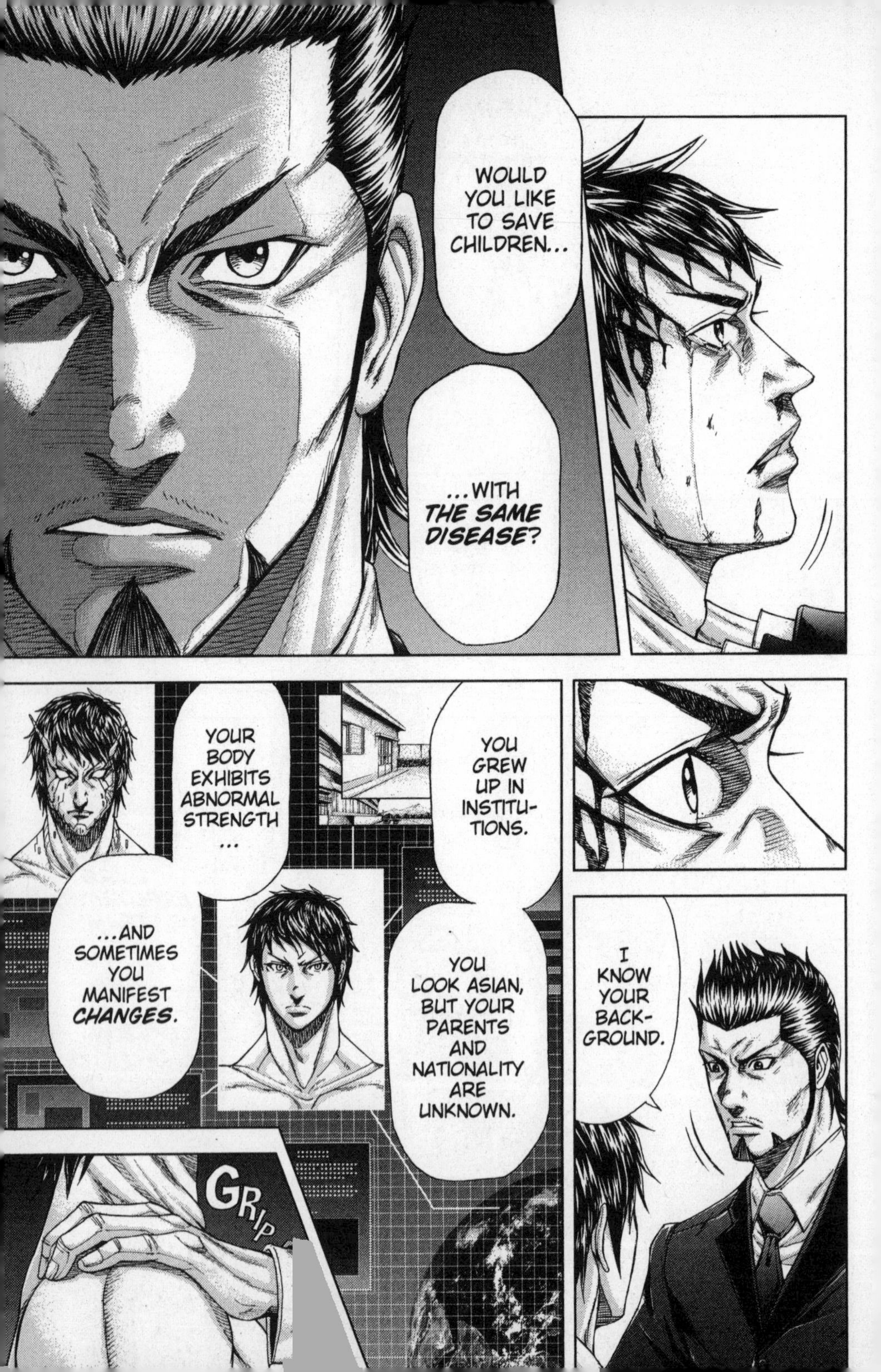
WOULD YOU LIKE TO SAVE CHILDREN...
...WITH *THE SAME DISEASE*?
I KNOW YOUR BACK-GROUND.
YOU GREW UP IN INSTITU-TIONS.
YOUR BODY EXHIBITS ABNORMAL STRENGTH ...
YOU LOOK ASIAN, BUT YOUR PARENTS AND NATIONALITY ARE UNKNOWN.
...AND SOMETIMES YOU MANIFEST ***CHANGES***.
GRIP

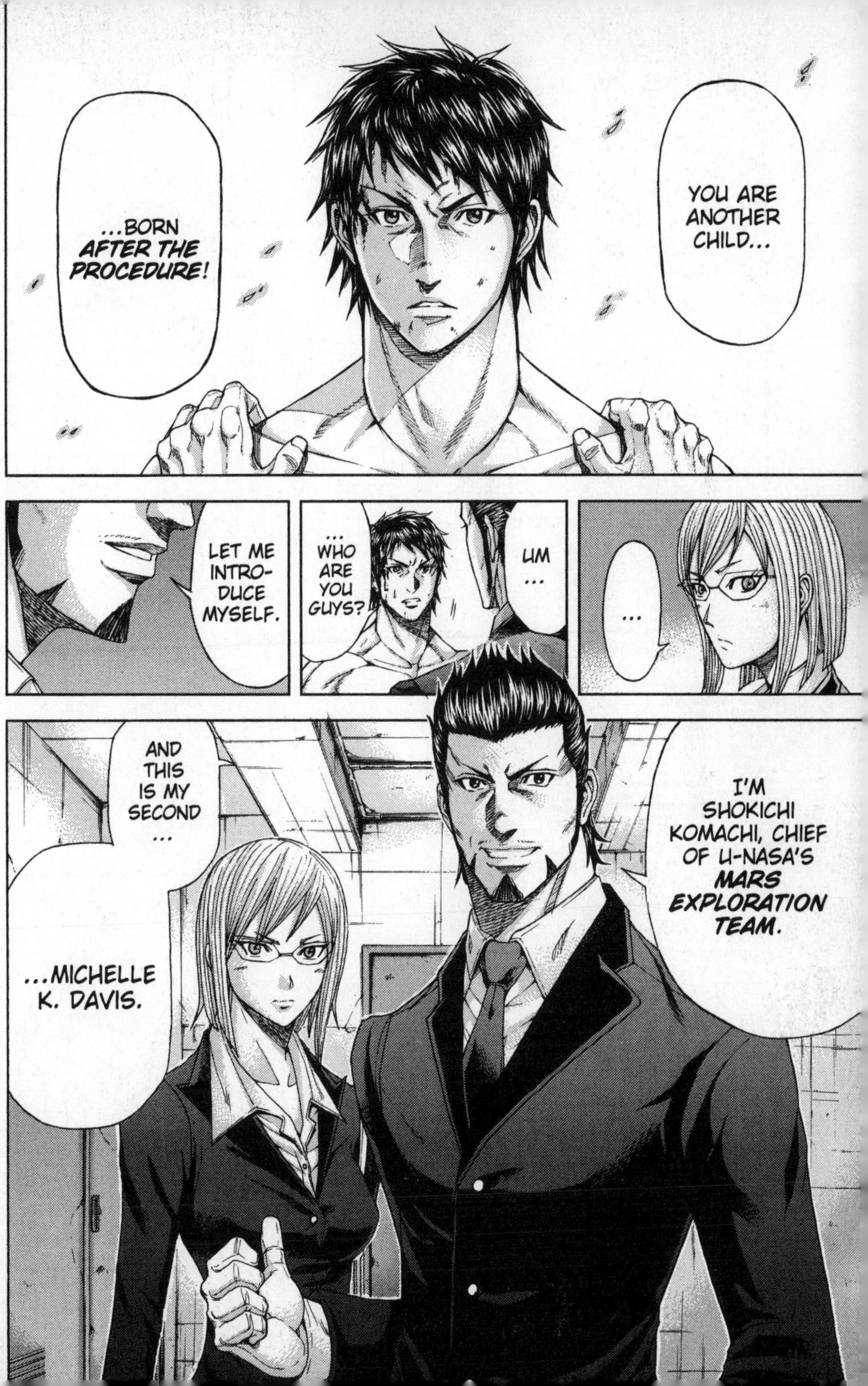
YOU ARE ANOTHER CHILD...
...BORN AFTER THE PROCEDURE!
...
UM ...
... WHO ARE YOU GUYS?
LET ME INTRO-DUCE MYSELF.
I'M SHOKICHI KOMACHI, CHIEF OF U-NASA'S MARS EXPLORATION TEAM.
AND THIS IS MY SECOND ...
...MICHELLE K. DAVIS.

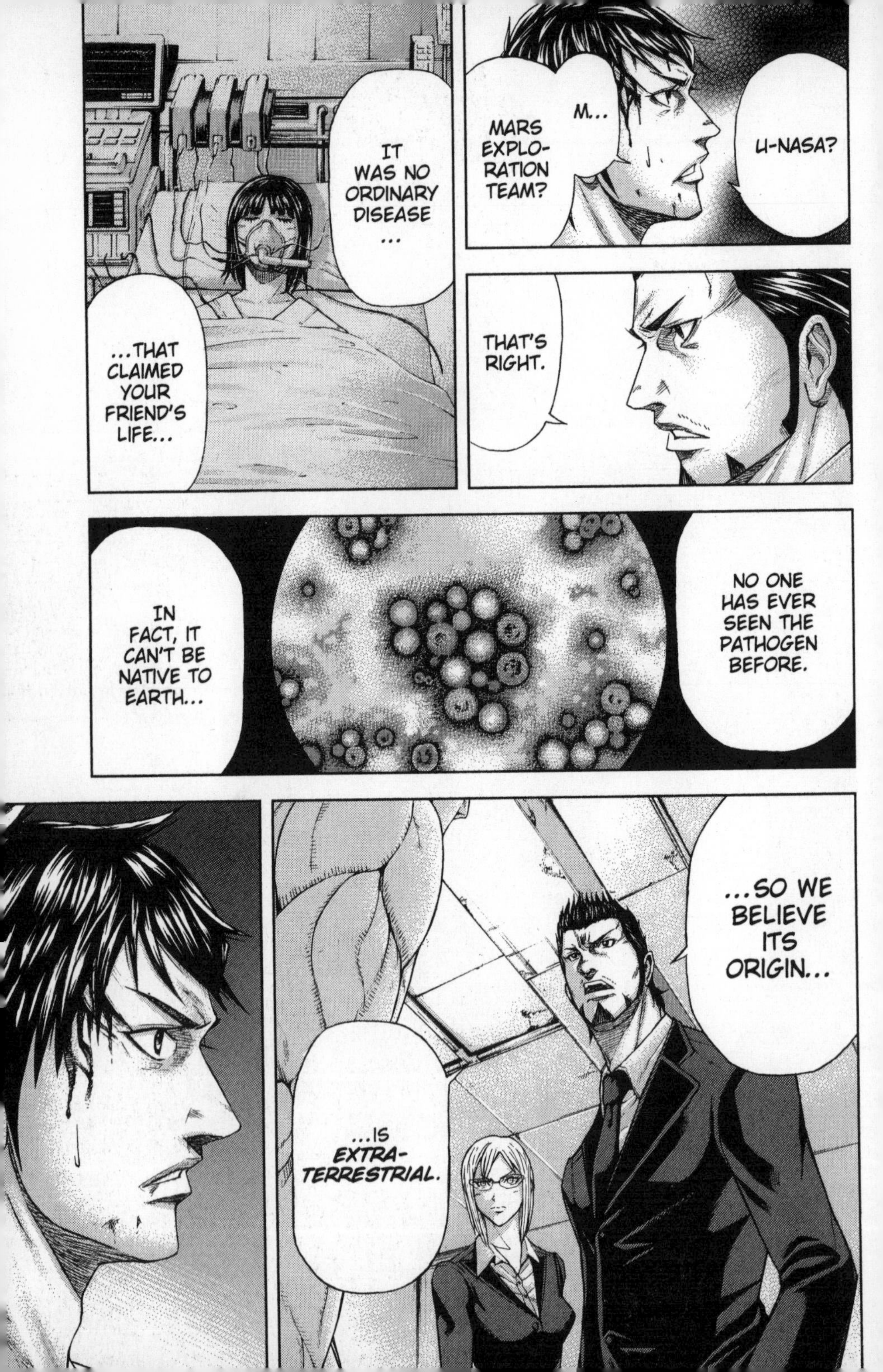
U-NASA?
M...
MARS EXPLORATION TEAM?
THAT'S RIGHT.
IT WAS NO ORDINARY DISEASE...
...THAT CLAIMED YOUR FRIEND'S LIFE...
NO ONE HAS EVER SEEN THE PATHOGEN BEFORE.
IN FACT, IT CAN'T BE NATIVE TO EARTH...
...SO WE BELIEVE ITS ORIGIN...
...IS *EXTRA-TERRESTRIAL*.

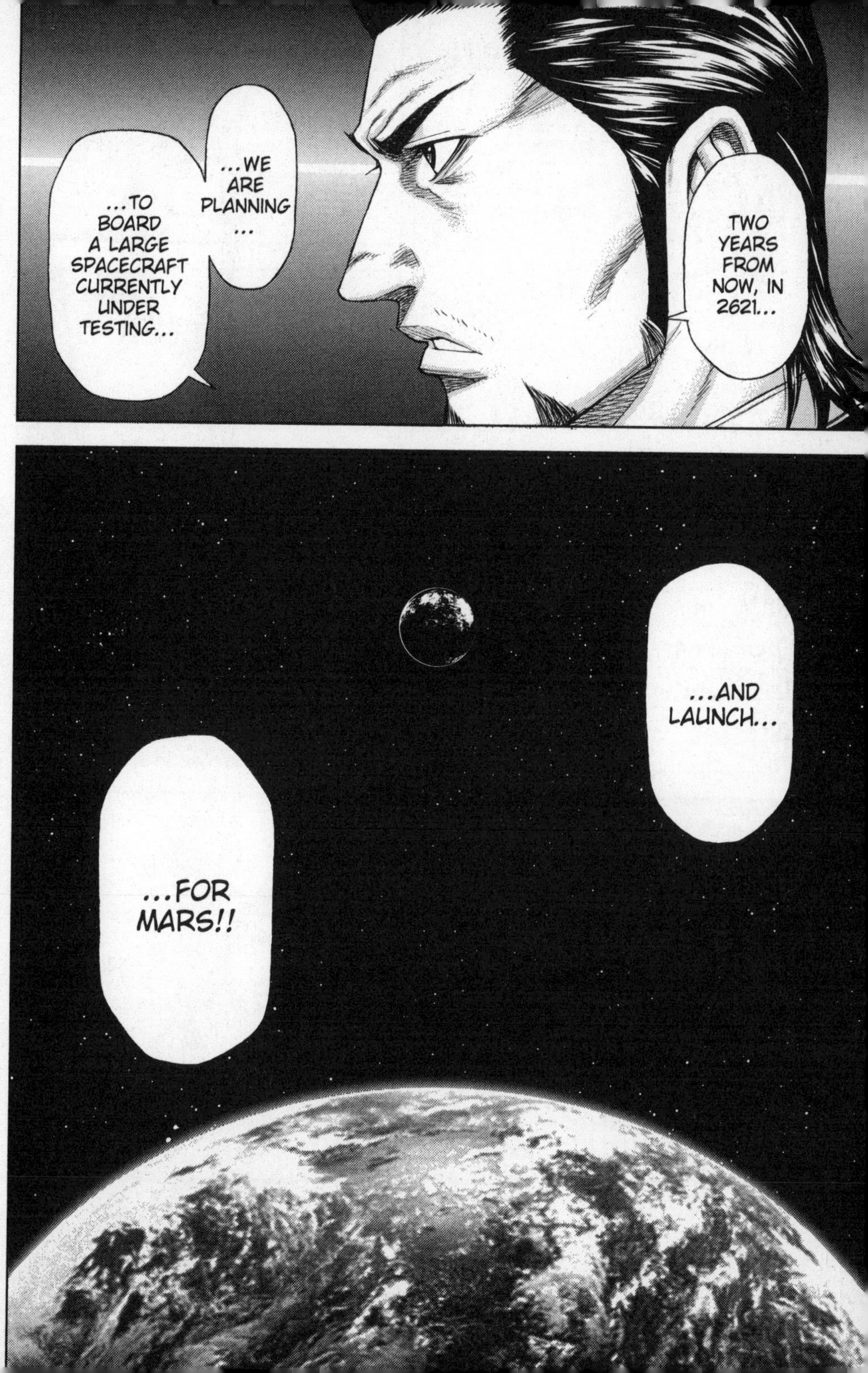
TWO YEARS FROM NOW, IN 2621...
...WE ARE PLANNING...
...TO BOARD A LARGE SPACECRAFT CURRENTLY UNDER TESTING...
...AND LAUNCH...
...FOR MARS!!

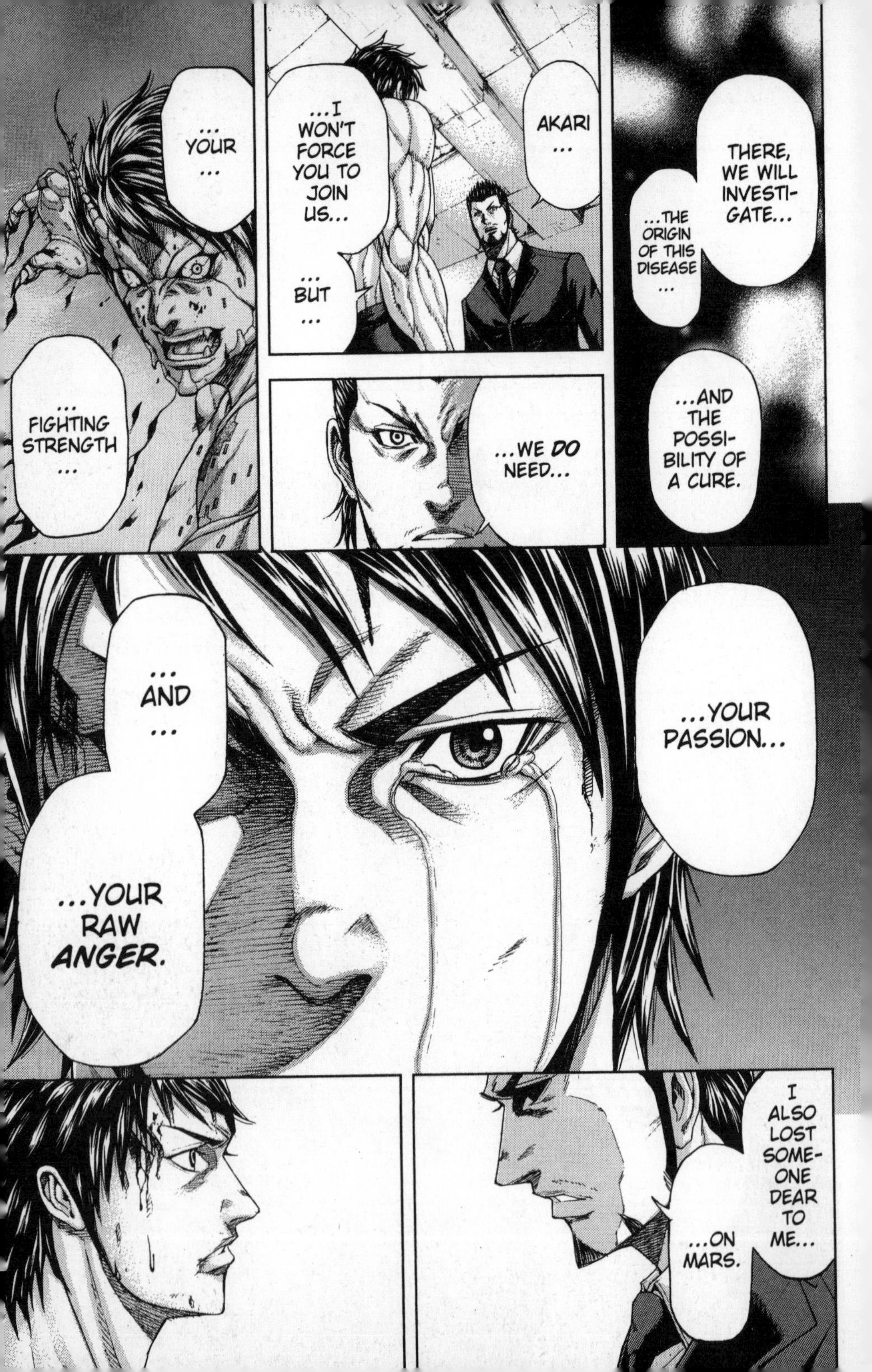
THERE, WE WILL INVESTIGATE...
...THE ORIGIN OF THIS DISEASE...
...AND THE POSSIBILITY OF A CURE.
AKARI...
...I WON'T FORCE YOU TO JOIN US...
...BUT...
...WE *DO* NEED...
...YOUR...
...FIGHTING STRENGTH...
...YOUR PASSION...
...AND...
...YOUR RAW *ANGER*.
I ALSO LOST SOMEONE DEAR TO ME...
...ON MARS.

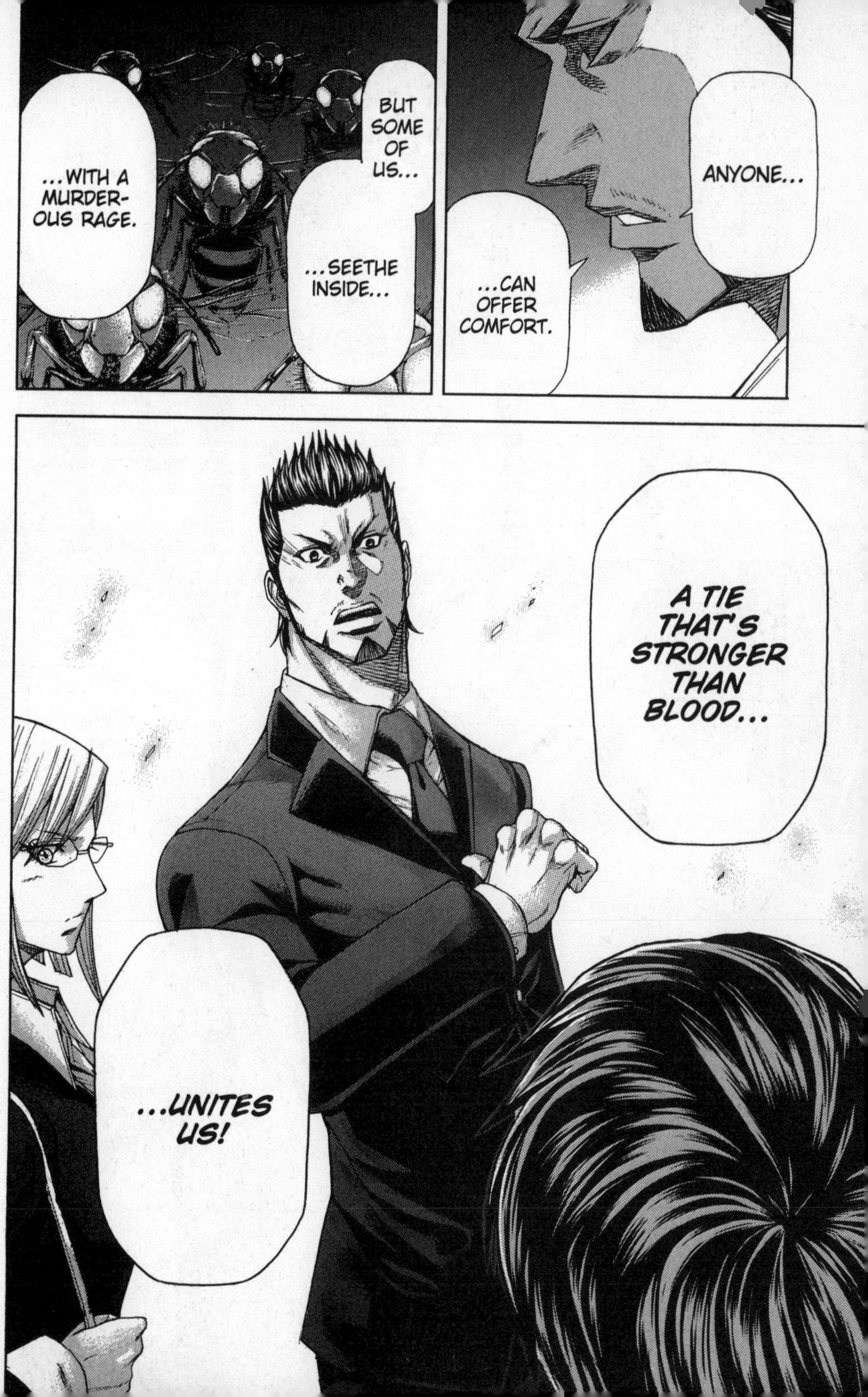
ANYONE...
...CAN OFFER COMFORT.
BUT SOME OF US...
...SEETHE INSIDE...
...WITH A MURDER-OUS RAGE.
A TIE THAT'S STRONGER THAN BLOOD...
...UNITES US!

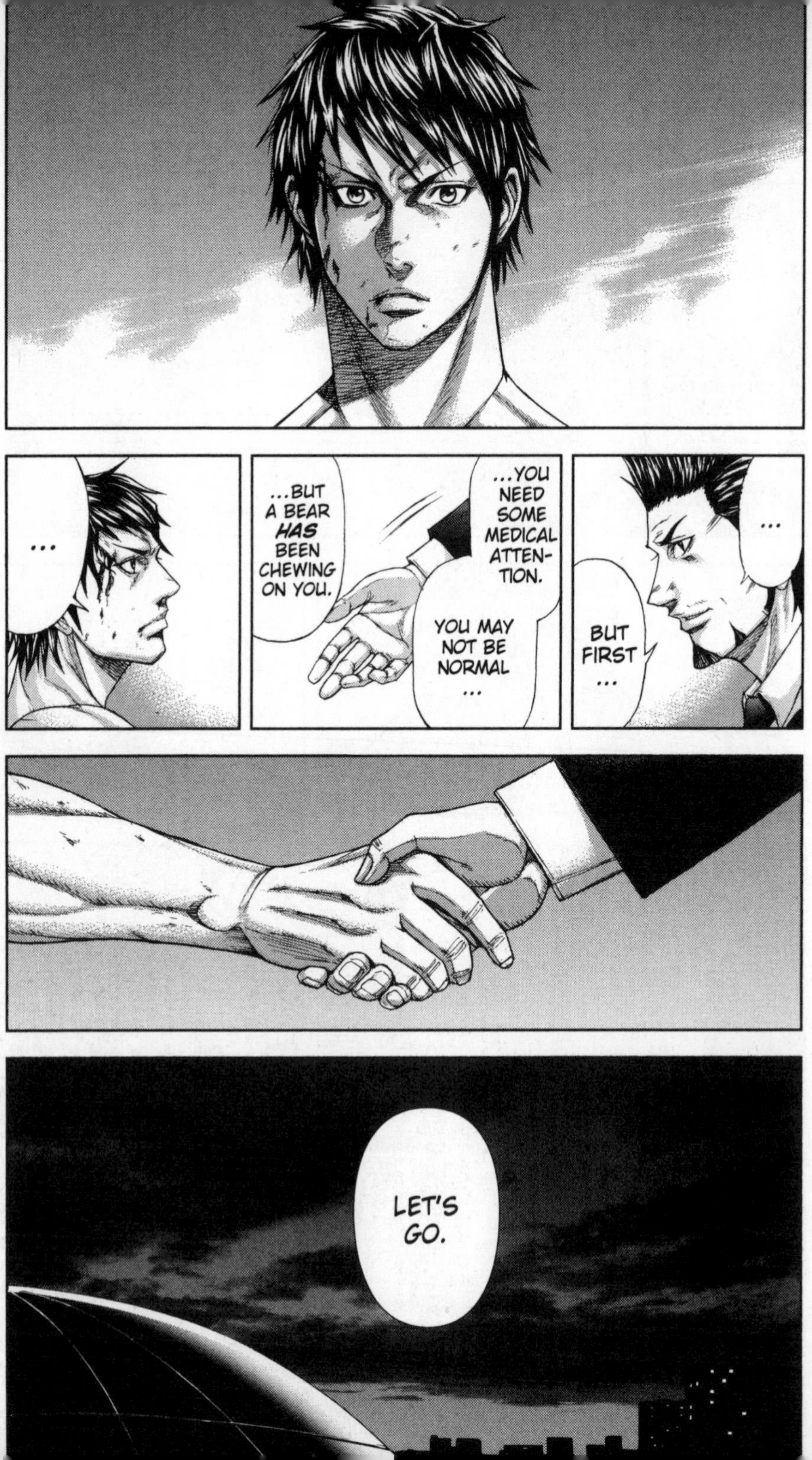
...
BUT FIRST ...
...YOU NEED SOME MEDICAL ATTENTION.
YOU MAY NOT BE NORMAL ...
...BUT A BEAR **HAS** BEEN CHEWING ON YOU.
...
LET'S GO.

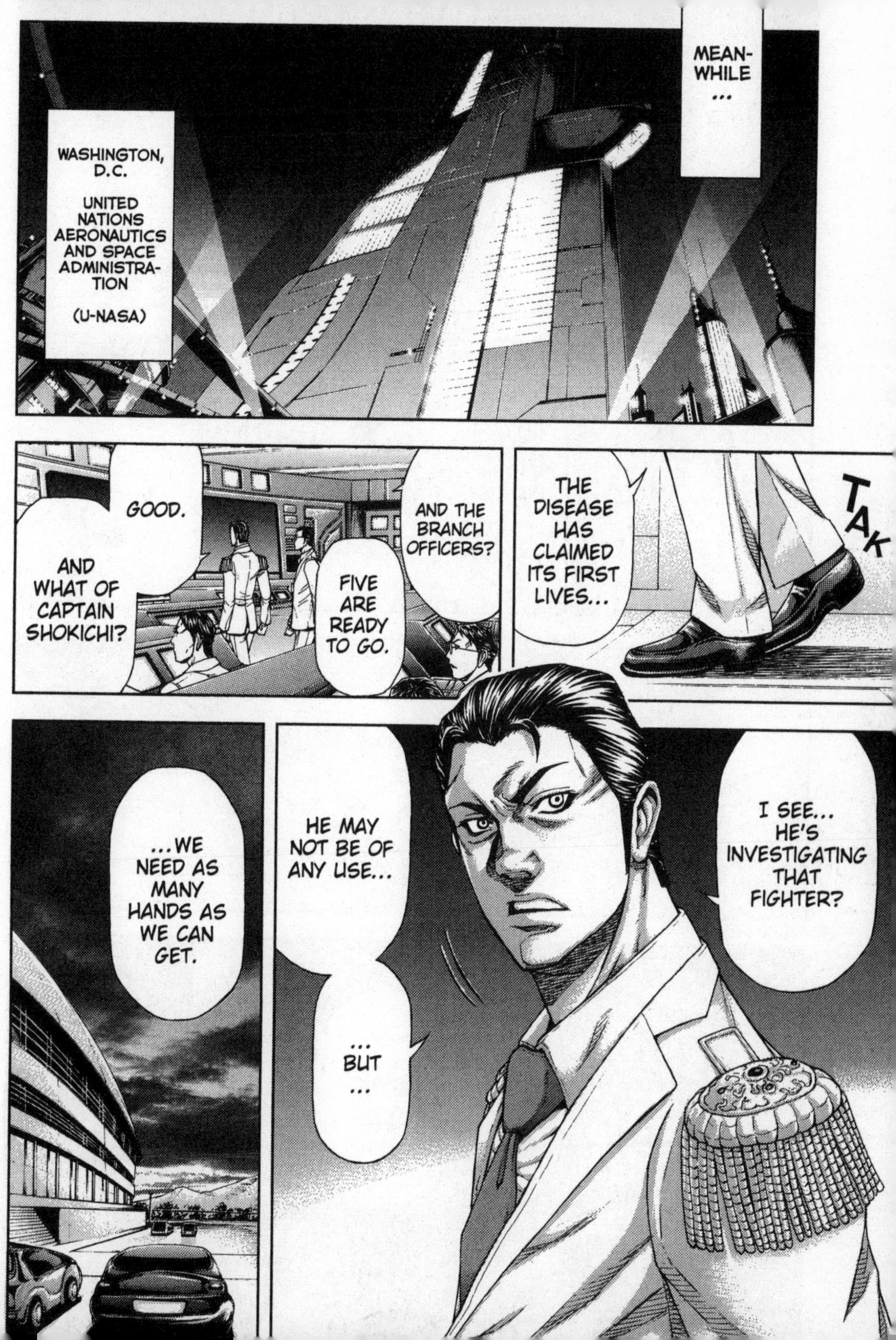
MEAN-WHILE...
WASHINGTON, D.C.
UNITED NATIONS AERONAUTICS AND SPACE ADMINISTRATION
(U-NASA)
TAK
THE DISEASE HAS CLAIMED ITS FIRST LIVES...
AND THE BRANCH OFFICERS?
FIVE ARE READY TO GO.
GOOD.
AND WHAT OF CAPTAIN SHOKICHI?
I SEE... HE'S INVESTIGATING THAT FIGHTER?
HE MAY NOT BE OF ANY USE...
...BUT...
...WE NEED AS MANY HANDS AS WE CAN GET.

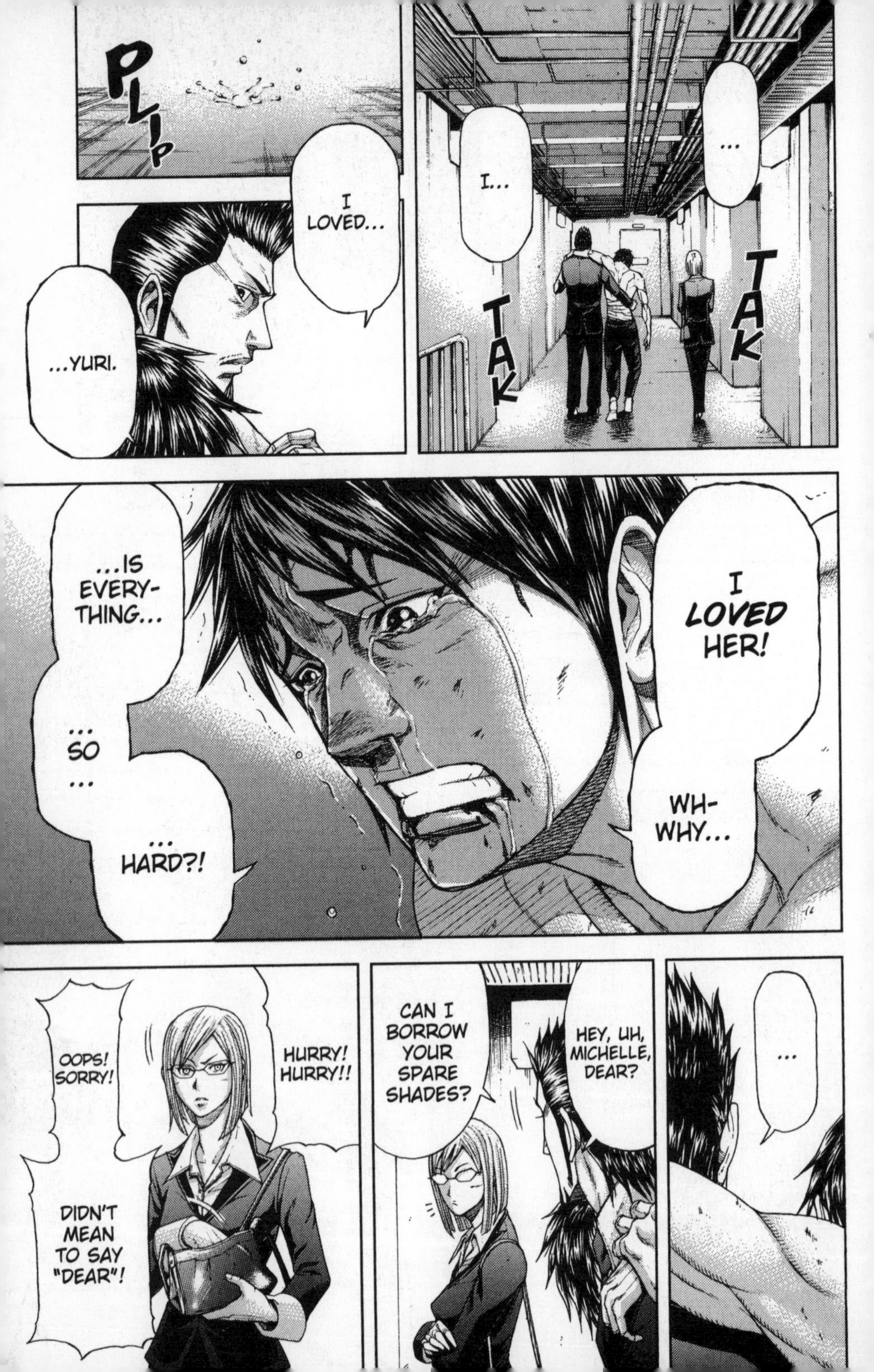
...
TAK
I...
TAK
PLIP
I LOVED...
...YURI.
I LOVED HER!
WH-WHY...
...IS EVERYTHING...
...SO...
...HARD?!
...
HEY, UH, MICHELLE, DEAR?
CAN I BORROW YOUR SPARE SHADES?
HURRY! HURRY!!
OOPS! SORRY!
DIDN'T MEAN TO SAY "DEAR"!

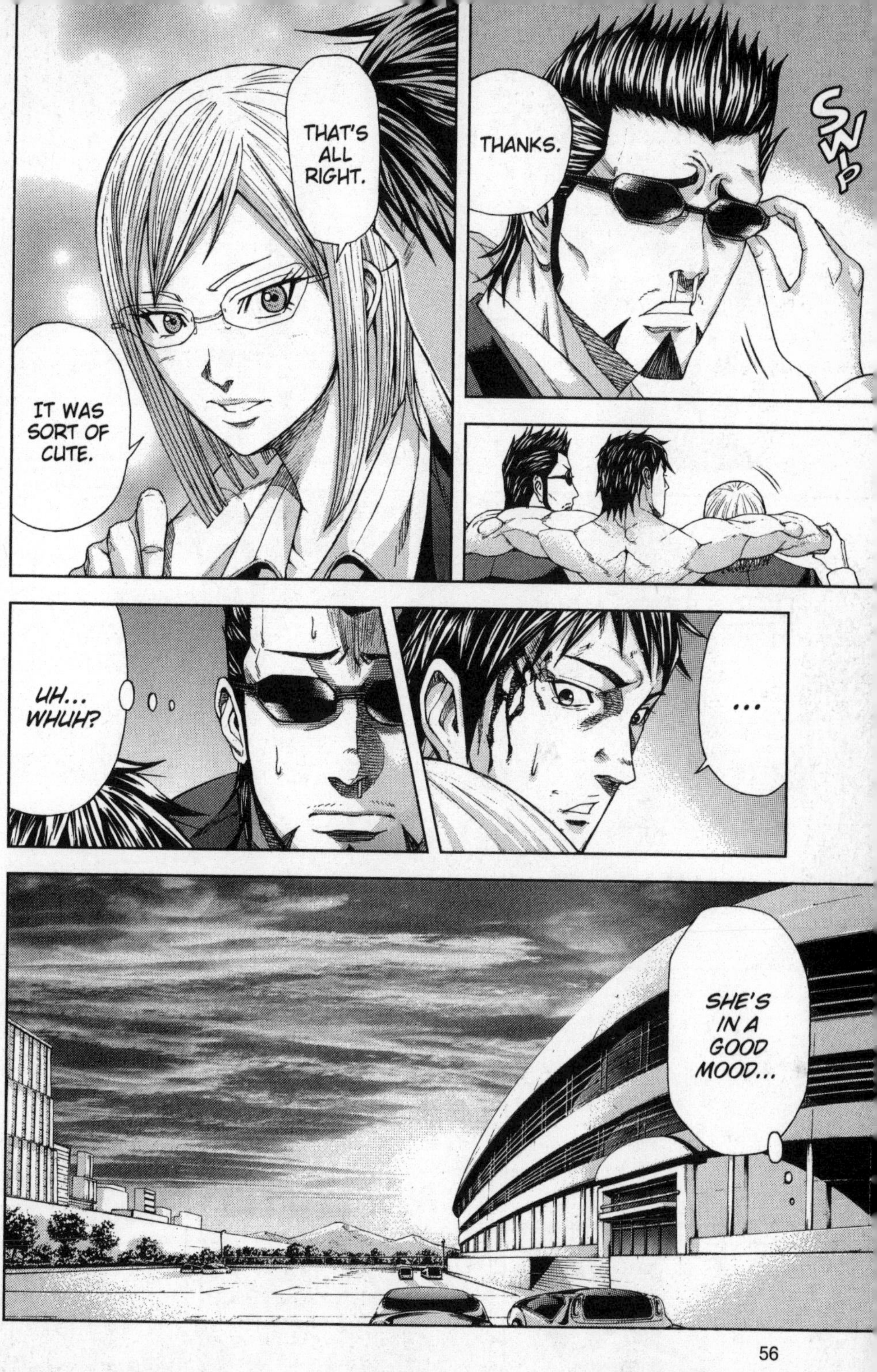
SWIP
THANKS.
THAT'S ALL RIGHT.
IT WAS SORT OF CUTE.
...
UH... WHUH?
SHE'S IN A GOOD MOOD...

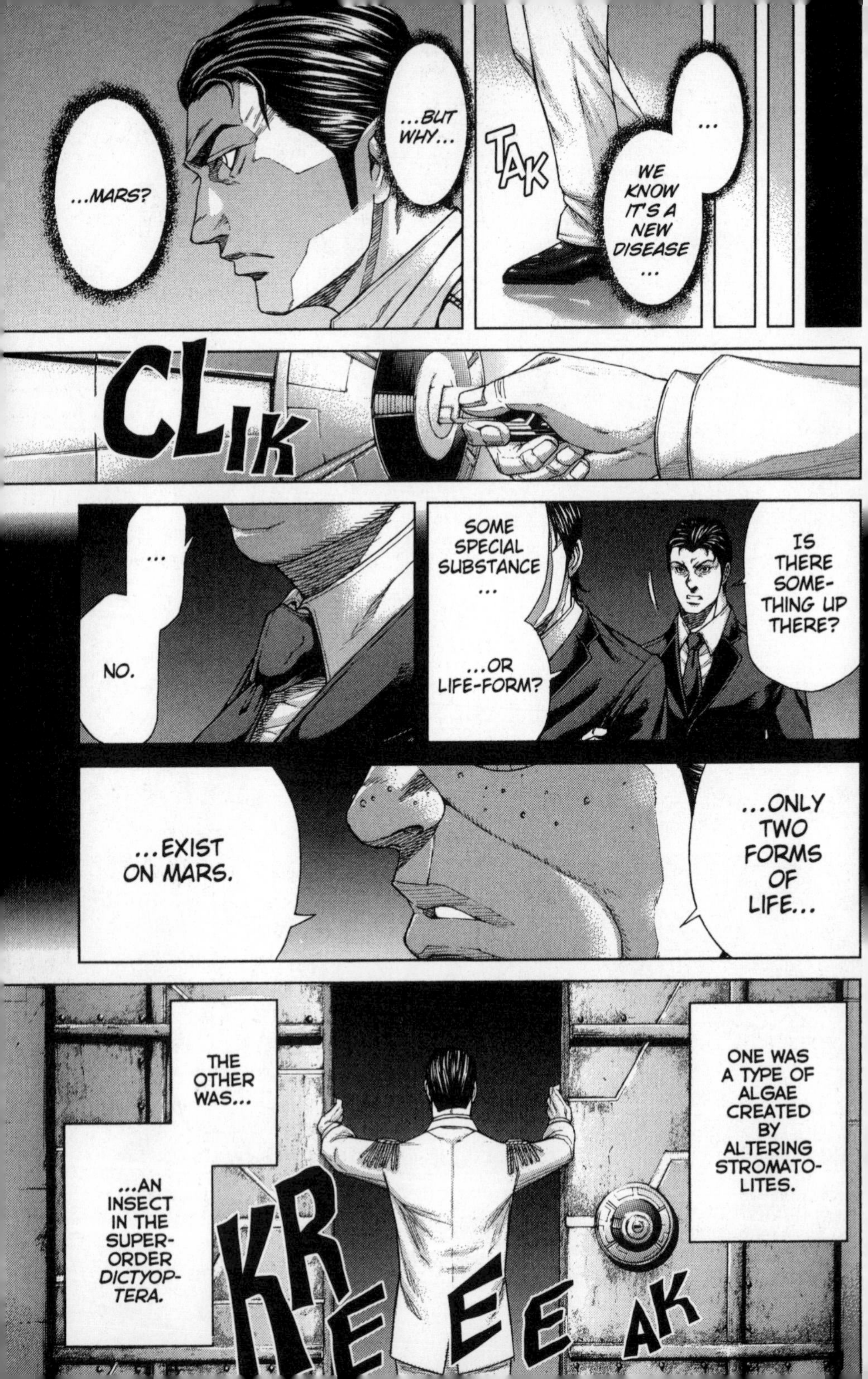
...
WE KNOW IT'S A NEW DISEASE ...
TAK
...BUT WHY...
...MARS?
CLIK
IS THERE SOME-THING UP THERE?
SOME SPECIAL SUBSTANCE ...
...OR LIFE-FORM?
...
NO.
...ONLY TWO FORMS OF LIFE...
...EXIST ON MARS.
ONE WAS A TYPE OF ALGAE CREATED BY ALTERING STROMATO-LITES.
THE OTHER WAS...
...AN INSECT IN THE SUPER-ORDER DICTYOP-TERA.
KREEEAK

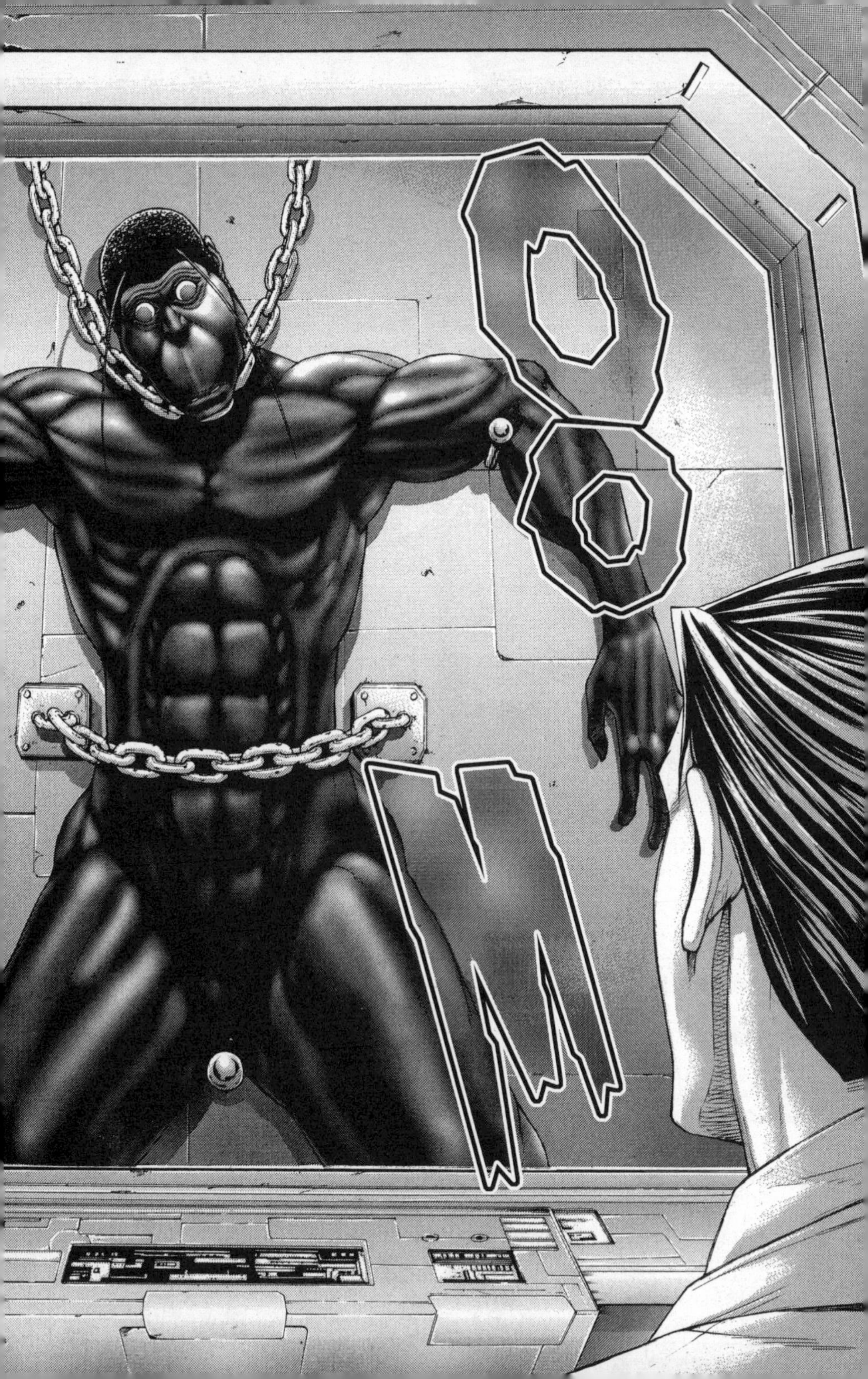
OOM

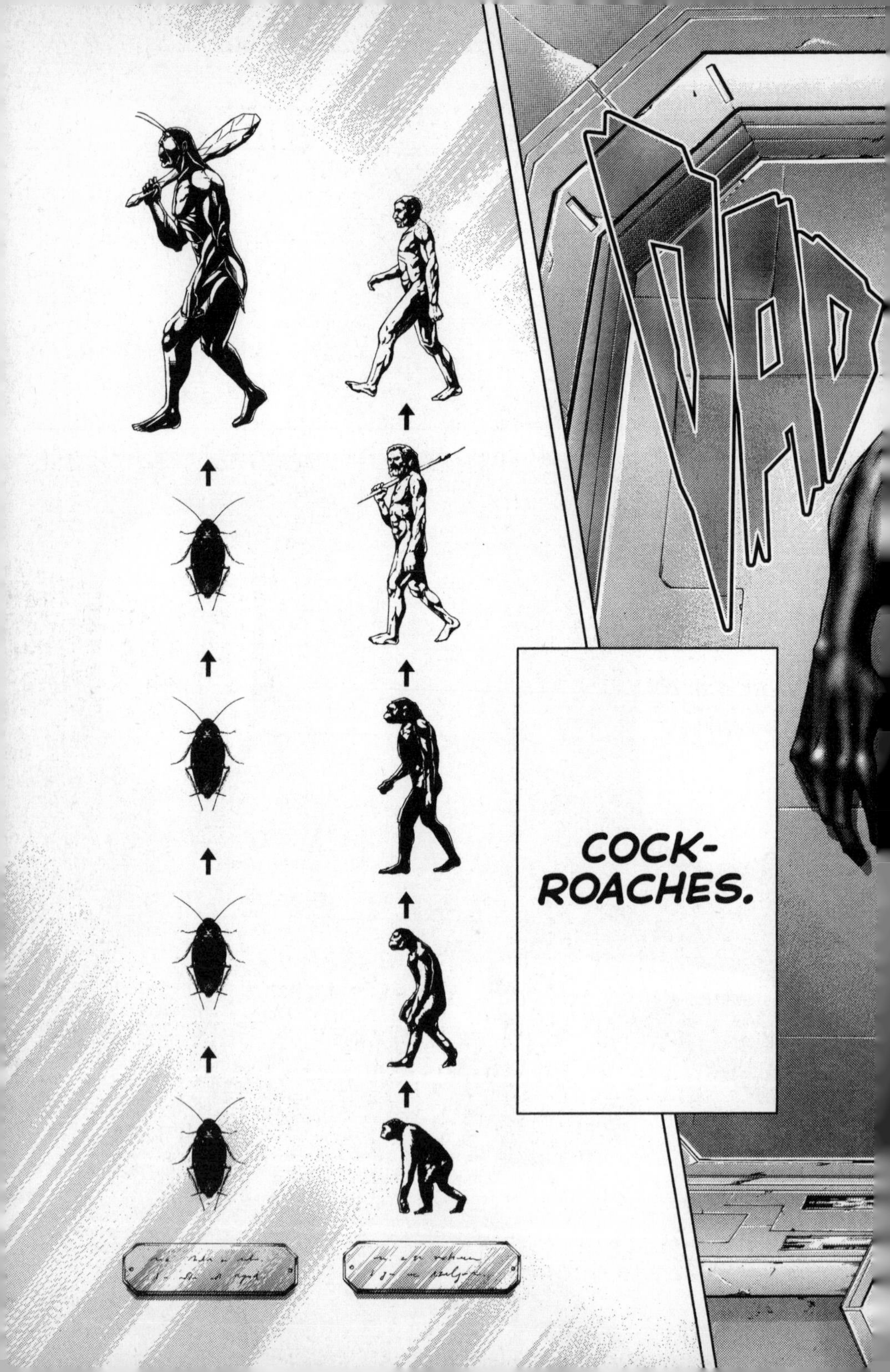
COCK-
ROACHES.

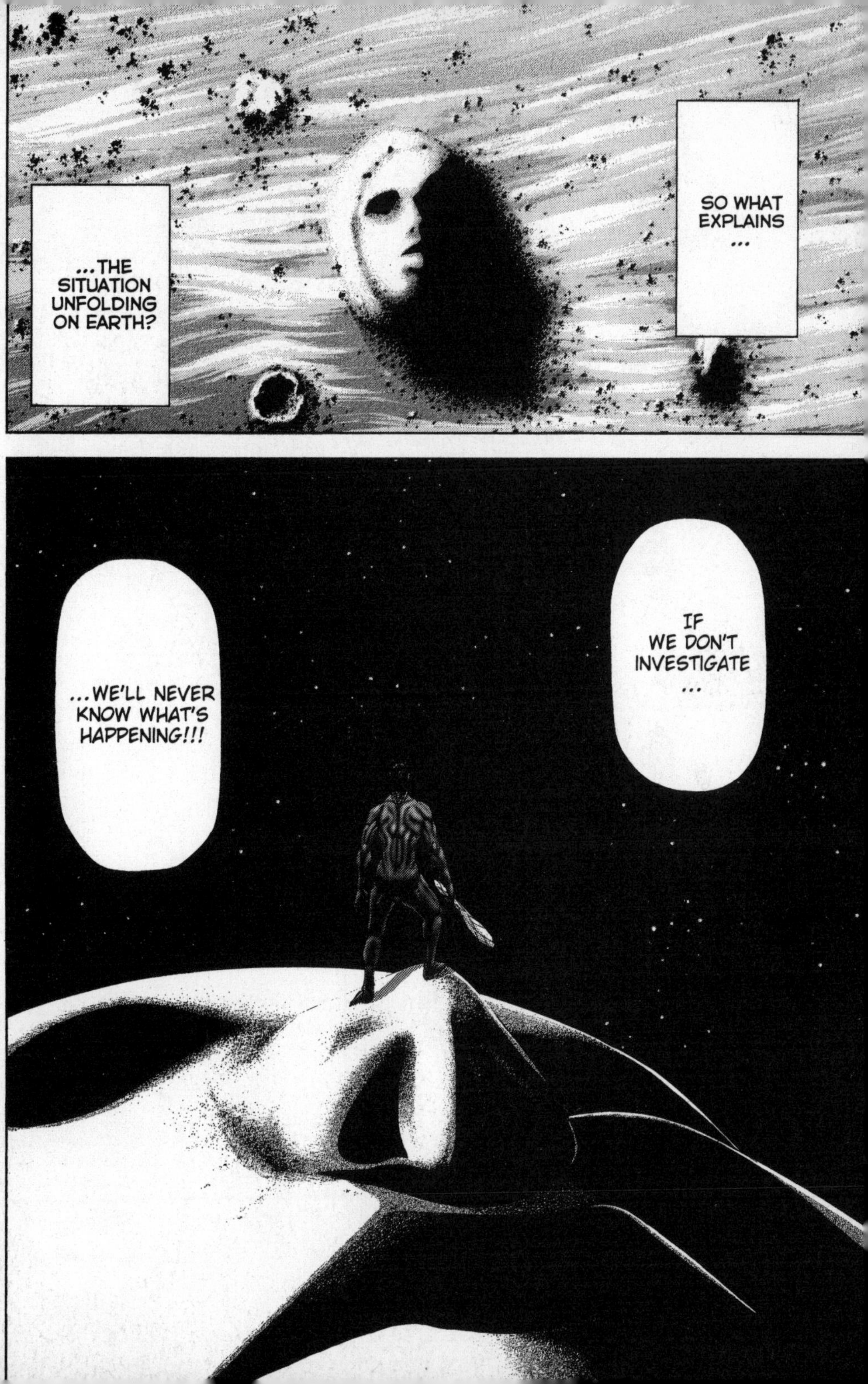
SO WHAT EXPLAINS ...
...THE SITUATION UNFOLDING ON EARTH?
IF WE DON'T INVESTIGATE ...
...WE'LL NEVER KNOW WHAT'S HAPPENING!!!

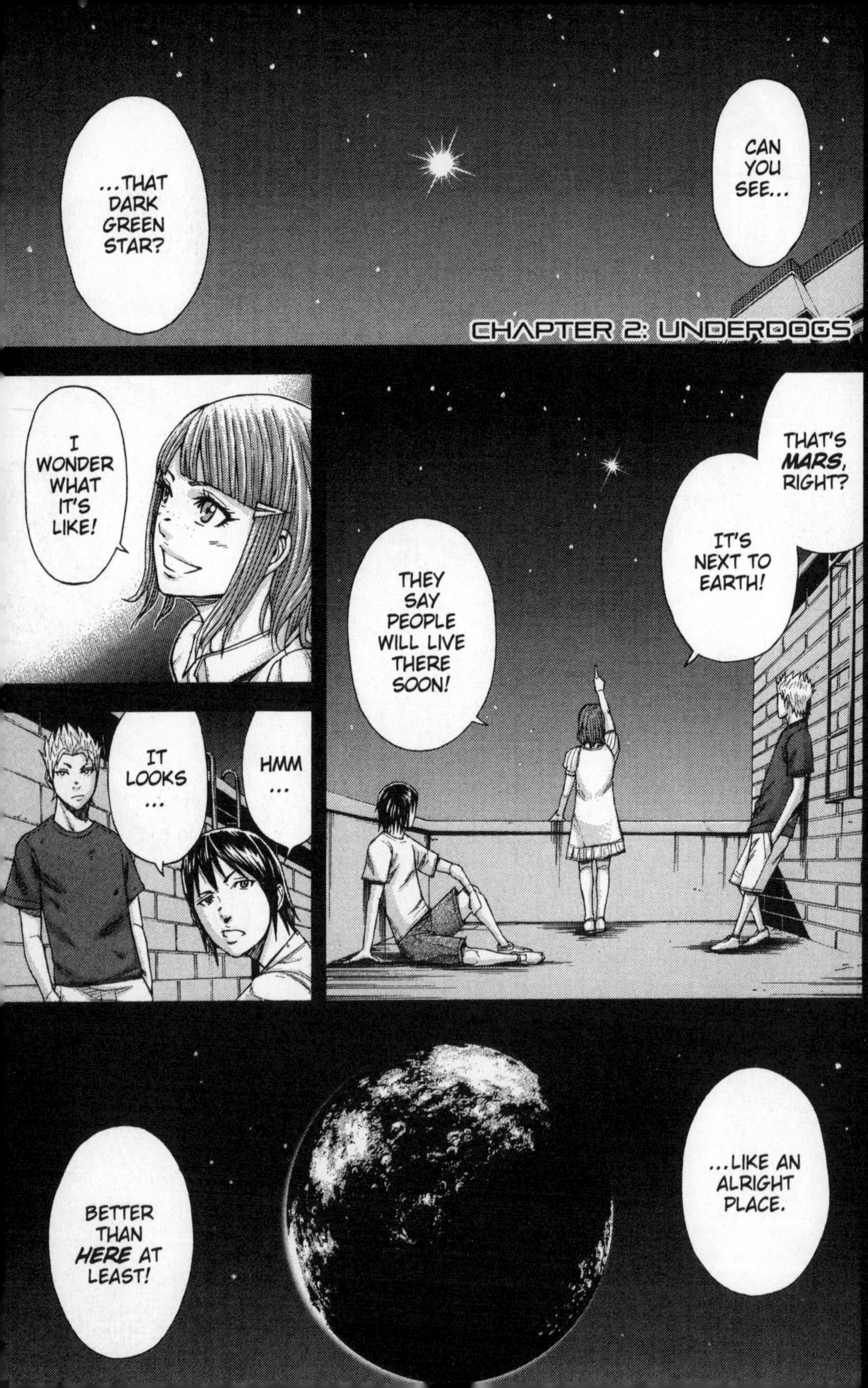
CAN YOU SEE...
...THAT DARK GREEN STAR?
CHAPTER 2: UNDERDOGS
THAT'S MARS, RIGHT?
IT'S NEXT TO EARTH!
THEY SAY PEOPLE WILL LIVE THERE SOON!
I WONDER WHAT IT'S LIKE!
HMM...
IT LOOKS...
...LIKE AN ALRIGHT PLACE.
BETTER THAN HERE AT LEAST!

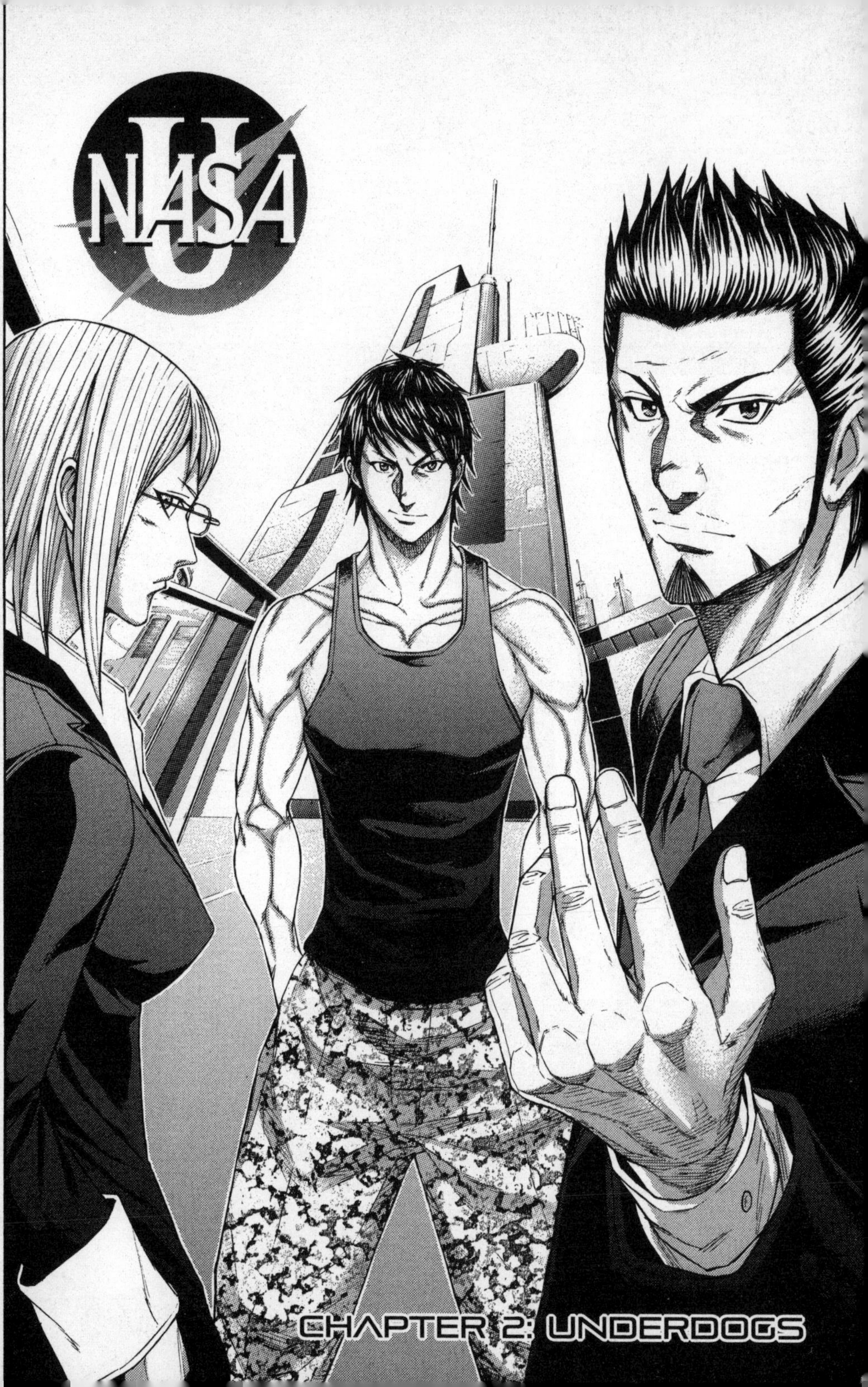
U NASA
CHAPTER 2: UNDERDOGS

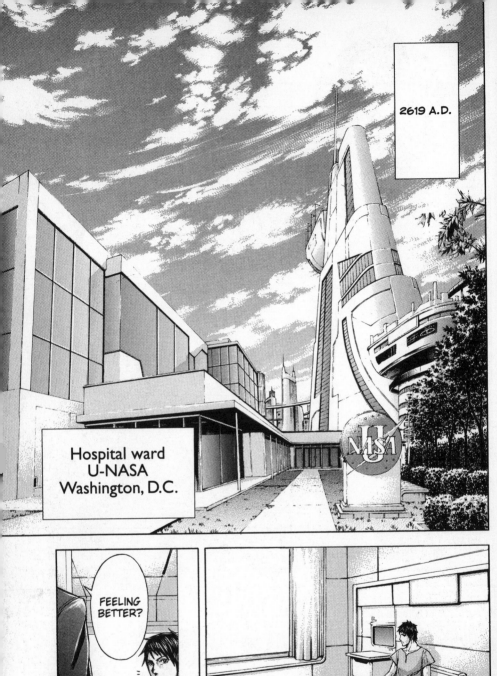

2619 A.D.

Hospital ward
U-NASA
Washington, D.C.

FEELING
BETTER?

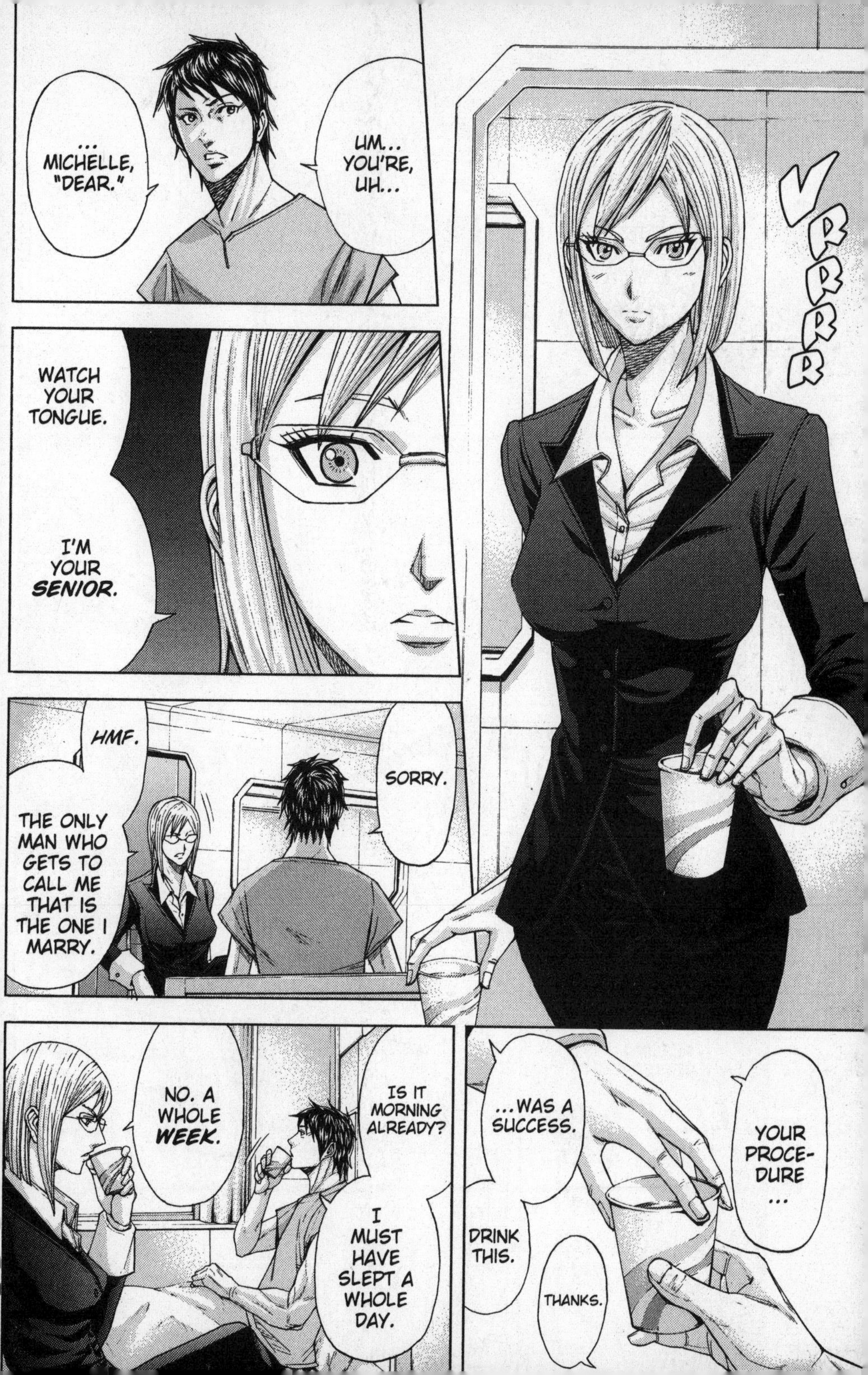
VRRRR
UM... YOU'RE, UH...
... MICHELLE, "DEAR."
WATCH YOUR TONGUE.
I'M YOUR SENIOR.
SORRY.
HMF.
THE ONLY MAN WHO GETS TO CALL ME THAT IS THE ONE I MARRY.
YOUR PROCEDURE ...
...WAS A SUCCESS.
DRINK THIS.
THANKS.
IS IT MORNING ALREADY?
I MUST HAVE SLEPT A WHOLE DAY.
NO. A WHOLE WEEK.

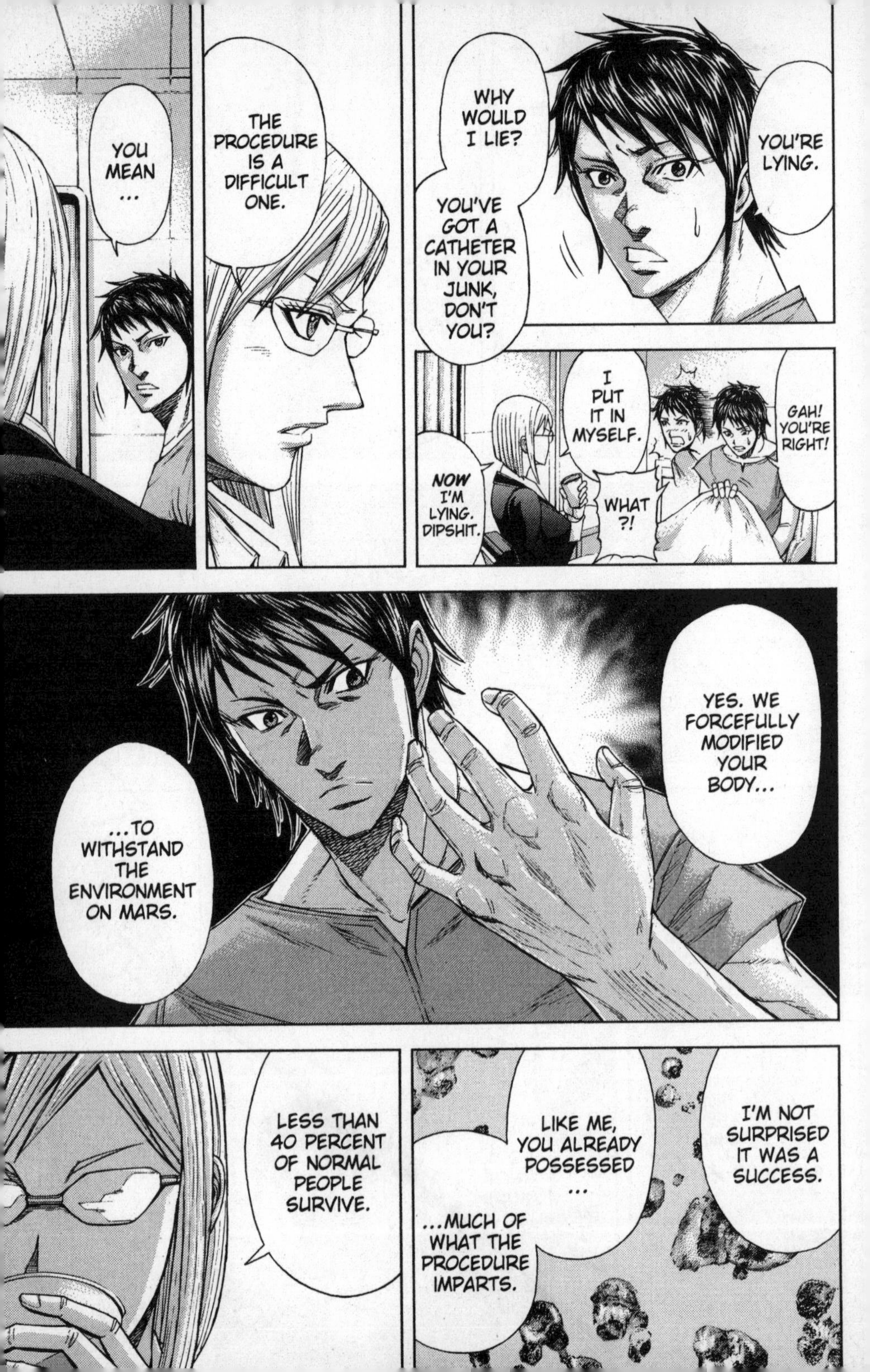
YOU'RE LYING.
WHY WOULD I LIE?
YOU'VE GOT A CATHETER IN YOUR JUNK, DON'T YOU?
GAH! YOU'RE RIGHT!
I PUT IT IN MYSELF.
WHAT?!
NOW I'M LYING. DIPSHIT.
THE PROCEDURE IS A DIFFICULT ONE.
YOU MEAN ...
YES. WE FORCEFULLY MODIFIED YOUR BODY...
...TO WITHSTAND THE ENVIRONMENT ON MARS.
I'M NOT SURPRISED IT WAS A SUCCESS.
LIKE ME, YOU ALREADY POSSESSED ...
...MUCH OF WHAT THE PROCEDURE IMPARTS.
LESS THAN 40 PERCENT OF NORMAL PEOPLE SURVIVE.

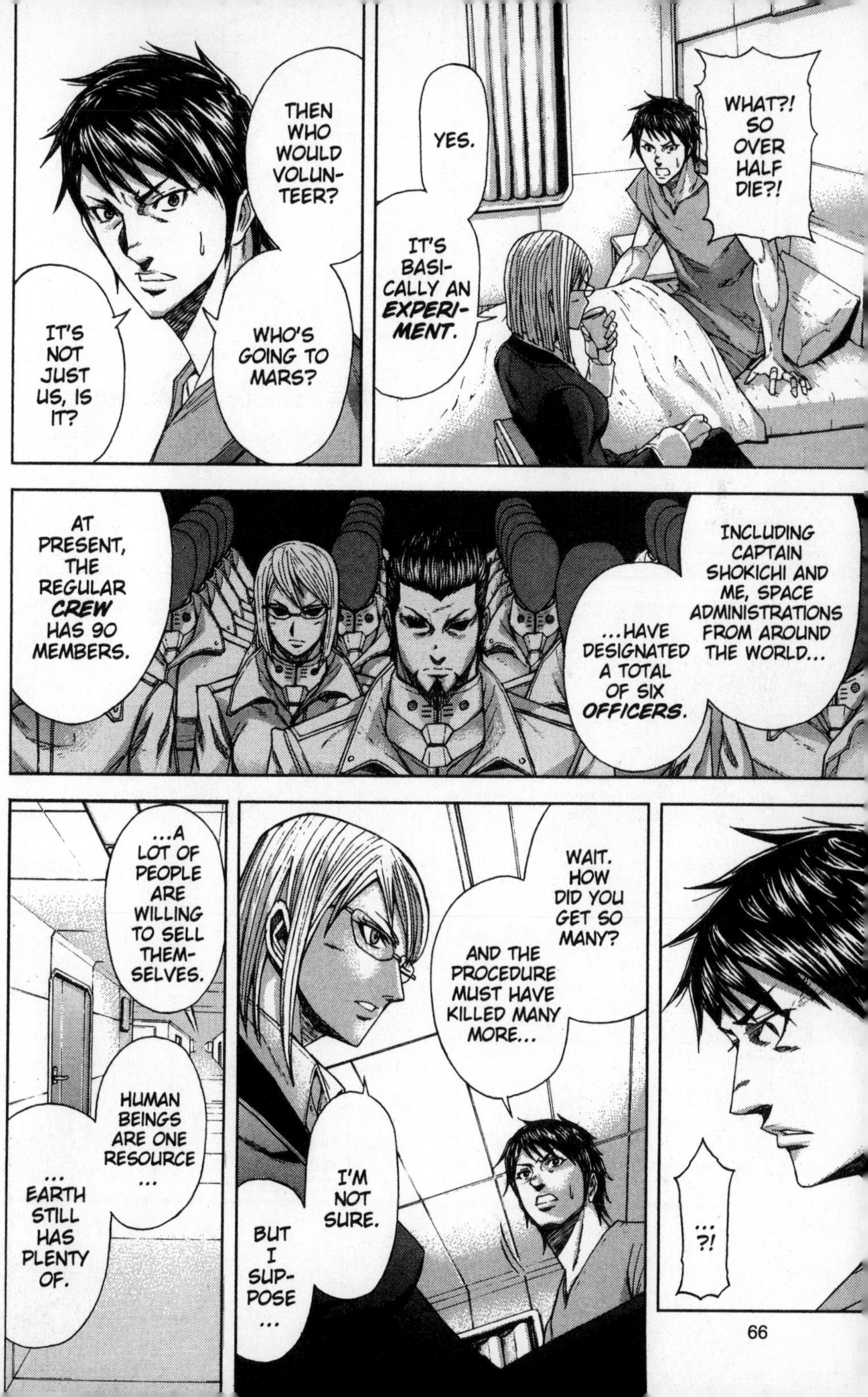
WHAT?! SO OVER HALF DIE?!
YES.
IT'S BASICALLY AN *EXPERIMENT*.
THEN WHO WOULD VOLUNTEER?
WHO'S GOING TO MARS?
IT'S NOT JUST US, IS IT?
INCLUDING CAPTAIN SHOKICHI AND ME, SPACE ADMINISTRATIONS FROM AROUND THE WORLD...
...HAVE DESIGNATED A TOTAL OF SIX *OFFICERS*.
AT PRESENT, THE REGULAR *CREW* HAS 90 MEMBERS.
...?!
WAIT. HOW DID YOU GET SO MANY?
AND THE PROCEDURE MUST HAVE KILLED MANY MORE...
I'M NOT SURE.
BUT I SUPPOSE...
...A LOT OF PEOPLE ARE WILLING TO SELL THEMSELVES.
HUMAN BEINGS ARE ONE RESOURCE...
...EARTH STILL HAS PLENTY OF.

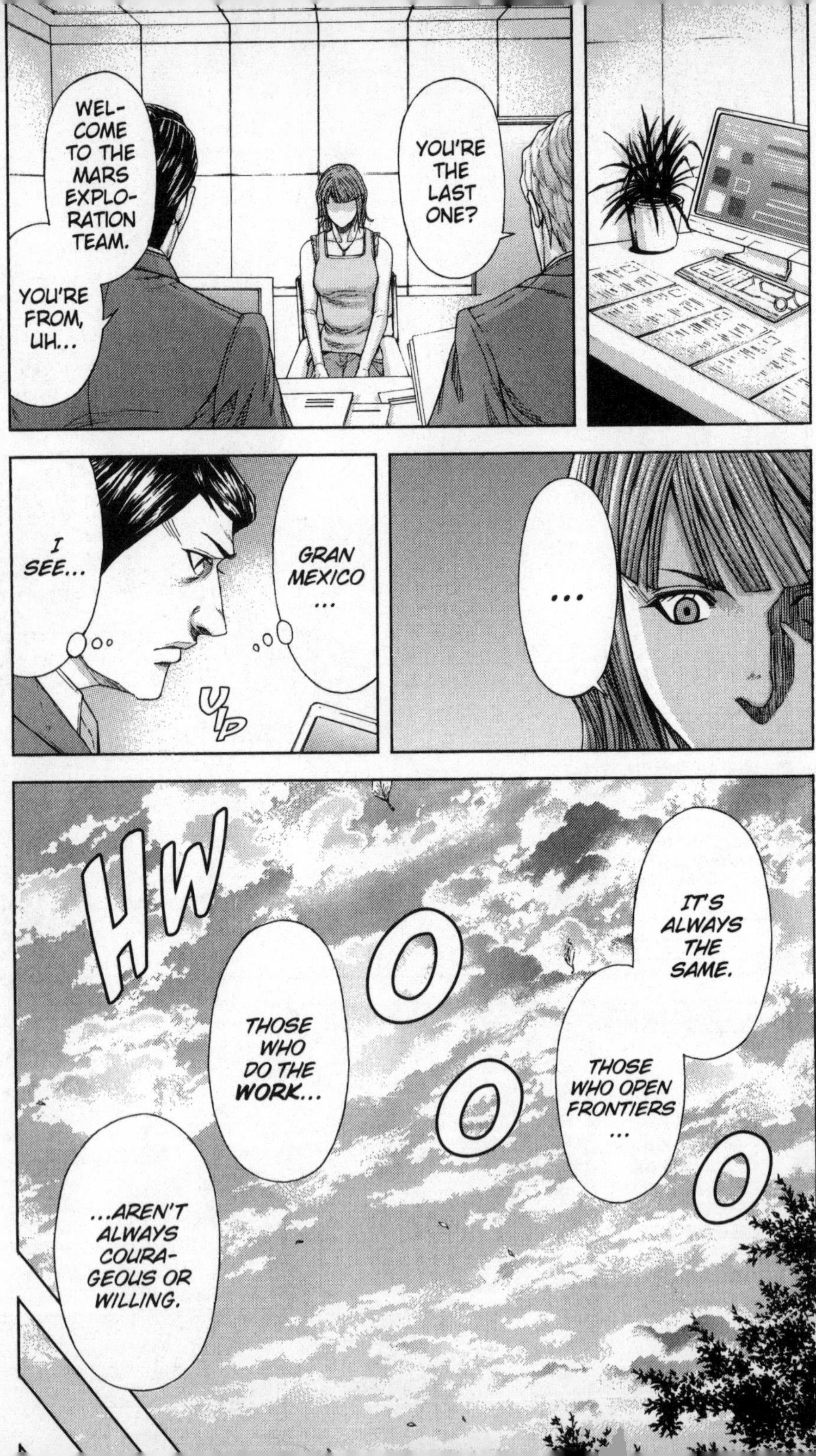
YOU'RE THE LAST ONE?
WEL-COME TO THE MARS EXPLO-RATION TEAM.
YOU'RE FROM, UH...
...
GRAN MEXICO ...
I SEE...
UP
HWOOOO
IT'S ALWAYS THE SAME.
THOSE WHO OPEN FRONTIERS ...
THOSE WHO DO THE **WORK**...
...AREN'T ALWAYS COURA-GEOUS OR WILLING.

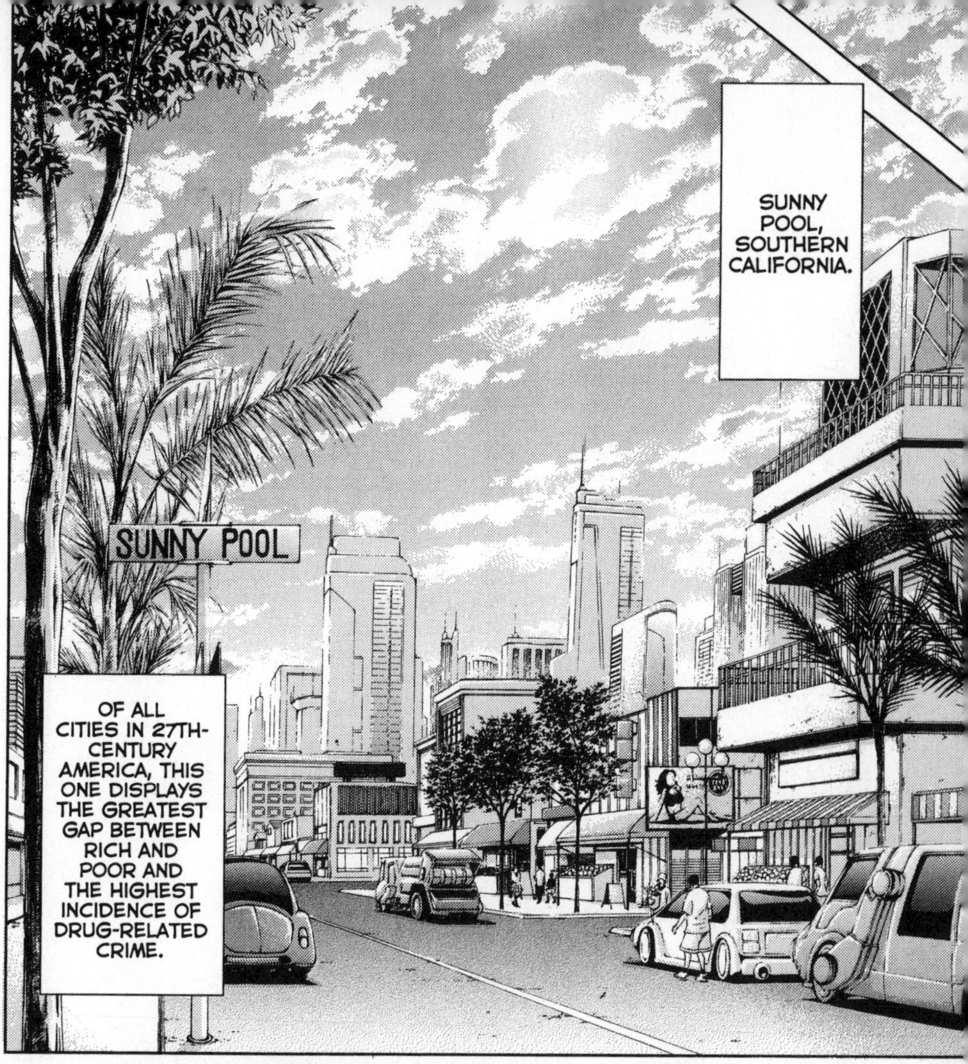
SUNNY POOL, SOUTHERN CALIFORNIA.
SUNNY POOL
OF ALL CITIES IN 27TH-CENTURY AMERICA, THIS ONE DISPLAYS THE GREATEST GAP BETWEEN RICH AND POOR AND THE HIGHEST INCIDENCE OF DRUG-RELATED CRIME.

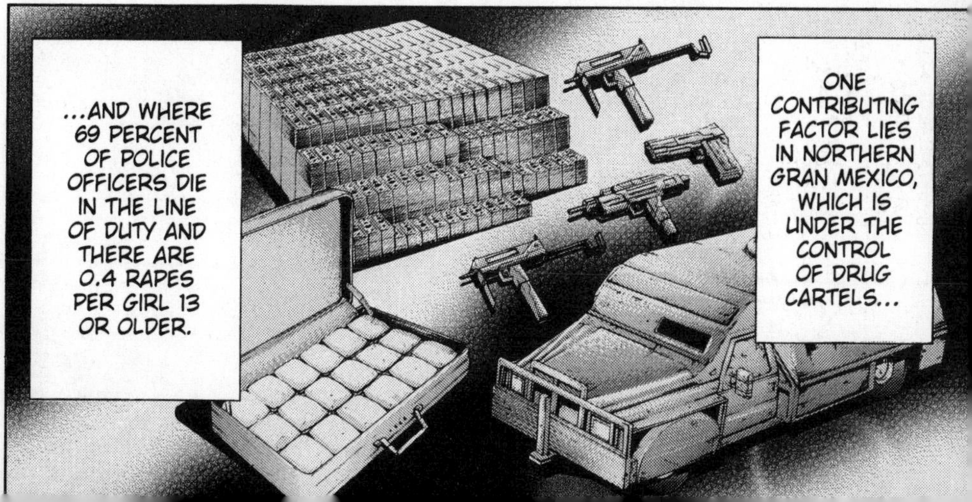
ONE CONTRIBUTING FACTOR LIES IN NORTHERN GRAN MEXICO, WHICH IS UNDER THE CONTROL OF DRUG CARTELS...
...AND WHERE 69 PERCENT OF POLICE OFFICERS DIE IN THE LINE OF DUTY AND THERE ARE 0.4 RAPES PER GIRL 13 OR OLDER.

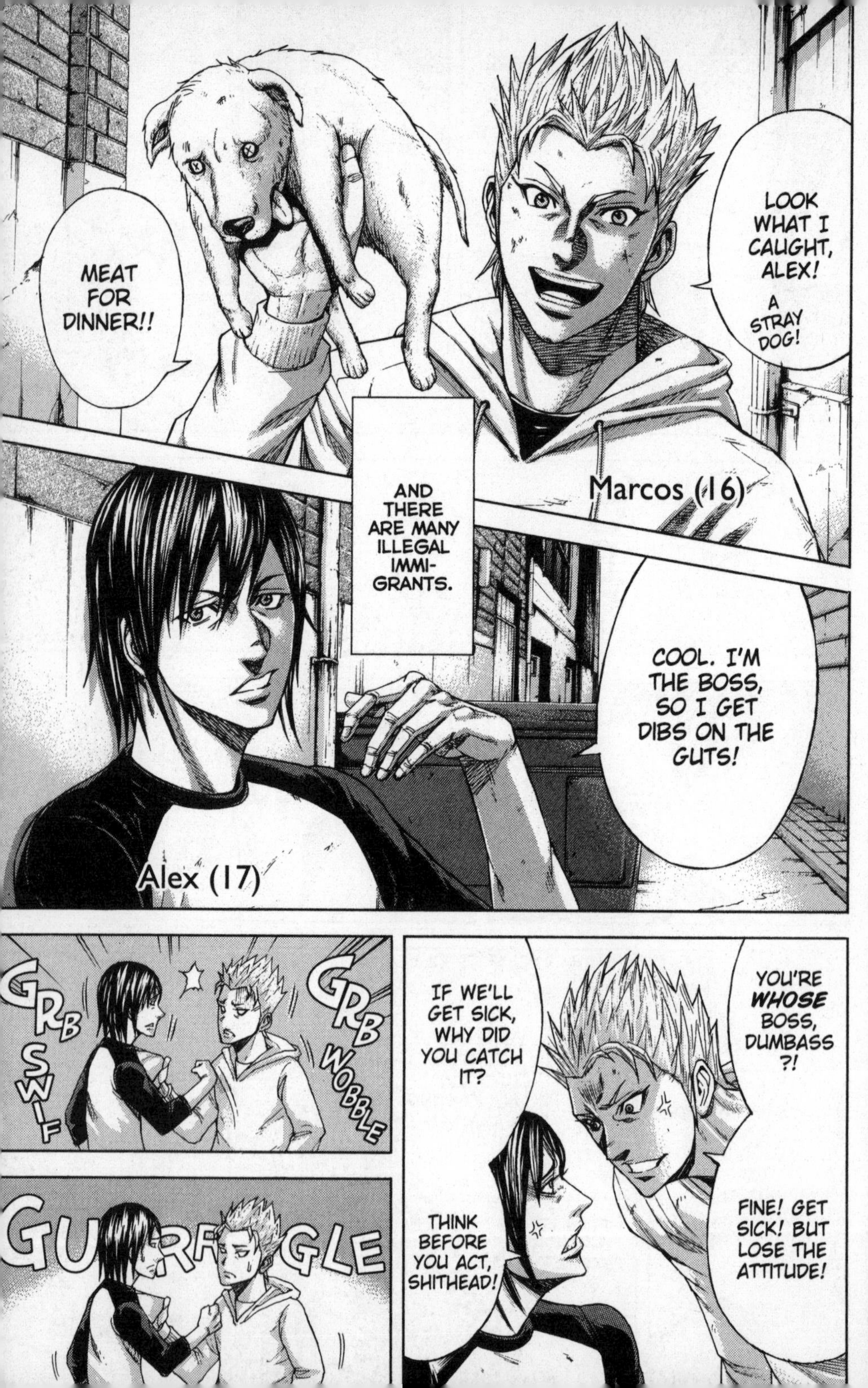
LOOK WHAT I CAUGHT, ALEX!
A STRAY DOG!
MEAT FOR DINNER!!
Marcos (16)
AND THERE ARE MANY ILLEGAL IMMI-GRANTS.
COOL. I'M THE BOSS, SO I GET DIBS ON THE GUTS!
Alex (17)
YOU'RE WHOSE BOSS, DUMBASS?!
IF WE'LL GET SICK, WHY DID YOU CATCH IT?
FINE! GET SICK! BUT LOSE THE ATTITUDE!
THINK BEFORE YOU ACT, SHITHEAD!
GRB
WOBBLE
GRB
SWIF
GURRGLE

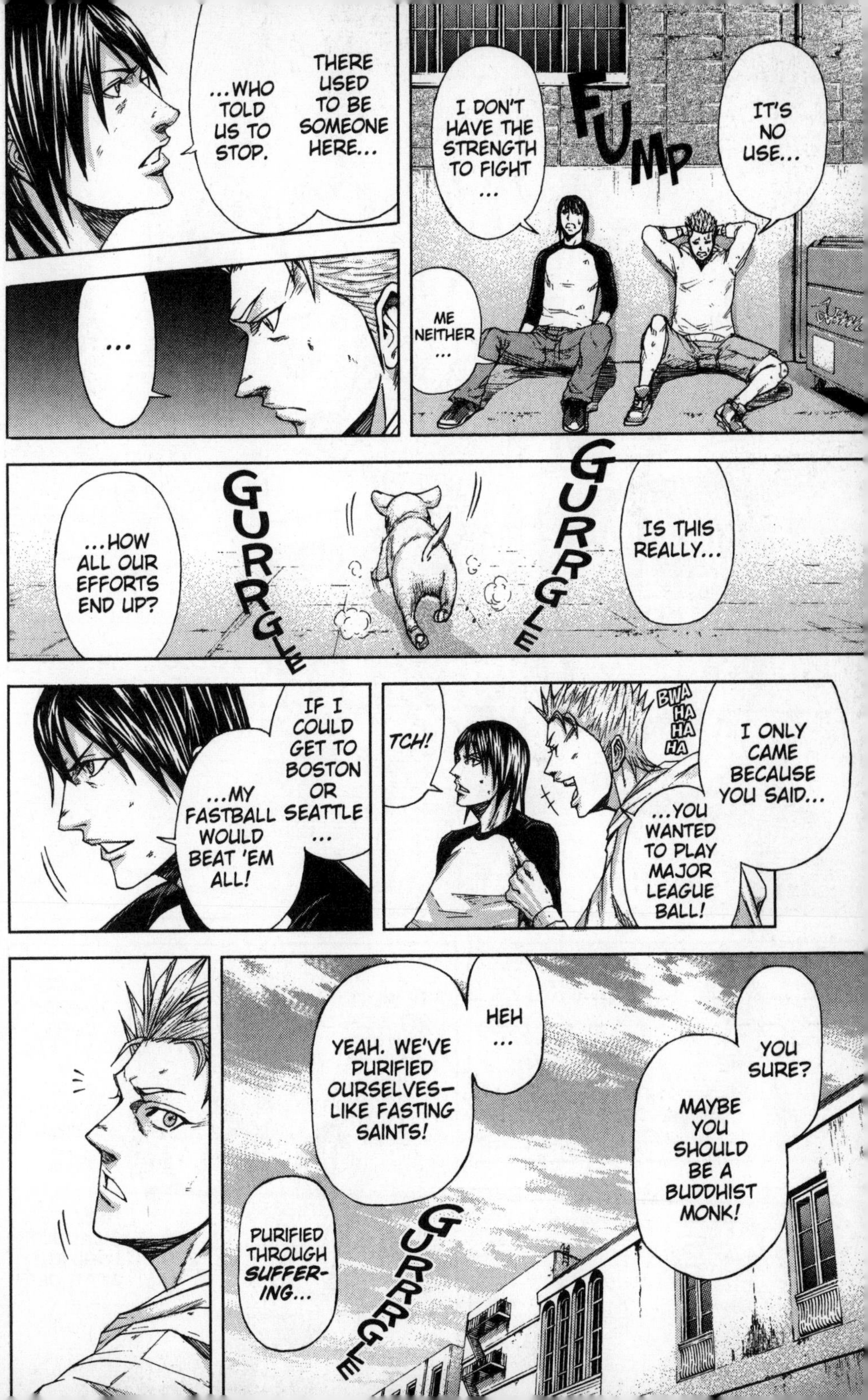
IT'S NO USE...
FUMP
I DON'T HAVE THE STRENGTH TO FIGHT...
ME NEITHER...
THERE USED TO BE SOMEONE HERE...
...WHO TOLD US TO STOP.
...
IS THIS REALLY...
GURRGLE
...HOW ALL OUR EFFORTS END UP?
GURRGLE
I ONLY CAME BECAUSE YOU SAID...
BWA HA HA HA
...YOU WANTED TO PLAY MAJOR LEAGUE BALL!
TCH!
IF I COULD GET TO BOSTON OR SEATTLE...
...MY FASTBALL WOULD BEAT 'EM ALL!
YOU SURE?
MAYBE YOU SHOULD BE A BUDDHIST MONK!
HEH...
YEAH. WE'VE PURIFIED OURSELVES-LIKE FASTING SAINTS!
GURRRGLE
PURIFIED THROUGH *SUFFER-ING*...

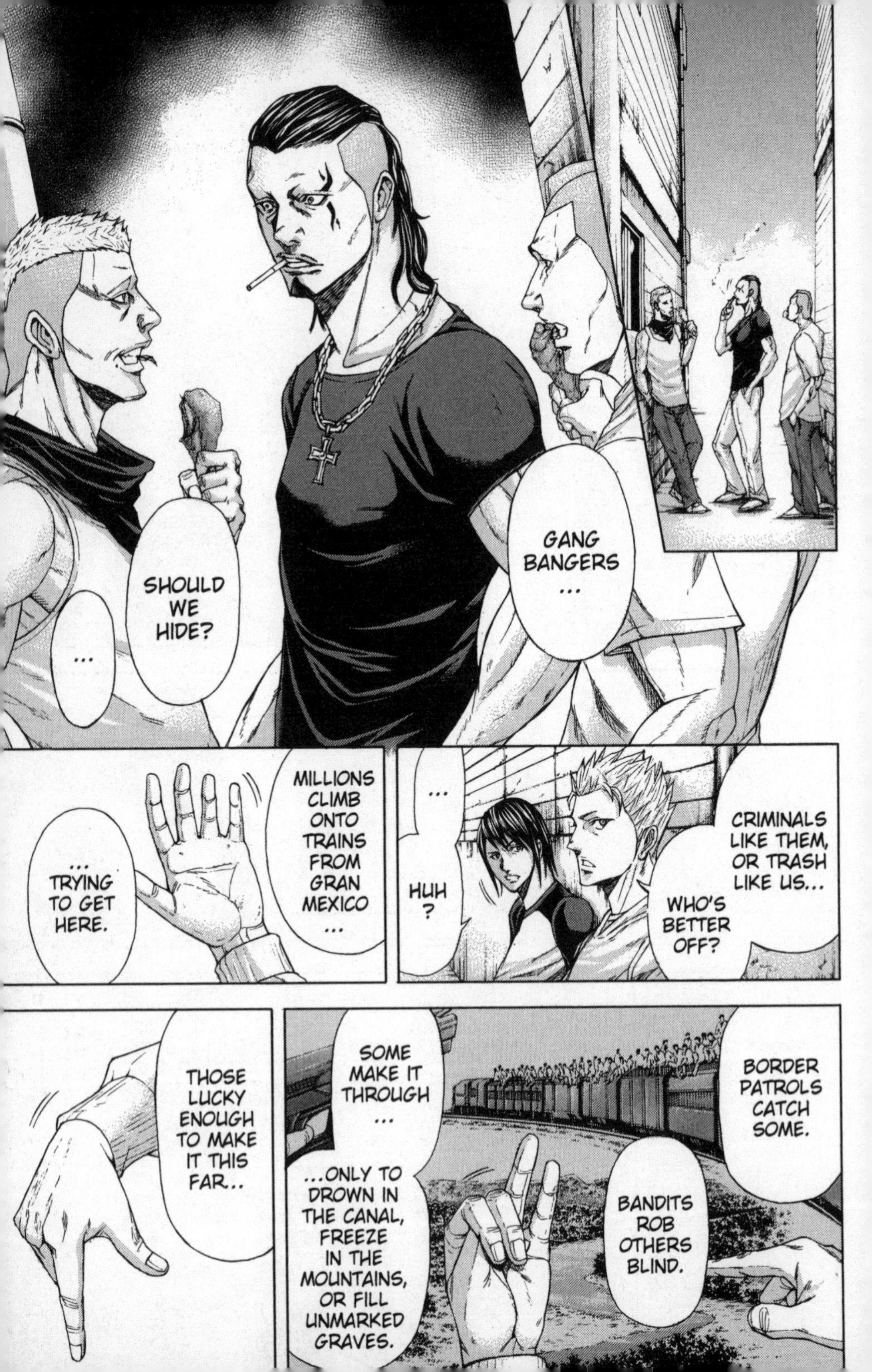
GANG BANGERS ...
SHOULD WE HIDE?
...
CRIMINALS LIKE THEM, OR TRASH LIKE US...
WHO'S BETTER OFF?
...
HUH?
MILLIONS CLIMB ONTO TRAINS FROM GRAN MEXICO ...
... TRYING TO GET HERE.
BORDER PATROLS CATCH SOME.
BANDITS ROB OTHERS BLIND.
SOME MAKE IT THROUGH ...
...ONLY TO DROWN IN THE CANAL, FREEZE IN THE MOUNTAINS, OR FILL UNMARKED GRAVES.
THOSE LUCKY ENOUGH TO MAKE IT THIS FAR...

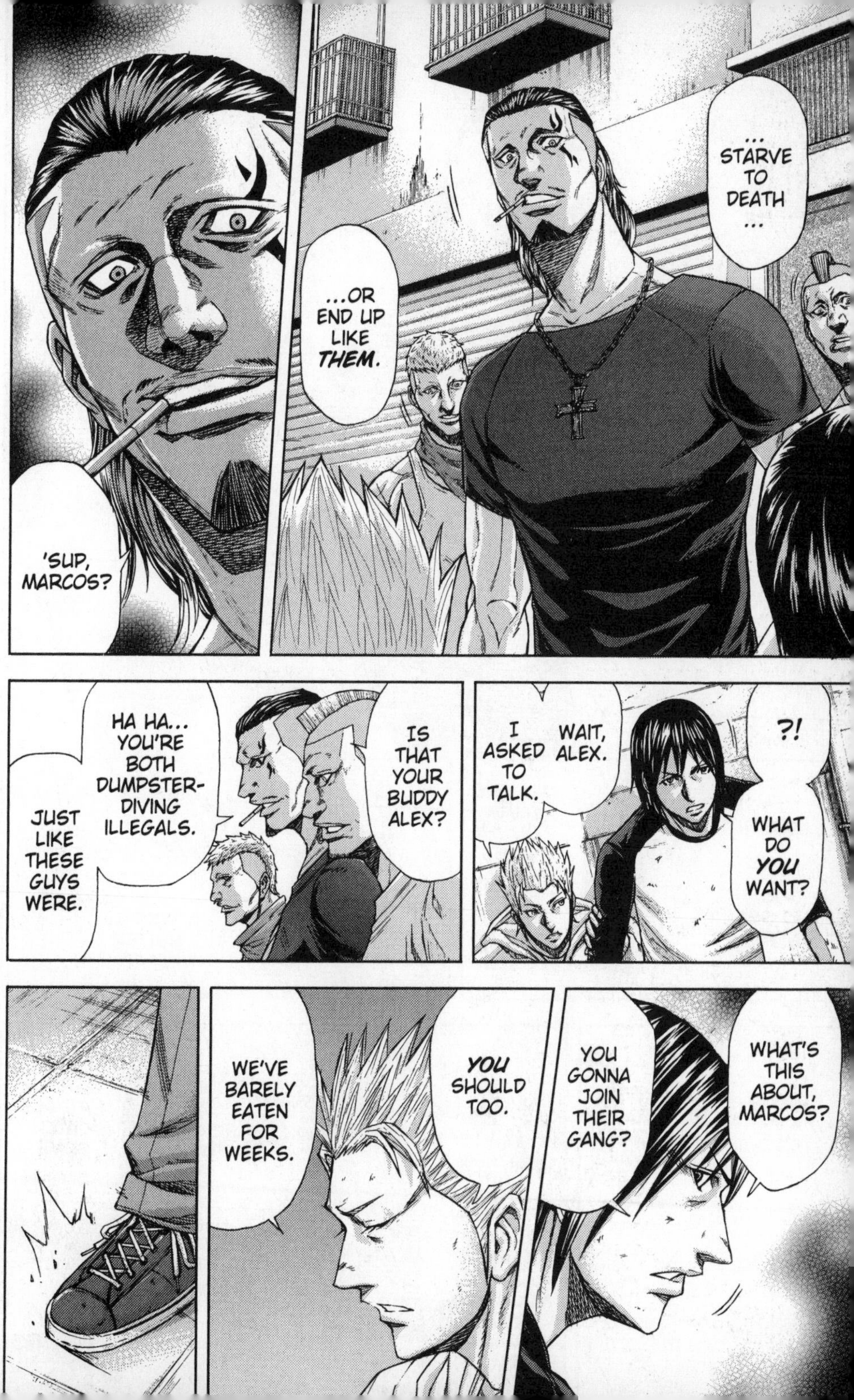
...STARVE TO DEATH...
...OR END UP LIKE *THEM*.
'SUP, MARCOS?
?!
WHAT DO *YOU* WANT?
WAIT, ALEX.
I ASKED TO TALK.
IS THAT YOUR BUDDY ALEX?
HA HA... YOU'RE BOTH DUMPSTER-DIVING ILLEGALS.
JUST LIKE THESE GUYS WERE.
WHAT'S THIS ABOUT, MARCOS?
YOU GONNA JOIN THEIR GANG?
YOU SHOULD TOO.
WE'VE BARELY EATEN FOR WEEKS.

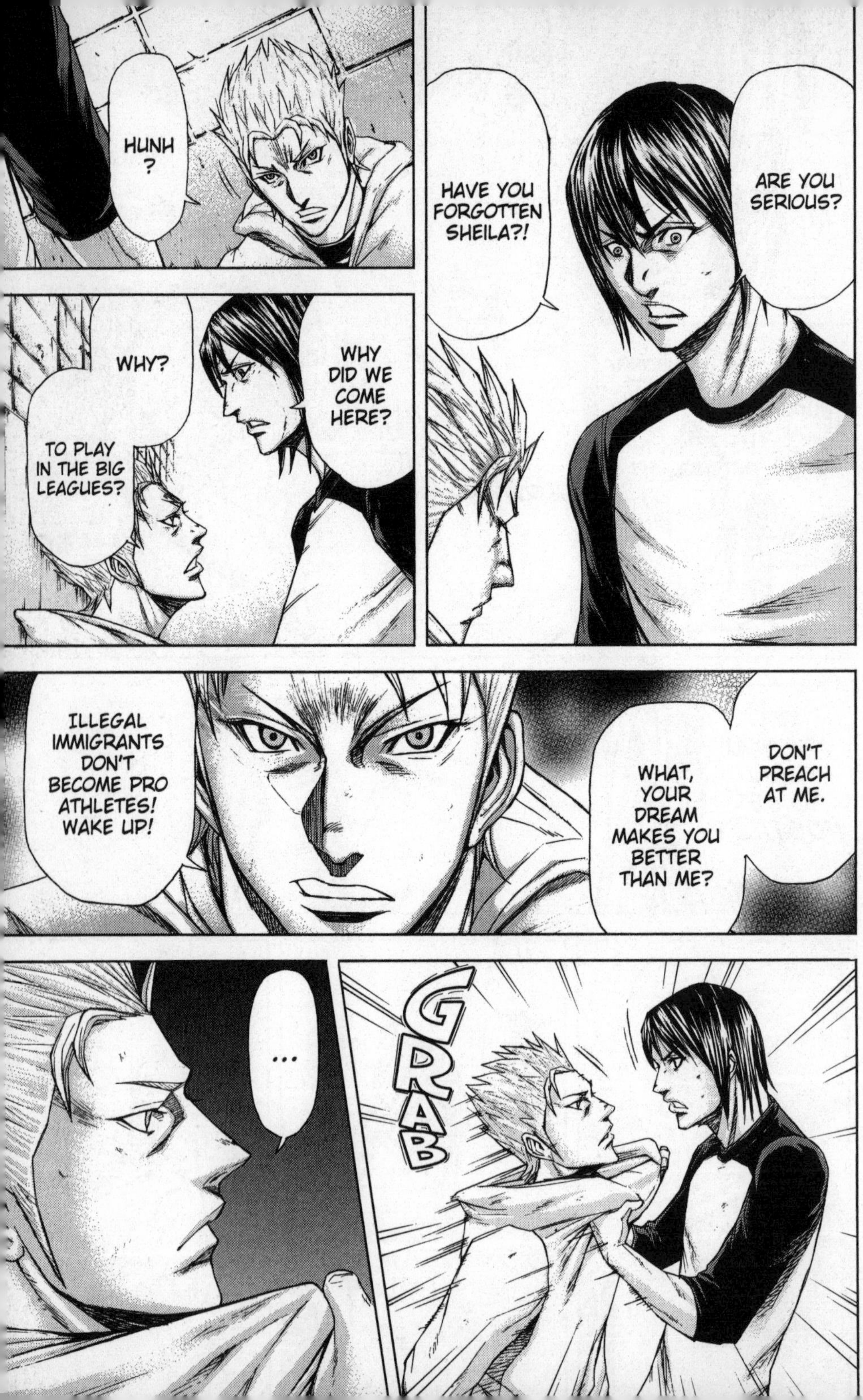
ARE YOU SERIOUS?
HAVE YOU FORGOTTEN SHEILA?!
HUNH?
WHY DID WE COME HERE?
WHY?
TO PLAY IN THE BIG LEAGUES?
DON'T PREACH AT ME.
WHAT, YOUR DREAM MAKES YOU BETTER THAN ME?
ILLEGAL IMMIGRANTS DON'T BECOME PRO ATHLETES! WAKE UP!
GRAB
...

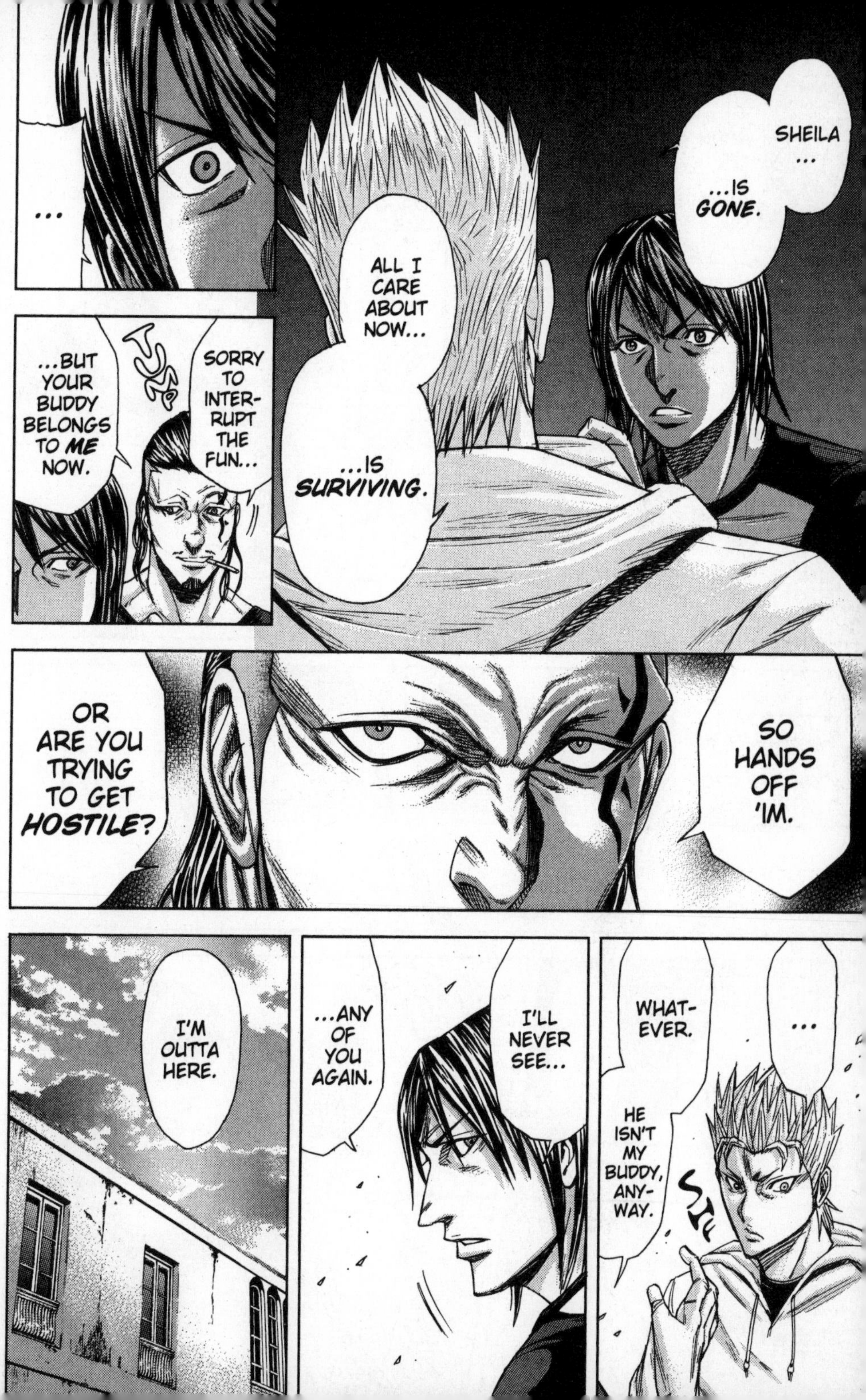
SHEILA ...
...IS GONE.
ALL I CARE ABOUT NOW...
...IS SURVIVING.
...
SORRY TO INTERRUPT THE FUN...
...BUT YOUR BUDDY BELONGS TO ME NOW.
SO HANDS OFF 'IM.
OR ARE YOU TRYING TO GET HOSTILE?
...
WHAT-EVER.
HE ISN'T MY BUDDY, ANY-WAY.
I'LL NEVER SEE...
...ANY OF YOU AGAIN.
I'M OUTTA HERE.

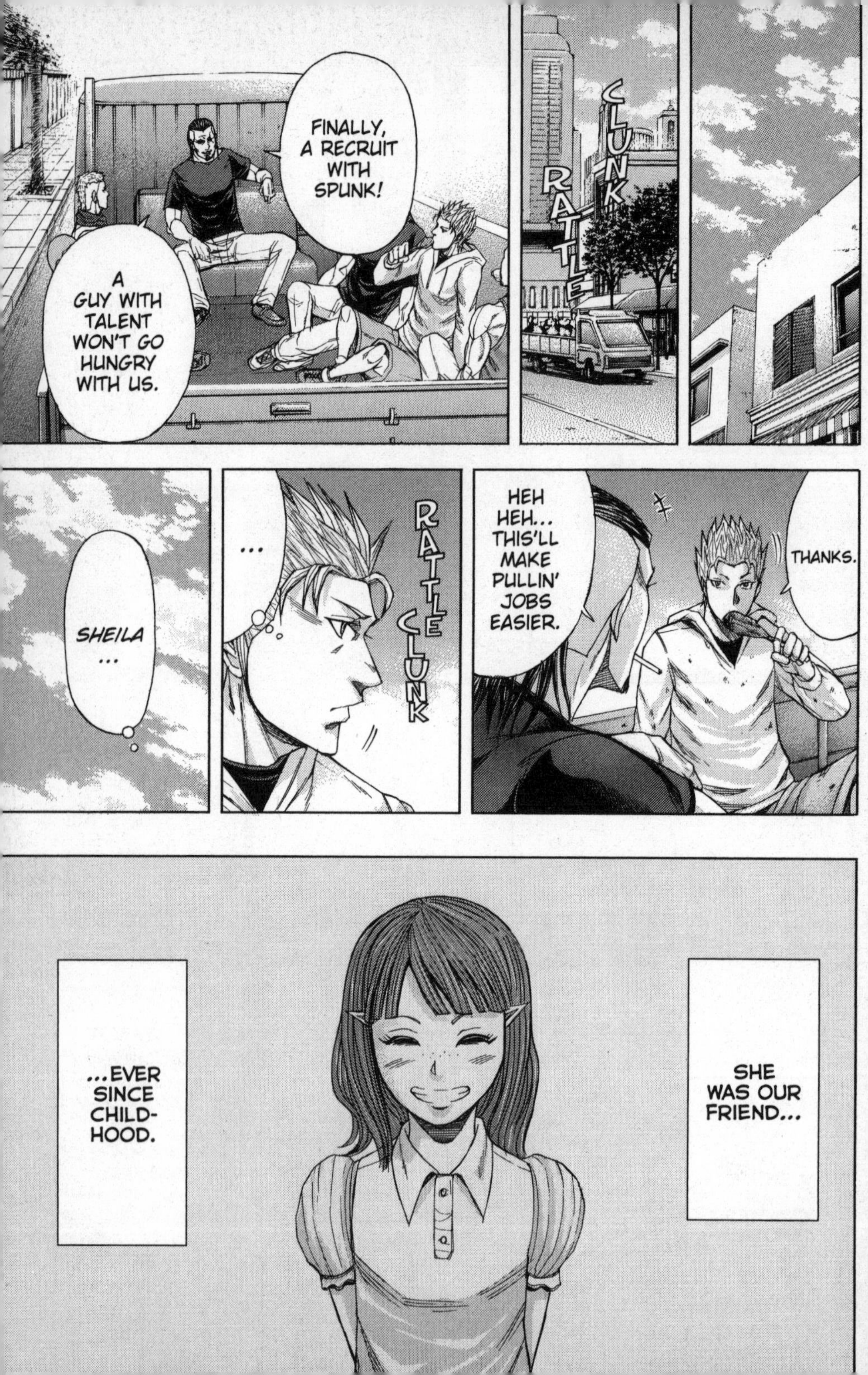
RATTLE
CLUNK
FINALLY, A RECRUIT WITH SPUNK!
A GUY WITH TALENT WON'T GO HUNGRY WITH US.
THANKS.
HEH HEH... THIS'LL MAKE PULLIN' JOBS EASIER.
RATTLE
CLUNK
...
SHEILA...
SHE WAS OUR FRIEND...
...EVER SINCE CHILD-HOOD.

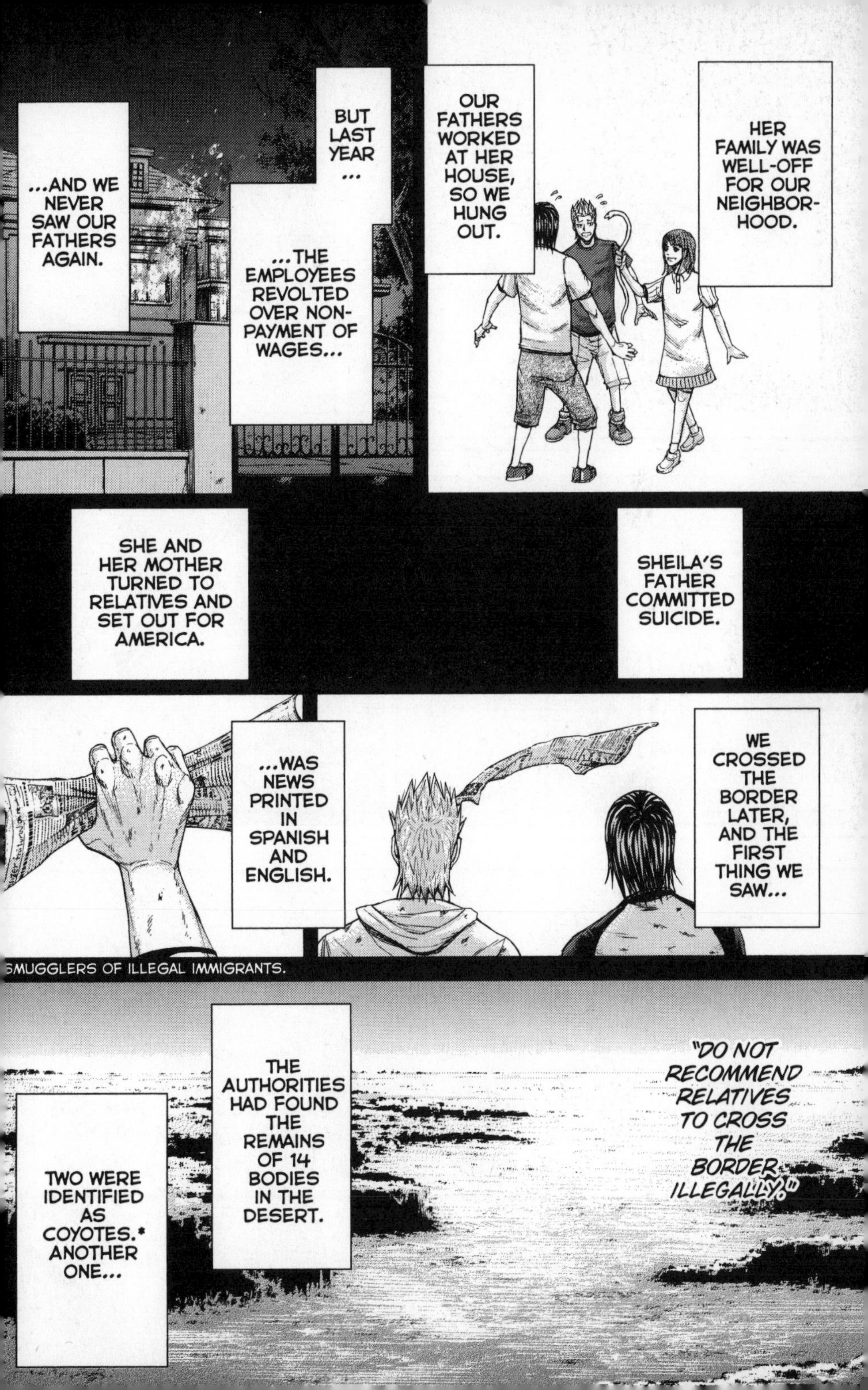
HER FAMILY WAS WELL-OFF FOR OUR NEIGHBOR-HOOD.
OUR FATHERS WORKED AT HER HOUSE, SO WE HUNG OUT.
BUT LAST YEAR...
...THE EMPLOYEES REVOLTED OVER NON-PAYMENT OF WAGES...
...AND WE NEVER SAW OUR FATHERS AGAIN.
SHEILA'S FATHER COMMITTED SUICIDE.
SHE AND HER MOTHER TURNED TO RELATIVES AND SET OUT FOR AMERICA.
WE CROSSED THE BORDER LATER, AND THE FIRST THING WE SAW...
...WAS NEWS PRINTED IN SPANISH AND ENGLISH.
"DO NOT RECOMMEND RELATIVES TO CROSS THE BORDER ILLEGALLY."
THE AUTHORITIES HAD FOUND THE REMAINS OF 14 BODIES IN THE DESERT.
TWO WERE IDENTIFIED AS COYOTES.* ANOTHER ONE...

SMUGGLERS OF ILLEGAL IMMIGRANTS.

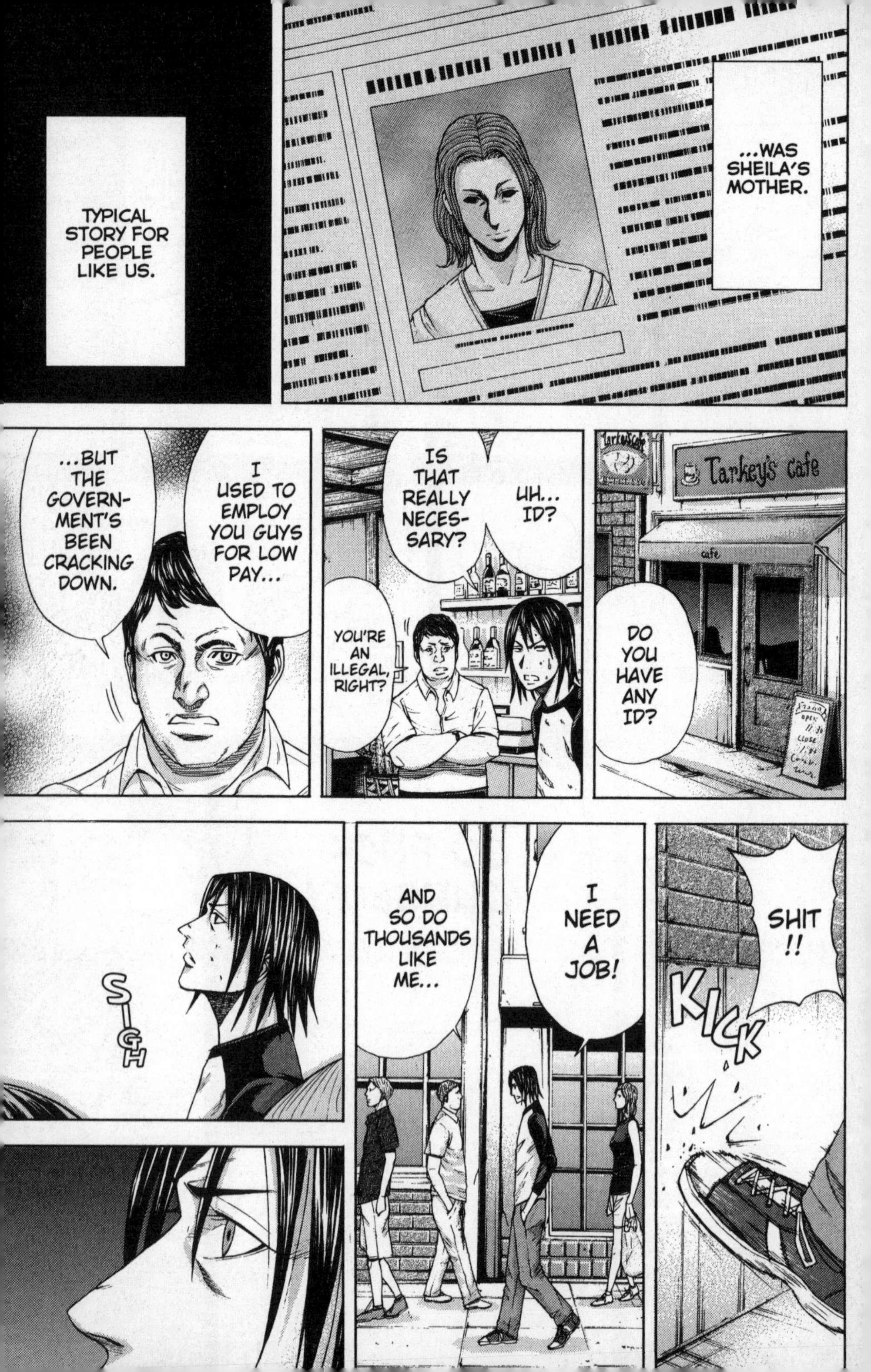
...WAS SHEILA'S MOTHER.
TYPICAL STORY FOR PEOPLE LIKE US.
Tarkey's cafe
cafe
DO YOU HAVE ANY ID?
UH... ID?
IS THAT REALLY NECESSARY?
YOU'RE AN ILLEGAL, RIGHT?
I USED TO EMPLOY YOU GUYS FOR LOW PAY...
...BUT THE GOVERNMENT'S BEEN CRACKING DOWN.
SHIT!!
KICK
I NEED A JOB!
AND SO DO THOUSANDS LIKE ME...
SIGH

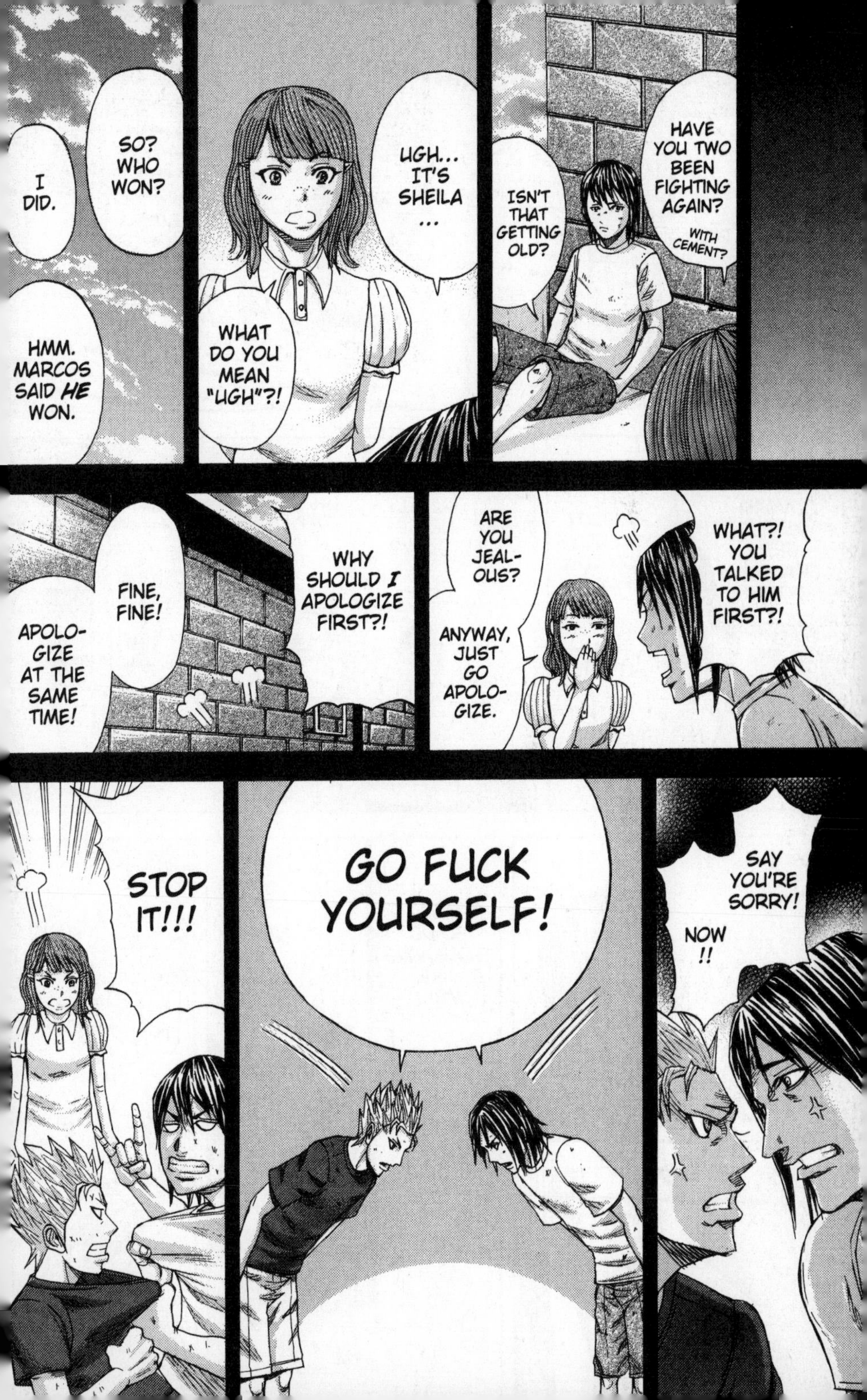
HAVE YOU TWO BEEN FIGHTING AGAIN?
WITH CEMENT?
ISN'T THAT GETTING OLD?
UGH... IT'S SHEILA ...
WHAT DO YOU MEAN "UGH"?!
SO? WHO WON?
I DID.
HMM. MARCOS SAID HE WON.
WHAT?! YOU TALKED TO HIM FIRST?!
ARE YOU JEAL-OUS?
ANYWAY, JUST GO APOLO-GIZE.
WHY SHOULD I APOLOGIZE FIRST?!
FINE, FINE!
APOLO-GIZE AT THE SAME TIME!
SAY YOU'RE SORRY!
NOW!!
GO FUCK YOURSELF!
STOP IT!!!

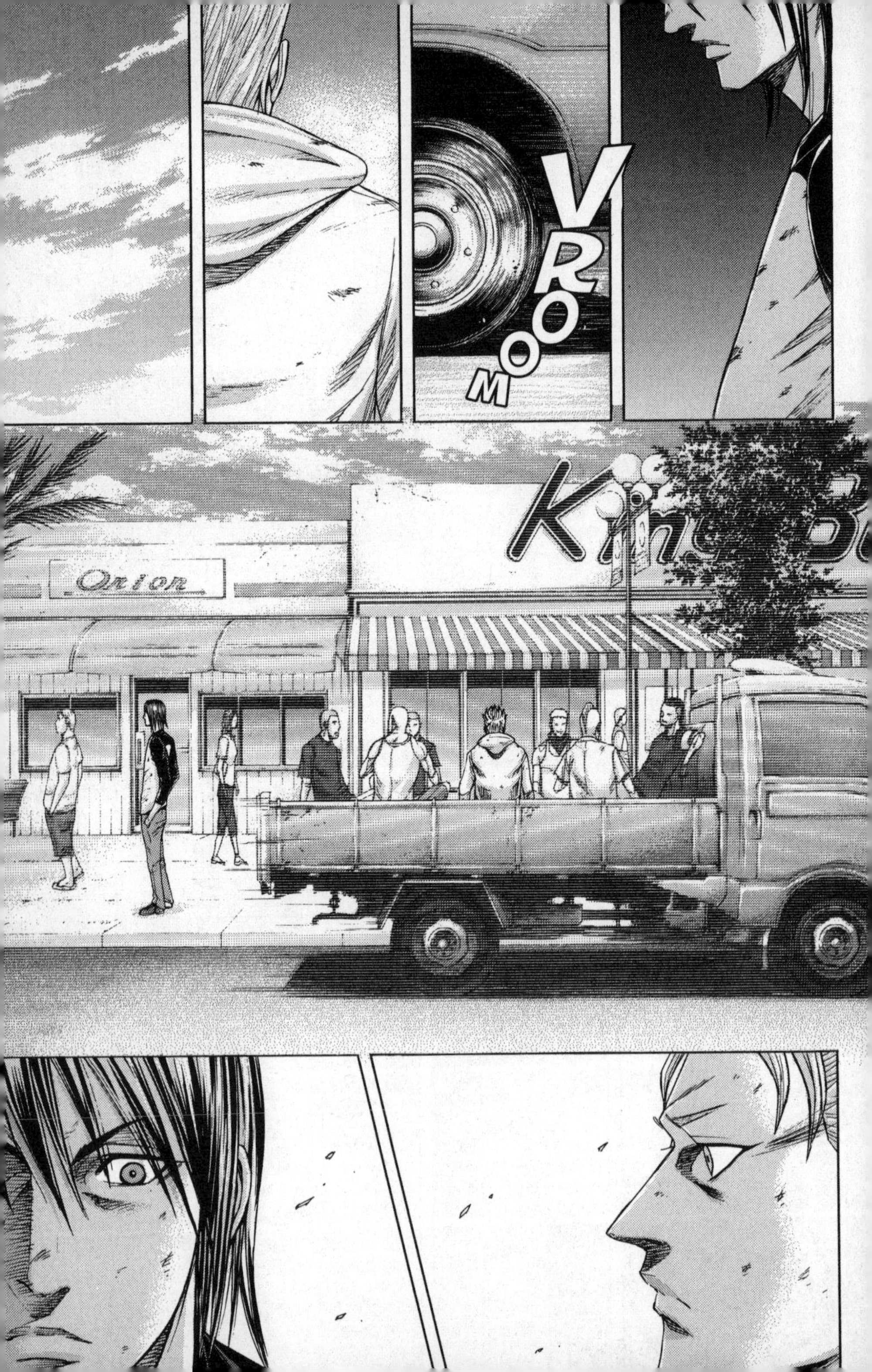
VROOOM
Orion

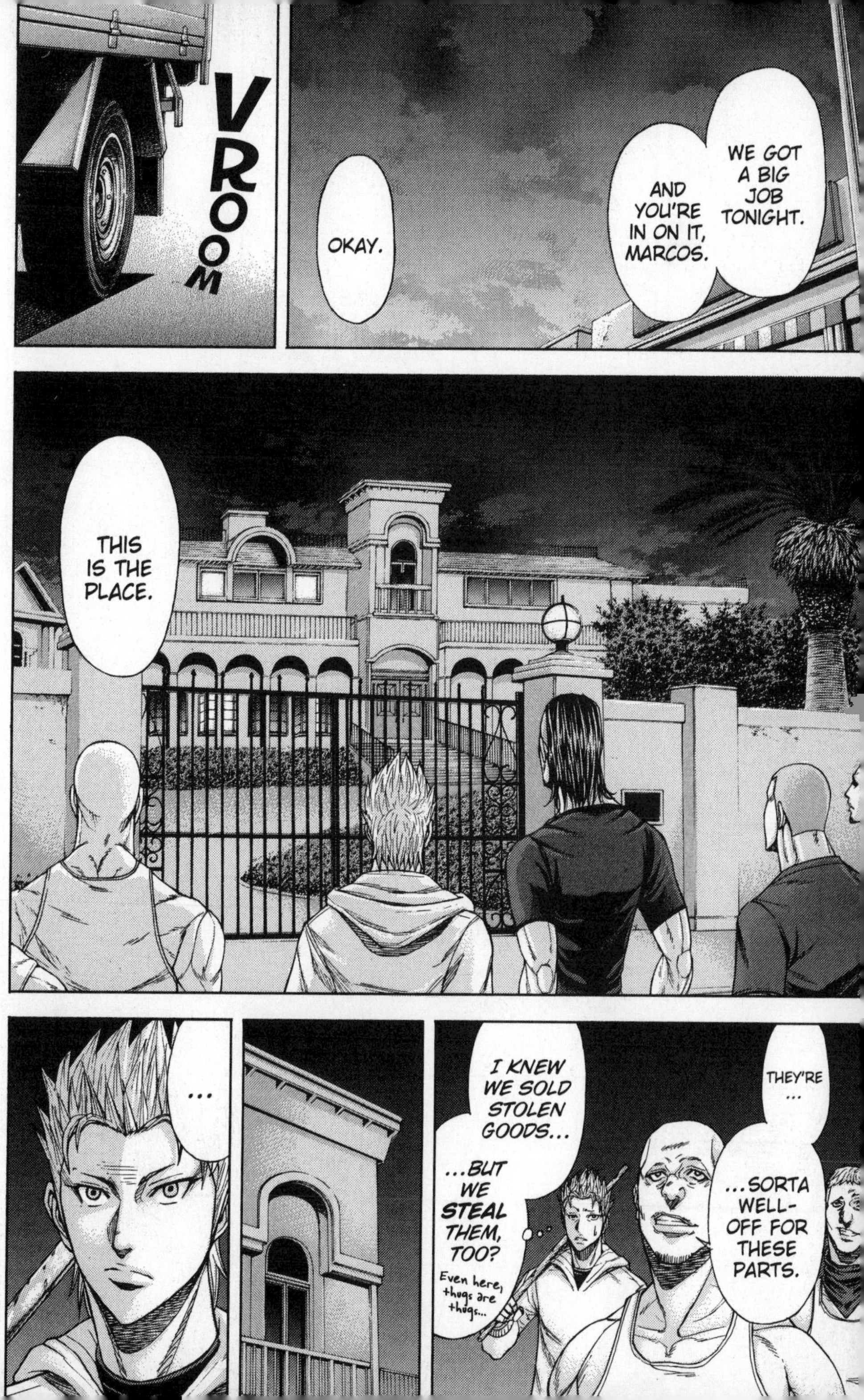
WE GOT A BIG JOB TONIGHT.
AND YOU'RE IN ON IT, MARCOS.
OKAY.
VROOM
THIS IS THE PLACE.
THEY'RE ...
...SORTA WELL-OFF FOR THESE PARTS.
I KNEW WE SOLD STOLEN GOODS...
...BUT WE STEAL THEM, TOO?
Even here, thugs are thugs...
...

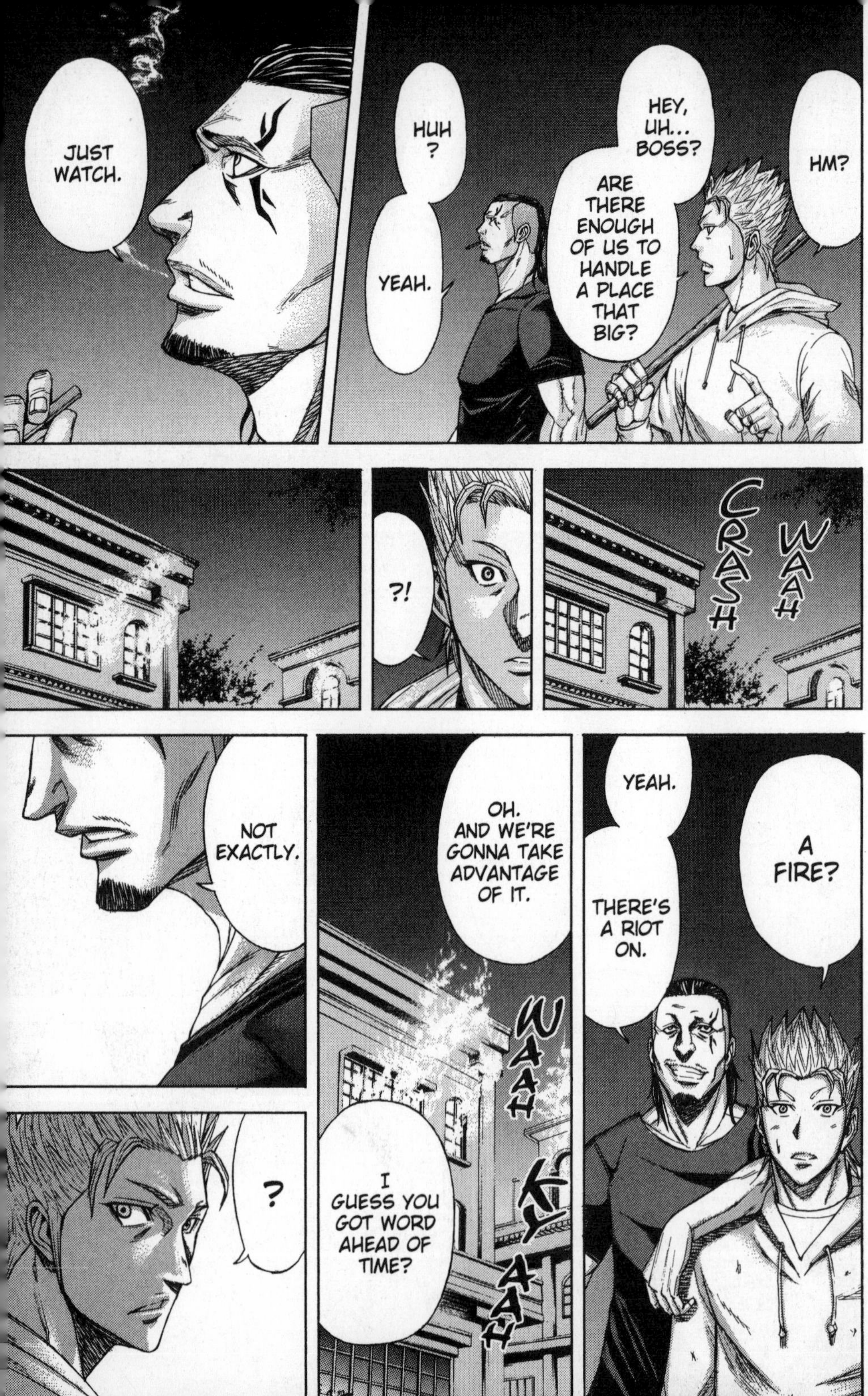
HM?
HEY, UH... BOSS?
ARE THERE ENOUGH OF US TO HANDLE A PLACE THAT BIG?
HUH?
YEAH.
JUST WATCH.
WAAH
CRASH
?!
A FIRE?
YEAH.
THERE'S A RIOT ON.
OH. AND WE'RE GONNA TAKE ADVANTAGE OF IT.
WAAH
KYAAH
I GUESS YOU GOT WORD AHEAD OF TIME?
NOT EXACTLY.
?

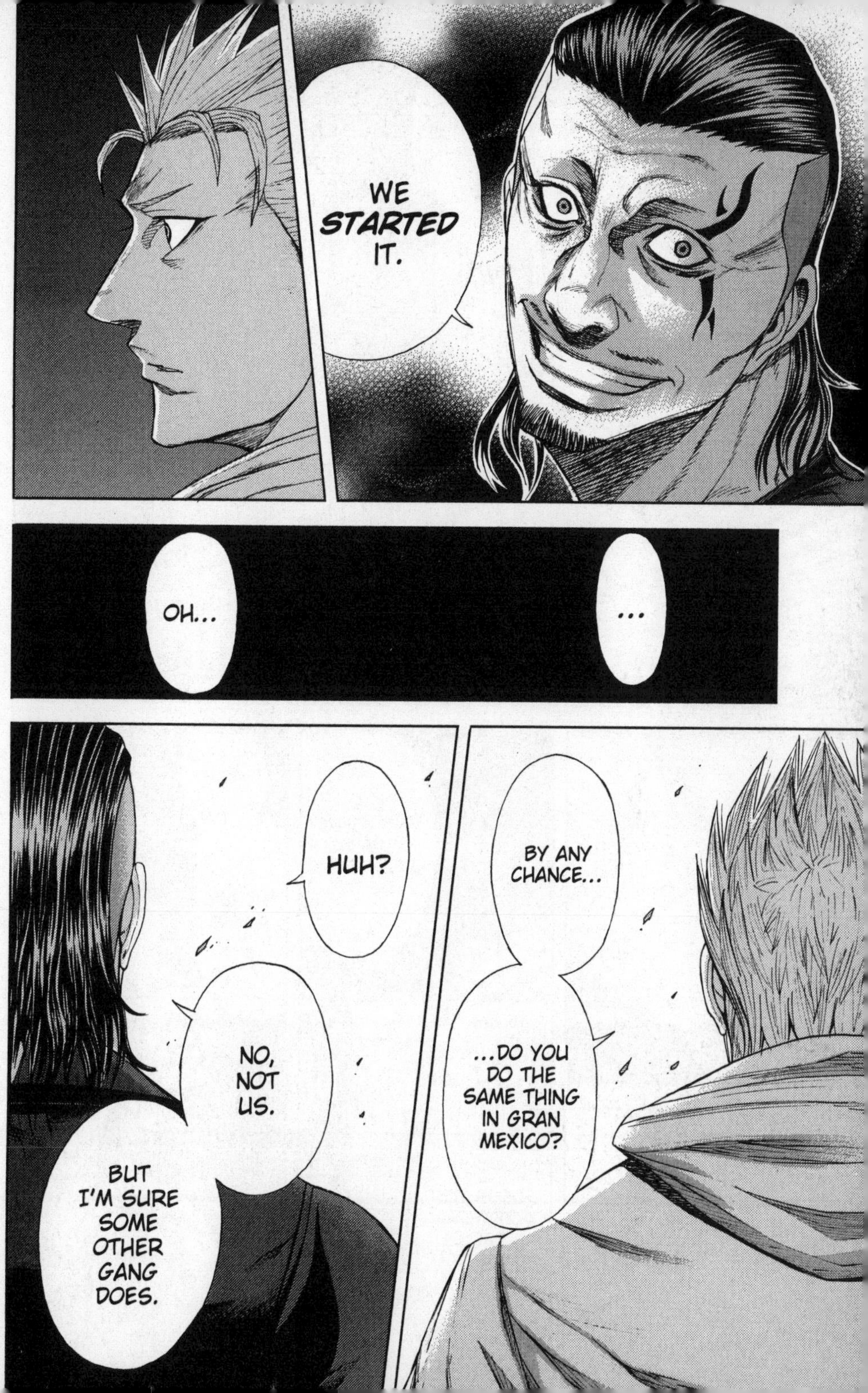
WE STARTED IT.
...
OH...
BY ANY CHANCE...
...DO YOU DO THE SAME THING IN GRAN MEXICO?
HUH?
NO, NOT US.
BUT I'M SURE SOME OTHER GANG DOES.

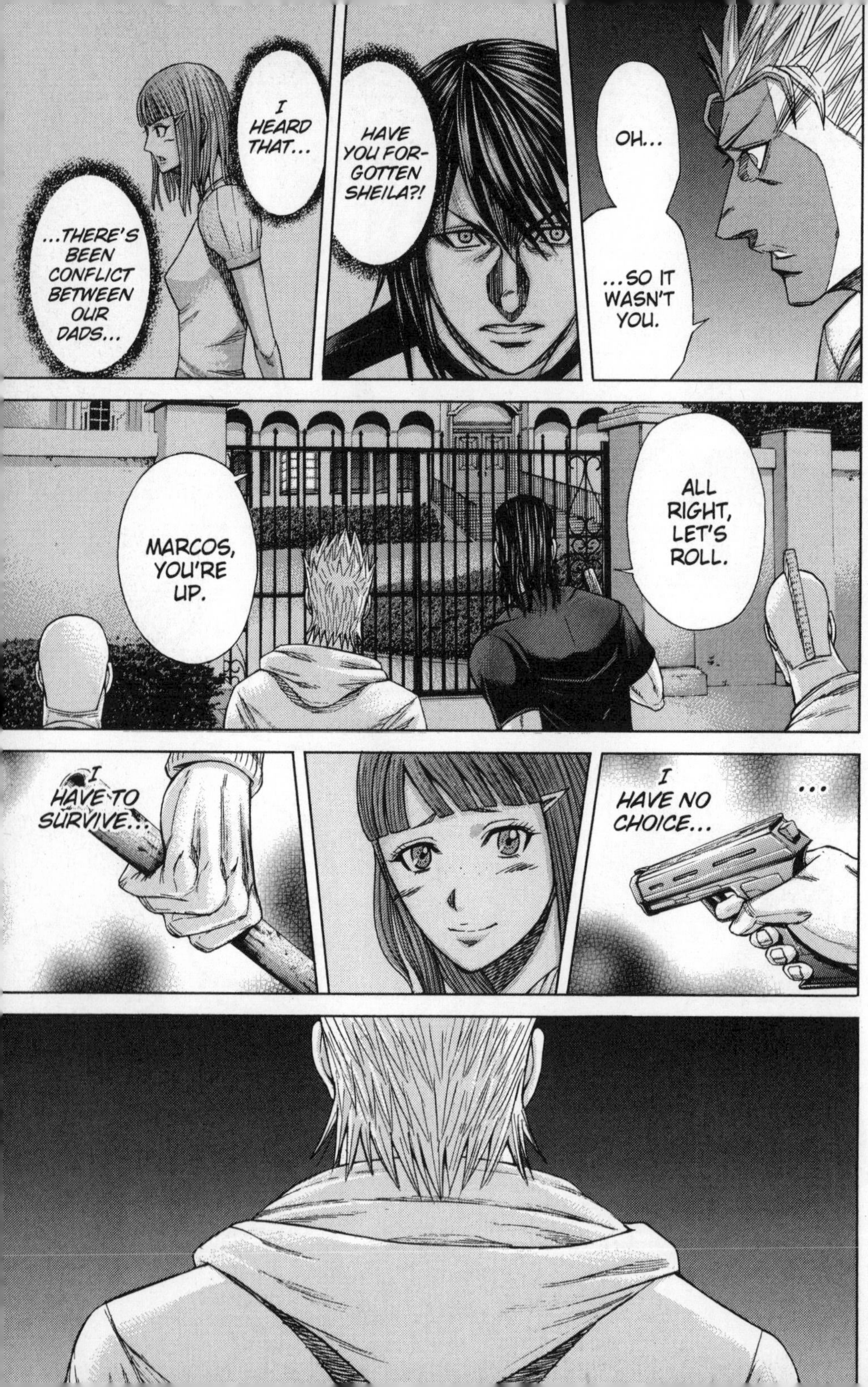
OH...
...SO IT WASN'T YOU.
HAVE YOU FOR-GOTTEN SHEILA?!
I HEARD THAT...
...THERE'S BEEN CONFLICT BETWEEN OUR DADS...
ALL RIGHT, LET'S ROLL.
MARCOS, YOU'RE UP.
...
I HAVE NO CHOICE...
I HAVE TO SURVIVE...

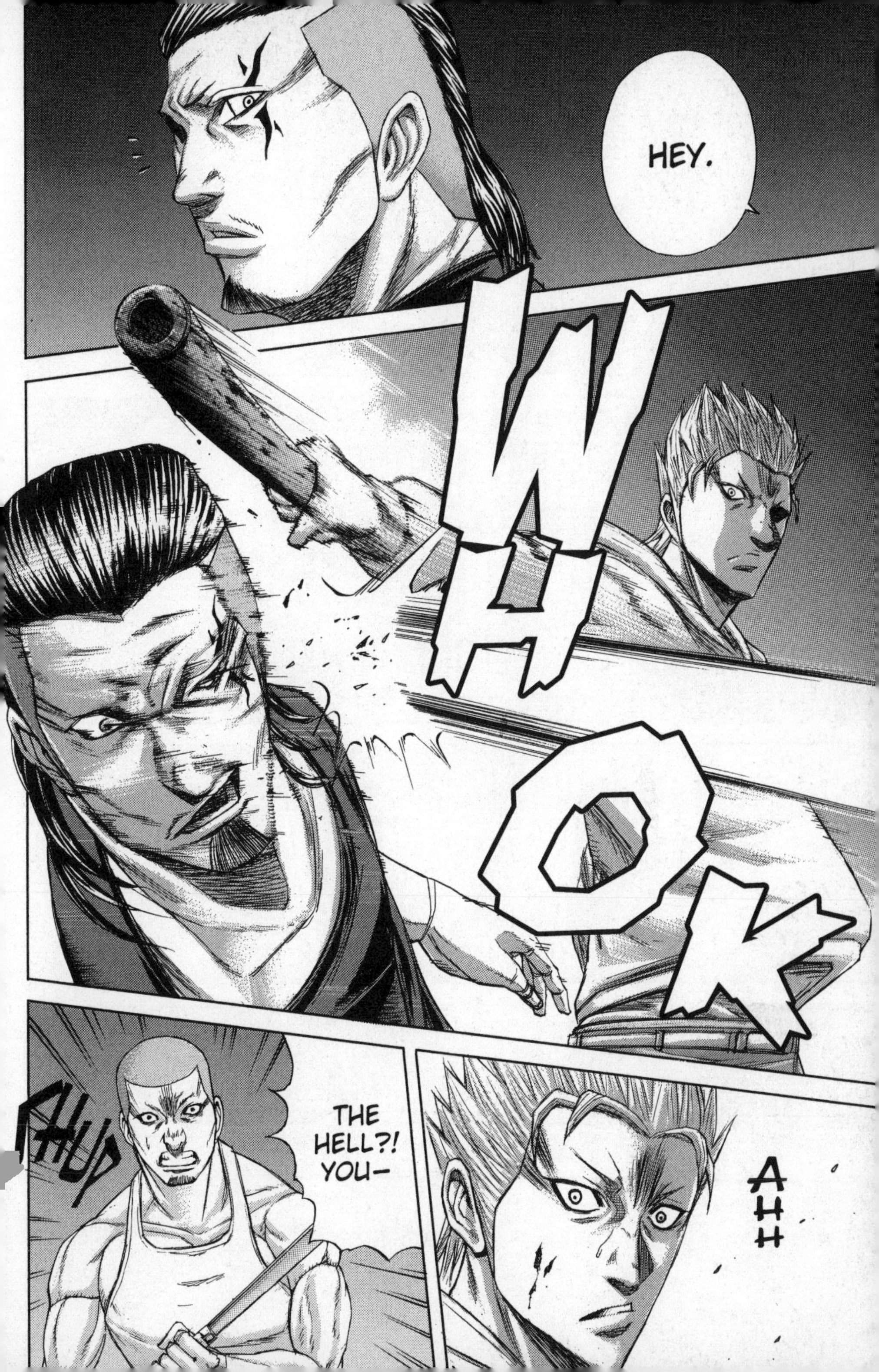
HEY.
WHOK
AHH
THUD
THE HELL?! YOU–

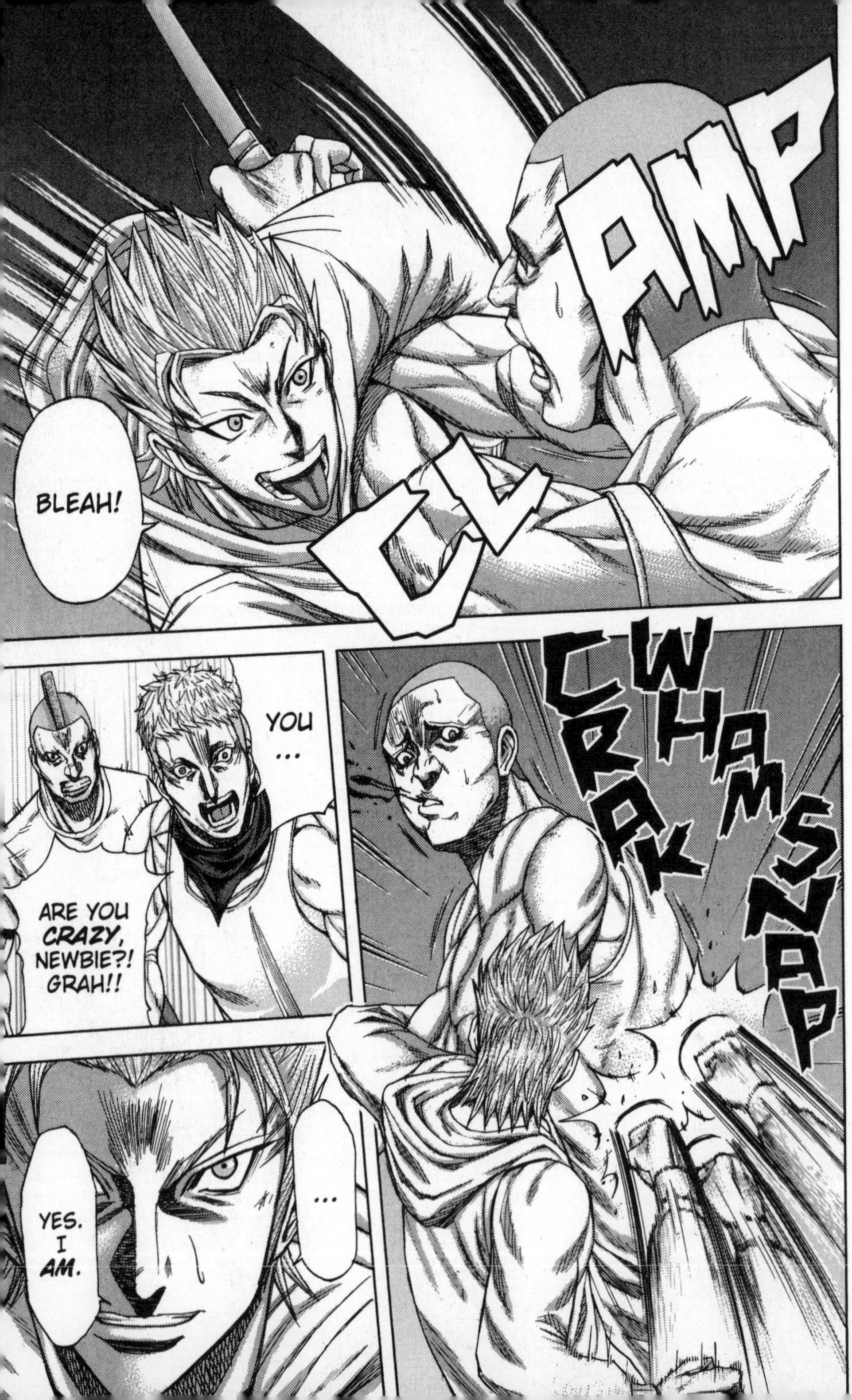
AMP
BLEAH!
WHAM
CRAK
SNAP
YOU ...
ARE YOU *CRAZY*, NEWBIE?! GRAH!!
...
YES. I *AM*.

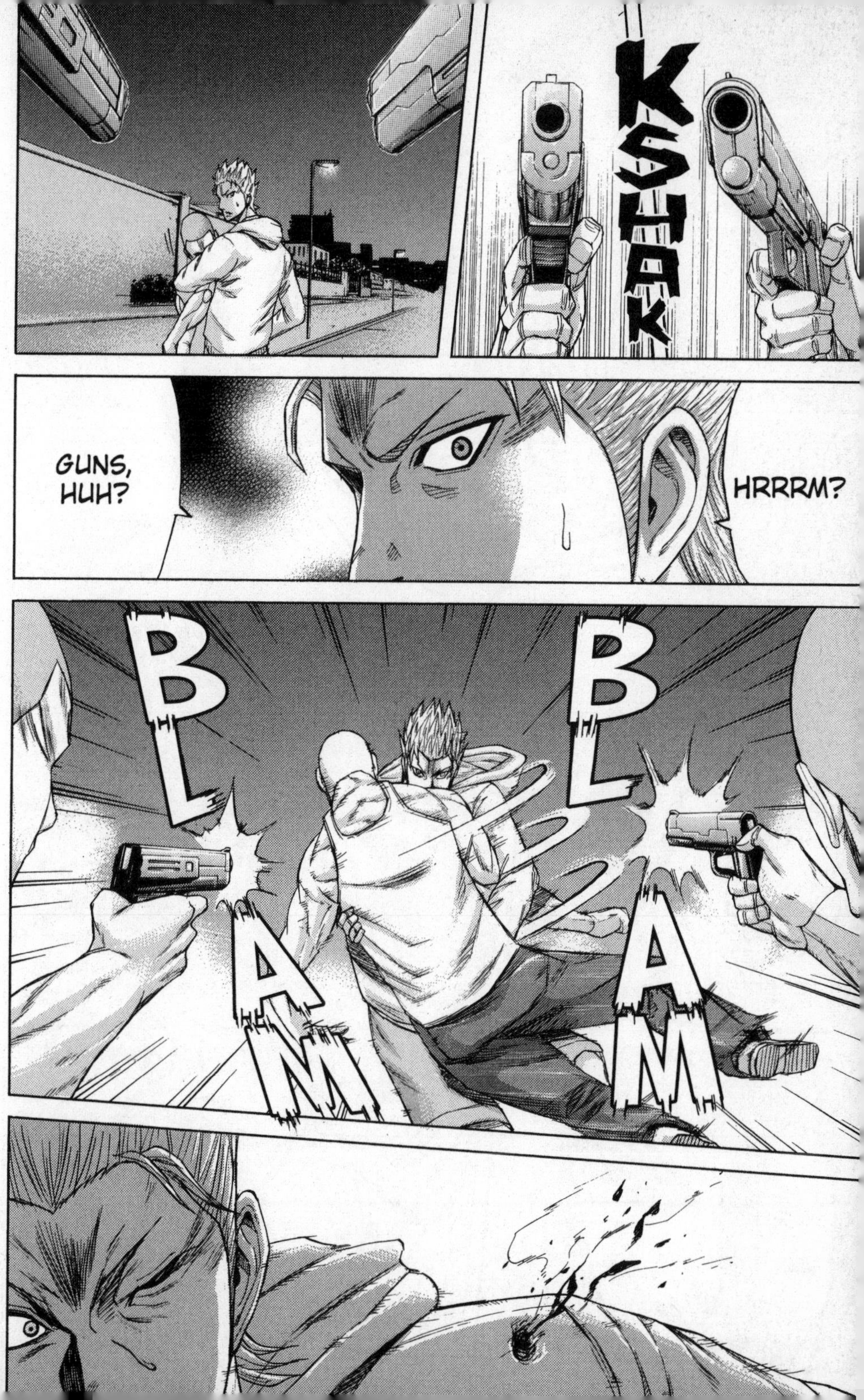
KSHAK
HRRRM?
GUNS, HUH?
BLAM
BLAM

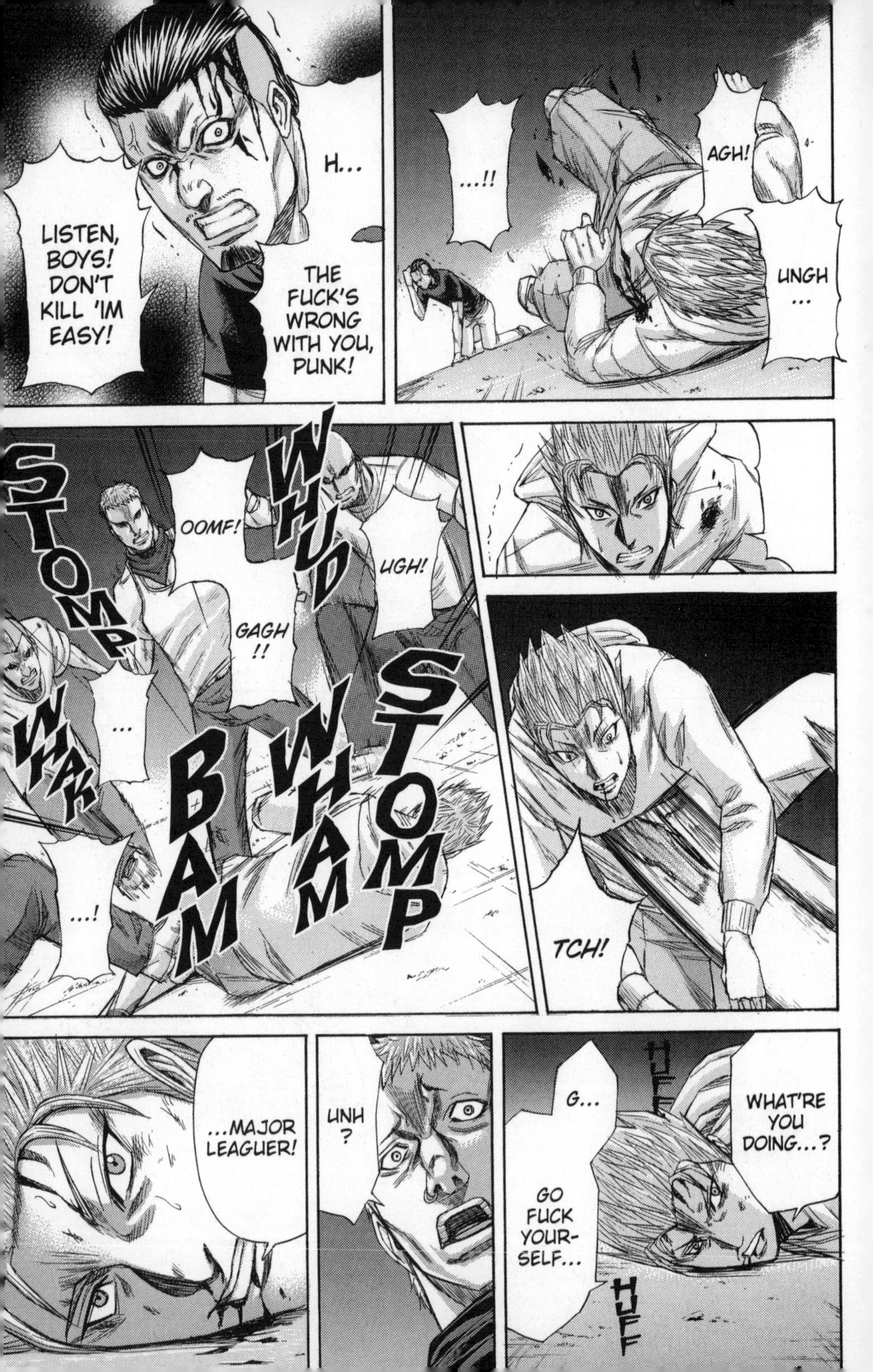
AGH!
UNGH ...
...!!
H...
THE FUCK'S WRONG WITH YOU, PUNK!
LISTEN, BOYS! DON'T KILL 'IM EASY!
TCH!
WHUD
UGH!
OOMF!
STOMP
GAGH !!
STOMP
WHAM
BAM
...
WHAK
...!
HUFF
WHAT'RE YOU DOING...?
G...
GO FUCK YOUR-SELF...
HUFF
UNH ?
...MAJOR LEAGUER!

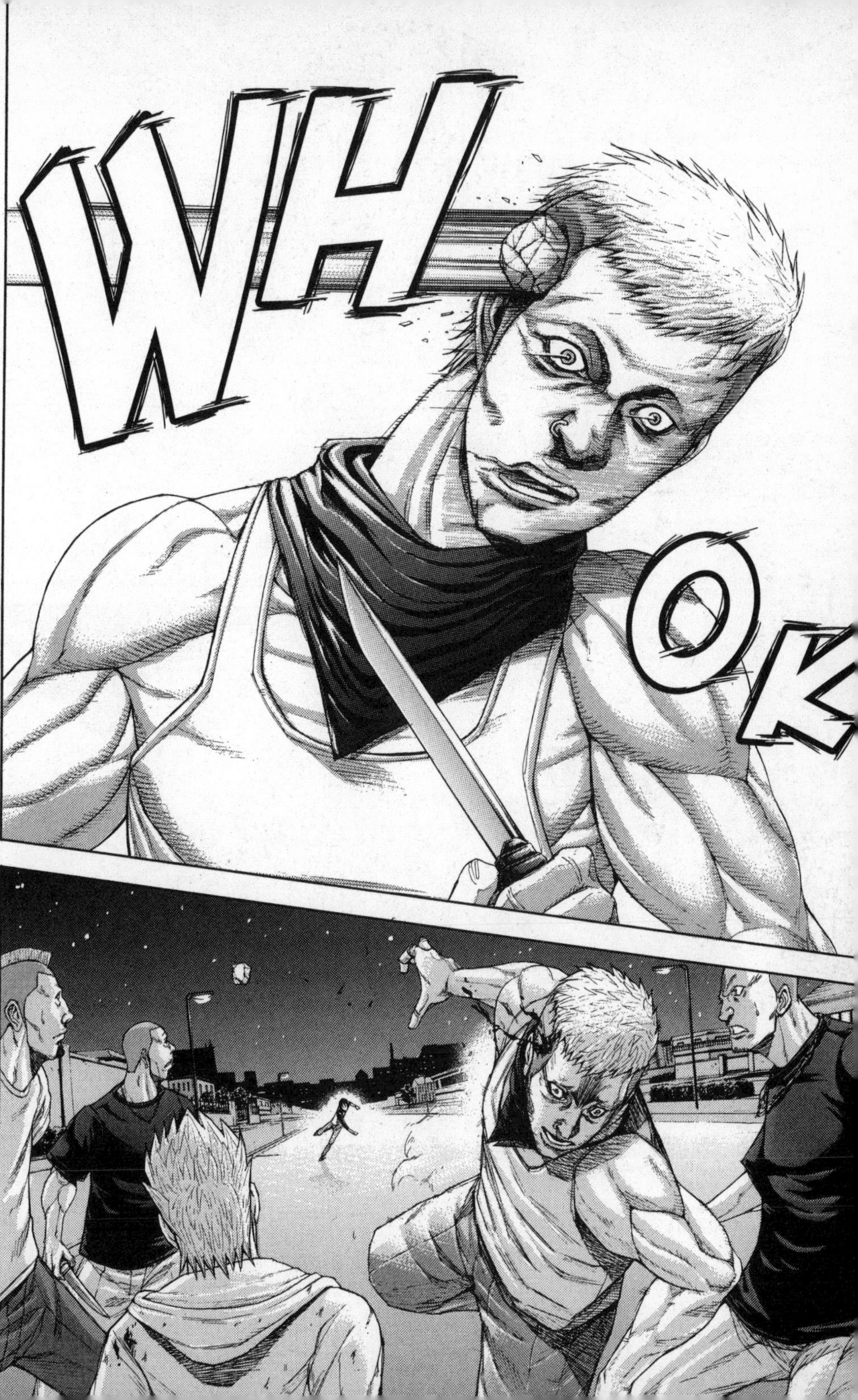
WH
OK

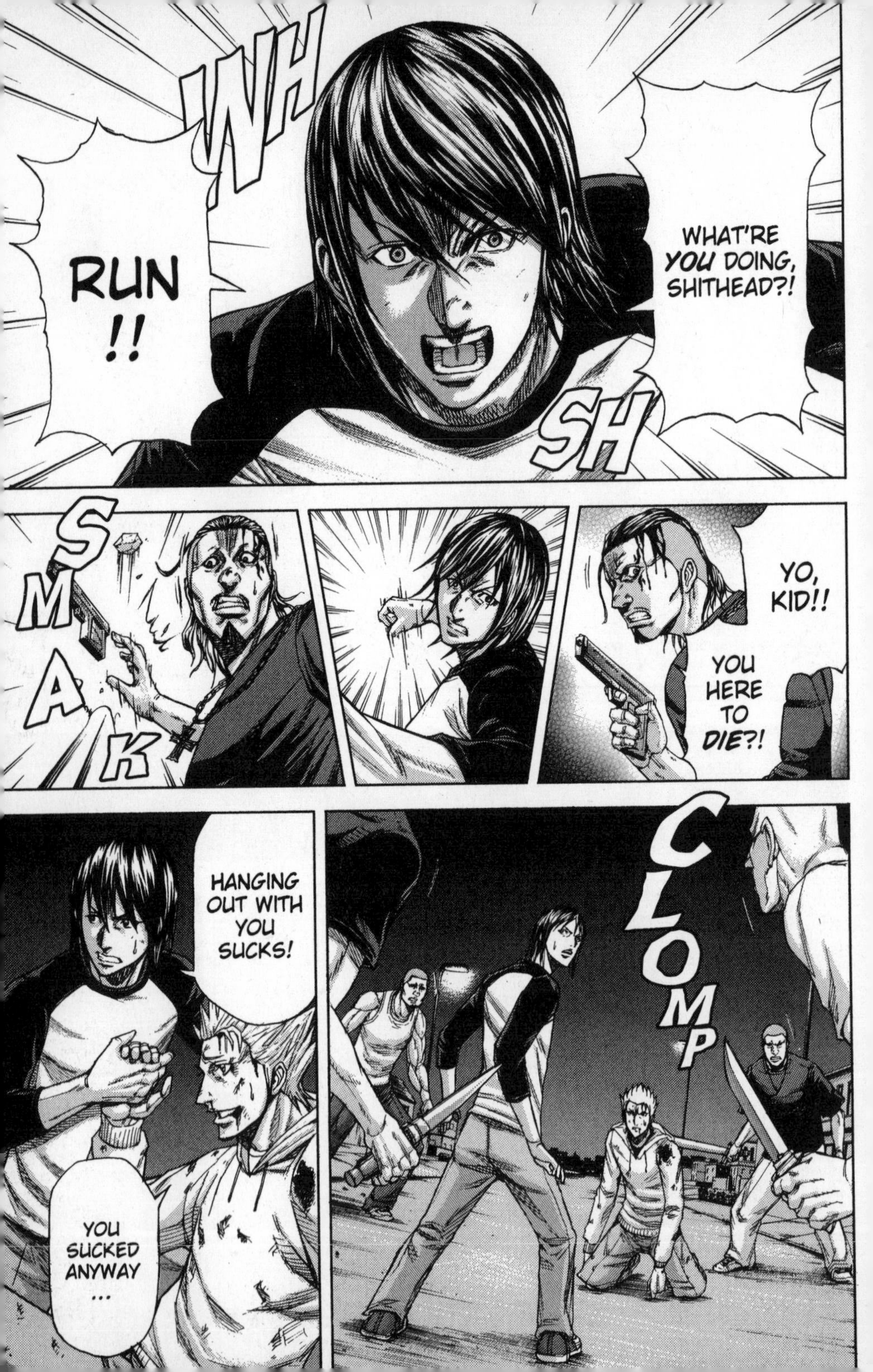
WHAT'RE *YOU* DOING, SHITHEAD?!
WH
RUN !!
SH
YO, KID!!
YOU HERE TO *DIE*?!
SMAK
CLOMP
HANGING OUT WITH YOU SUCKS!
YOU SUCKED ANYWAY ...

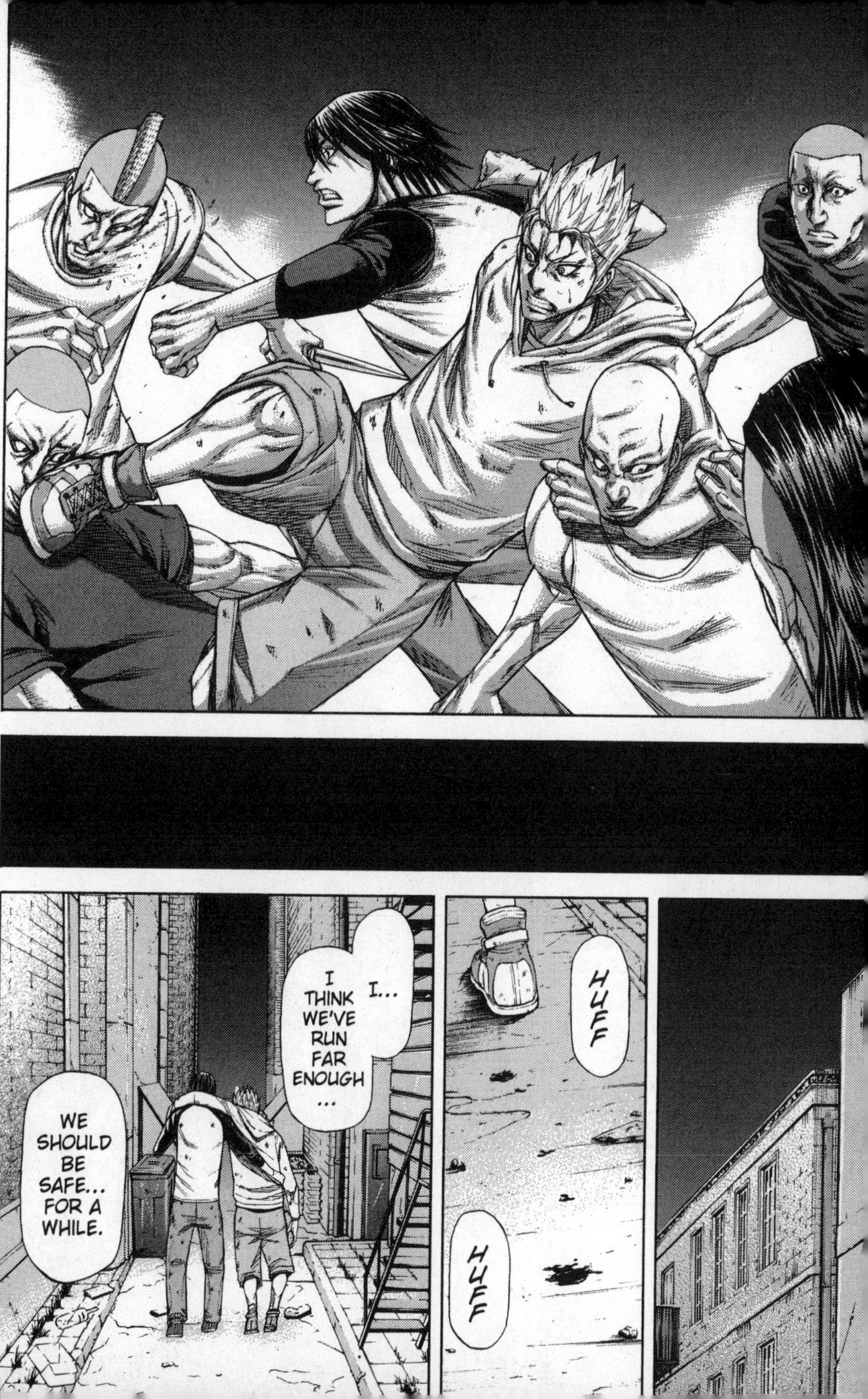
HUFF
HUFF
I...
I THINK WE'VE RUN FAR ENOUGH...
WE SHOULD BE SAFE... FOR A WHILE.

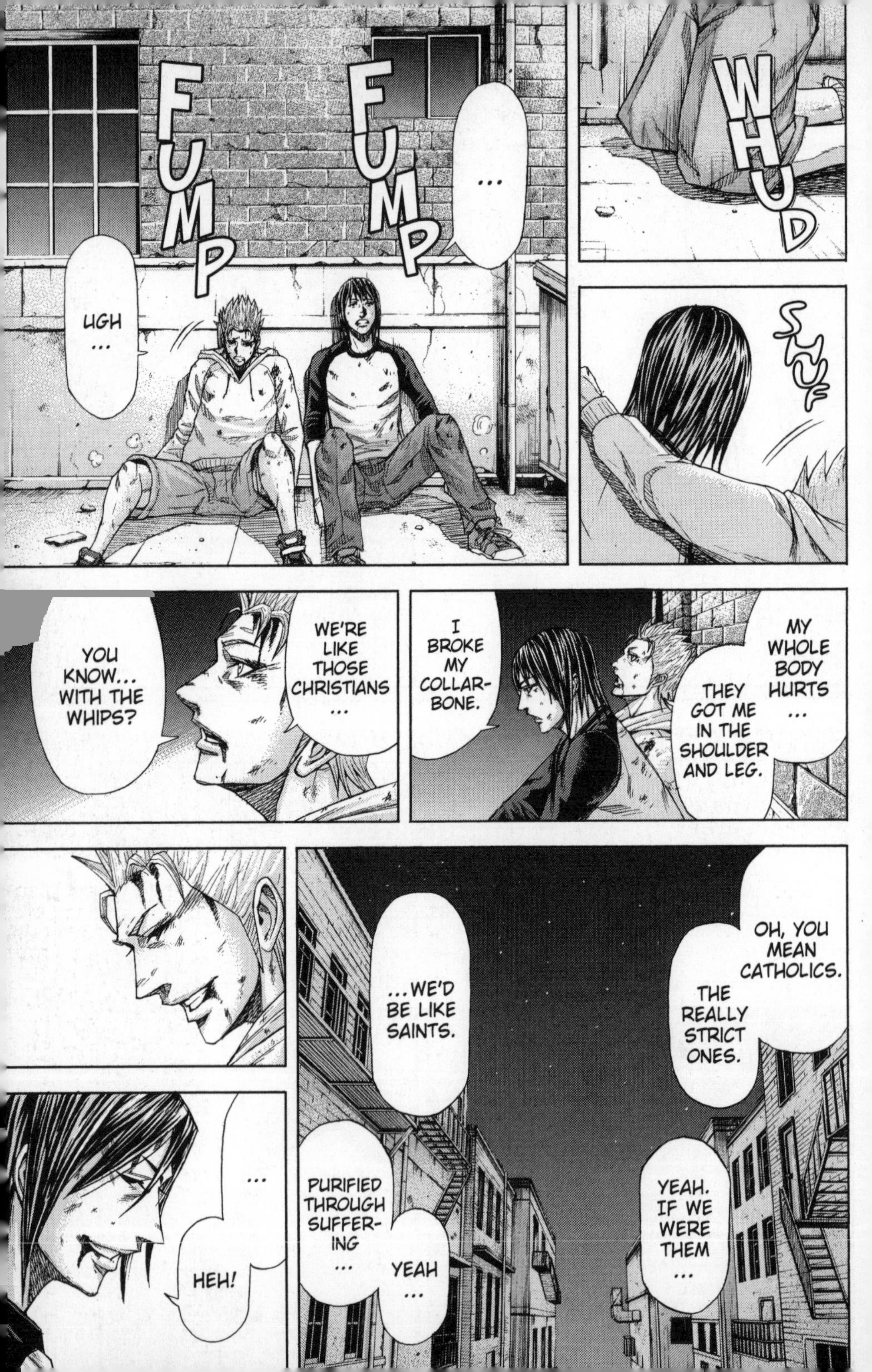
WHUD
SHUF
...
FUMP
FUMP
UGH ...
MY WHOLE BODY HURTS ...
THEY GOT ME IN THE SHOULDER AND LEG.
I BROKE MY COLLAR-BONE.
WE'RE LIKE THOSE CHRISTIANS ...
YOU KNOW... WITH THE WHIPS?
OH, YOU MEAN CATHOLICS.
THE REALLY STRICT ONES.
YEAH. IF WE WERE THEM ...
...WE'D BE LIKE SAINTS.
PURIFIED THROUGH SUFFER-ING ...
YEAH ...
...
HEH!

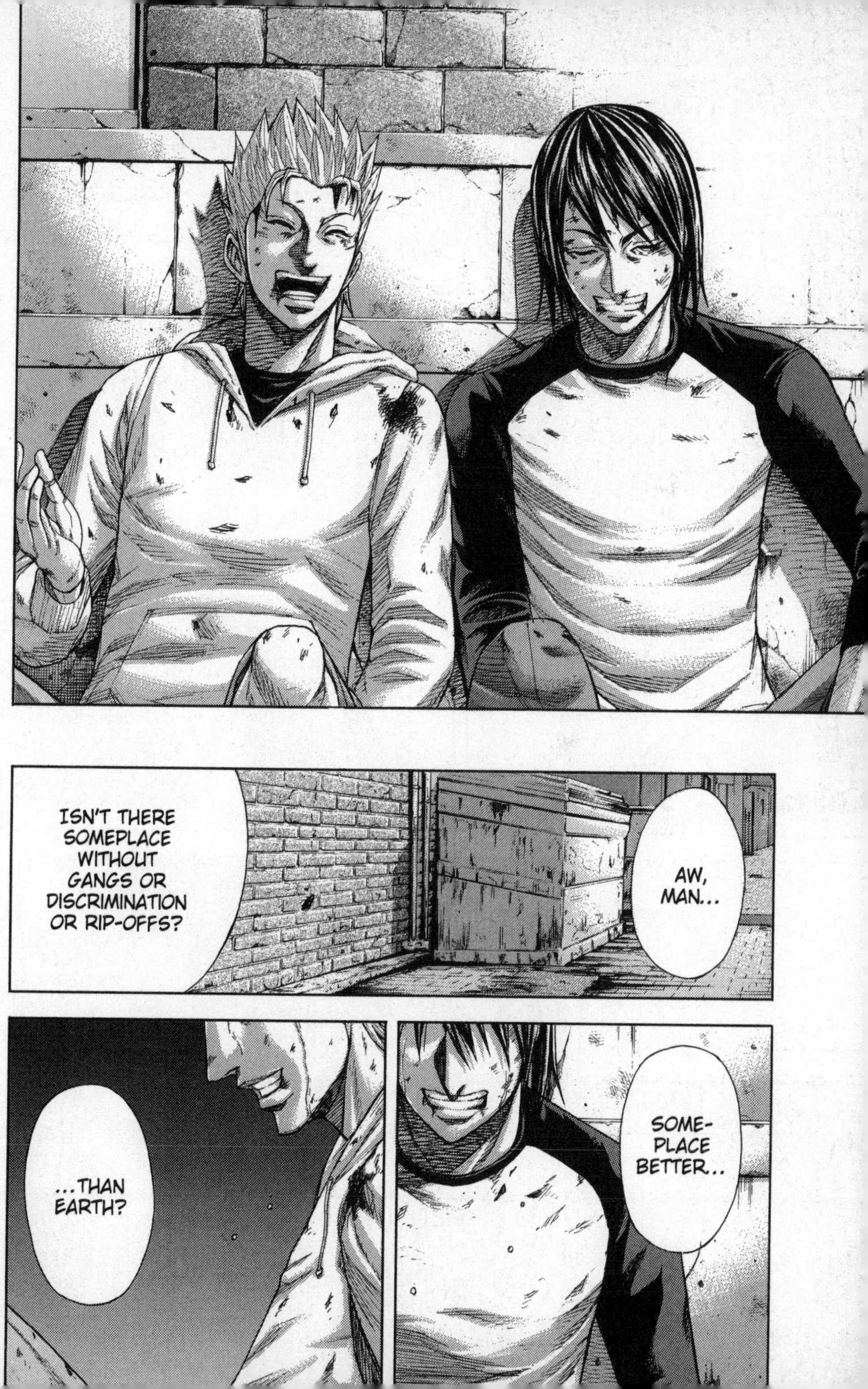
AW, MAN...
ISN'T THERE SOMEPLACE WITHOUT GANGS OR DISCRIMINATION OR RIP-OFFS?
SOME-PLACE BETTER...
...THAN EARTH?

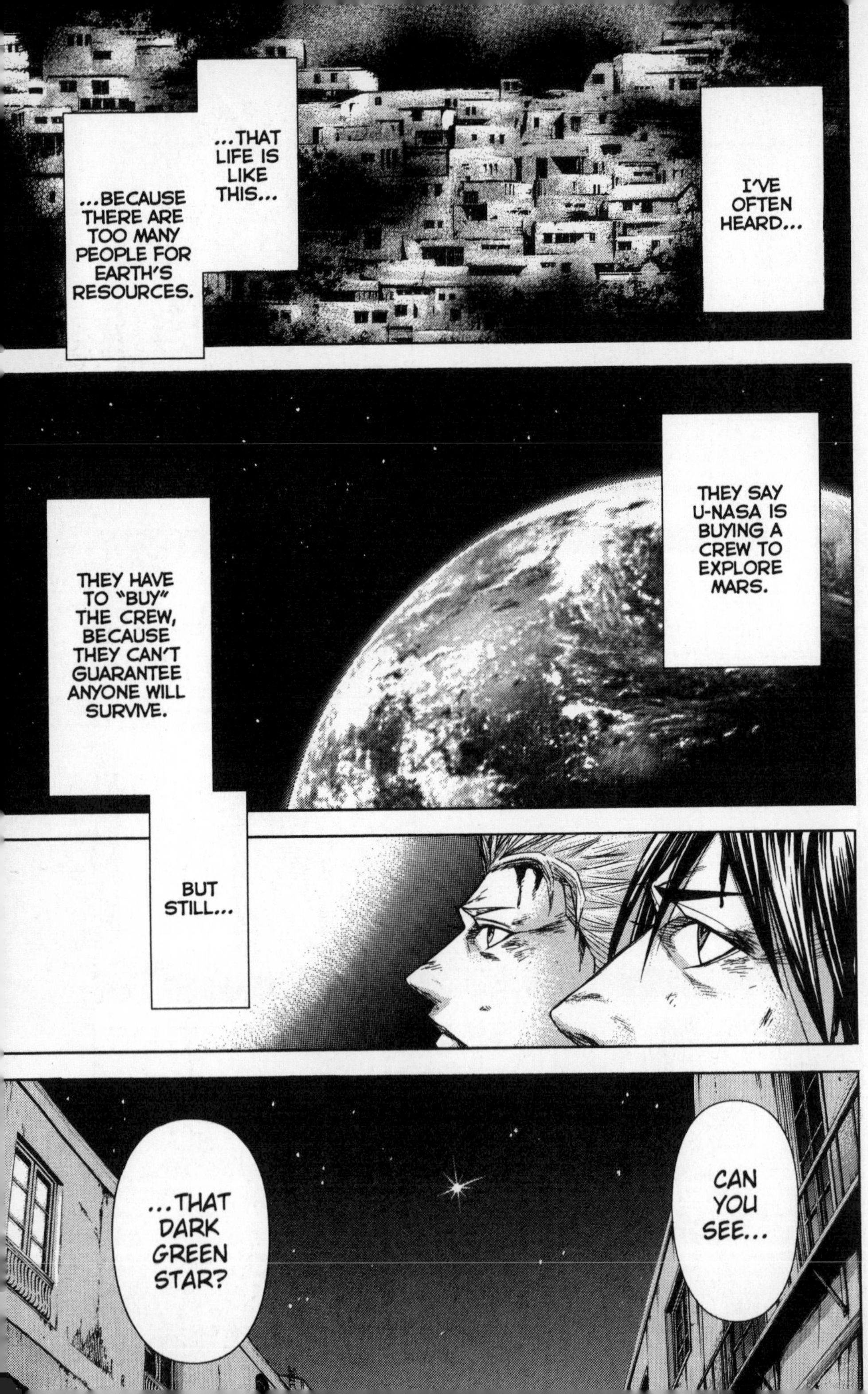
I'VE OFTEN HEARD...
...THAT LIFE IS LIKE THIS...
...BECAUSE THERE ARE TOO MANY PEOPLE FOR EARTH'S RESOURCES.
THEY SAY U-NASA IS BUYING A CREW TO EXPLORE MARS.
THEY HAVE TO "BUY" THE CREW, BECAUSE THEY CAN'T GUARANTEE ANYONE WILL SURVIVE.
BUT STILL...
CAN YOU SEE...
...THAT DARK GREEN STAR?

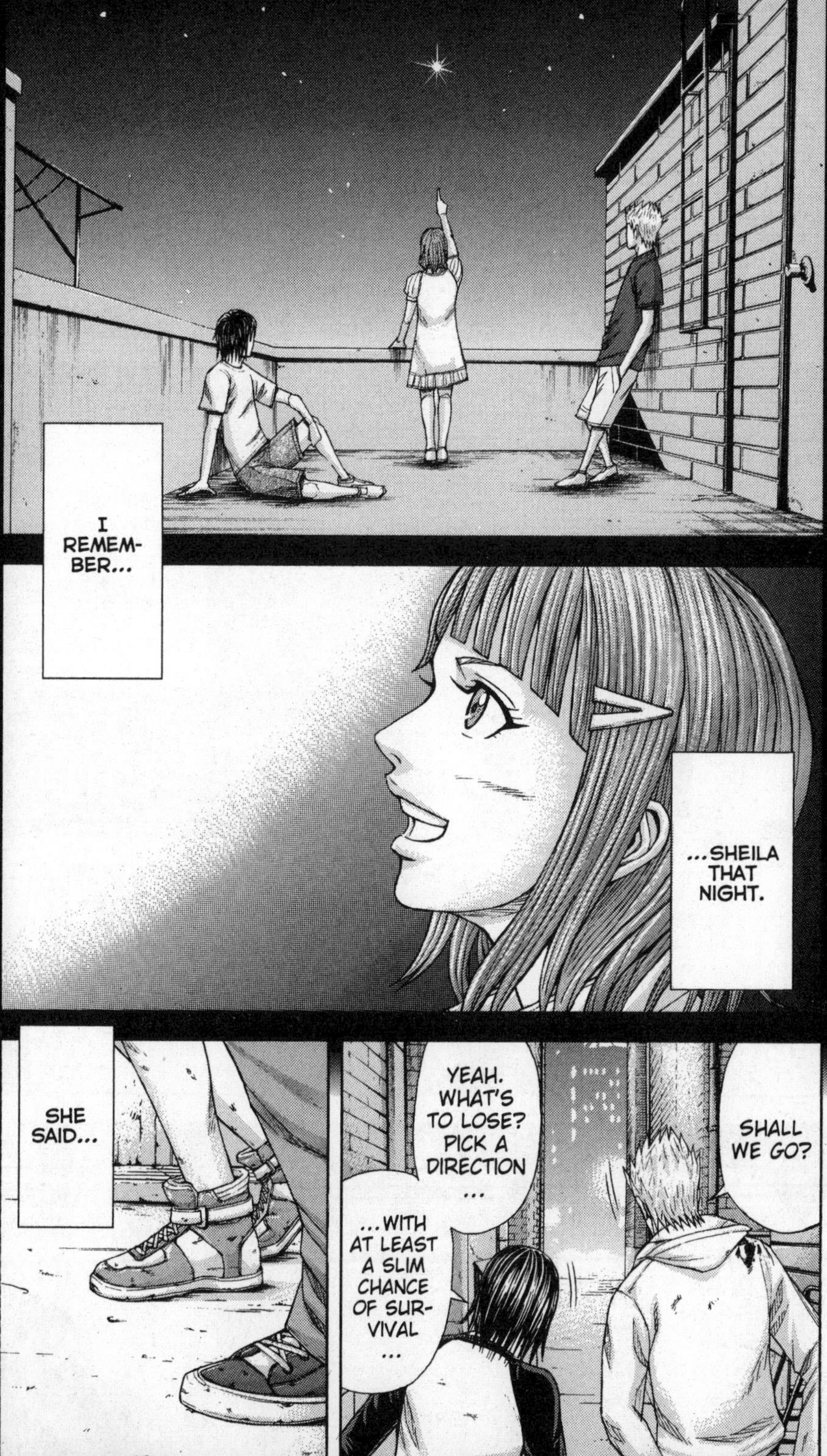
I REMEMBER...
...SHEILA THAT NIGHT.
SHALL WE GO?
YEAH. WHAT'S TO LOSE? PICK A DIRECTION ...
...WITH AT LEAST A SLIM CHANCE OF SURVIVAL ...
SHE SAID...

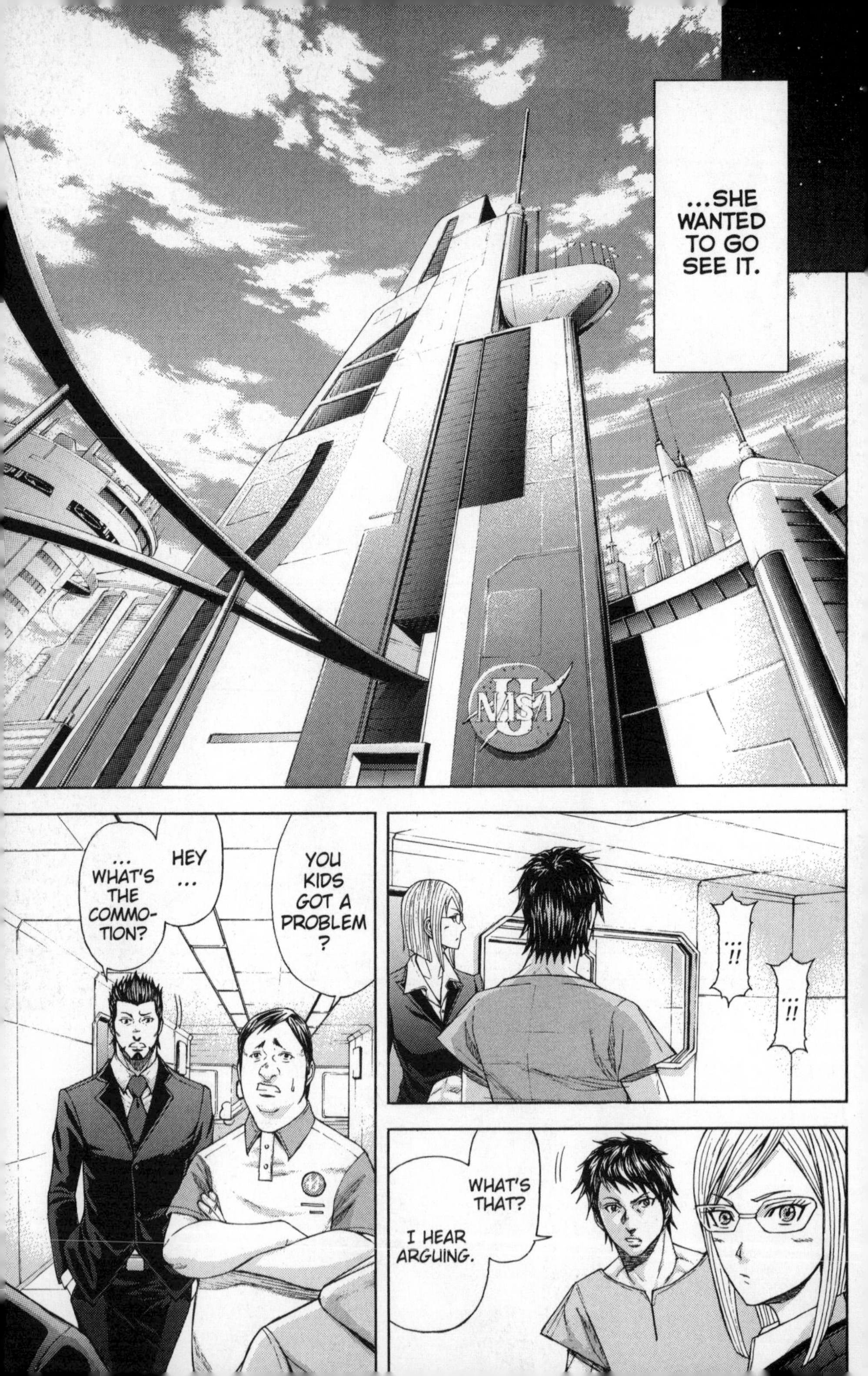
...SHE WANTED TO GO SEE IT.
NASA
...!!
...!!
WHAT'S THAT?
I HEAR ARGUING.
YOU KIDS GOT A PROBLEM?
HEY...
...WHAT'S THE COMMOTION?

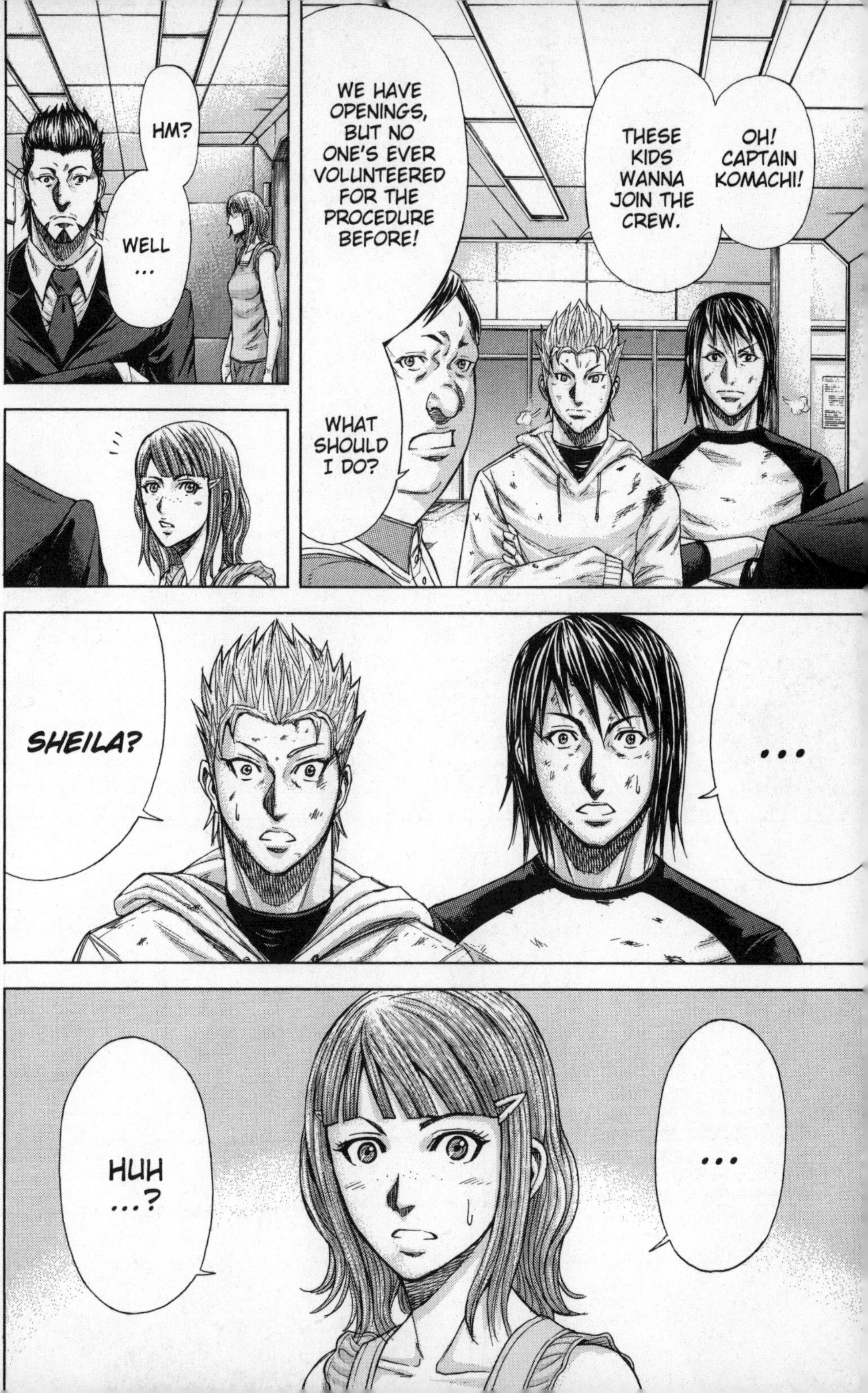
OH! CAPTAIN KOMACHI!
THESE KIDS WANNA JOIN THE CREW.
WE HAVE OPENINGS, BUT NO ONE'S EVER VOLUNTEERED FOR THE PROCEDURE BEFORE!
WHAT SHOULD I DO?
HM?
WELL ...
...
SHEILA?
...
HUH ...?

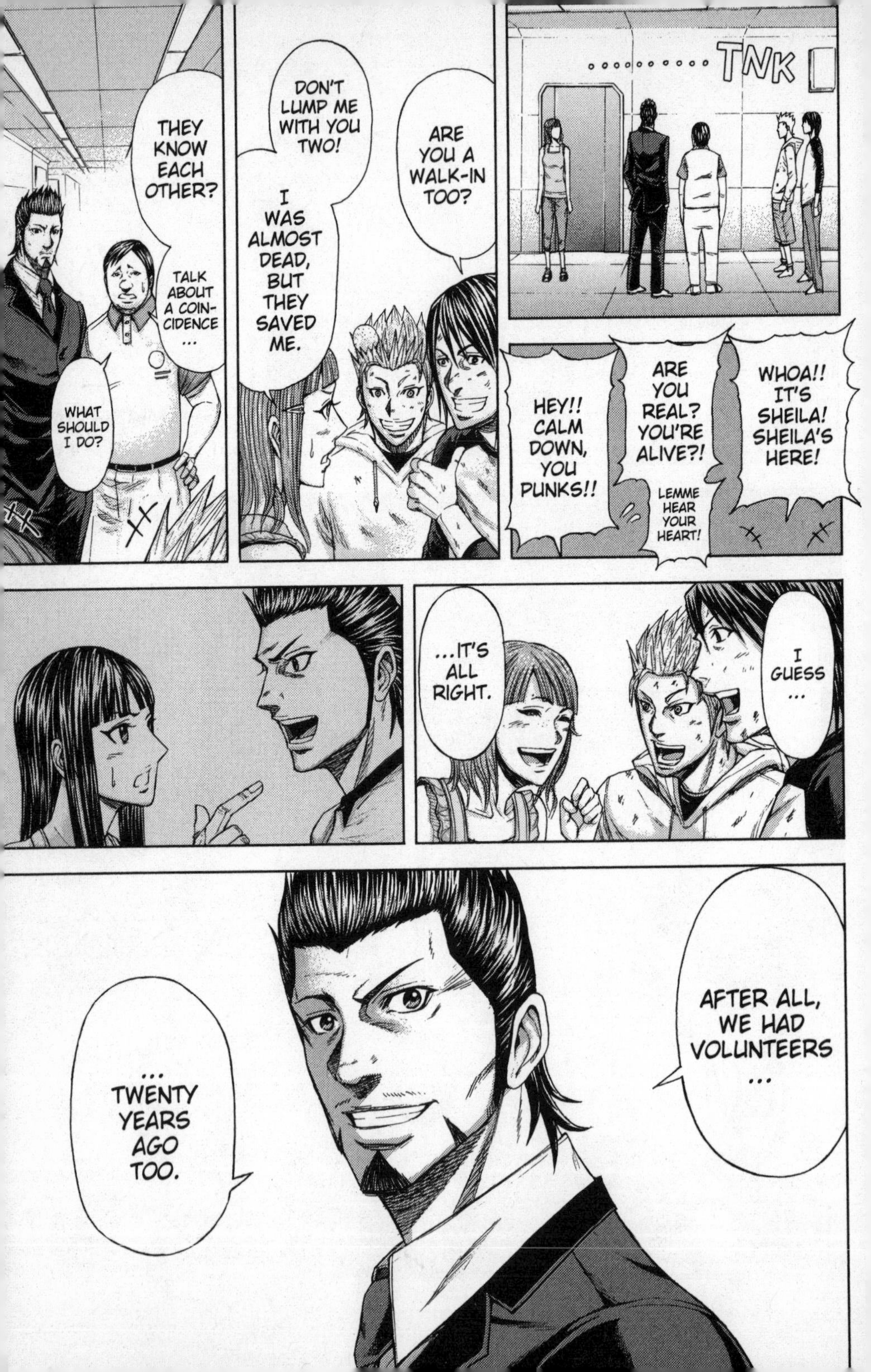

..........TNK
WHOA!! IT'S SHEILA! SHEILA'S HERE!
ARE YOU REAL? YOU'RE ALIVE?!
LEMME HEAR YOUR HEART!
HEY!! CALM DOWN, YOU PUNKS!!
ARE YOU A WALK-IN TOO?
DON'T LUMP ME WITH YOU TWO!
I WAS ALMOST DEAD, BUT THEY SAVED ME.
THEY KNOW EACH OTHER?
TALK ABOUT A COIN-CIDENCE...
WHAT SHOULD I DO?
I GUESS...
...IT'S ALL RIGHT.
AFTER ALL, WE HAD VOLUNTEERS...
...TWENTY YEARS AGO TOO.

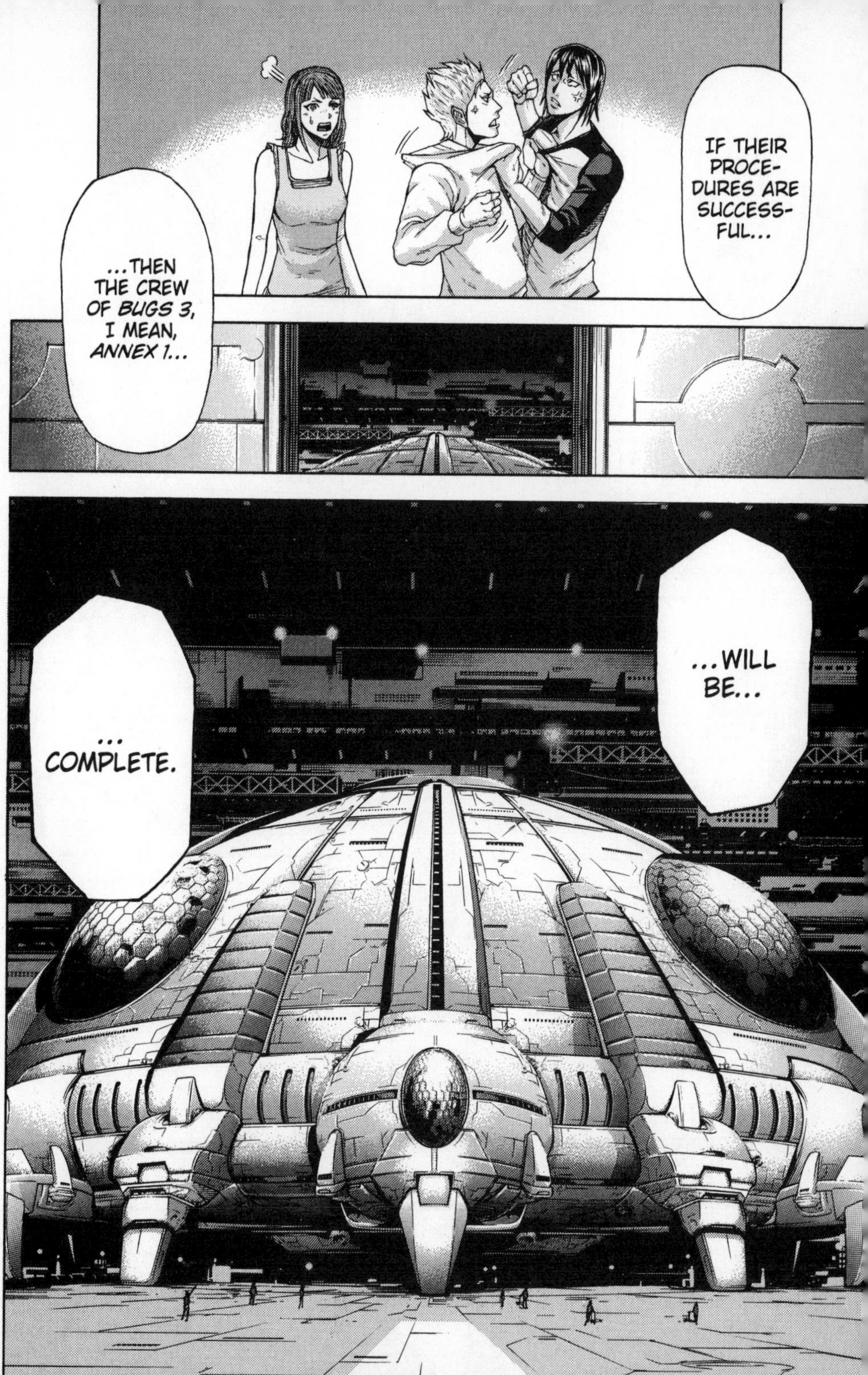
IF THEIR PROCE- DURES ARE SUCCESS- FUL...
...THEN THE CREW OF BUGS 3, I MEAN, ANNEX 1...
...WILL BE...
... COMPLETE.

Annex

(noun) (to…) an extension or addition to a building
(verb) to add a territory (country, etc.) to another (especially
through the use of force)

From *The Genius English-Japanese Dictionary*, with
omissions. Publisher: Taishukan Shoten.

U-NASA Preliminary File I - Cockroaches

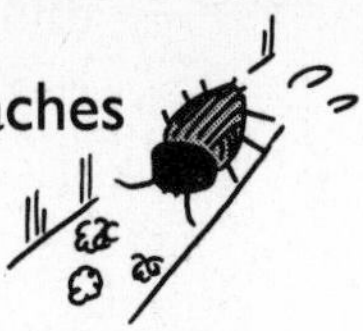

●The white liquid that comes out when a cockroach is smashed isn't muscle, it's "fat body." Fat body stores fat, glycogen and protein. It is said that by efficiently converting this into energy, cockroaches are able to withstand hunger for a long time. In experiments, female American cockroaches have survived for one month without eating or sleeping.

●It is true that cockroaches are weak against cold. In general, temperatures under 25°C will impair growth or cause death, but some individuals show greater resistance. In the case of sending cockroaches to Mars, they would be bred to increase stability and resistance to cold.

●Cockroaches love to feed on onion skin.

●Cockroaches actually like cleanliness. They often lick their antennae (to apply an antibacterial substance in their saliva) to clean themselves. Thus, they hate passing through dusty areas.

●One of the most common routes cockroaches use to invade homes is the doorway. They slip in when people are going in or out. Using a pesticide around entrances is an effective preventive measure.

●Cockroach egg cases can be steeped in hot sake and whiskey for drinking. According to a book by someone who has drunk such a beverage, it helps round out the taste.

●Dried and grilled cockroaches, as well as alcohol seasoned with egg cases, have been used as medicine. According to tradition, the uses are many, including treatment of colds, cirrhosis and irregular menstruation.

●Cockroaches secrete their aggregation pheromone from a part of their rectum called a "rectal pad," so it is mixed with excrement when emitted. The exposed excrement attracts other cockroaches.

●Cockroach larvae grow more quickly in a group rather than alone, and differences between individuals are small. The reason for this remains unclear.

●Mature cockroaches have relatively long lives compared to other insects. The eggs, larvae and adults live together congenially.

—What do you think about this?

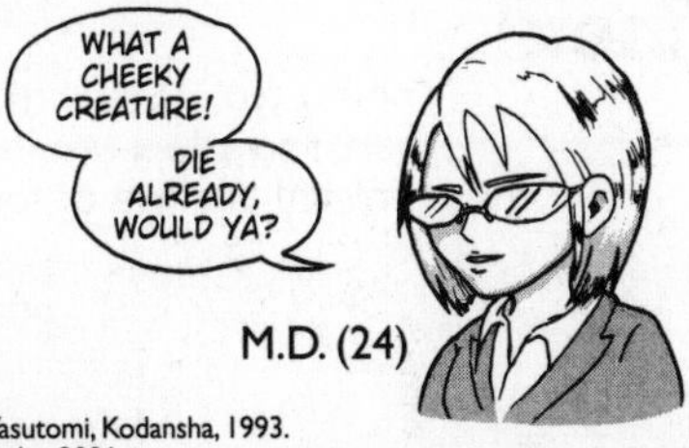
WHAT A CHEEKY CREATURE!
DIE ALREADY, WOULD YA?

M.D. (24)

References:
About Cockroaches, Kazuo Yasutomi (editor), Gihodo Shuppan, 1991.
Cockroaches: A 300-Million-Year-Old Secret—The Living Fossil in Your Kitchen, Kazuo Yasutomi, Kodansha, 1993.
The Taste of Bugs (New Edition), Satoshi Shinonaga and Akifumi Hayashi, Yasaka Shobo, 2006.

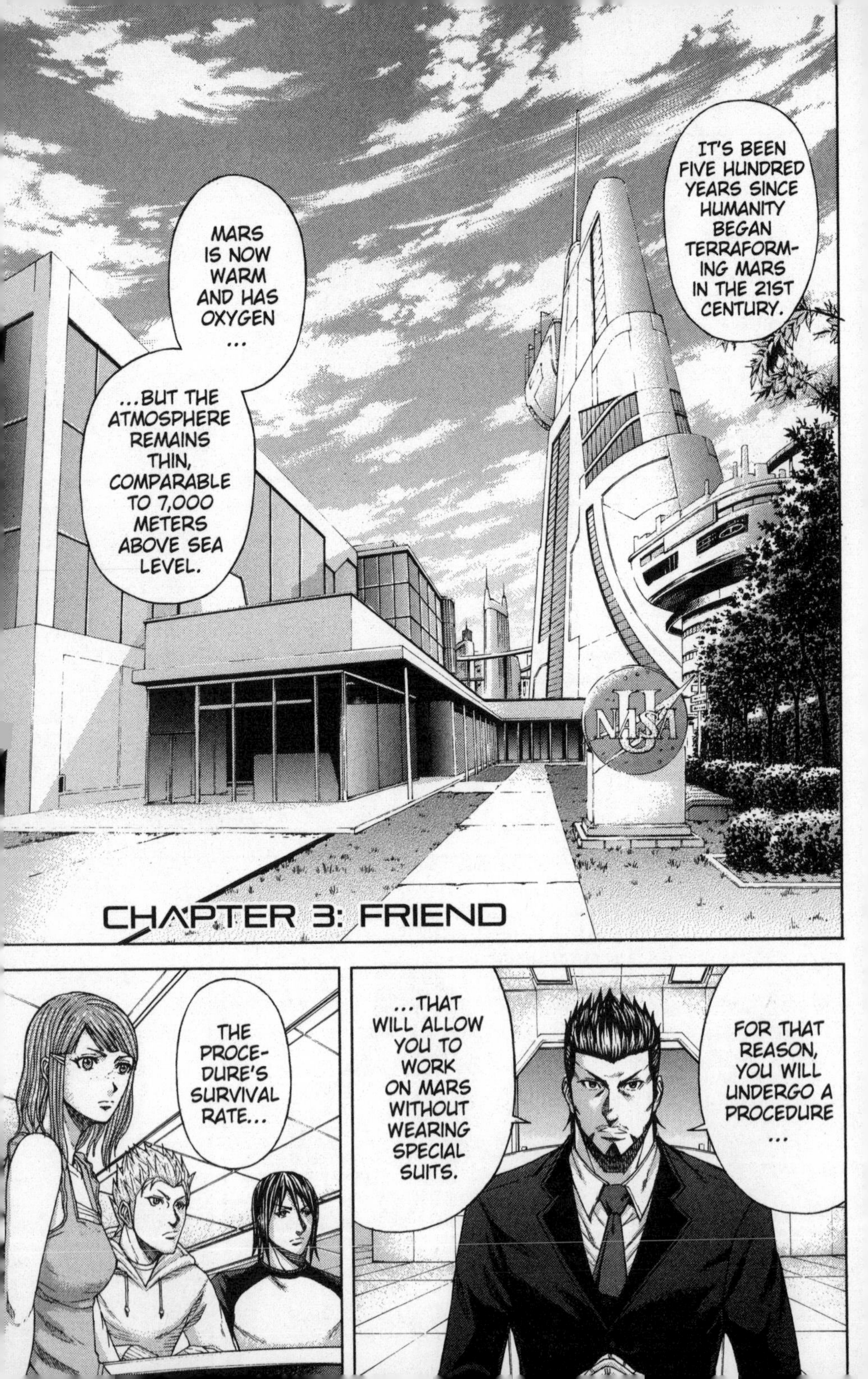
IT'S BEEN FIVE HUNDRED YEARS SINCE HUMANITY BEGAN TERRAFORM-ING MARS IN THE 21ST CENTURY.
MARS IS NOW WARM AND HAS OXYGEN ...
...BUT THE ATMOSPHERE REMAINS THIN, COMPARABLE TO 7,000 METERS ABOVE SEA LEVEL.
CHAPTER 3: FRIEND
FOR THAT REASON, YOU WILL UNDERGO A PROCEDURE ...
...THAT WILL ALLOW YOU TO WORK ON MARS WITHOUT WEARING SPECIAL SUITS.
THE PROCE-DURE'S SURVIVAL RATE...

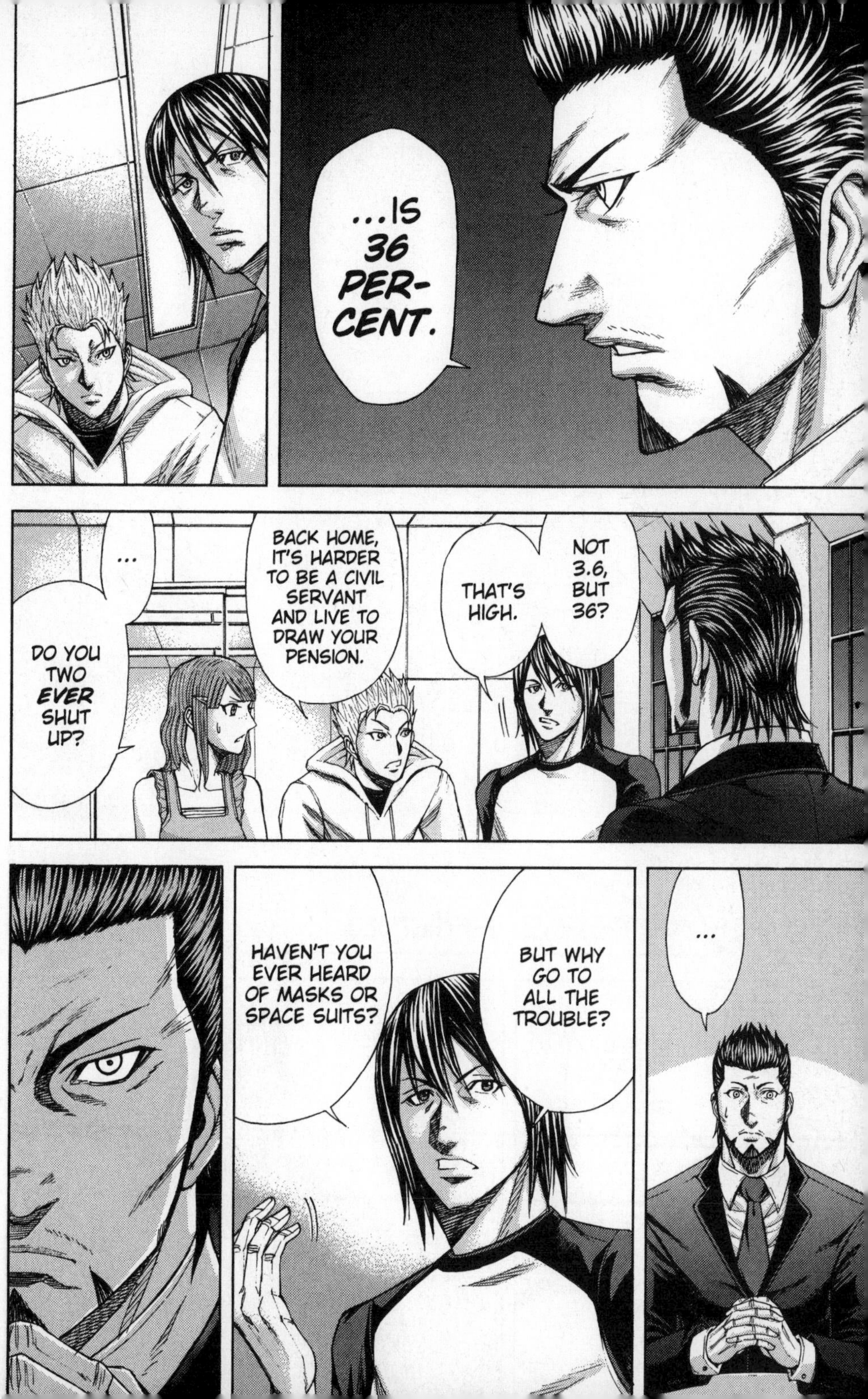
...IS 36 PER-CENT.
NOT 3.6, BUT 36?
THAT'S HIGH.
BACK HOME, IT'S HARDER TO BE A CIVIL SERVANT AND LIVE TO DRAW YOUR PENSION.
...
DO YOU TWO *EVER* SHUT UP?
...
BUT WHY GO TO ALL THE TROUBLE?
HAVEN'T YOU EVER HEARD OF MASKS OR SPACE SUITS?

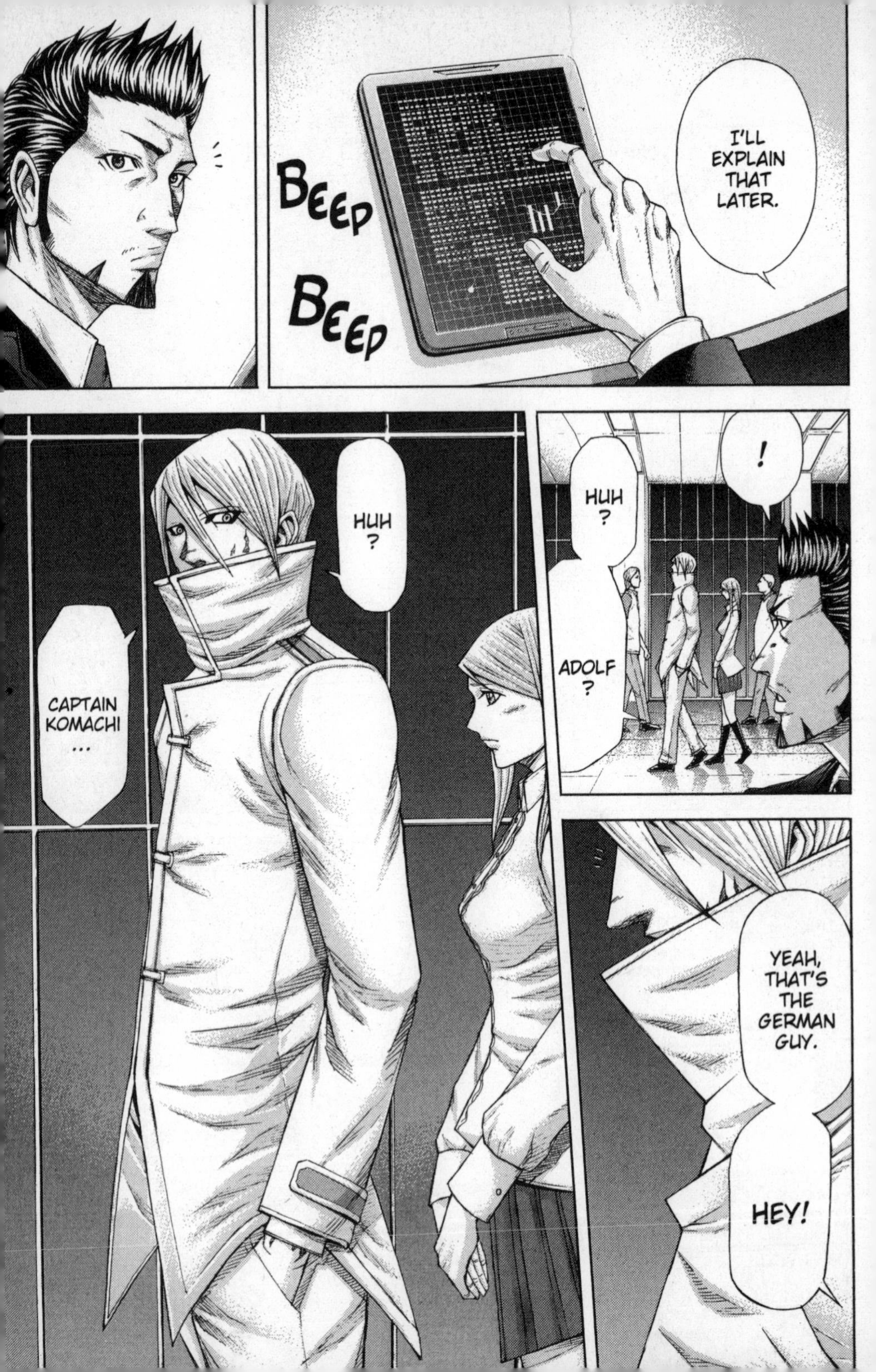
I'LL EXPLAIN THAT LATER.
BEEP
BEEP
!
HUH?
ADOLF?
YEAH, THAT'S THE GERMAN GUY.
HEY!
HUH?
CAPTAIN KOMACHI ...

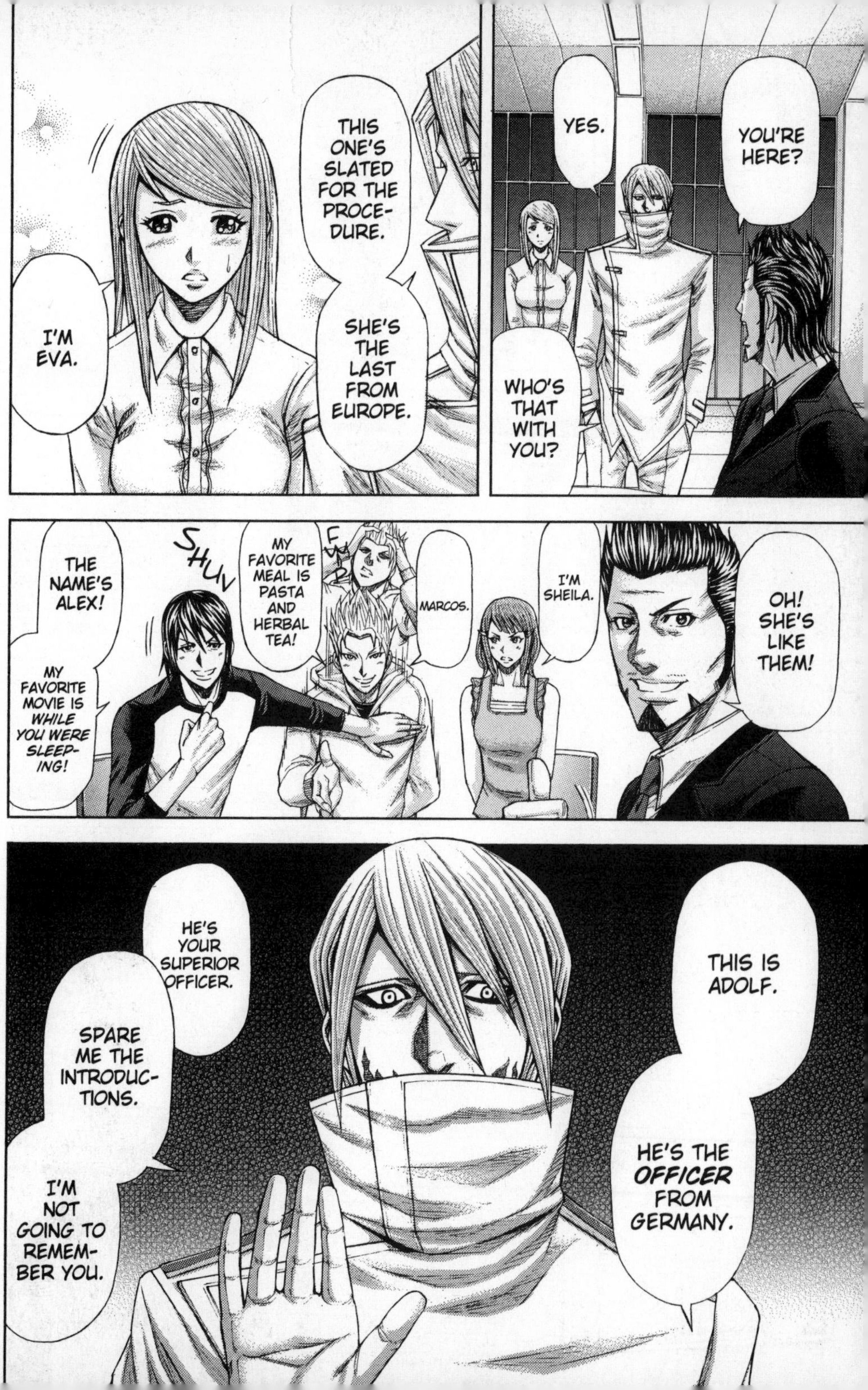
YOU'RE HERE?
YES.
WHO'S THAT WITH YOU?
THIS ONE'S SLATED FOR THE PROCEDURE.
SHE'S THE LAST FROM EUROPE.
I'M EVA.
OH! SHE'S LIKE THEM!
I'M SHEILA.
MARCOS.
MY FAVORITE MEAL IS PASTA AND HERBAL TEA!
SHUV
THE NAME'S ALEX!
MY FAVORITE MOVIE IS *WHILE YOU WERE SLEEPING!*
THIS IS ADOLF.
HE'S THE ***OFFICER*** FROM GERMANY.
HE'S YOUR SUPERIOR OFFICER.
SPARE ME THE INTRODUCTIONS.
I'M NOT GOING TO REMEMBER YOU.

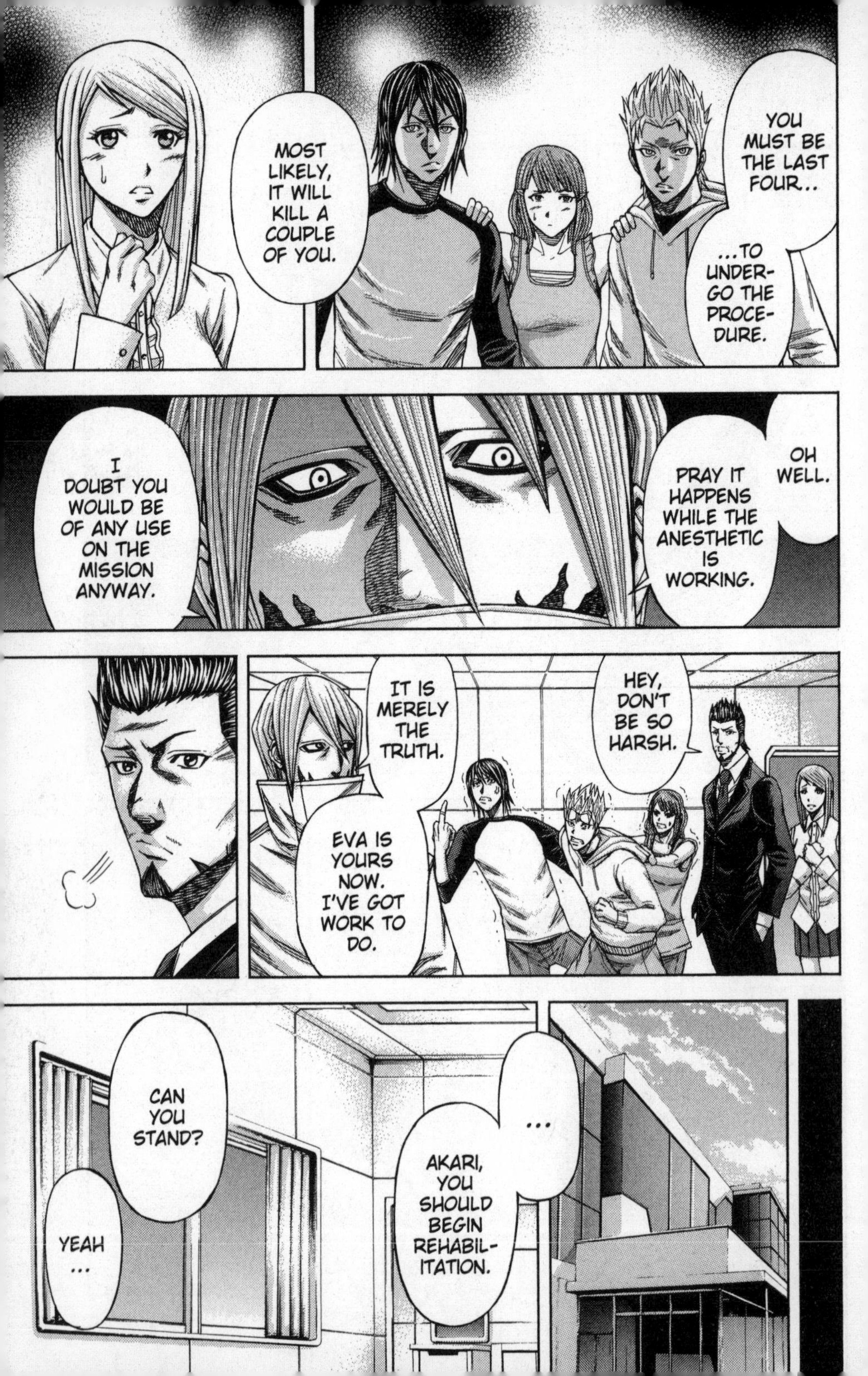
YOU MUST BE THE LAST FOUR..
...TO UNDER-GO THE PROCE-DURE.
MOST LIKELY, IT WILL KILL A COUPLE OF YOU.
OH WELL.
PRAY IT HAPPENS WHILE THE ANESTHETIC IS WORKING.
I DOUBT YOU WOULD BE OF ANY USE ON THE MISSION ANYWAY.
HEY, DON'T BE SO HARSH.
IT IS MERELY THE TRUTH.
EVA IS YOURS NOW. I'VE GOT WORK TO DO.
...
AKARI, YOU SHOULD BEGIN REHABIL-ITATION.
CAN YOU STAND?
YEAH ...

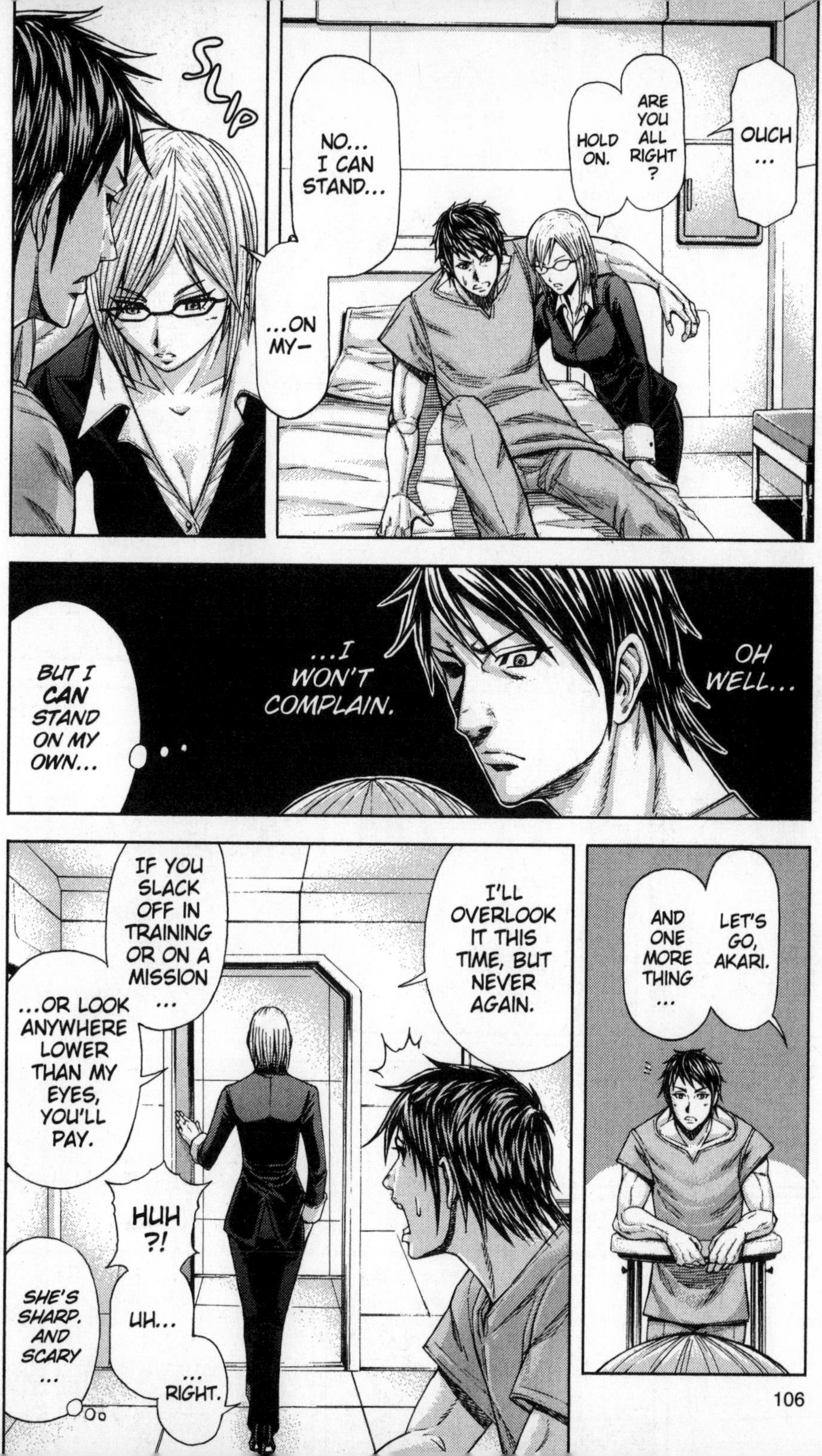
OUCH...
ARE YOU ALL RIGHT?
HOLD ON.
NO... I CAN STAND...
...ON MY—
SLIP
OH WELL...
...I WON'T COMPLAIN.
BUT I CAN STAND ON MY OWN...
LET'S GO, AKARI.
AND ONE MORE THING...
I'LL OVERLOOK IT THIS TIME, BUT NEVER AGAIN.
IF YOU SLACK OFF IN TRAINING OR ON A MISSION...
...OR LOOK ANYWHERE LOWER THAN MY EYES, YOU'LL PAY.
HUH?!
UH...
...RIGHT.
SHE'S SHARP. AND SCARY...

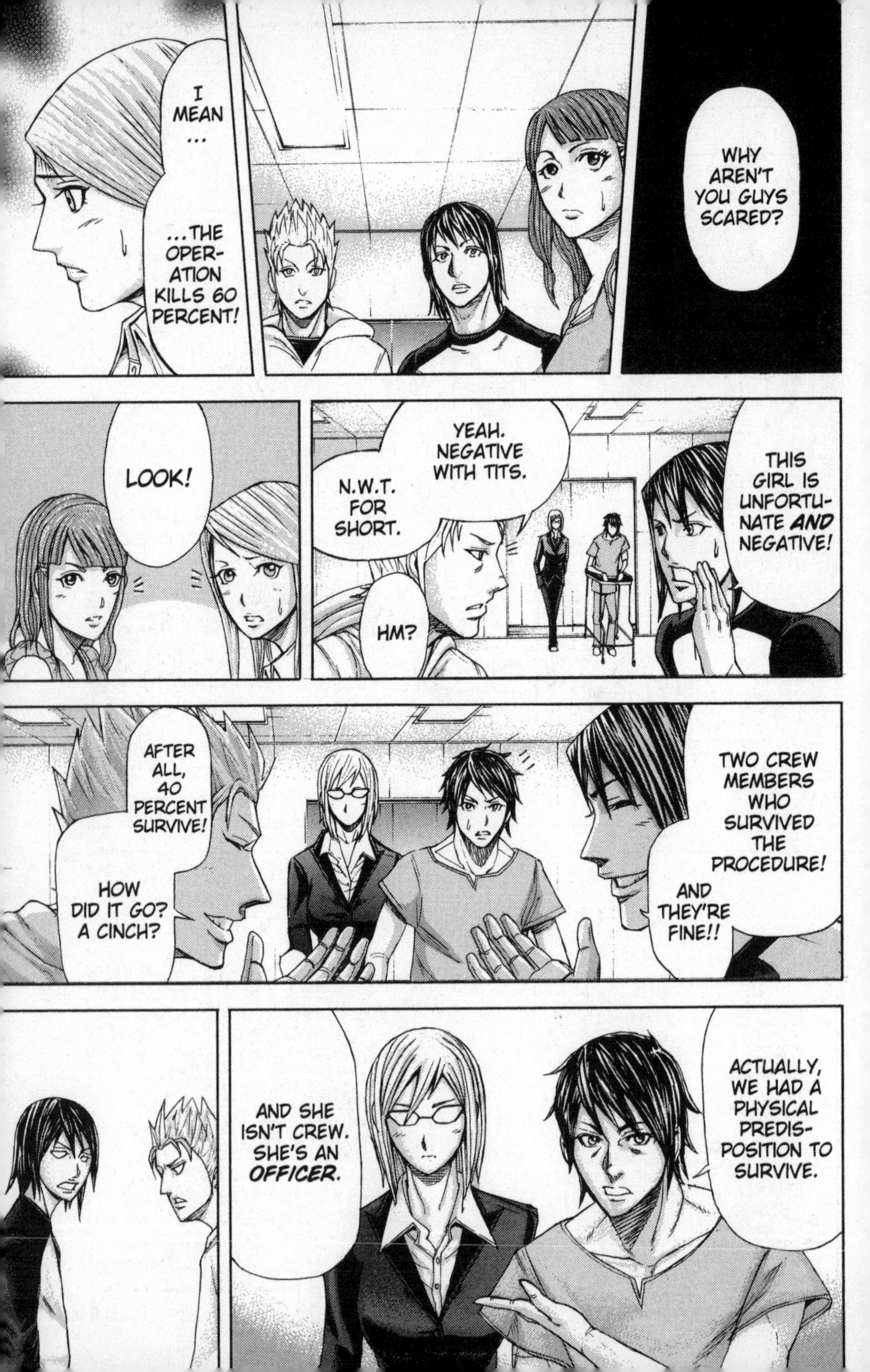
WHY AREN'T YOU GUYS SCARED?
I MEAN ...
...THE OPERATION KILLS 60 PERCENT!
THIS GIRL IS UNFORTUNATE *AND* NEGATIVE!
YEAH. NEGATIVE WITH TITS.
N.W.T. FOR SHORT.
HM?
LOOK!
TWO CREW MEMBERS WHO SURVIVED THE PROCEDURE!
AND THEY'RE FINE!!
AFTER ALL, 40 PERCENT SURVIVE!
HOW DID IT GO? A CINCH?
ACTUALLY, WE HAD A PHYSICAL PREDISPOSITION TO SURVIVE.
AND SHE ISN'T CREW. SHE'S AN *OFFICER*.

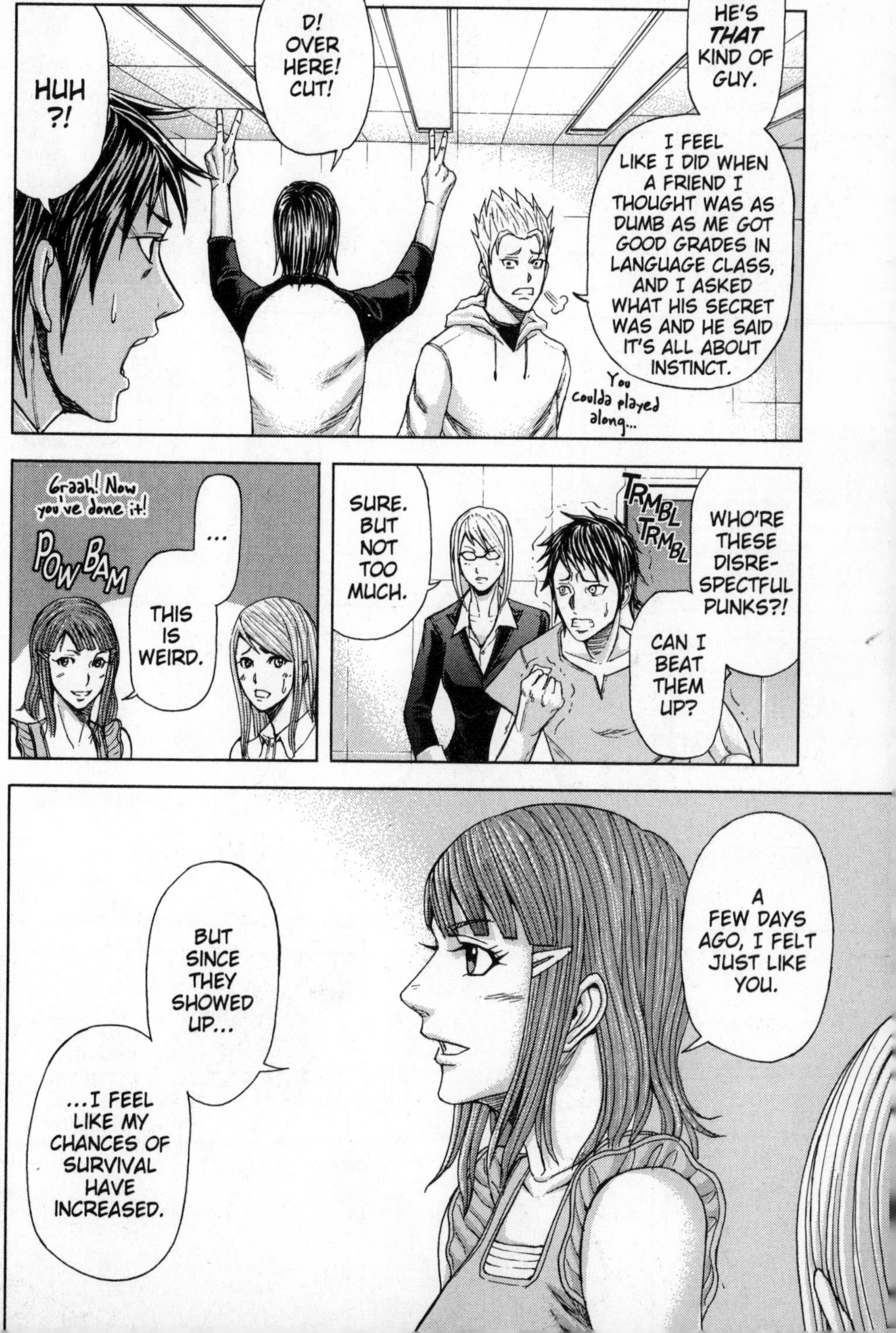
UGH. HE'S THAT KIND OF GUY.
I FEEL LIKE I DID WHEN A FRIEND I THOUGHT WAS AS DUMB AS ME GOT GOOD GRADES IN LANGUAGE CLASS, AND I ASKED WHAT HIS SECRET WAS AND HE SAID IT'S ALL ABOUT INSTINCT.
You coulda played along...
D! OVER HERE! CUT!
HUH?!
TRMBL TRMBL
WHO'RE THESE DISRE-SPECTFUL PUNKS?!
CAN I BEAT THEM UP?
SURE. BUT NOT TOO MUCH.
Graah! Now you've done it!
POW BAM
...
THIS IS WEIRD.
A FEW DAYS AGO, I FELT JUST LIKE YOU.
BUT SINCE THEY SHOWED UP...
...I FEEL LIKE MY CHANCES OF SURVIVAL HAVE INCREASED.

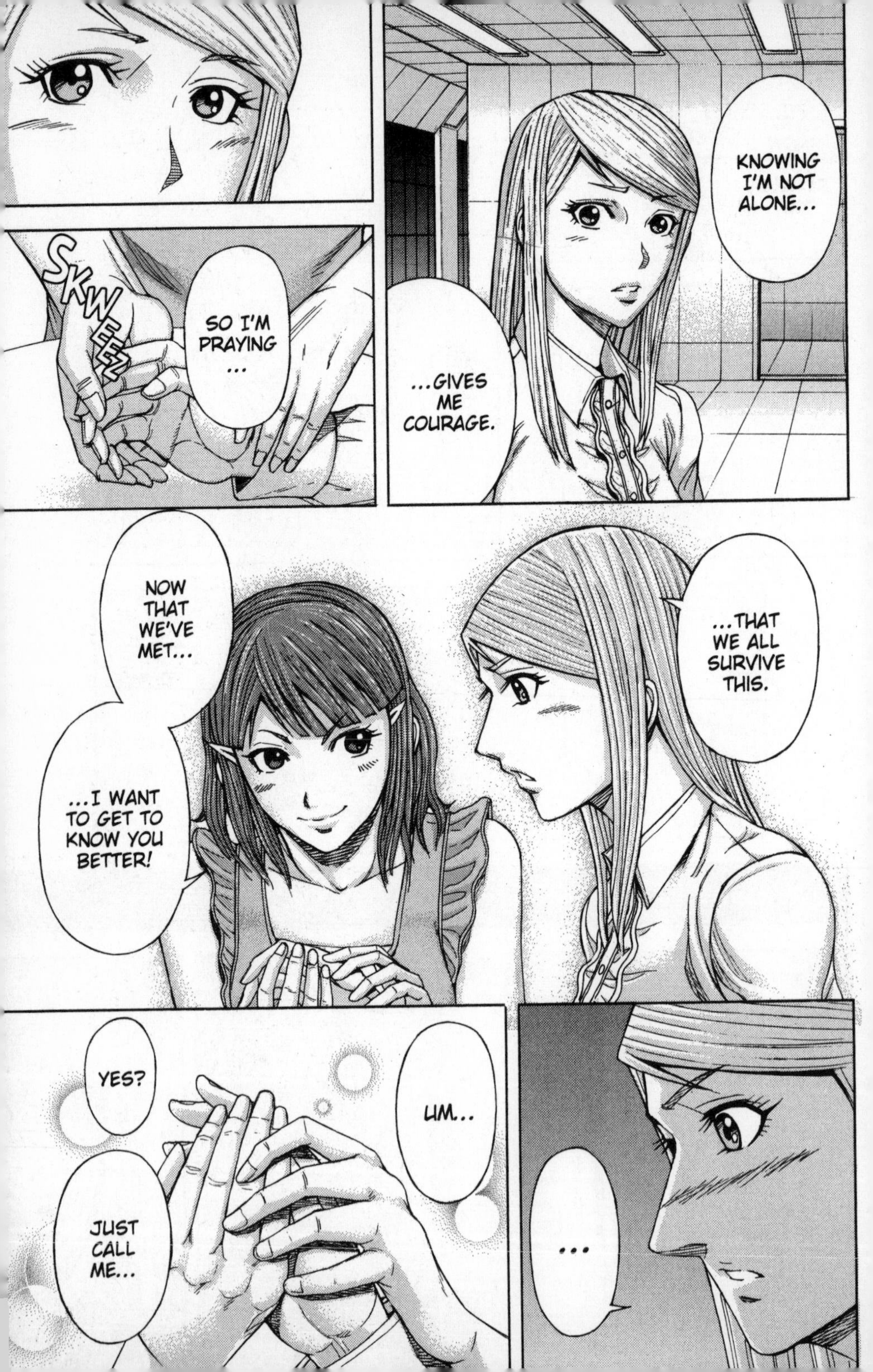
KNOWING I'M NOT ALONE...
...GIVES ME COURAGE.
SKWEEZ
SO I'M PRAYING ...
...THAT WE ALL SURVIVE THIS.
NOW THAT WE'VE MET...
...I WANT TO GET TO KNOW YOU BETTER!
...
UM...
YES?
JUST CALL ME...

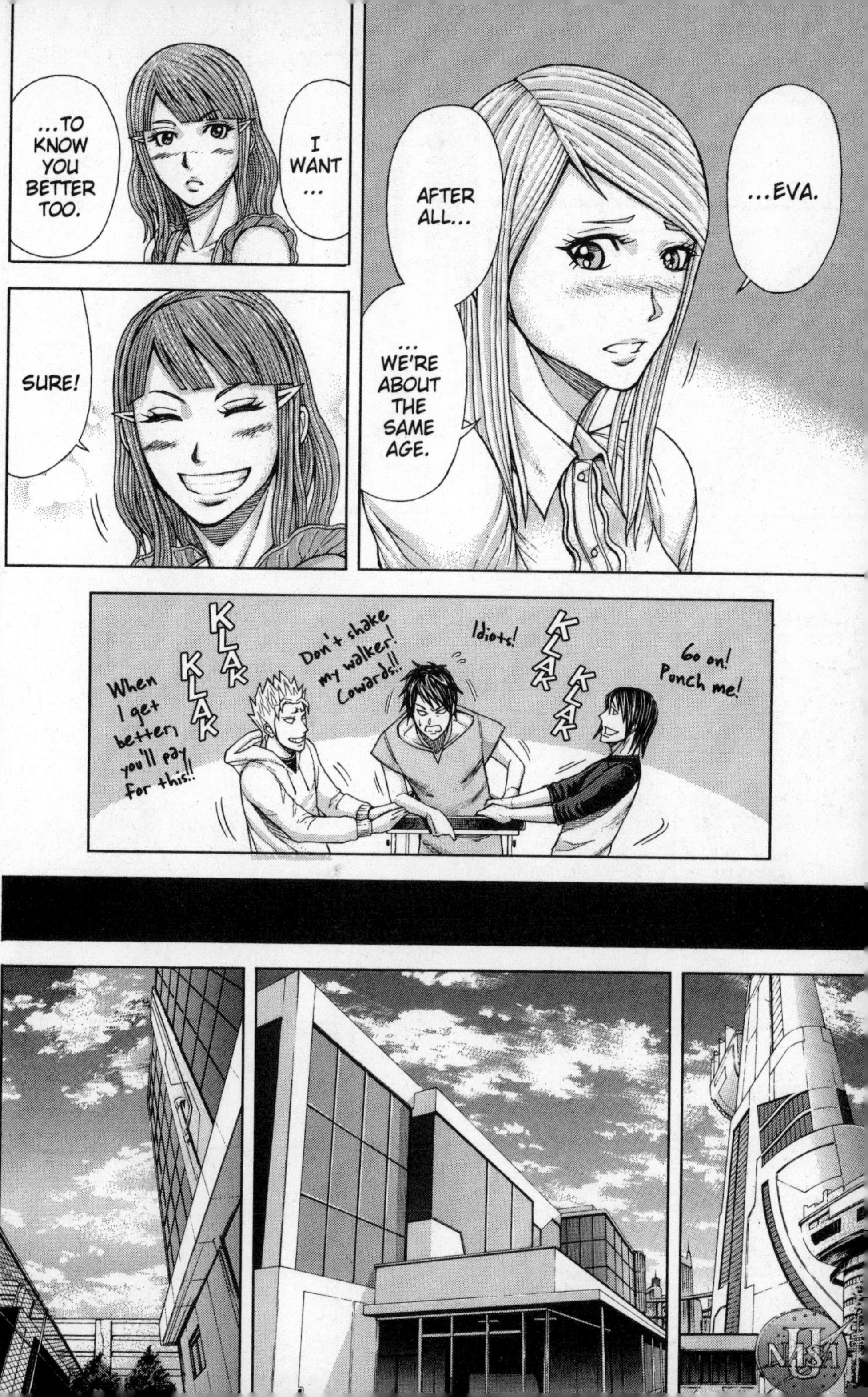
...EVA.
AFTER ALL...
...WE'RE ABOUT THE SAME AGE.
I WANT...
...TO KNOW YOU BETTER TOO.
SURE!
Go on! Punch me!
KLAK KLAK
Idiots!
Don't shake my walker! Cowards!!
KLAK KLAK
When I get better you'll pay for this!!

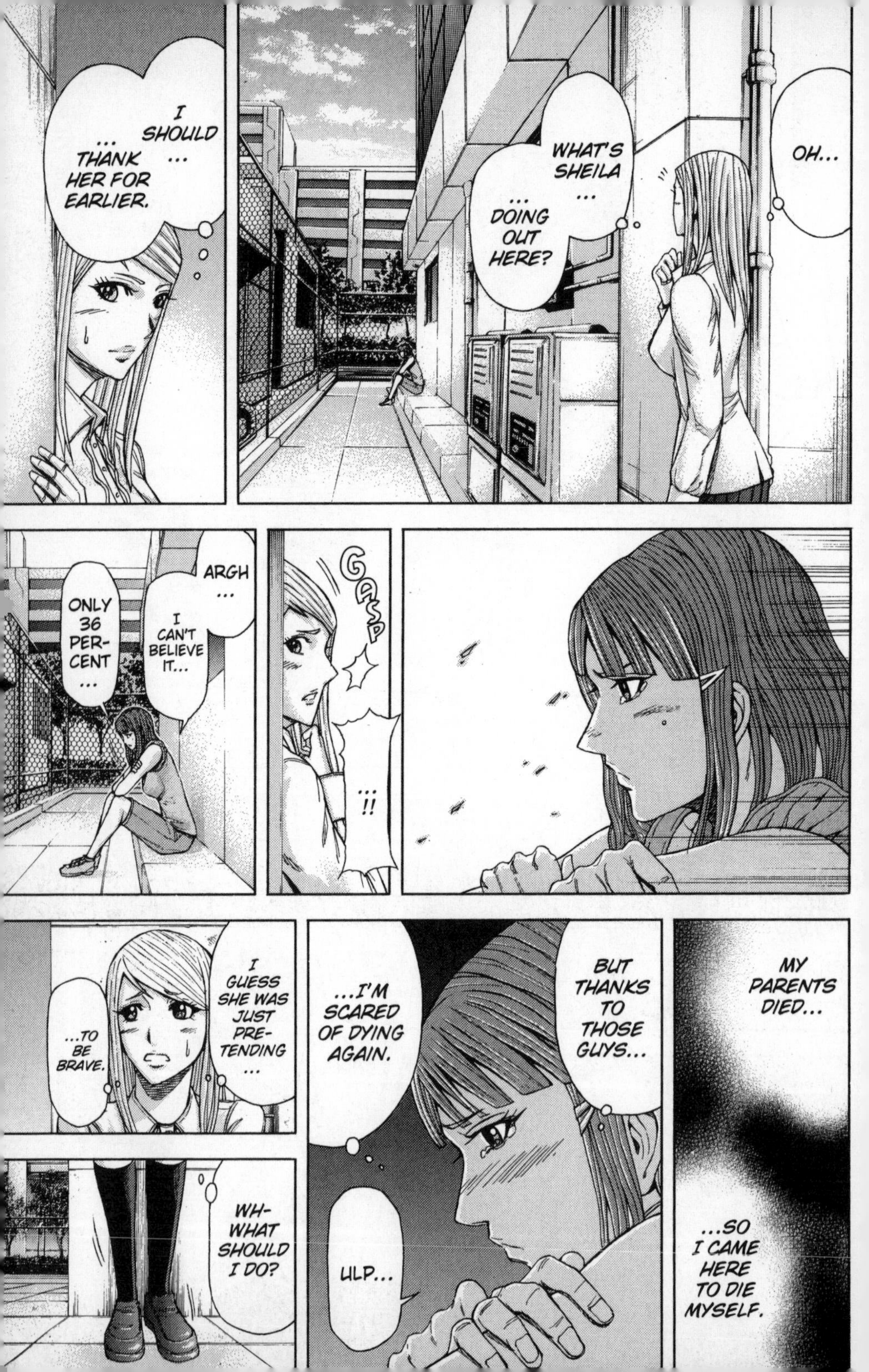
OH...
WHAT'S SHEILA ... DOING OUT HERE?
I SHOULD ... THANK HER FOR EARLIER.
GASP
...!!
ARGH ...
I CAN'T BELIEVE IT...
ONLY 36 PERCENT ...
MY PARENTS DIED...
...SO I CAME HERE TO DIE MYSELF.
BUT THANKS TO THOSE GUYS...
...I'M SCARED OF DYING AGAIN.
ULP...
I GUESS SHE WAS JUST PRETENDING ...
...TO BE BRAVE.
WH-WHAT SHOULD I DO?

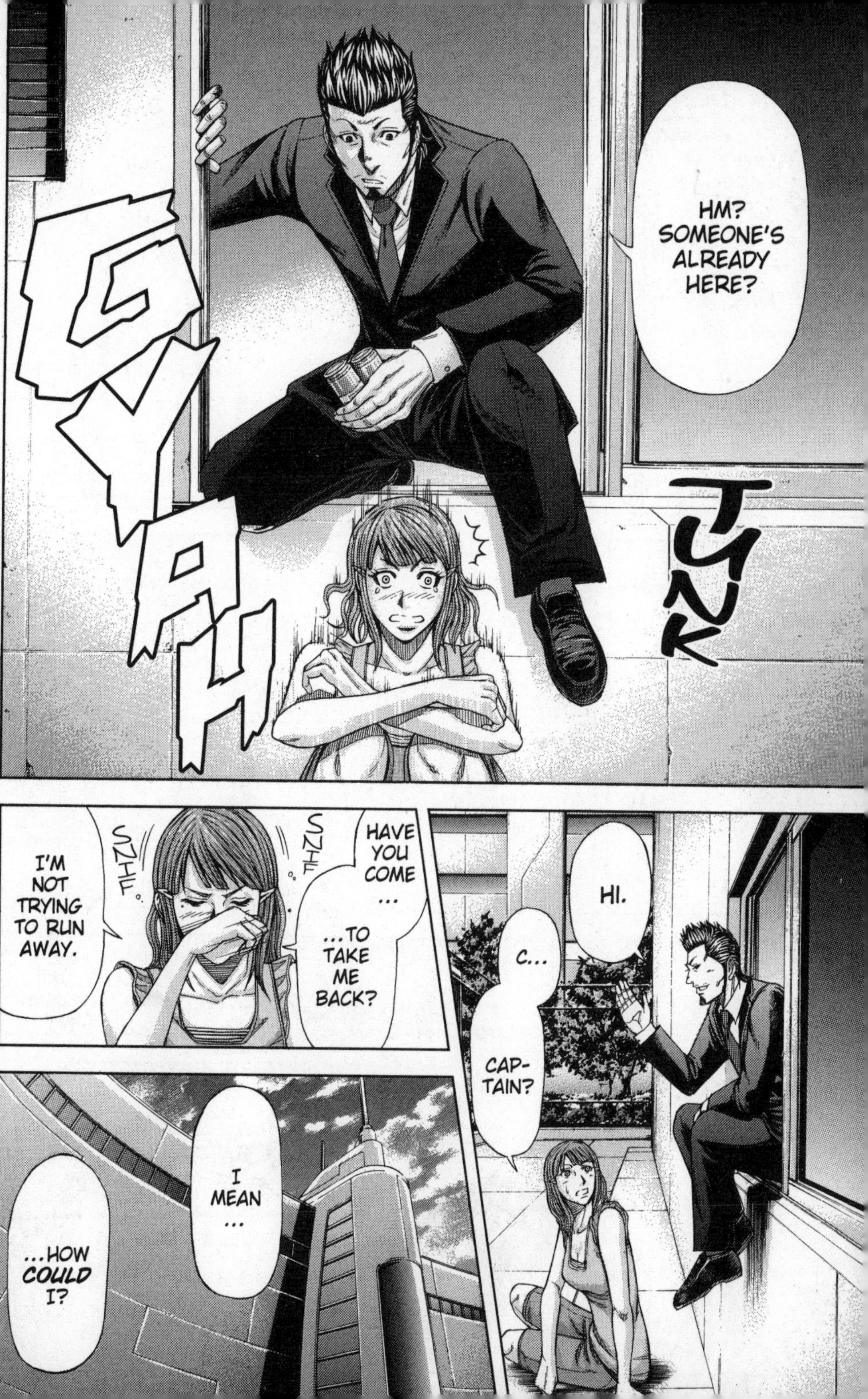
HM? SOMEONE'S ALREADY HERE?
JUNK
GYAAH
HI.
C...
CAP-TAIN?
SNIFF
HAVE YOU COME ...
...TO TAKE ME BACK?
SNIFF
I'M NOT TRYING TO RUN AWAY.
I MEAN ...
...HOW **COULD** I?

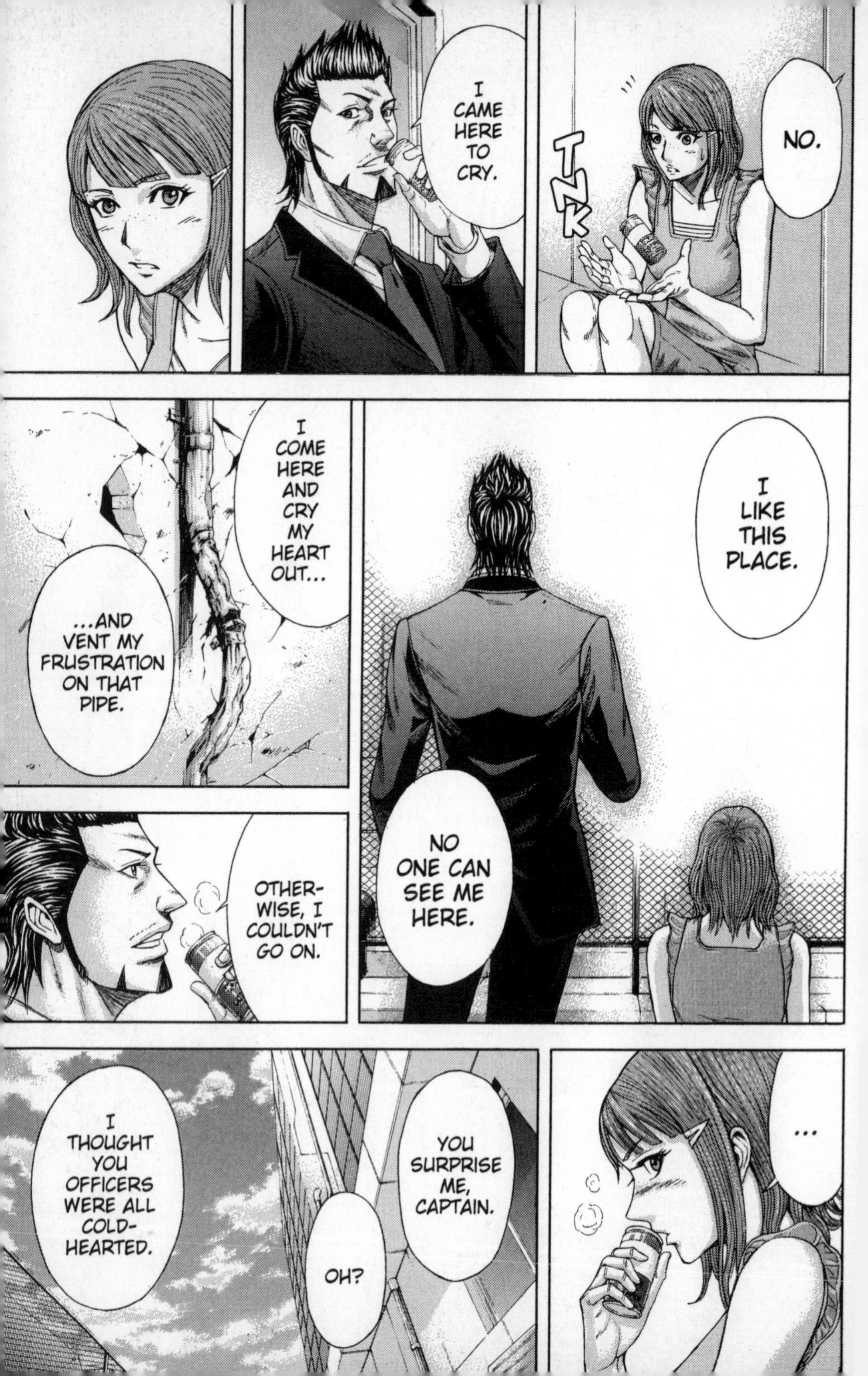
NO.
TNK
I CAME HERE TO CRY.
I LIKE THIS PLACE.
NO ONE CAN SEE ME HERE.
I COME HERE AND CRY MY HEART OUT...
...AND VENT MY FRUSTRATION ON THAT PIPE.
OTHER-WISE, I COULDN'T GO ON.
...
YOU SURPRISE ME, CAPTAIN.
OH?
I THOUGHT YOU OFFICERS WERE ALL COLD-HEARTED.

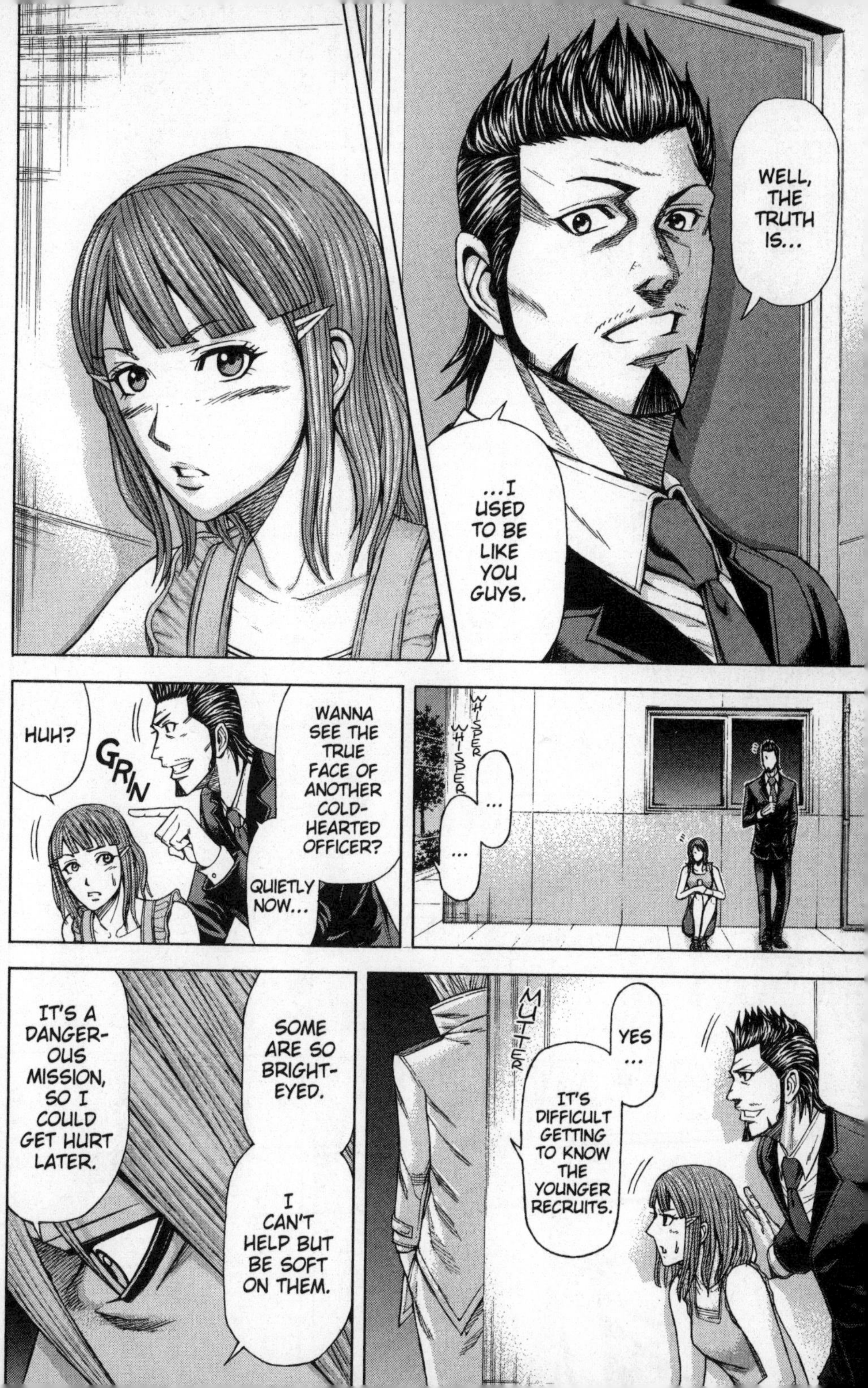
WELL, THE TRUTH IS...
...I USED TO BE LIKE YOU GUYS.
WHISPER
WHISPER
...
...
WANNA SEE THE TRUE FACE OF ANOTHER COLD-HEARTED OFFICER?
QUIETLY NOW...
GRIN
HUH?
MUTTER
YES ...
IT'S DIFFICULT GETTING TO KNOW THE YOUNGER RECRUITS.
SOME ARE SO BRIGHT-EYED.
I CAN'T HELP BUT BE SOFT ON THEM.
IT'S A DANGER-OUS MISSION, SO I COULD GET HURT LATER.

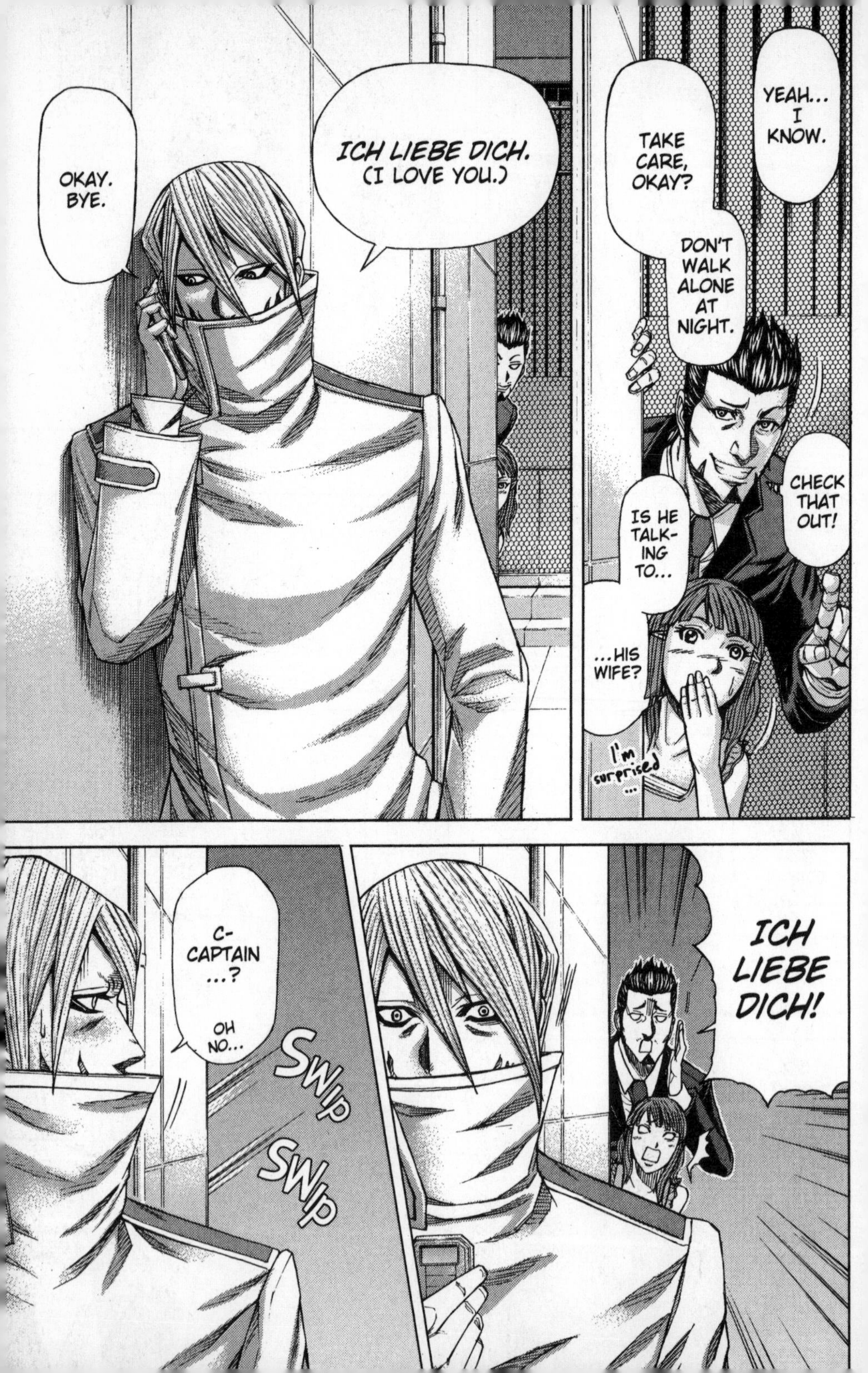
YEAH... I KNOW.
TAKE CARE, OKAY?
DON'T WALK ALONE AT NIGHT.
CHECK THAT OUT!
IS HE TALKING TO...
...HIS WIFE?
I'm surprised...
ICH LIEBE DICH. (I LOVE YOU.)
OKAY. BYE.
ICH LIEBE DICH!
SWIP
SWIP
C-CAPTAIN...?
OH NO...

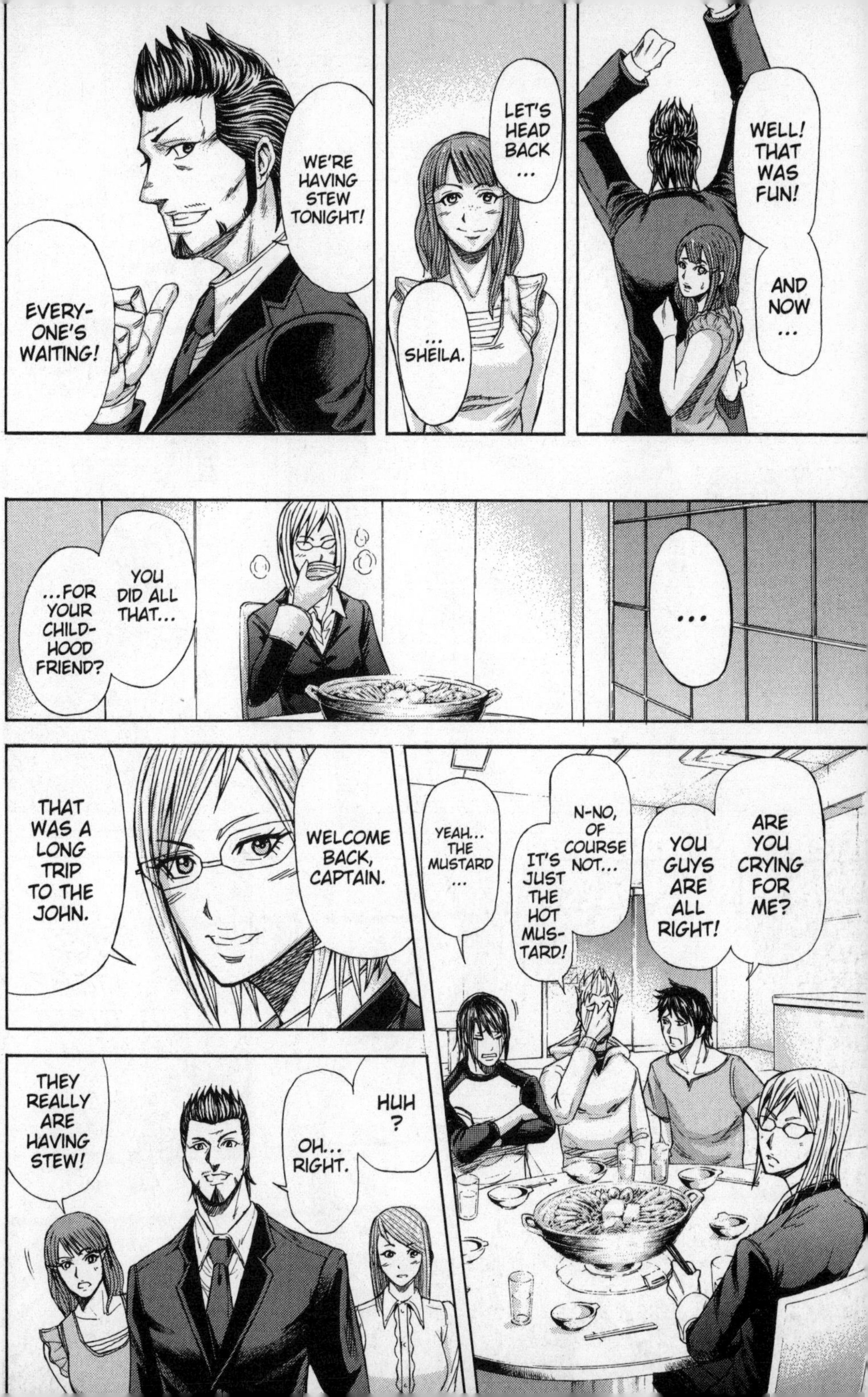
WELL! THAT WAS FUN!
AND NOW ...
LET'S HEAD BACK ...
... SHEILA.
WE'RE HAVING STEW TONIGHT!
EVERY-ONE'S WAITING!
...
YOU DID ALL THAT...
...FOR YOUR CHILD-HOOD FRIEND?
ARE YOU CRYING FOR ME?
YOU GUYS ARE ALL RIGHT!
N-NO, OF COURSE NOT...
IT'S JUST THE HOT MUS-TARD!
YEAH... THE MUSTARD ...
WELCOME BACK, CAPTAIN.
THAT WAS A LONG TRIP TO THE JOHN.
HUH ?
OH... RIGHT.
THEY REALLY ARE HAVING STEW!

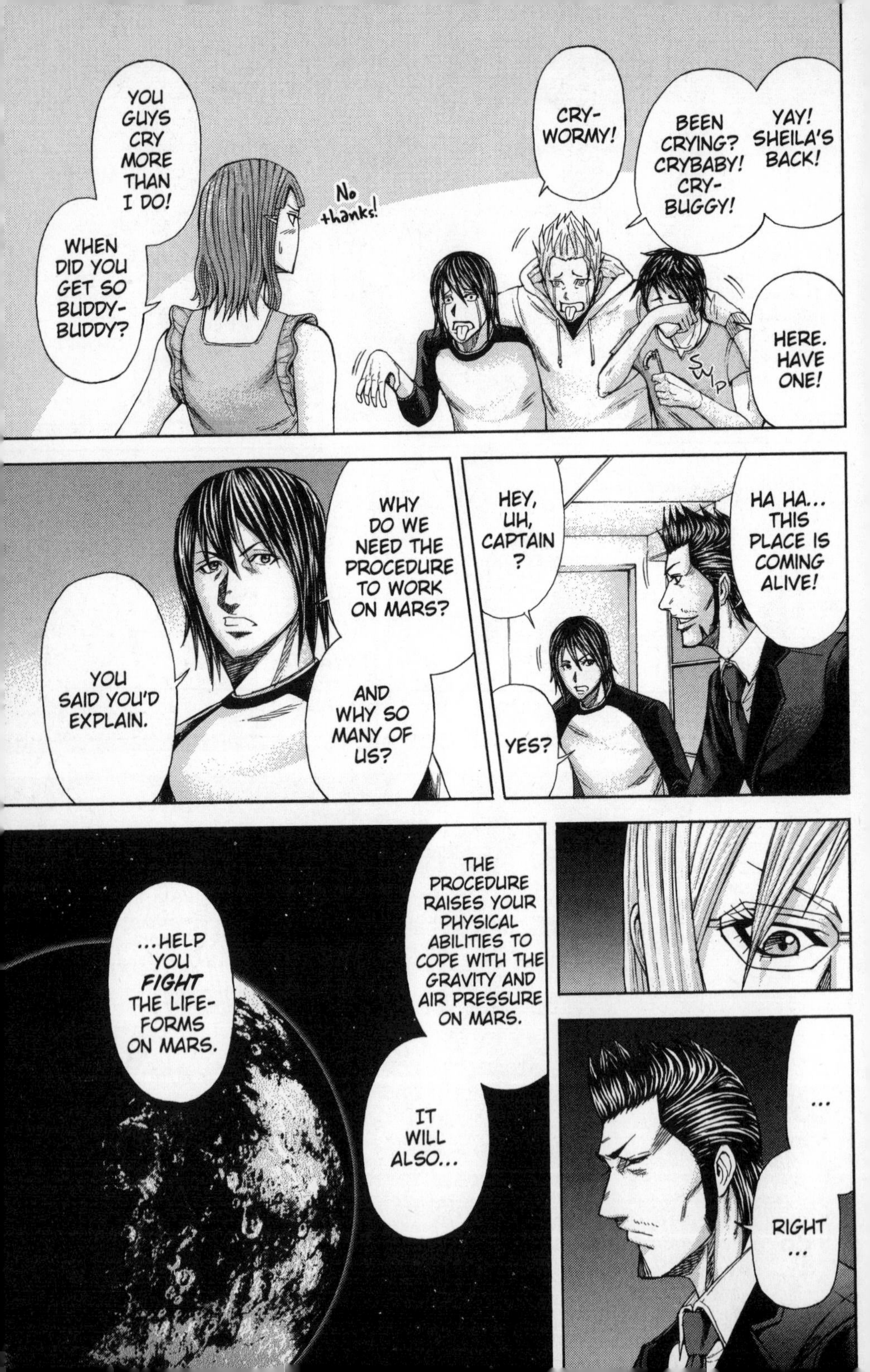
YAY! SHEILA'S BACK!
BEEN CRYING? CRYBABY! CRY-BUGGY!
HERE. HAVE ONE!
SWIP
CRY-WORMY!
No thanks!
YOU GUYS CRY MORE THAN I DO!
WHEN DID YOU GET SO BUDDY-BUDDY?
HA HA... THIS PLACE IS COMING ALIVE!
HEY, UH, CAPTAIN?
YES?
WHY DO WE NEED THE PROCEDURE TO WORK ON MARS?
AND WHY SO MANY OF US?
YOU SAID YOU'D EXPLAIN.
...
RIGHT ...
THE PROCEDURE RAISES YOUR PHYSICAL ABILITIES TO COPE WITH THE GRAVITY AND AIR PRESSURE ON MARS.
IT WILL ALSO...
...HELP YOU FIGHT THE LIFE-FORMS ON MARS.

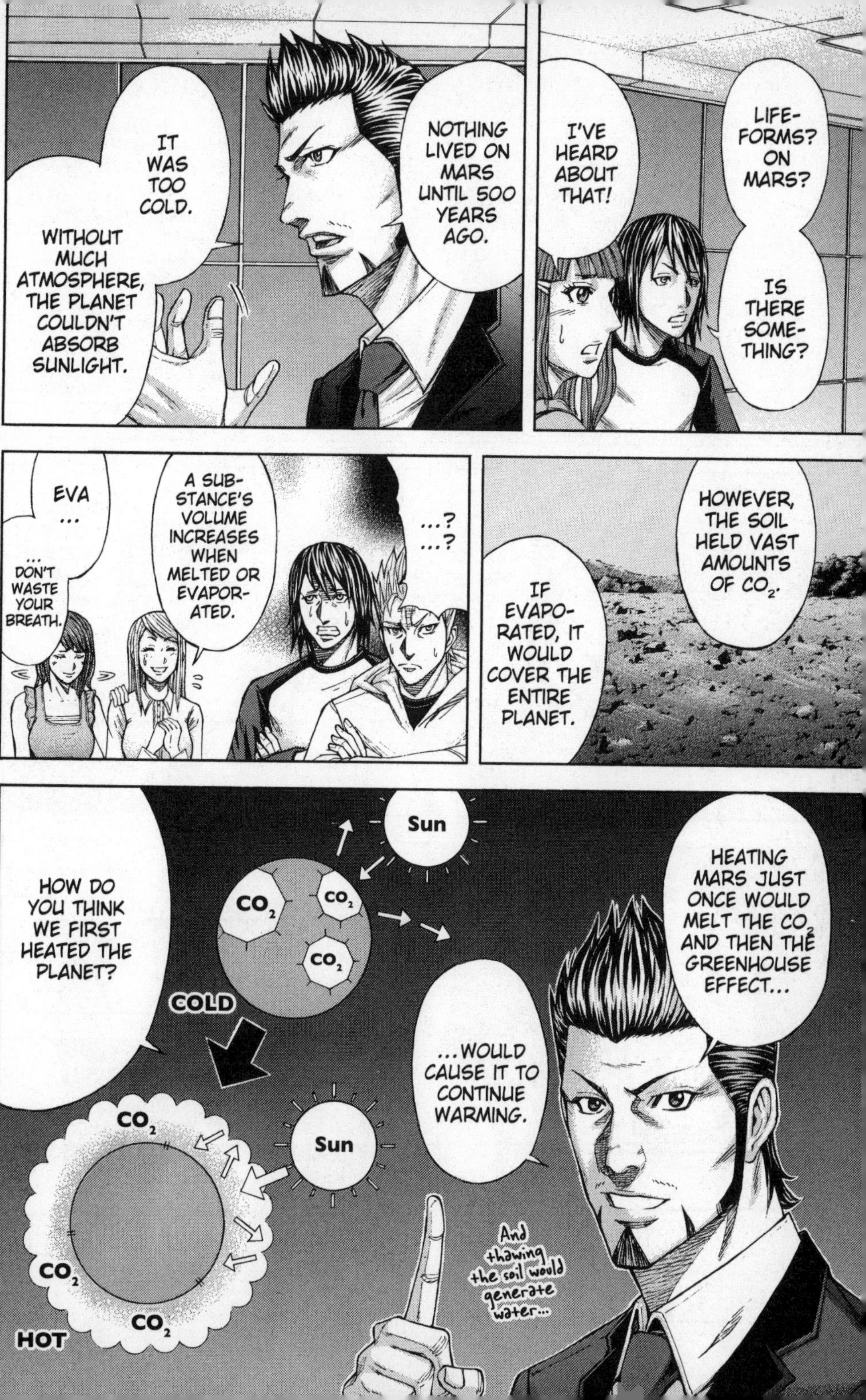
LIFE-FORMS? ON MARS?
IS THERE SOMETHING?
I'VE HEARD ABOUT THAT!
NOTHING LIVED ON MARS UNTIL 500 YEARS AGO.
IT WAS TOO COLD.
WITHOUT MUCH ATMOSPHERE, THE PLANET COULDN'T ABSORB SUNLIGHT.
HOWEVER, THE SOIL HELD VAST AMOUNTS OF CO_2.
IF EVAPORATED, IT WOULD COVER THE ENTIRE PLANET.
...? ...?
A SUBSTANCE'S VOLUME INCREASES WHEN MELTED OR EVAPORATED.
EVA...
...DON'T WASTE YOUR BREATH.
HEATING MARS JUST ONCE WOULD MELT THE CO_2 AND THEN THE GREENHOUSE EFFECT...
...WOULD CAUSE IT TO CONTINUE WARMING.
And thawing the soil would generate water...
HOW DO YOU THINK WE FIRST HEATED THE PLANET?
Sun
CO_2
CO_2
CO_2
COLD
Sun
CO_2
CO_2
CO_2
HOT

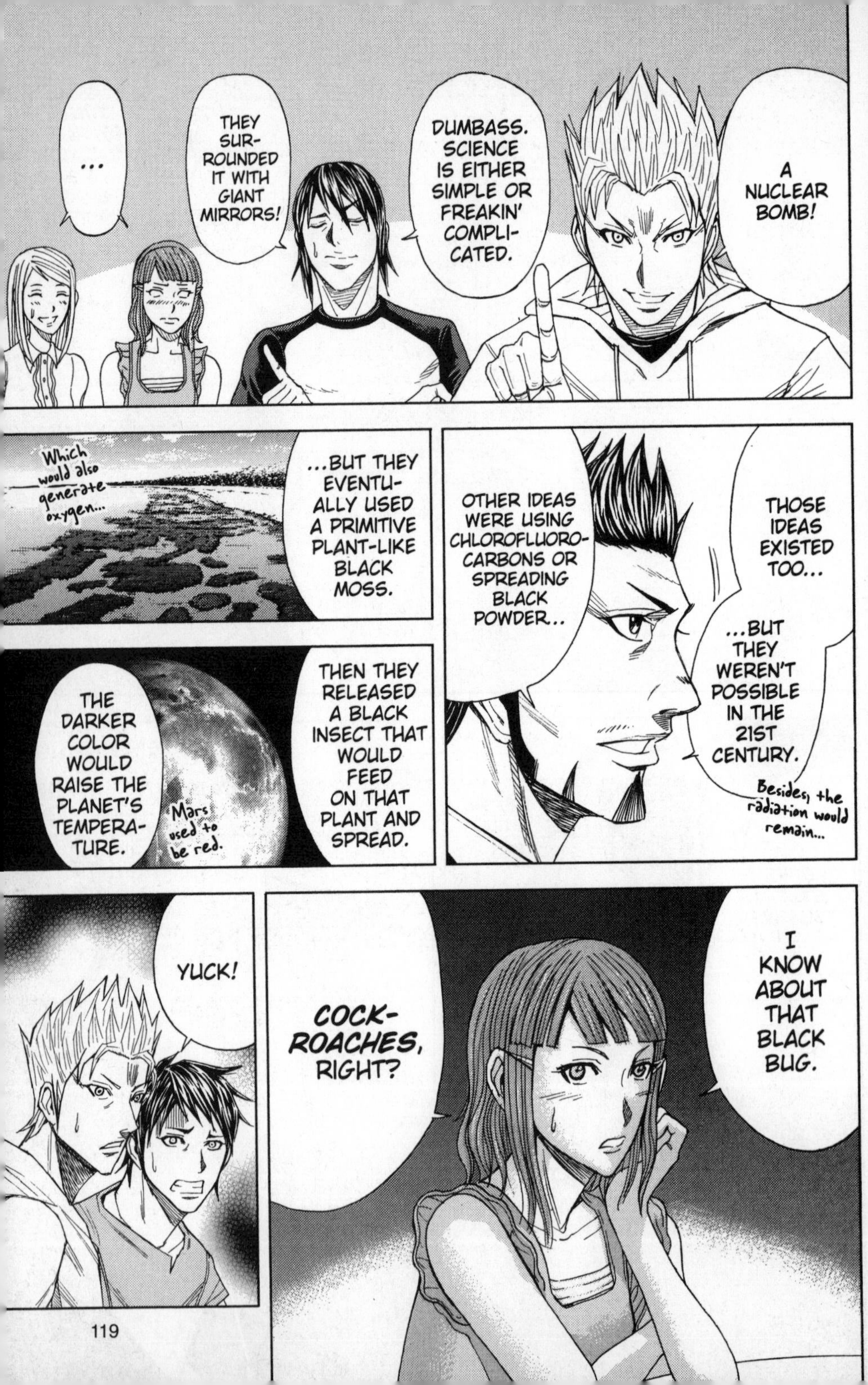
A NUCLEAR BOMB!
DUMBASS. SCIENCE IS EITHER SIMPLE OR FREAKIN' COMPLICATED.
THEY SURROUNDED IT WITH GIANT MIRRORS!
...
THOSE IDEAS EXISTED TOO...
...BUT THEY WEREN'T POSSIBLE IN THE 21ST CENTURY.
Besides, the radiation would remain...
OTHER IDEAS WERE USING CHLOROFLUOROCARBONS OR SPREADING BLACK POWDER...
...BUT THEY EVENTUALLY USED A PRIMITIVE PLANT-LIKE BLACK MOSS.
Which would also generate oxygen...
THEN THEY RELEASED A BLACK INSECT THAT WOULD FEED ON THAT PLANT AND SPREAD.
THE DARKER COLOR WOULD RAISE THE PLANET'S TEMPERATURE.
Mars used to be red.
I KNOW ABOUT THAT BLACK BUG.
COCKROACHES, RIGHT?
YUCK!

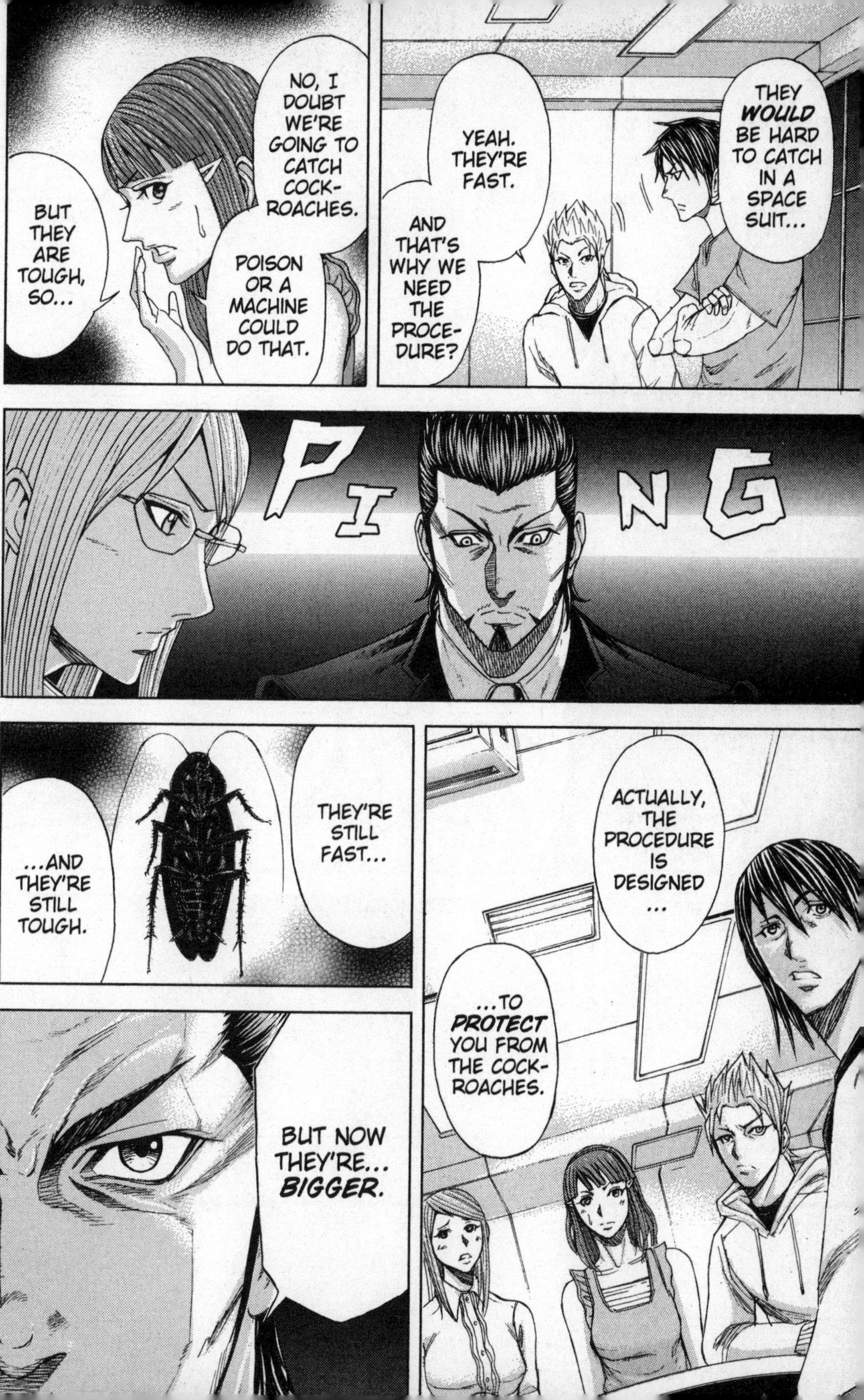
THEY WOULD BE HARD TO CATCH IN A SPACE SUIT...
YEAH. THEY'RE FAST.
AND THAT'S WHY WE NEED THE PROCEDURE?
NO, I DOUBT WE'RE GOING TO CATCH COCKROACHES.
POISON OR A MACHINE COULD DO THAT.
BUT THEY ARE TOUGH, SO...
PING
ACTUALLY, THE PROCEDURE IS DESIGNED...
...TO PROTECT YOU FROM THE COCKROACHES.
THEY'RE STILL FAST...
...AND THEY'RE STILL TOUGH.
BUT NOW THEY'RE... BIGGER.

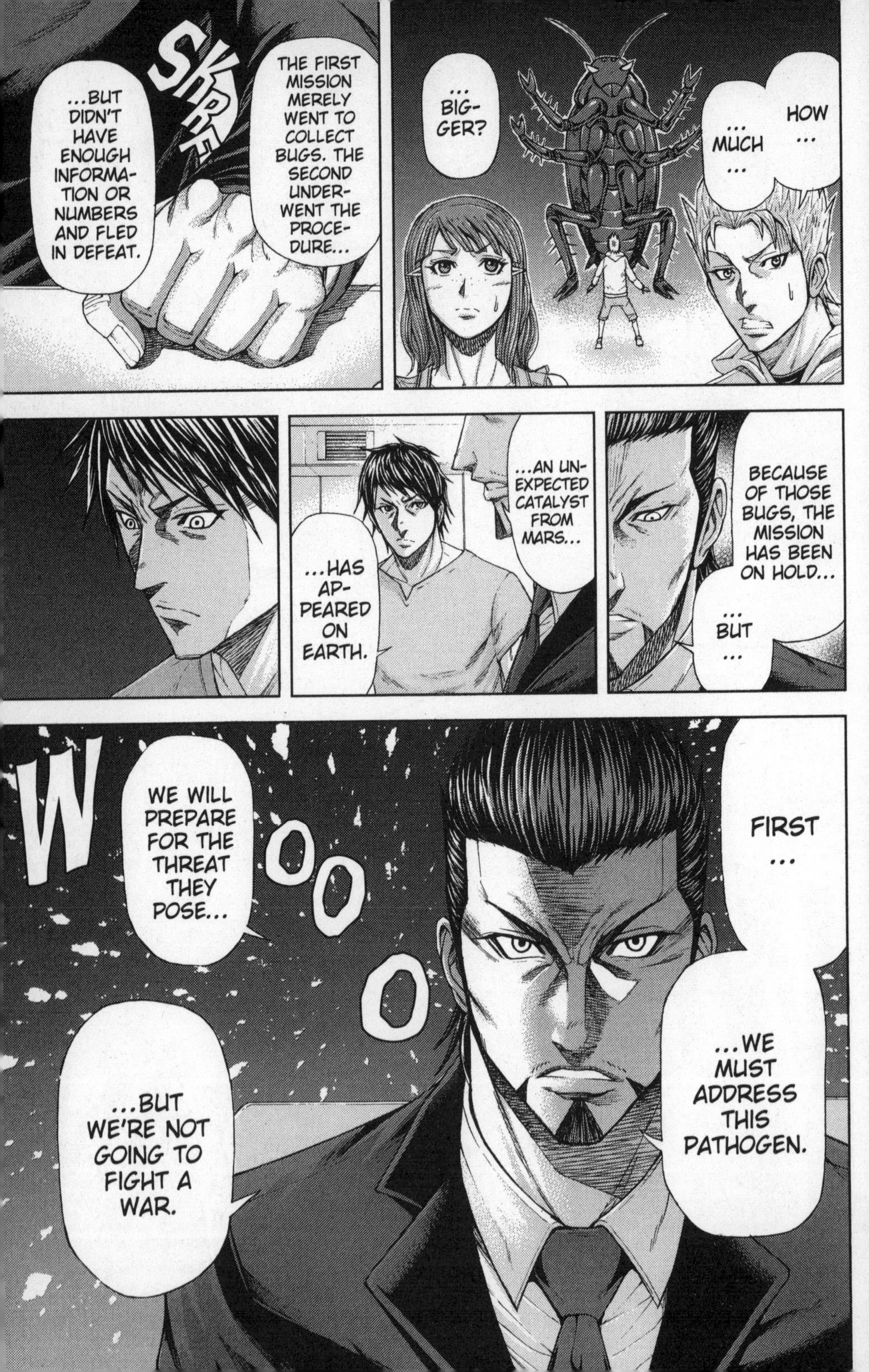
HOW ... MUCH ...
... BIG-GER?
THE FIRST MISSION MERELY WENT TO COLLECT BUGS. THE SECOND UNDER-WENT THE PROCE-DURE...
...BUT DIDN'T HAVE ENOUGH INFORMA-TION OR NUMBERS AND FLED IN DEFEAT.
SKRF
BECAUSE OF THOSE BUGS, THE MISSION HAS BEEN ON HOLD...
... BUT ...
...AN UN-EXPECTED CATALYST FROM MARS...
...HAS AP-PEARED ON EARTH.
FIRST ...
...WE MUST ADDRESS THIS PATHOGEN.
WOOO
WE WILL PREPARE FOR THE THREAT THEY POSE...
...BUT WE'RE NOT GOING TO FIGHT A WAR.

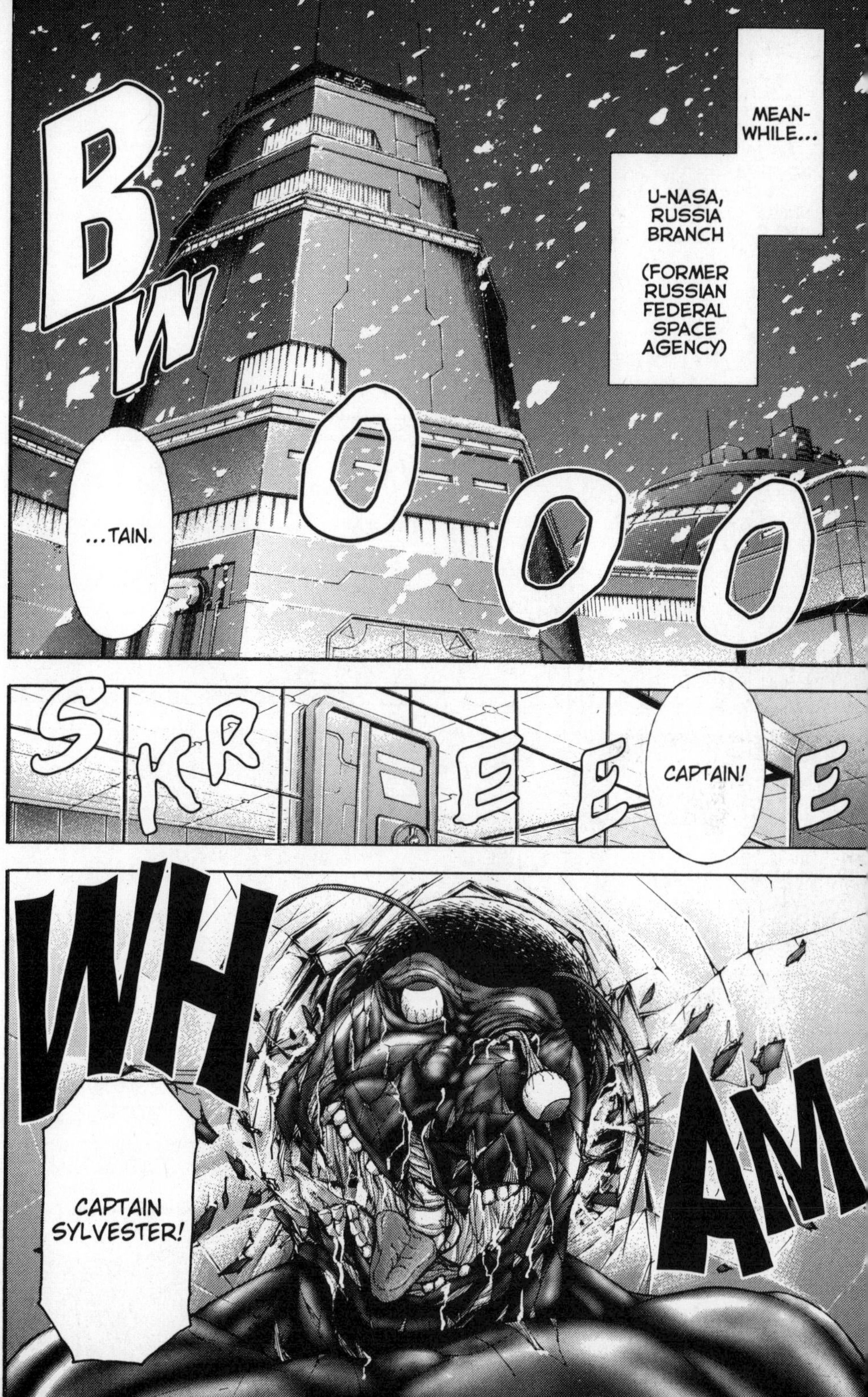
MEAN-WHILE...
U-NASA, RUSSIA BRANCH
(FORMER RUSSIAN FEDERAL SPACE AGENCY)
BWOOO
...TAIN.
CAPTAIN!
SKREEE
WHAM
CAPTAIN SYLVESTER!

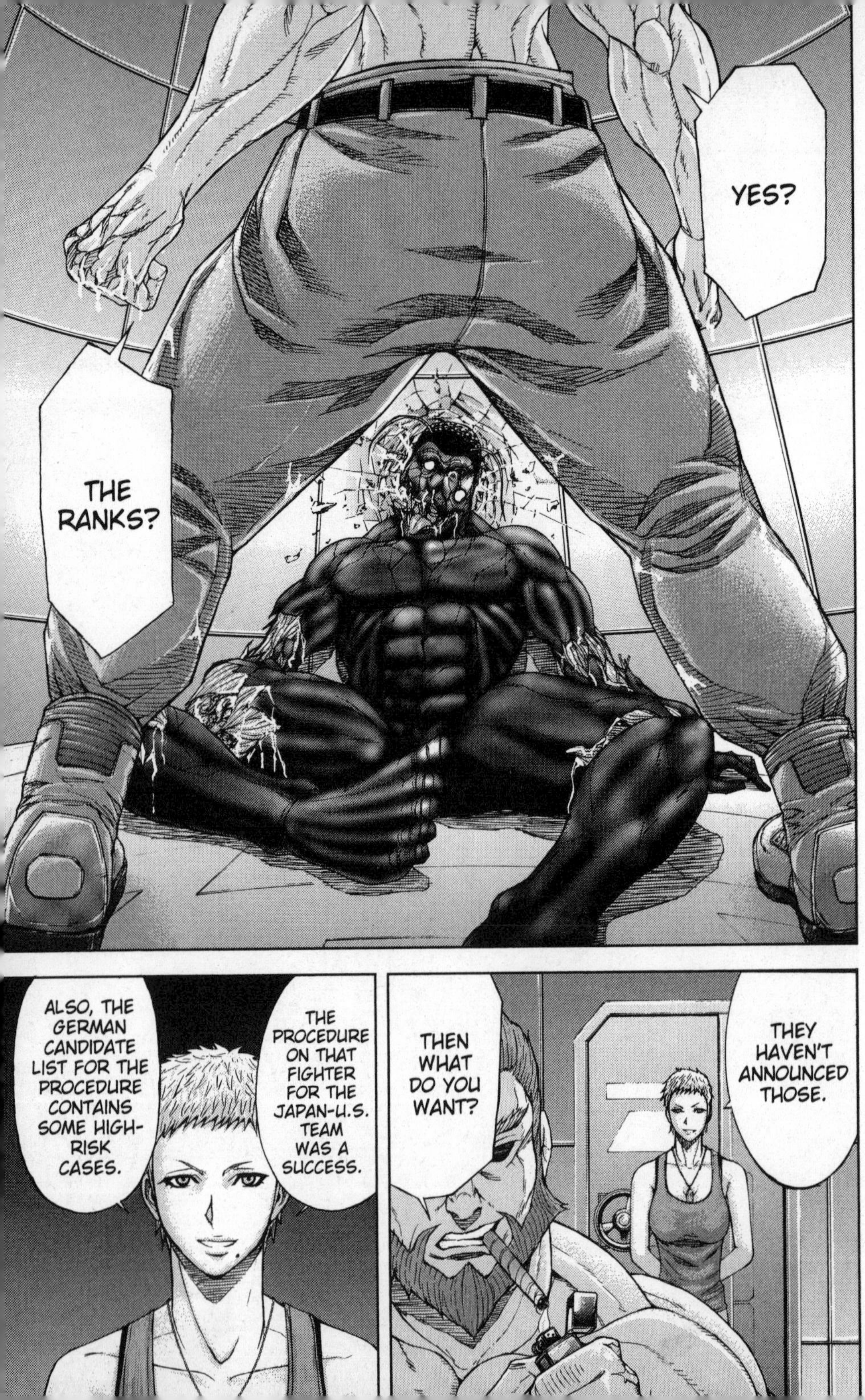
YES?
THE RANKS?
THEY HAVEN'T ANNOUNCED THOSE.
THEN WHAT DO YOU WANT?
THE PROCEDURE ON THAT FIGHTER FOR THE JAPAN-U.S. TEAM WAS A SUCCESS.
ALSO, THE GERMAN CANDIDATE LIST FOR THE PROCEDURE CONTAINS SOME HIGH-RISK CASES.

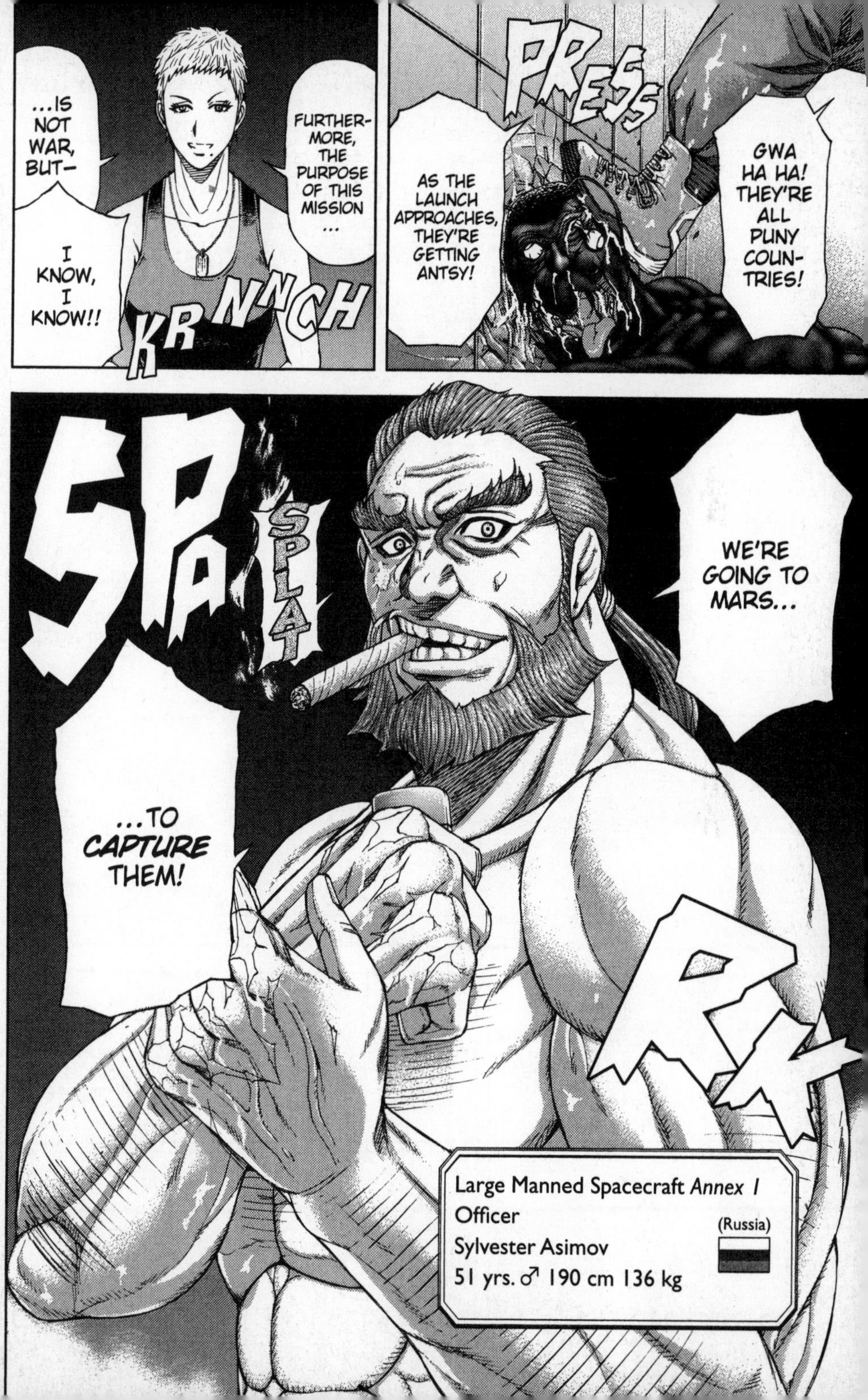
PRESS
GWA HA HA! THEY'RE ALL PUNY COUNTRIES!
AS THE LAUNCH APPROACHES, THEY'RE GETTING ANTSY!
FURTHERMORE, THE PURPOSE OF THIS MISSION …
…IS NOT WAR, BUT—
I KNOW, I KNOW!!
KRNNCH
WE'RE GOING TO MARS…
SPLAT
…TO *CAPTURE* THEM!
Large Manned Spacecraft *Annex 1*
Officer
Sylvester Asimov
(Russia)
51 yrs. ♂ 190 cm 136 kg

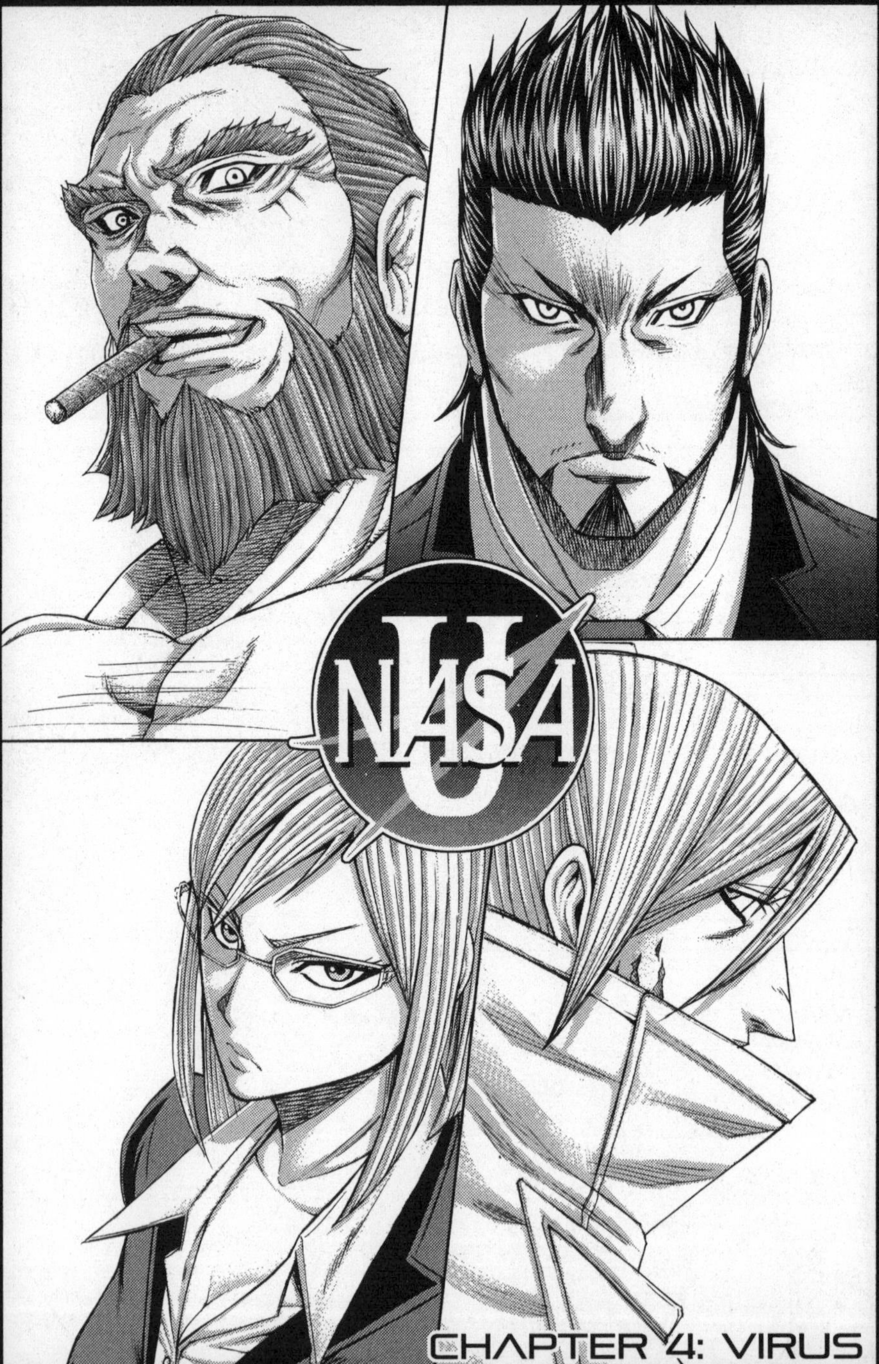
U NASA
CHAPTER 4: VIRUS

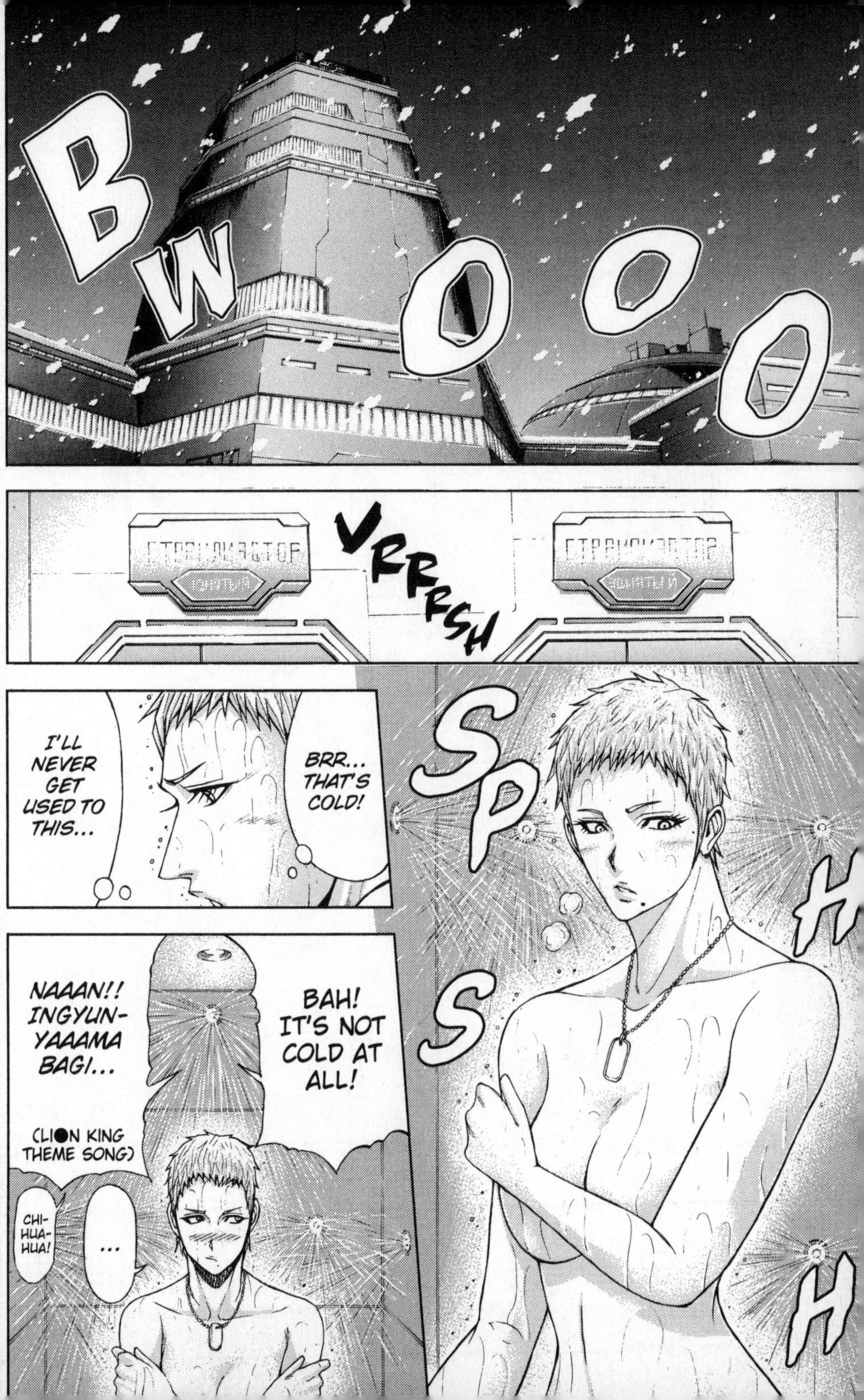
BWOOOO
VRRRSH
SP
H
S
H
BRR... THAT'S COLD!
I'LL NEVER GET USED TO THIS...
BAH! IT'S NOT COLD AT ALL!
NAAAN!! INGYUN-YAAAMA BAGI...
(LI●N KING THEME SONG)
...
CHI-HUA-HUA!

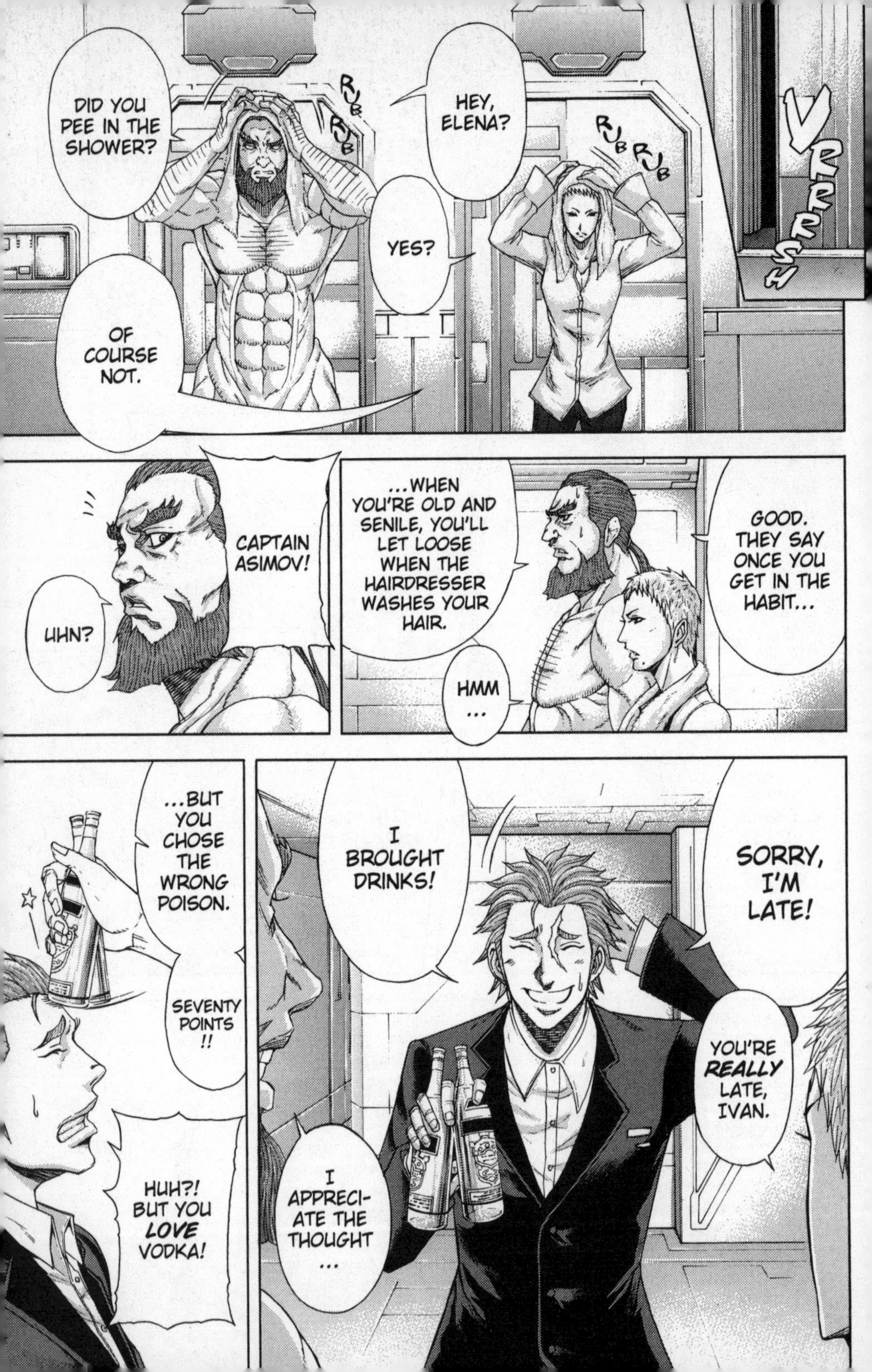
VRRRSH
HEY, ELENA?
RUB RUB
YES?
RUB RUB
DID YOU PEE IN THE SHOWER?
OF COURSE NOT.
GOOD. THEY SAY ONCE YOU GET IN THE HABIT...
...WHEN YOU'RE OLD AND SENILE, YOU'LL LET LOOSE WHEN THE HAIRDRESSER WASHES YOUR HAIR.
HMM ...
CAPTAIN ASIMOV!
UHN?
SORRY, I'M LATE!
I BROUGHT DRINKS!
YOU'RE *REALLY* LATE, IVAN.
I APPRECI-ATE THE THOUGHT ...
...BUT YOU CHOSE THE WRONG POISON.
SEVENTY POINTS !!
HUH?! BUT YOU *LOVE* VODKA!

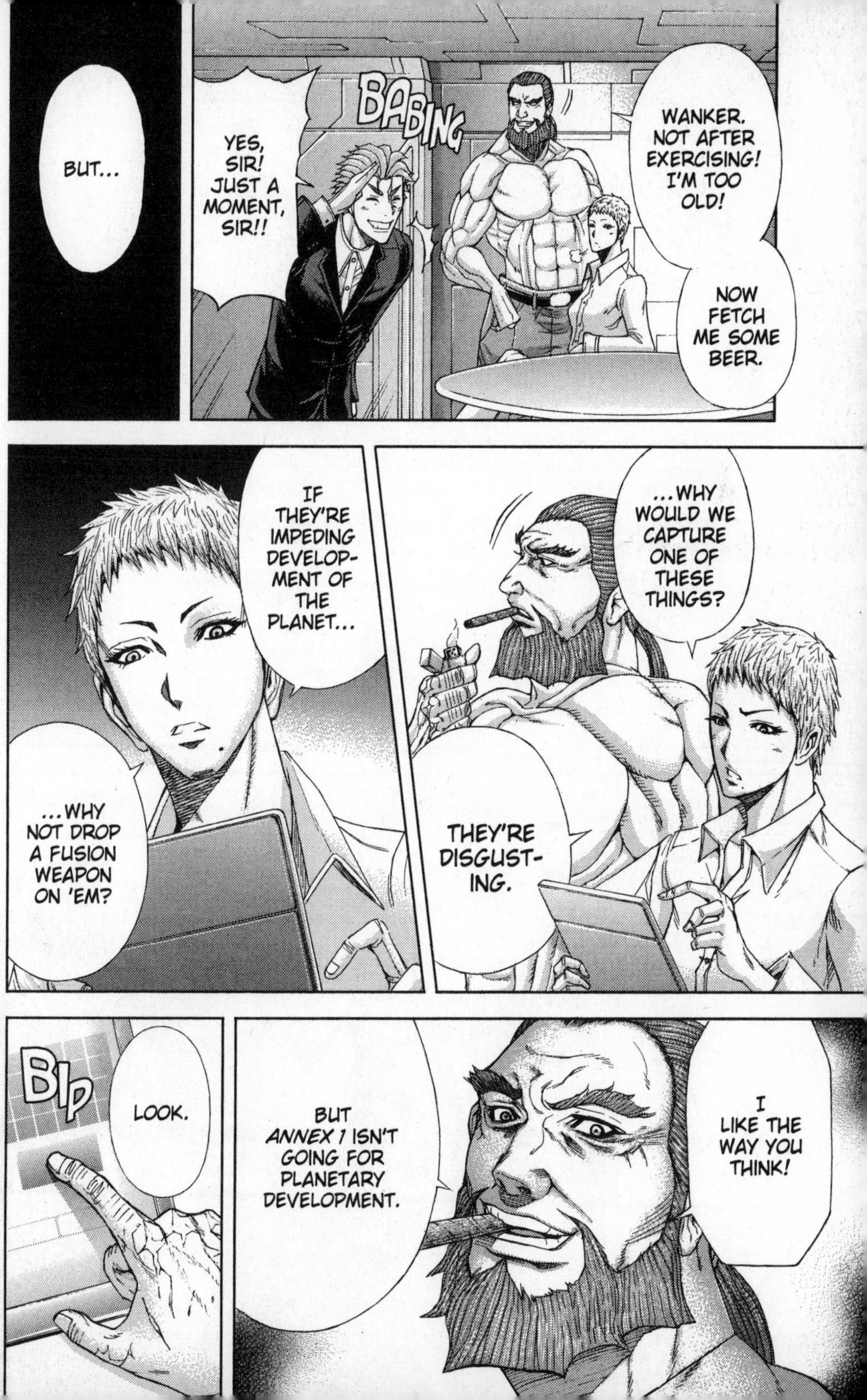
WANKER. NOT AFTER EXERCISING! I'M TOO OLD!
NOW FETCH ME SOME BEER.
BABING
YES, SIR! JUST A MOMENT, SIR!!
BUT...
...WHY WOULD WE CAPTURE ONE OF THESE THINGS?
THEY'RE DISGUST-ING.
IF THEY'RE IMPEDING DEVELOP-MENT OF THE PLANET...
...WHY NOT DROP A FUSION WEAPON ON 'EM?
I LIKE THE WAY YOU THINK!
BUT *ANNEX 1* ISN'T GOING FOR PLANETARY DEVELOPMENT.
BIP
LOOK.

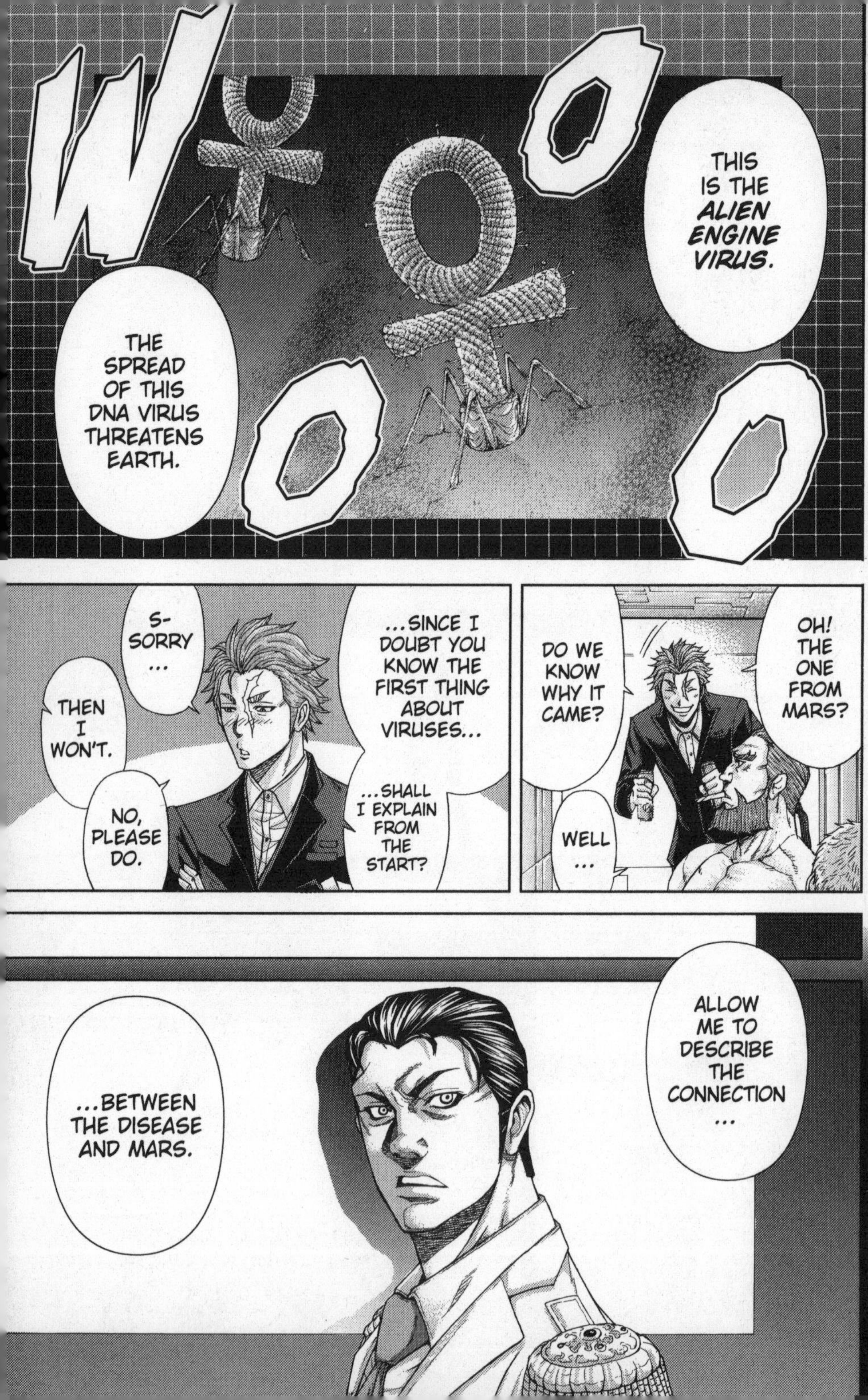
THIS IS THE *ALIEN ENGINE VIRUS.*
WOOO
THE SPREAD OF THIS DNA VIRUS THREATENS EARTH.
OH! THE ONE FROM MARS?
DO WE KNOW WHY IT CAME?
WELL ...
...SINCE I DOUBT YOU KNOW THE FIRST THING ABOUT VIRUSES...
...SHALL I EXPLAIN FROM THE START?
S-SORRY ...
THEN I WON'T.
NO, PLEASE DO.
ALLOW ME TO DESCRIBE THE CONNECTION ...
...BETWEEN THE DISEASE AND MARS.

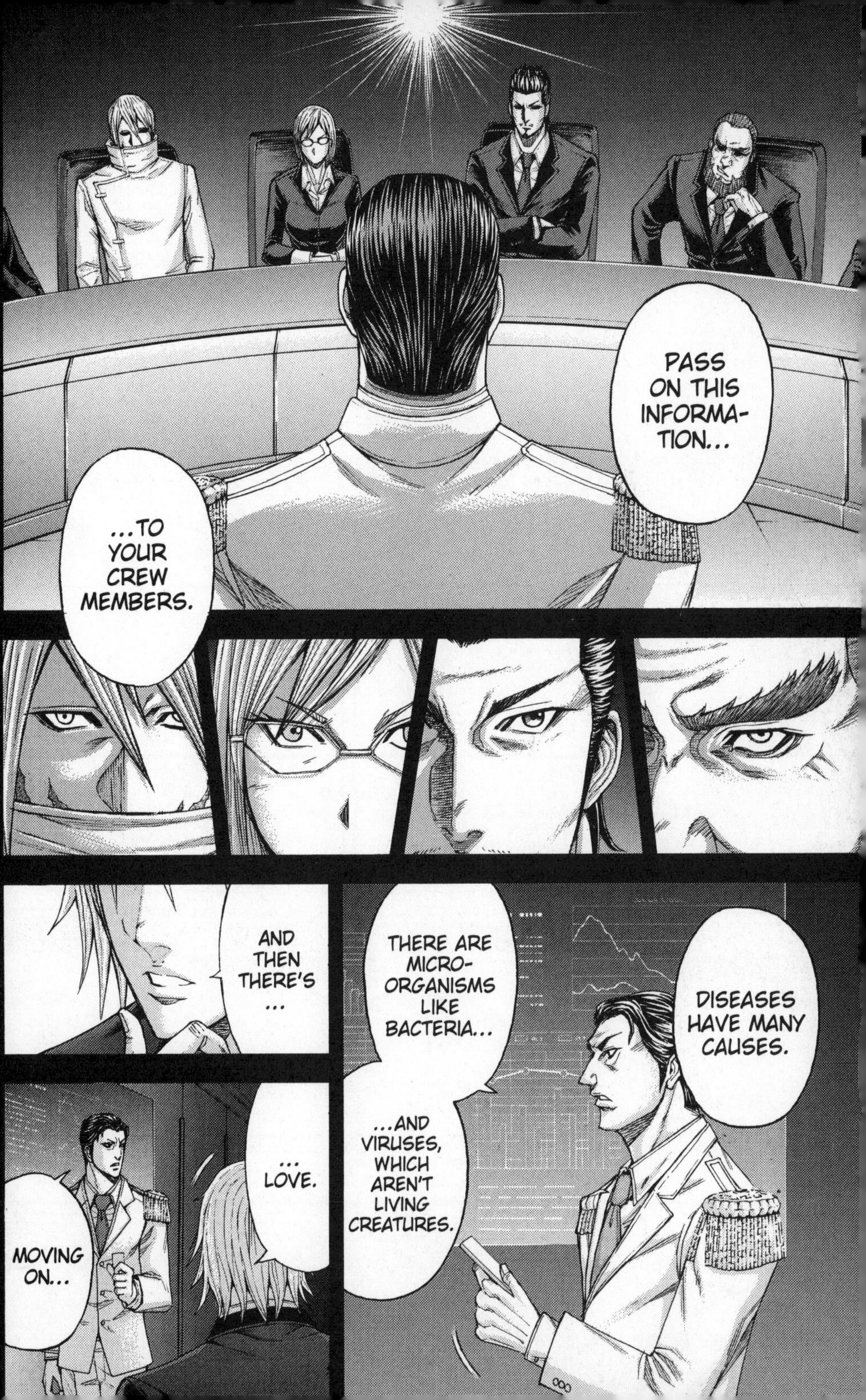
PASS ON THIS INFORMATION...
...TO YOUR CREW MEMBERS.
DISEASES HAVE MANY CAUSES.
THERE ARE MICRO-ORGANISMS LIKE BACTERIA...
...AND VIRUSES, WHICH AREN'T LIVING CREATURES.
AND THEN THERE'S ...
... LOVE.
MOVING ON...

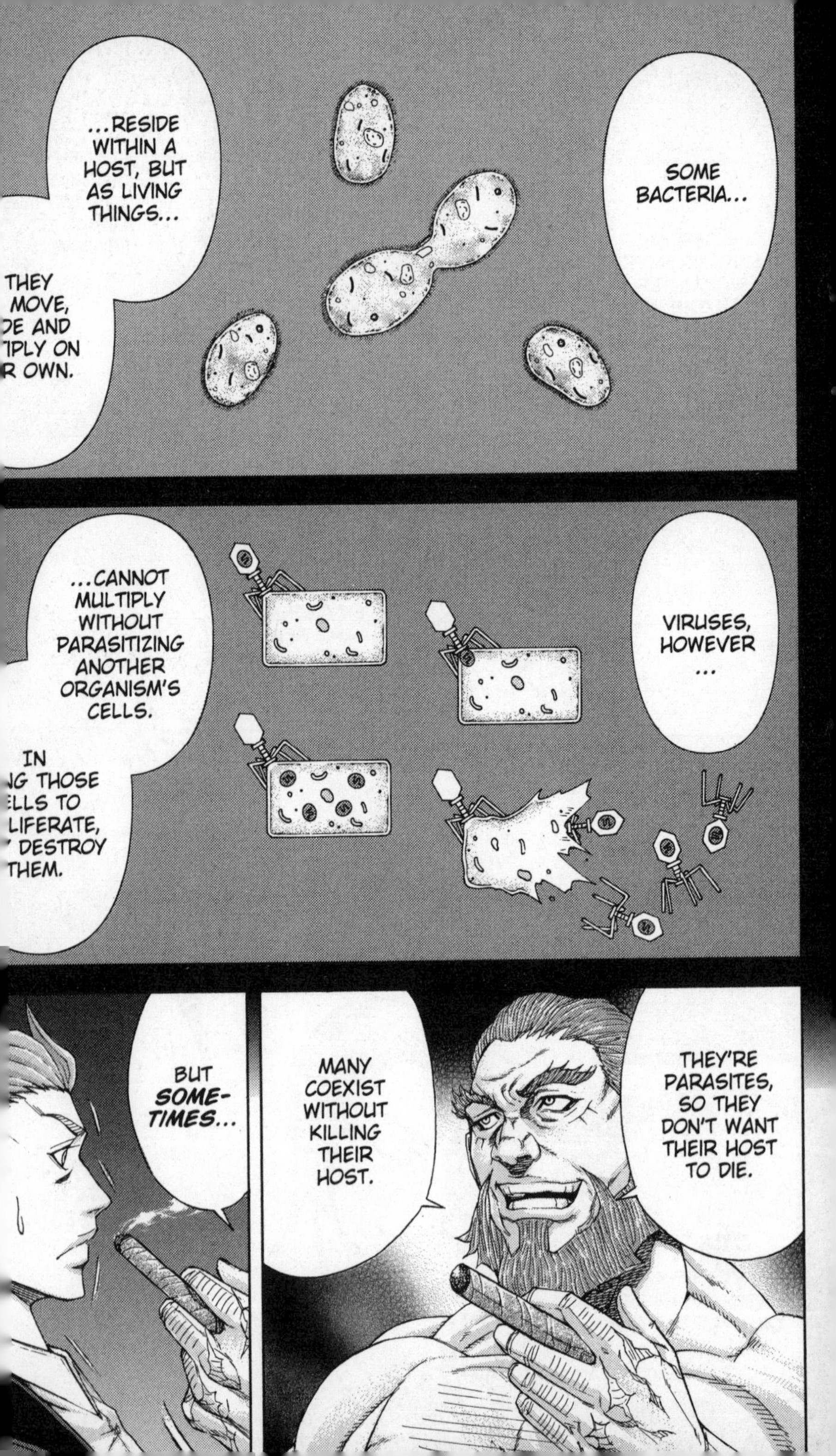
SOME BACTERIA...
...RESIDE WITHIN A HOST, BUT AS LIVING THINGS...
THEY MOVE, DE AND TIPLY ON R OWN.
VIRUSES, HOWEVER ...
...CANNOT MULTIPLY WITHOUT PARASITIZING ANOTHER ORGANISM'S CELLS.
IN NG THOSE ELLS TO LIFERATE, DESTROY THEM.
THEY'RE PARASITES, SO THEY DON'T WANT THEIR HOST TO DIE.
MANY COEXIST WITHOUT KILLING THEIR HOST.
BUT *SOME-TIMES*...

...A VIRUS MUTATES WHEN MOVING FROM ANIMAL TO HUMAN.

AFTER AN UNFORTUNATE ENCOUNTER WITH THE NEW ANIMAL...

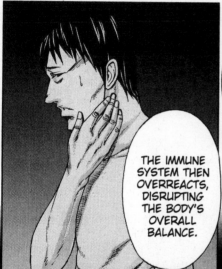

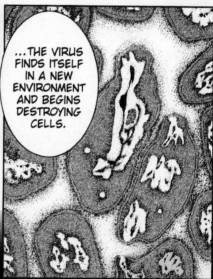

...THE VIRUS FINDS ITSELF IN A NEW ENVIRONMENT AND BEGINS DESTROYING CELLS.

THE IMMUNE SYSTEM THEN OVERREACTS, DISRUPTING THE BODY'S OVERALL BALANCE.

THAT IS THE BASIC MECHANISM OF HUMAN INFECTIOUS DISEASES.

IN OTHER WORDS...

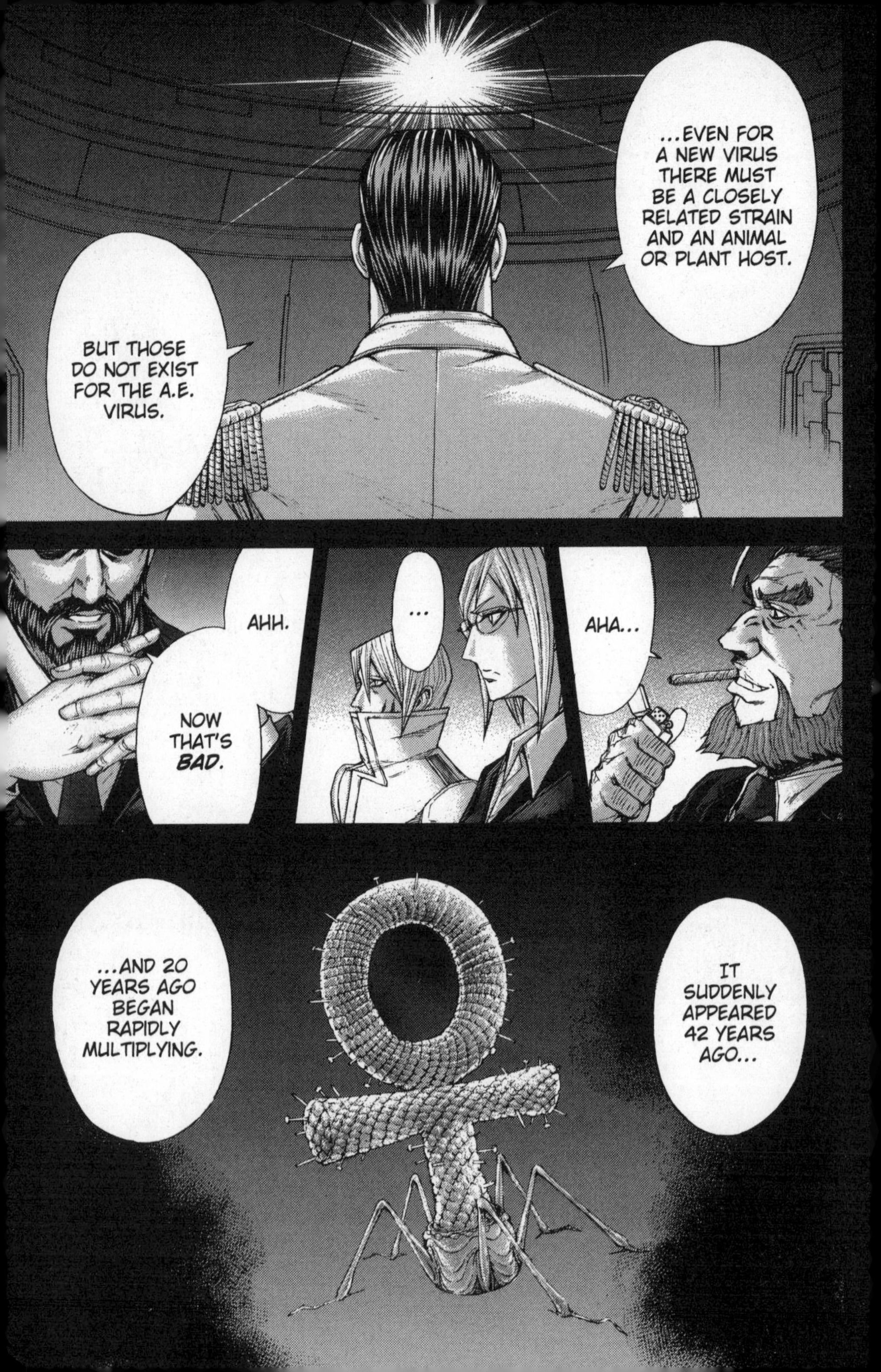
...EVEN FOR A NEW VIRUS THERE MUST BE A CLOSELY RELATED STRAIN AND AN ANIMAL OR PLANT HOST.
BUT THOSE DO NOT EXIST FOR THE A.E. VIRUS.
AHA...
...
AHH.
NOW THAT'S *BAD*.
IT SUDDENLY APPEARED 42 YEARS AGO...
...AND 20 YEARS AGO BEGAN RAPIDLY MULTIPLYING.

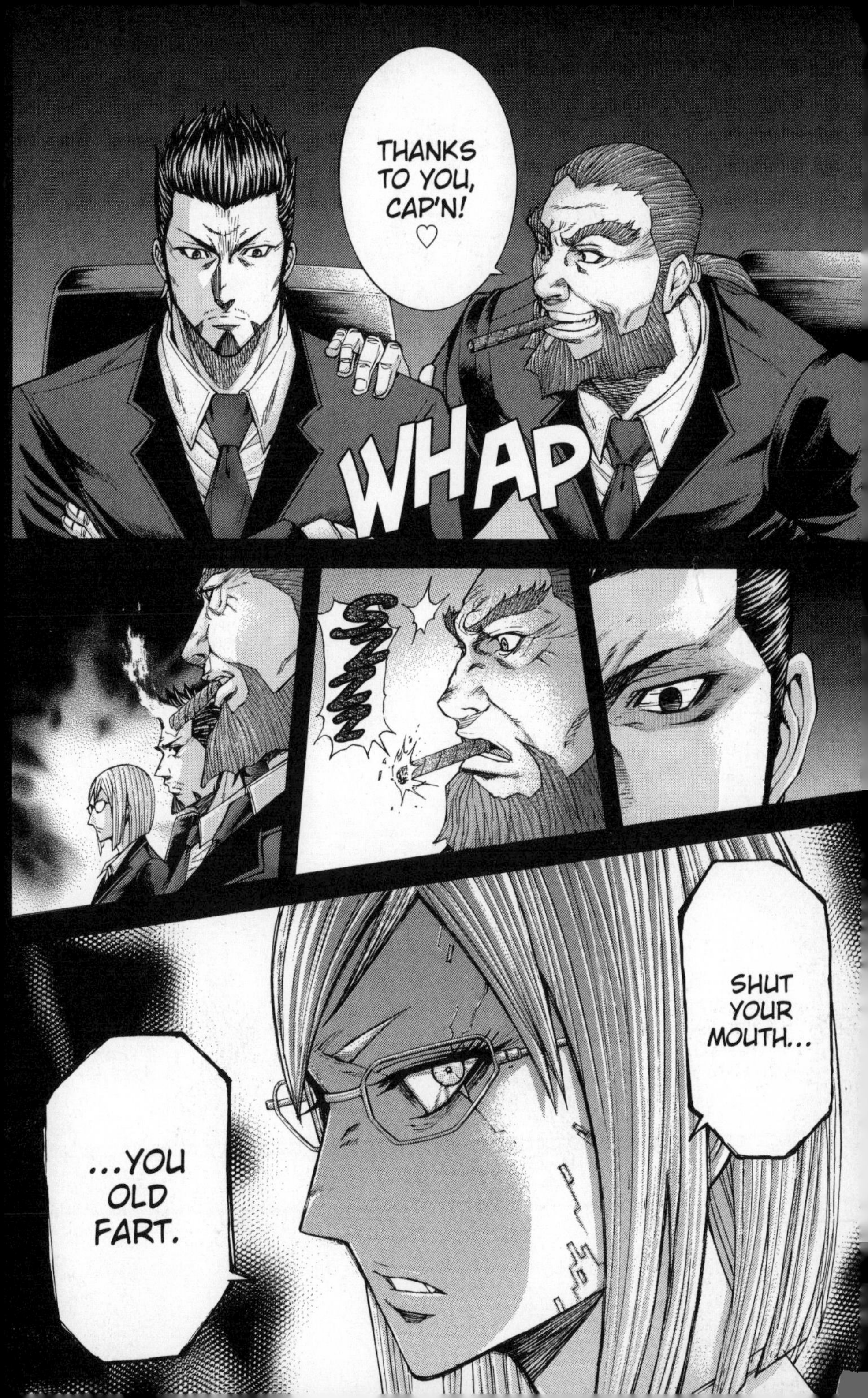
THANKS TO YOU, CAP'N! ♡
WHAP
SHUT YOUR MOUTH...
...YOU OLD FART.

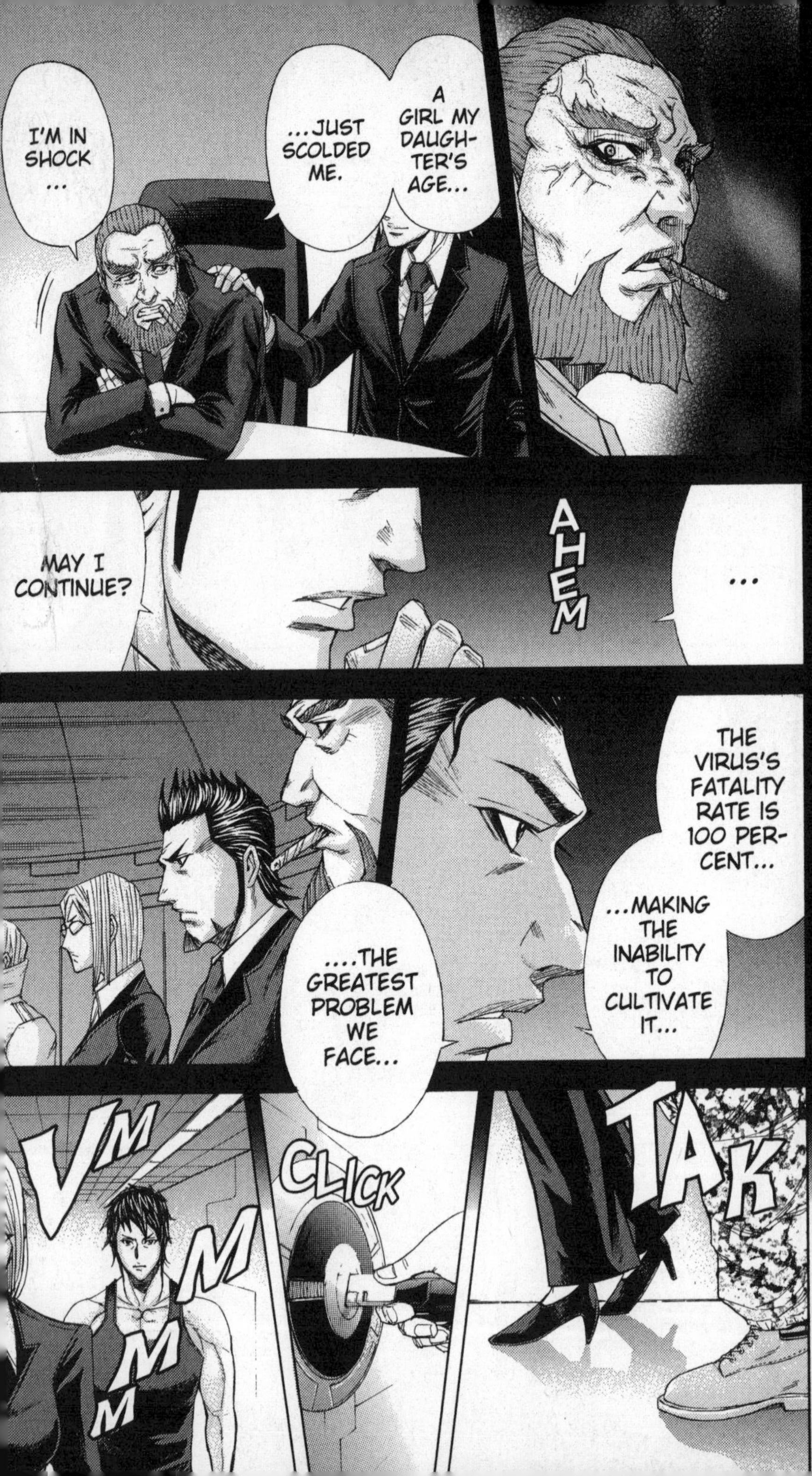
A GIRL MY DAUGHTER'S AGE...
...JUST SCOLDED ME.
I'M IN SHOCK ...
...
AHEM
MAY I CONTINUE?
THE VIRUS'S FATALITY RATE IS 100 PERCENT...
...MAKING THE INABILITY TO CULTIVATE IT...
....THE GREATEST PROBLEM WE FACE...
TAK
CLICK
VMMMMM

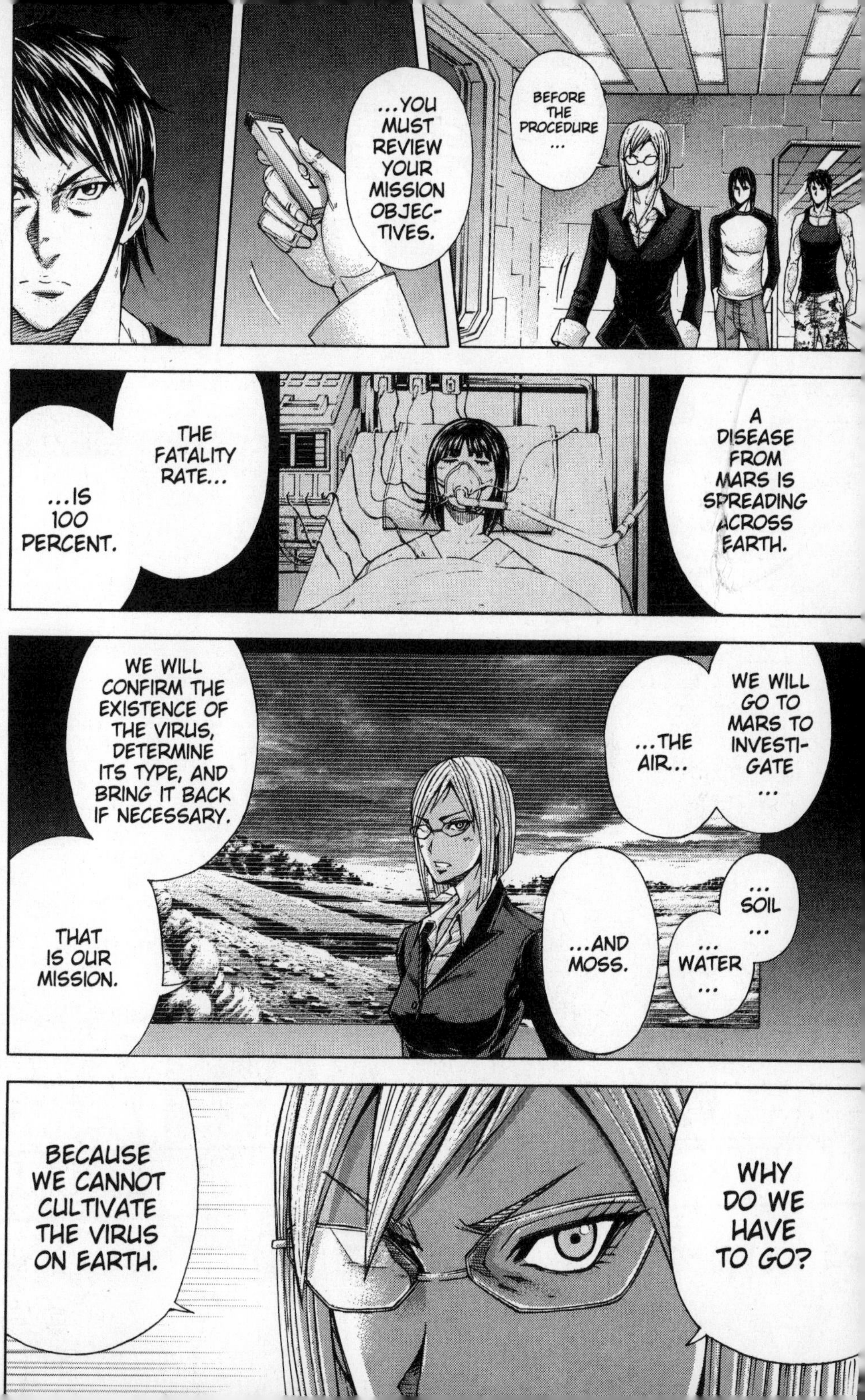
BEFORE THE PROCEDURE ...
...YOU MUST REVIEW YOUR MISSION OBJECTIVES.
A DISEASE FROM MARS IS SPREADING ACROSS EARTH.
THE FATALITY RATE...
...IS 100 PERCENT.
WE WILL GO TO MARS TO INVESTIGATE ...
...THE AIR...
... SOIL ...
... WATER ...
...AND MOSS.
WE WILL CONFIRM THE EXISTENCE OF THE VIRUS, DETERMINE ITS TYPE, AND BRING IT BACK IF NECESSARY.
THAT IS OUR MISSION.
WHY DO WE HAVE TO GO?
BECAUSE WE CANNOT CULTIVATE THE VIRUS ON EARTH.

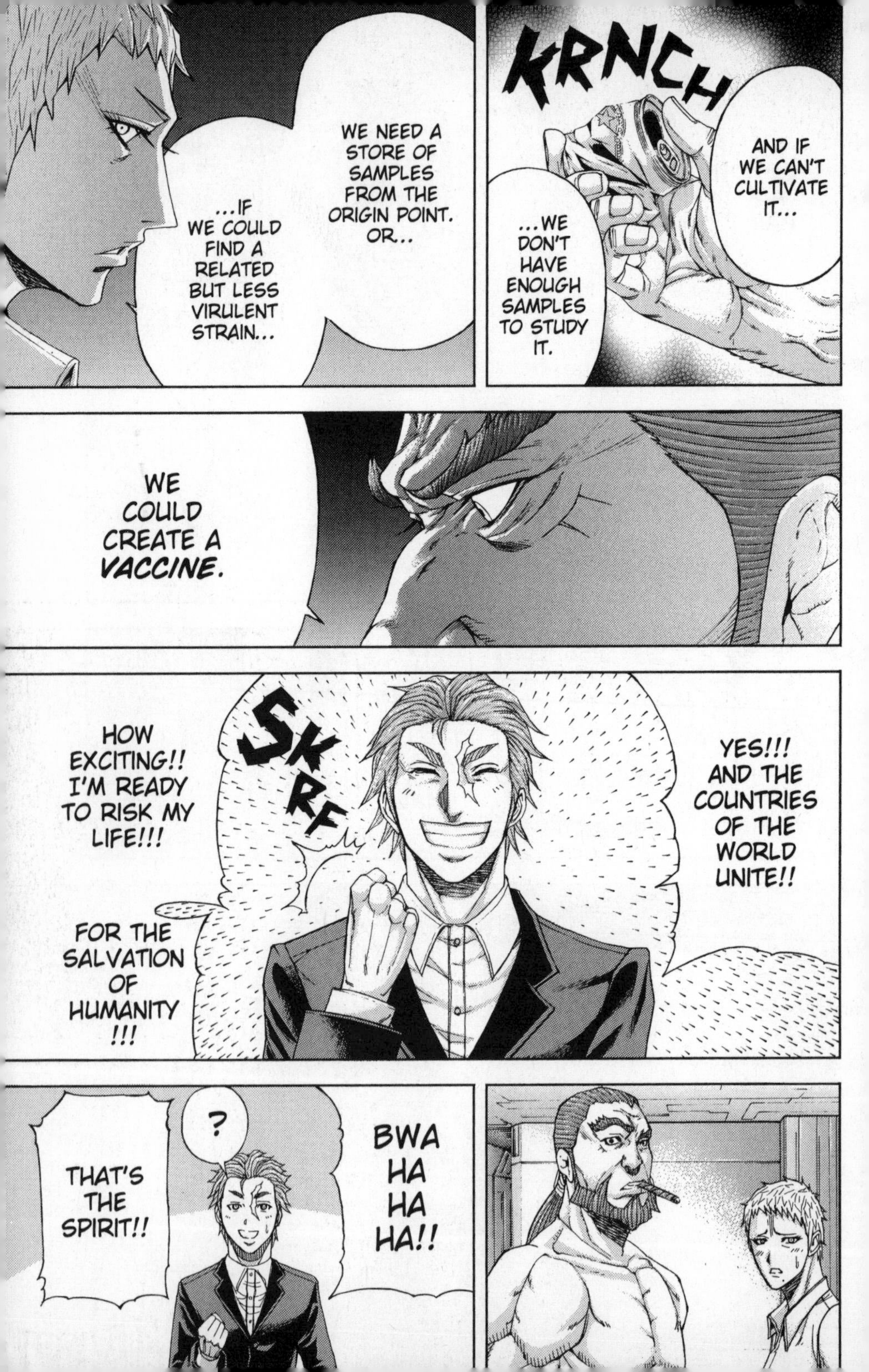
KRNCH
AND IF WE CAN'T CULTIVATE IT...
...WE DON'T HAVE ENOUGH SAMPLES TO STUDY IT.
WE NEED A STORE OF SAMPLES FROM THE ORIGIN POINT. OR...
...IF WE COULD FIND A RELATED BUT LESS VIRULENT STRAIN...
WE COULD CREATE A *VACCINE*.
YES!!! AND THE COUNTRIES OF THE WORLD UNITE!!
SKRF
HOW EXCITING!! I'M READY TO RISK MY LIFE!!!
FOR THE SALVATION OF HUMANITY!!!
BWA HA HA HA!!
?
THAT'S THE SPIRIT!!

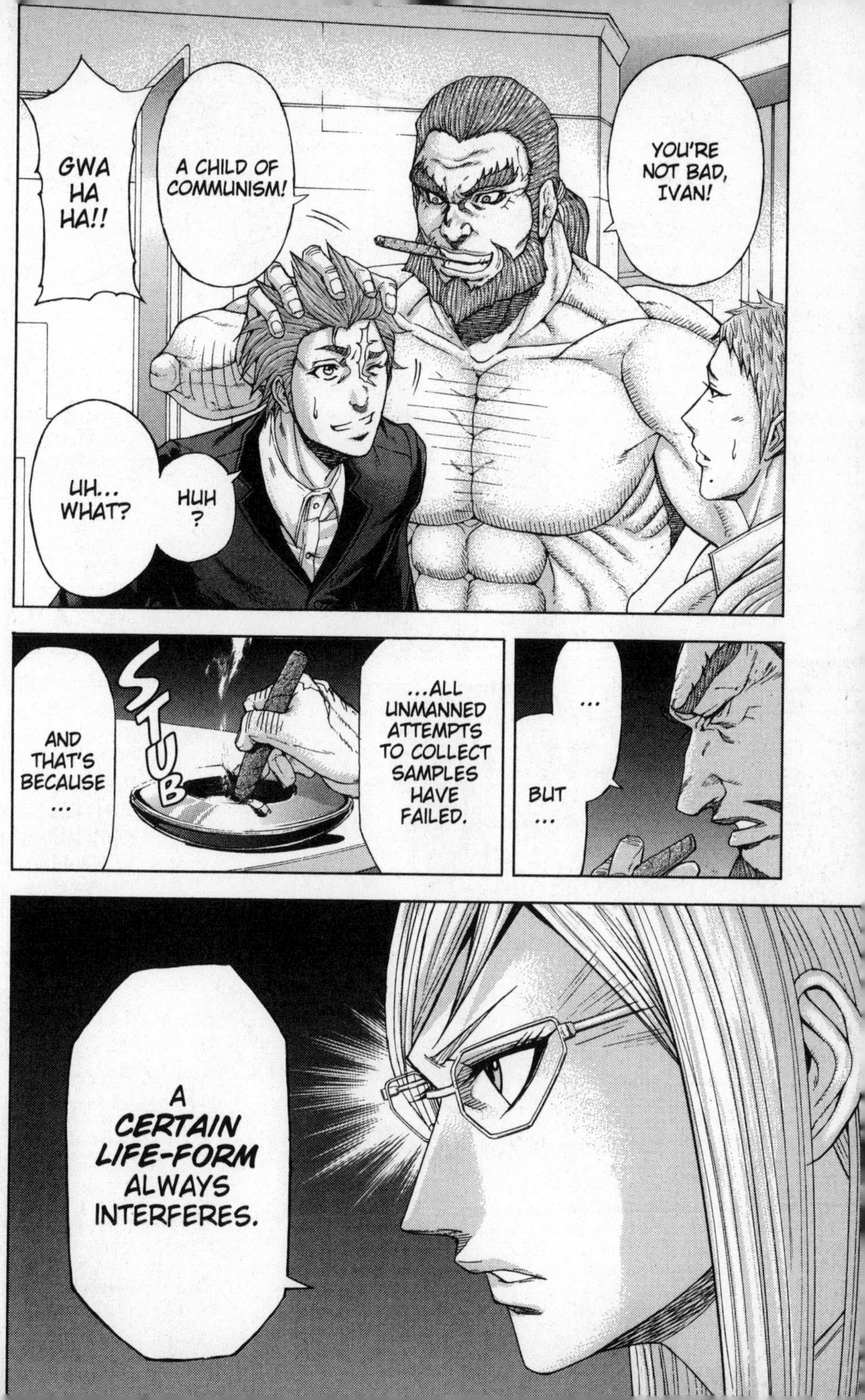
YOU'RE NOT BAD, IVAN!
A CHILD OF COMMUNISM!
GWA HA HA!!
HUH ?
UH... WHAT?
...
BUT ...
...ALL UNMANNED ATTEMPTS TO COLLECT SAMPLES HAVE FAILED.
STUB
AND THAT'S BECAUSE ...
A CERTAIN LIFE-FORM ALWAYS INTERFERES.

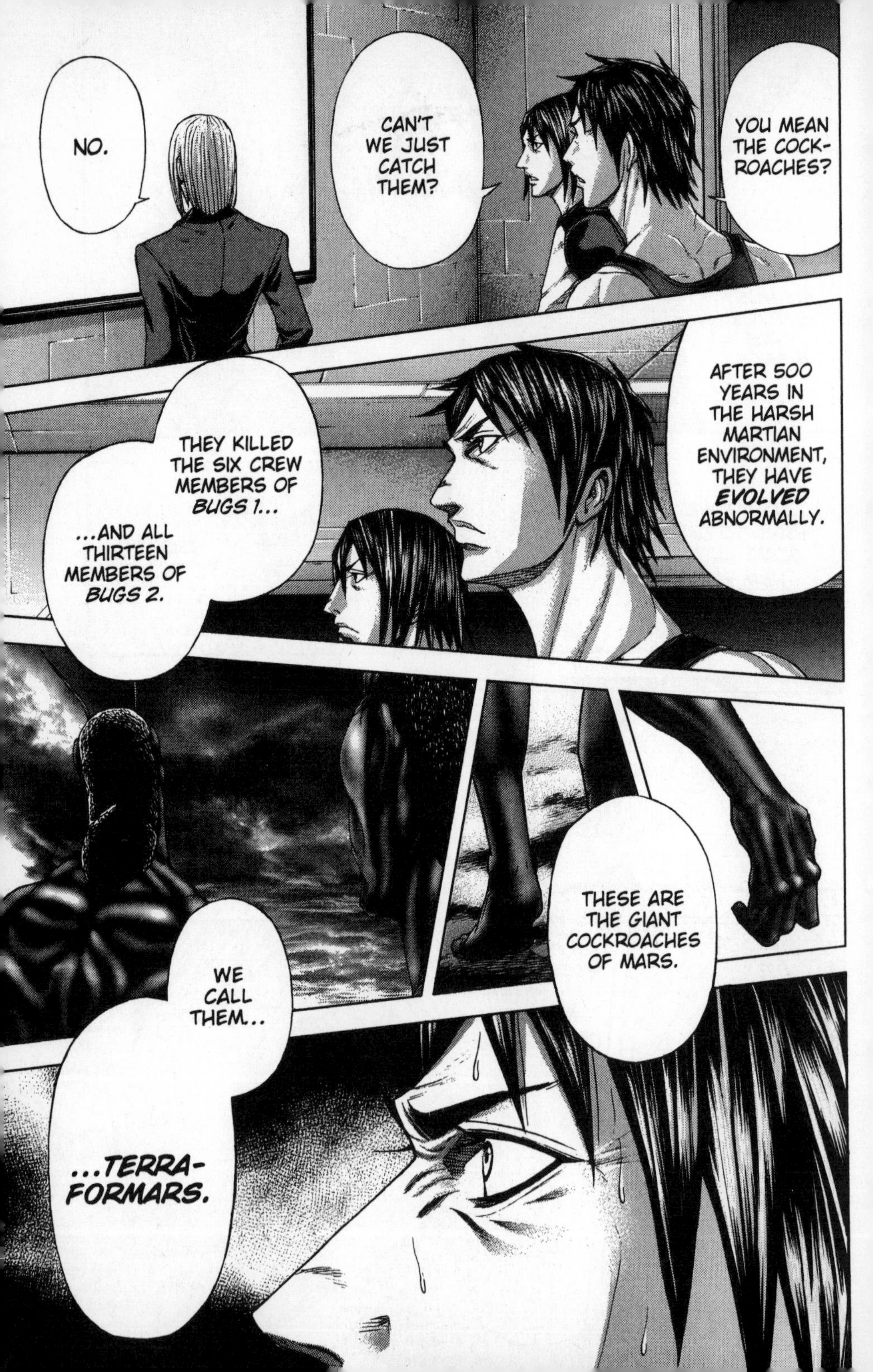
YOU MEAN THE COCK-ROACHES?
CAN'T WE JUST CATCH THEM?
NO.
AFTER 500 YEARS IN THE HARSH MARTIAN ENVIRONMENT, THEY HAVE ***EVOLVED*** ABNORMALLY.
THEY KILLED THE SIX CREW MEMBERS OF *BUGS 1*...
...AND ALL THIRTEEN MEMBERS OF *BUGS 2*.
THESE ARE THE GIANT COCKROACHES OF MARS.
WE CALL THEM...
...TERRA-FORMARS.

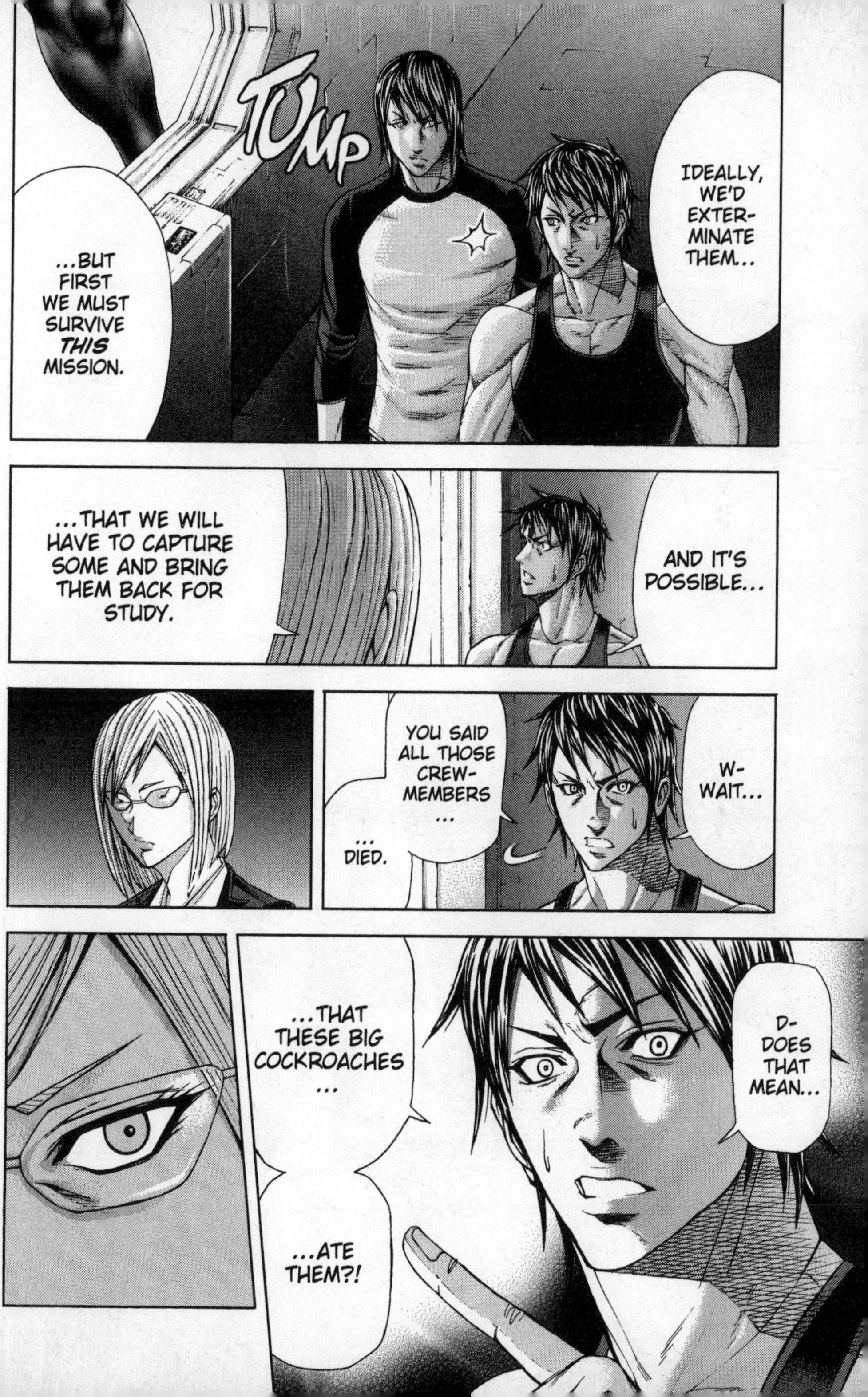
IDEALLY, WE'D EXTER-MINATE THEM...
TUMP
...BUT FIRST WE MUST SURVIVE *THIS* MISSION.
AND IT'S POSSIBLE...
...THAT WE WILL HAVE TO CAPTURE SOME AND BRING THEM BACK FOR STUDY.
W-WAIT...
YOU SAID ALL THOSE CREW-MEMBERS ...
... DIED.
D-DOES THAT MEAN...
...THAT THESE BIG COCKROACHES ...
...ATE THEM?!

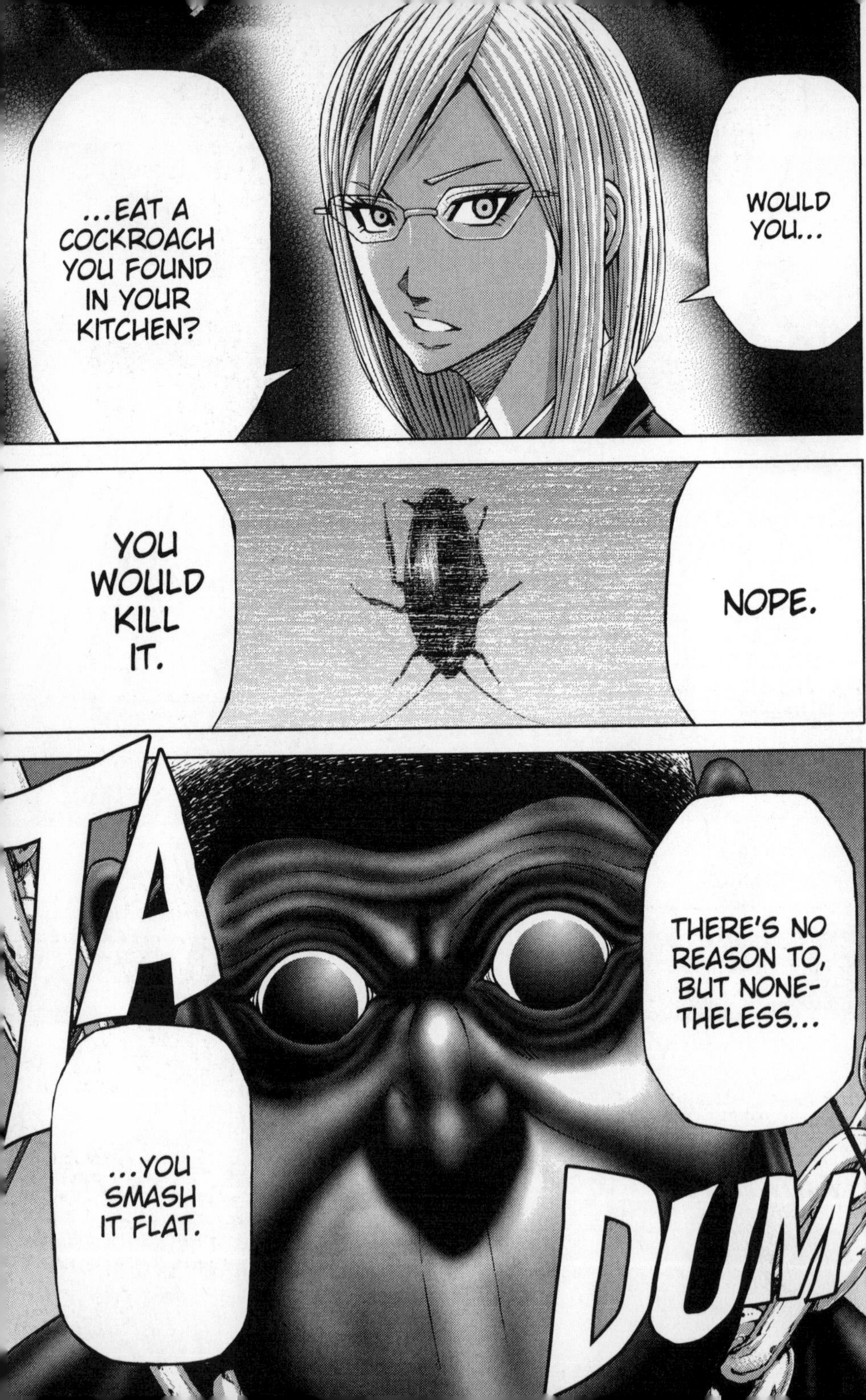
WOULD YOU...
...EAT A COCKROACH YOU FOUND IN YOUR KITCHEN?
NOPE.
YOU WOULD KILL IT.
THERE'S NO REASON TO, BUT NONE-THELESS...
...YOU SMASH IT FLAT.
TA
DUM

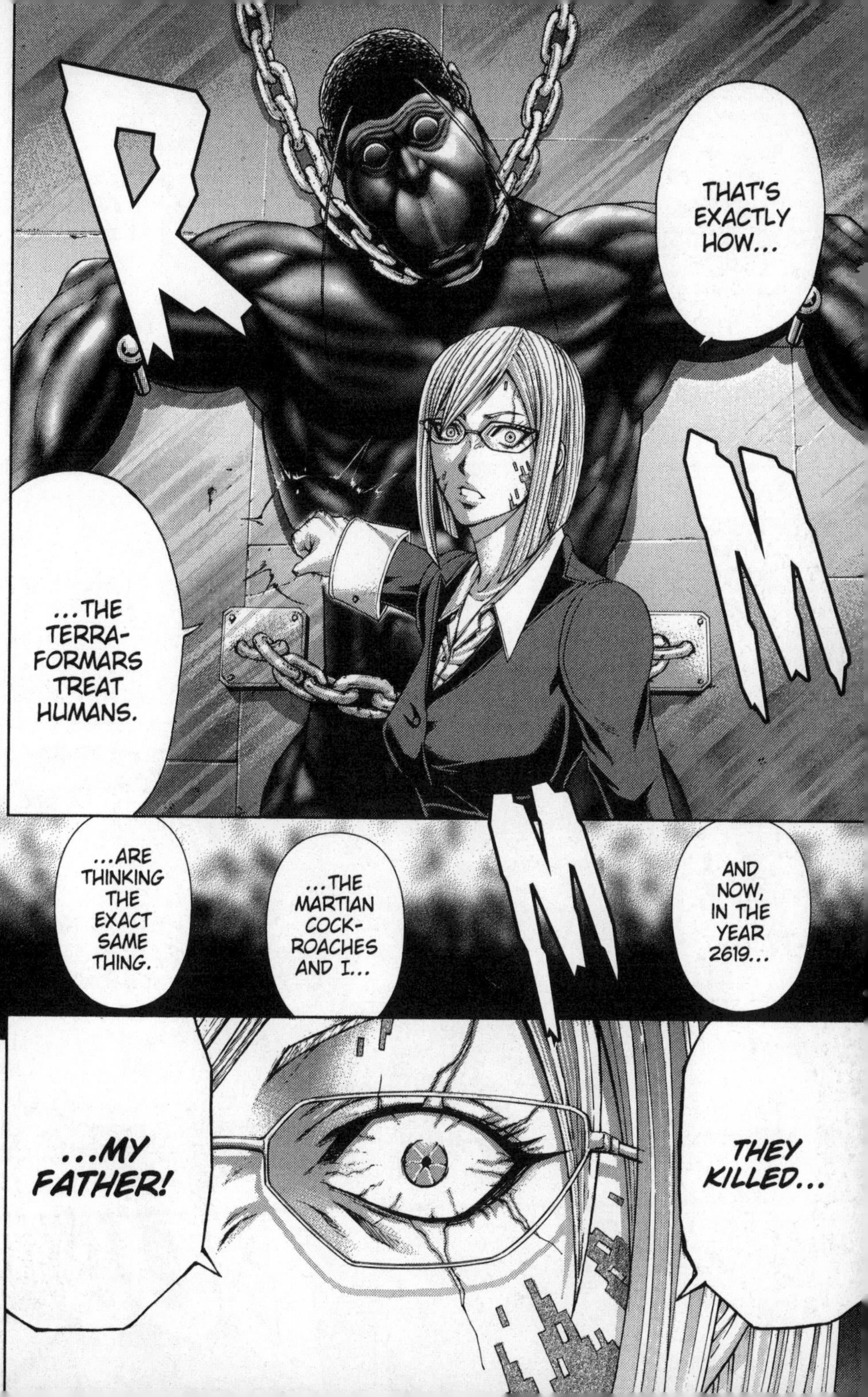
THAT'S EXACTLY HOW...
...THE TERRA-FORMARS TREAT HUMANS.
RMM
AND NOW, IN THE YEAR 2619...
...THE MARTIAN COCK-ROACHES AND I...
...ARE THINKING THE EXACT SAME THING.
THEY KILLED...
...MY FATHER!

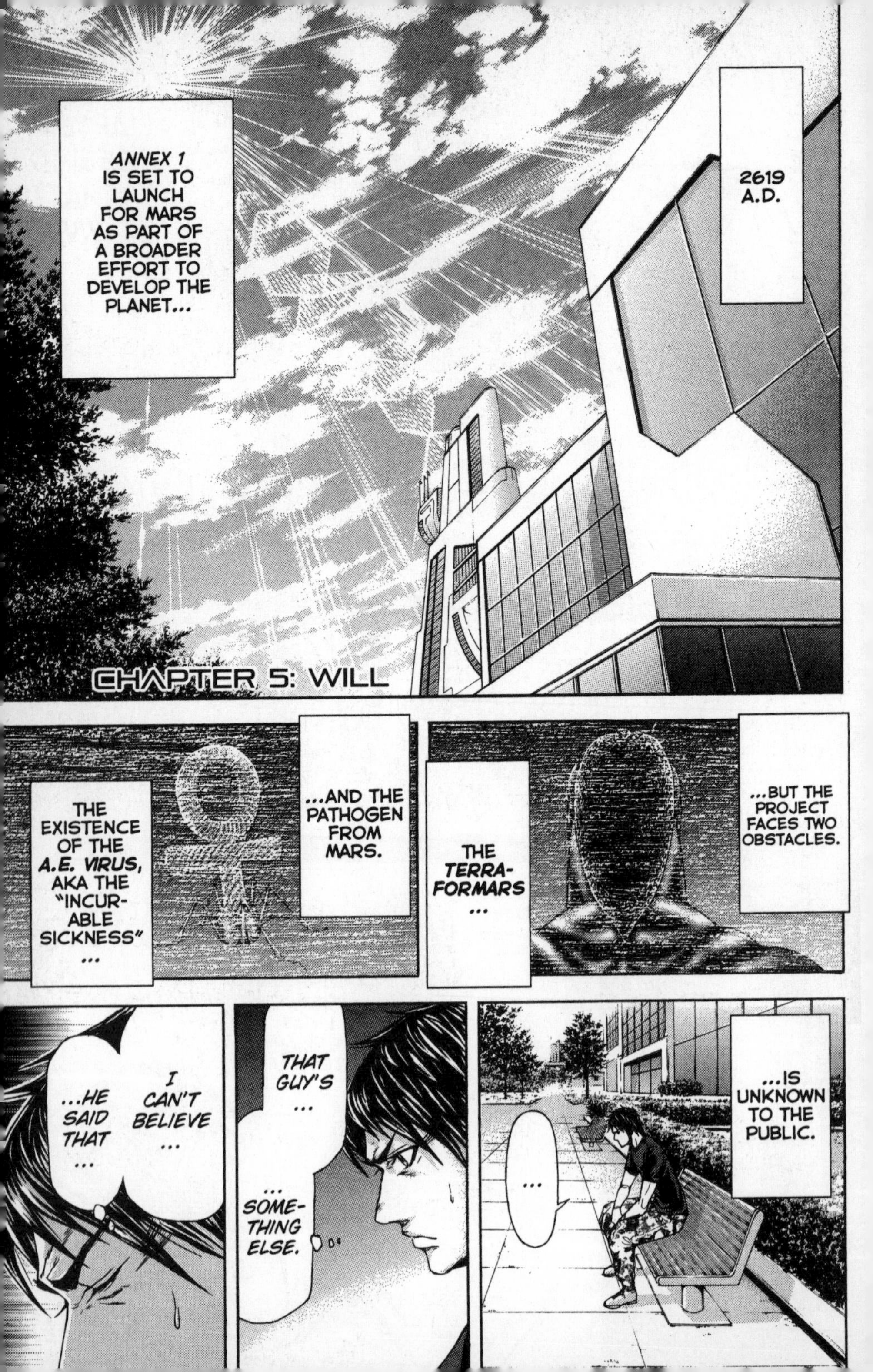
2619 A.D.
ANNEX 1 IS SET TO LAUNCH FOR MARS AS PART OF A BROADER EFFORT TO DEVELOP THE PLANET...
CHAPTER 5: WILL
...BUT THE PROJECT FACES TWO OBSTACLES.
THE TERRA-FORMARS...
...AND THE PATHOGEN FROM MARS.
THE EXISTENCE OF THE A.E. VIRUS, AKA THE "INCURABLE SICKNESS"...
...IS UNKNOWN TO THE PUBLIC.
...
THAT GUY'S...
...SOMETHING ELSE.
I CAN'T BELIEVE...
...HE SAID THAT...

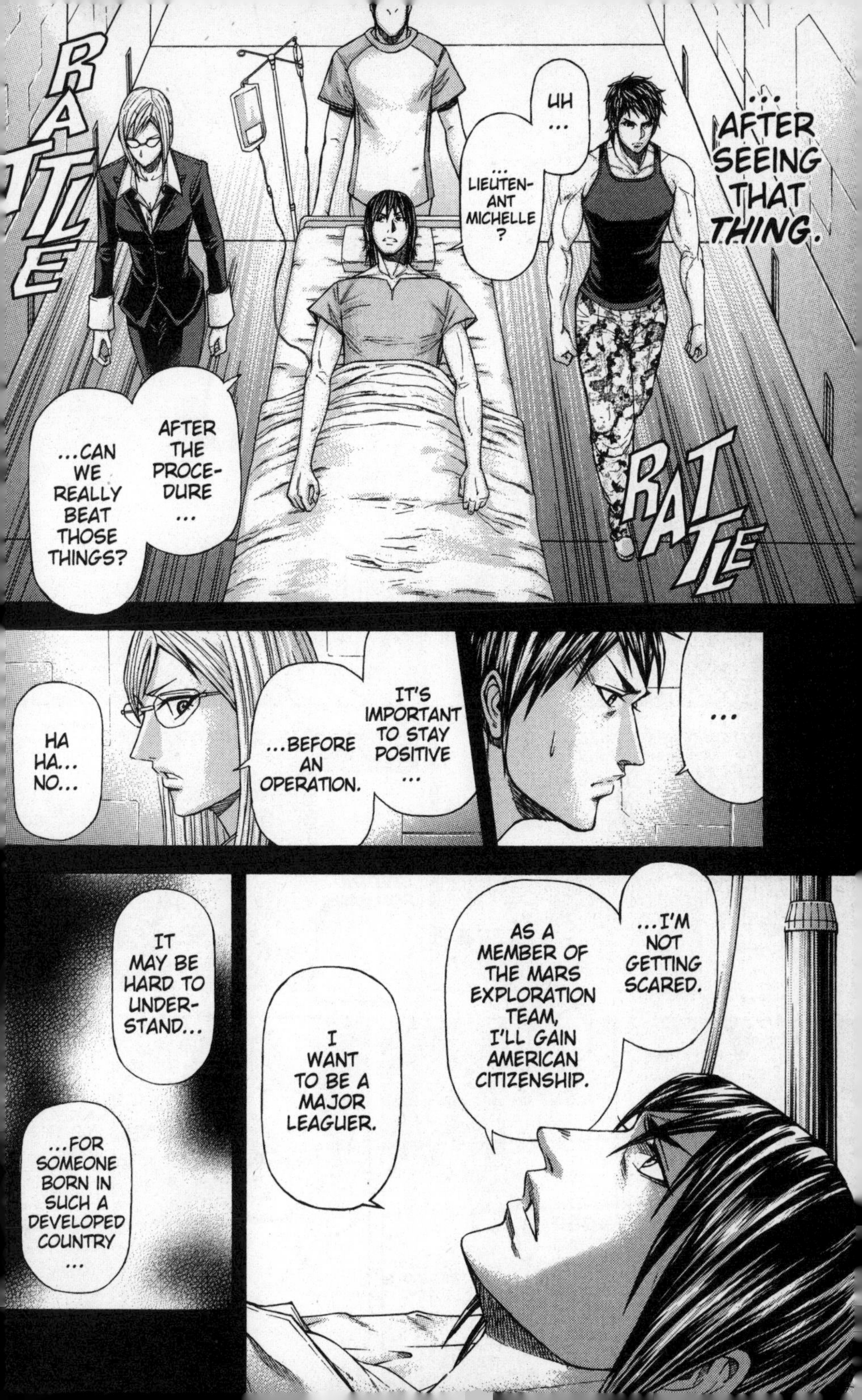
...AFTER SEEING THAT THING.
UH ...
...LIEUTENANT MICHELLE?
RATTLE
AFTER THE PROCEDURE ...
...CAN WE REALLY BEAT THOSE THINGS?
RATTLE
...
IT'S IMPORTANT TO STAY POSITIVE ...
...BEFORE AN OPERATION.
HA HA... NO...
...I'M NOT GETTING SCARED.
AS A MEMBER OF THE MARS EXPLORATION TEAM, I'LL GAIN AMERICAN CITIZENSHIP.
I WANT TO BE A MAJOR LEAGUER.
IT MAY BE HARD TO UNDERSTAND...
...FOR SOMEONE BORN IN SUCH A DEVELOPED COUNTRY ...

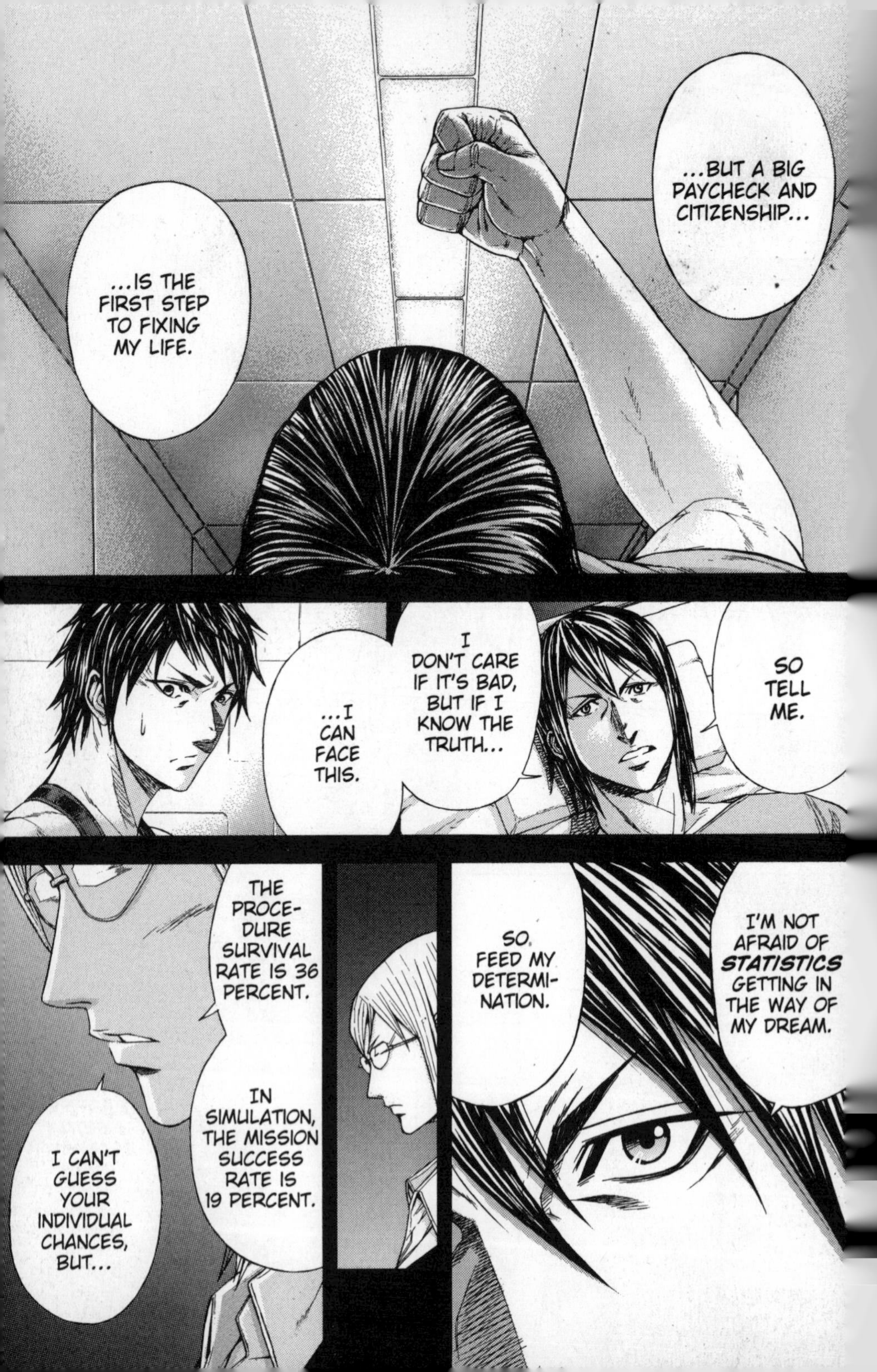
...BUT A BIG PAYCHECK AND CITIZENSHIP...
...IS THE FIRST STEP TO FIXING MY LIFE.
SO TELL ME.
I DON'T CARE IF IT'S BAD, BUT IF I KNOW THE TRUTH...
...I CAN FACE THIS.
I'M NOT AFRAID OF *STATISTICS* GETTING IN THE WAY OF MY DREAM.
SO, FEED MY DETERMINATION.
THE PROCEDURE SURVIVAL RATE IS 36 PERCENT.
IN SIMULATION, THE MISSION SUCCESS RATE IS 19 PERCENT.
I CAN'T GUESS YOUR INDIVIDUAL CHANCES, BUT...

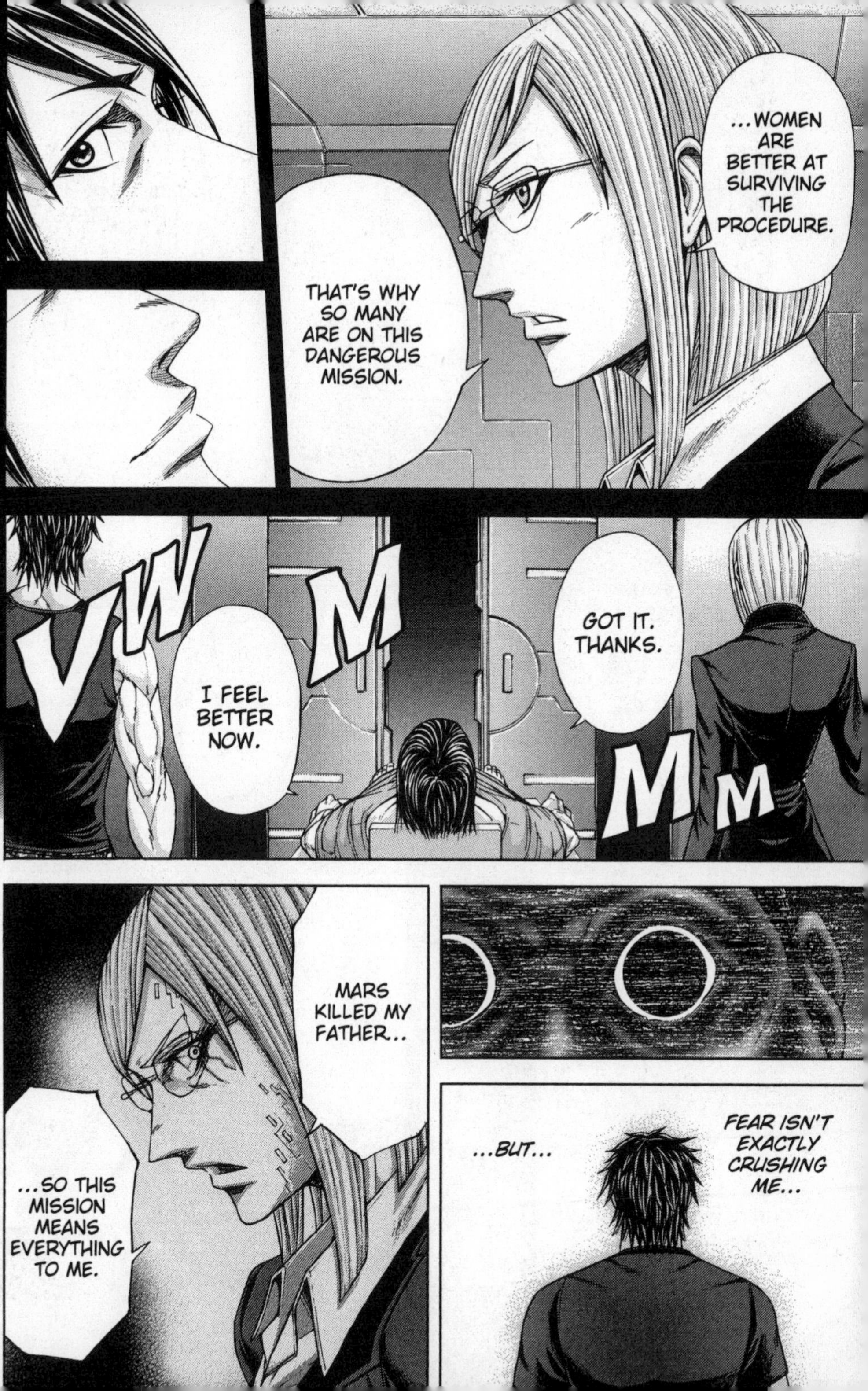
...WOMEN ARE BETTER AT SURVIVING THE PROCEDURE.
THAT'S WHY SO MANY ARE ON THIS DANGEROUS MISSION.
GOT IT. THANKS.
I FEEL BETTER NOW.
VWMMMM
FEAR ISN'T EXACTLY CRUSHING ME...
...BUT...
MARS KILLED MY FATHER...
...SO THIS MISSION MEANS EVERYTHING TO ME.

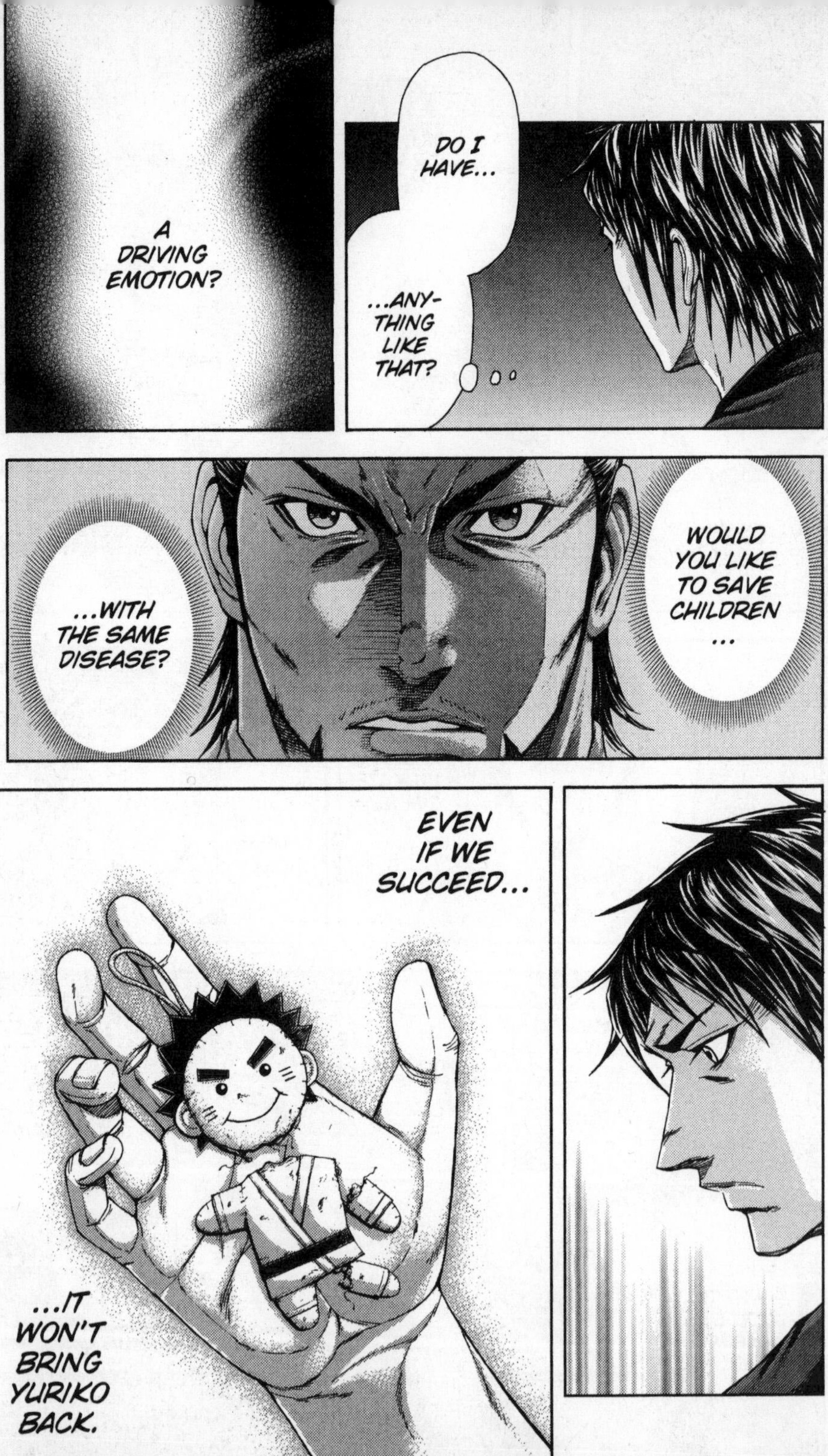
DO I HAVE...
...ANYTHING LIKE THAT?
A DRIVING EMOTION?
WOULD YOU LIKE TO SAVE CHILDREN ...
...WITH THE SAME DISEASE?
EVEN IF WE SUCCEED...
...IT WON'T BRING YURIKO BACK.

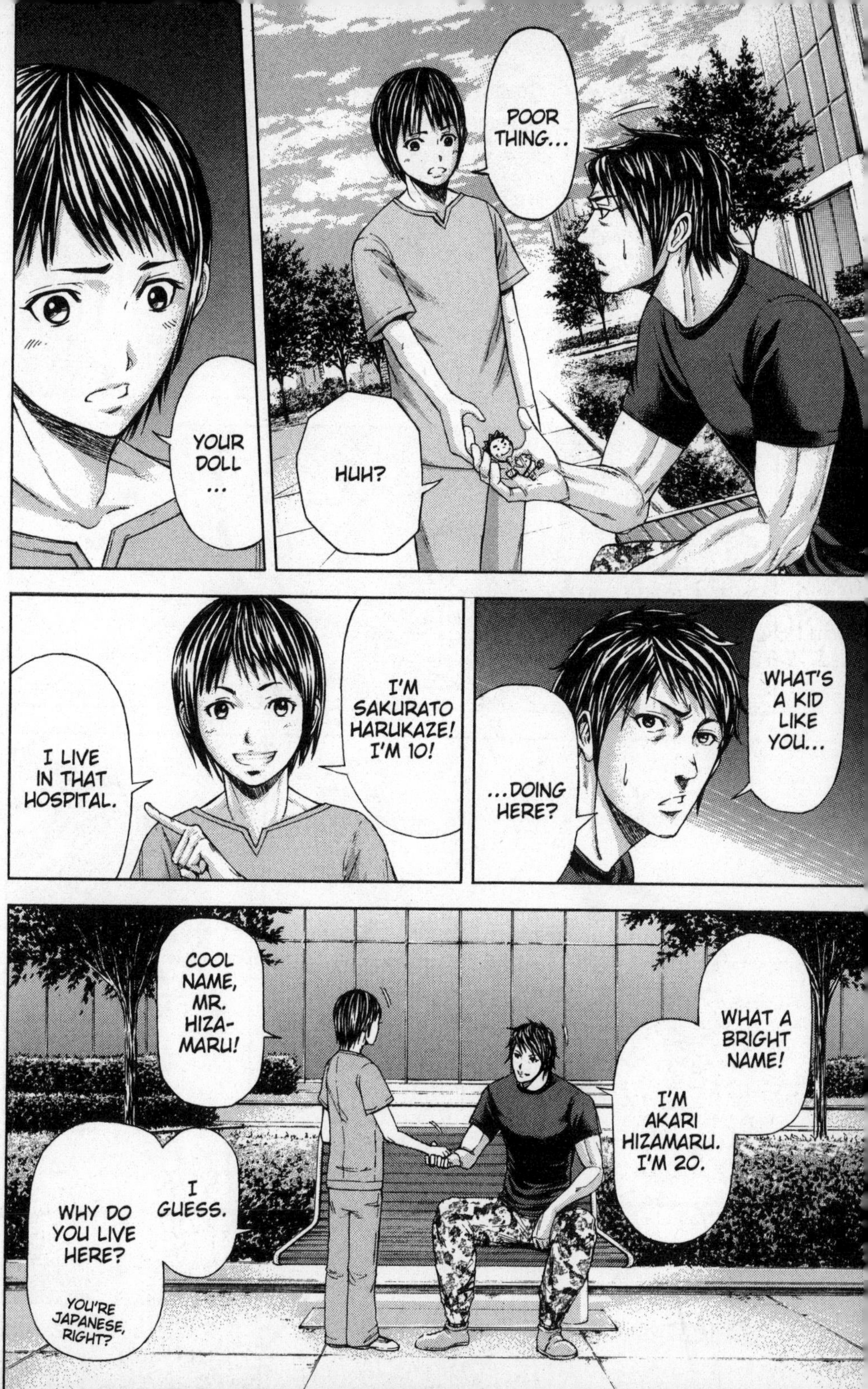
POOR THING...
HUH?
YOUR DOLL ...
WHAT'S A KID LIKE YOU...
...DOING HERE?
I'M SAKURATO HARUKAZE! I'M 10!
I LIVE IN THAT HOSPITAL.
WHAT A BRIGHT NAME!
I'M AKARI HIZAMARU. I'M 20.
COOL NAME, MR. HIZA-MARU!
I GUESS.
WHY DO YOU LIVE HERE?
YOU'RE JAPANESE, RIGHT?

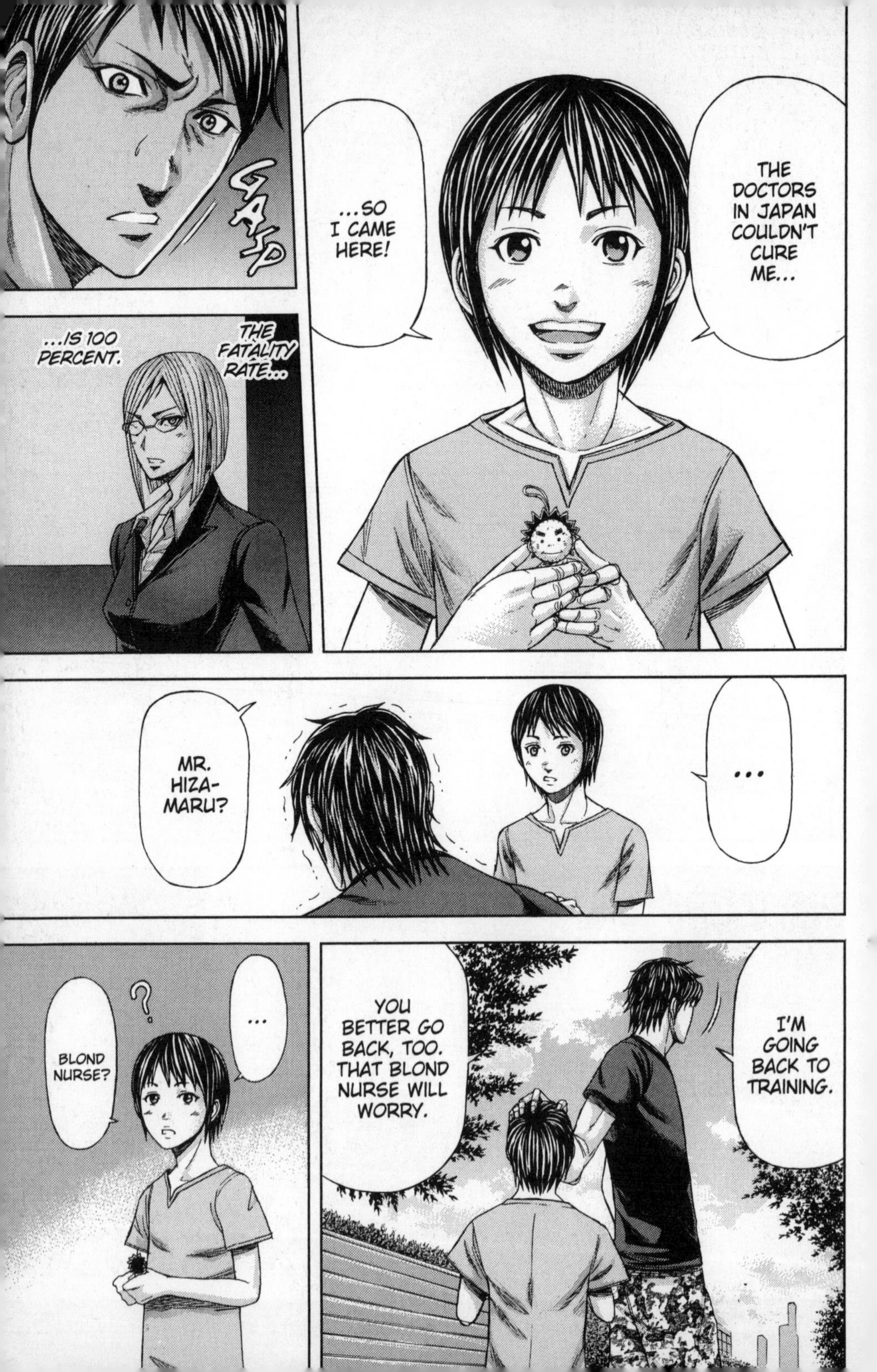
THE DOCTORS IN JAPAN COULDN'T CURE ME...
...SO I CAME HERE!
GASP
THE FATALITY RATE...
...IS 100 PERCENT.
...
MR. HIZA-MARU?
I'M GOING BACK TO TRAINING.
YOU BETTER GO BACK, TOO. THAT BLOND NURSE WILL WORRY.
...
?
BLOND NURSE?

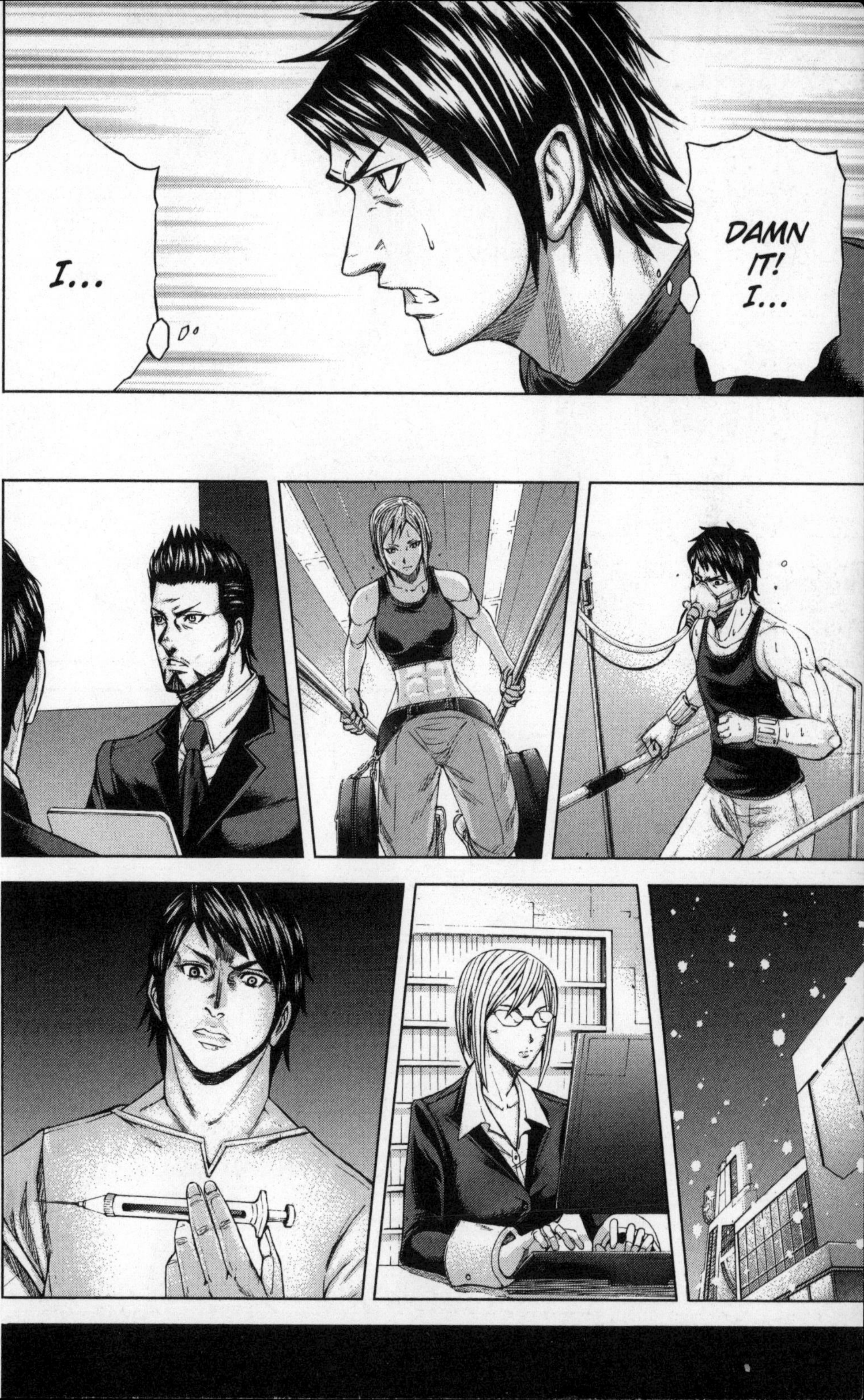
DAMN IT! I...
I...

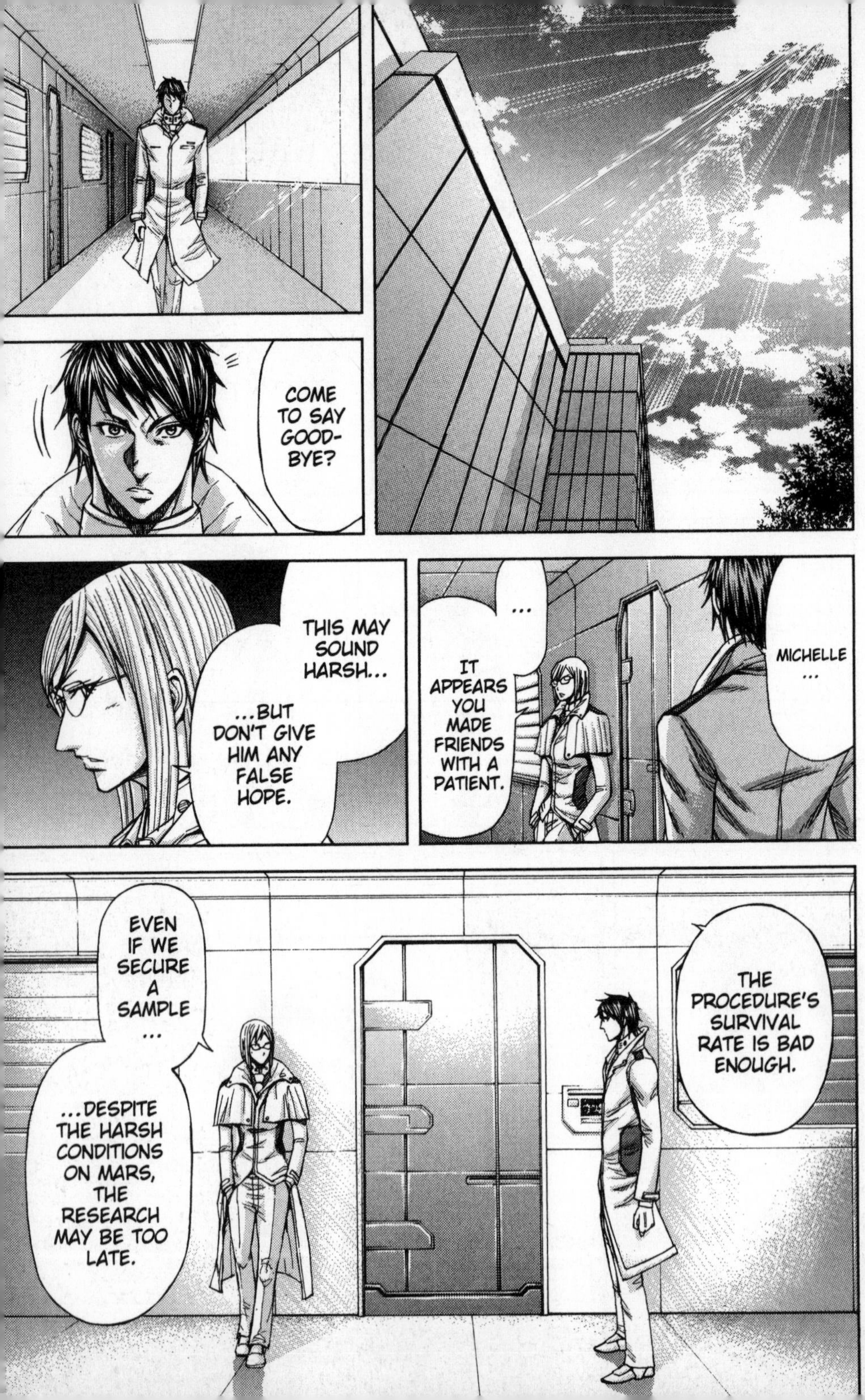
COME TO SAY GOOD-BYE?
MICHELLE ...
...
IT APPEARS YOU MADE FRIENDS WITH A PATIENT.
THIS MAY SOUND HARSH...
...BUT DON'T GIVE HIM ANY FALSE HOPE.
THE PROCEDURE'S SURVIVAL RATE IS BAD ENOUGH.
EVEN IF WE SECURE A SAMPLE ...
...DESPITE THE HARSH CONDITIONS ON MARS, THE RESEARCH MAY BE TOO LATE.

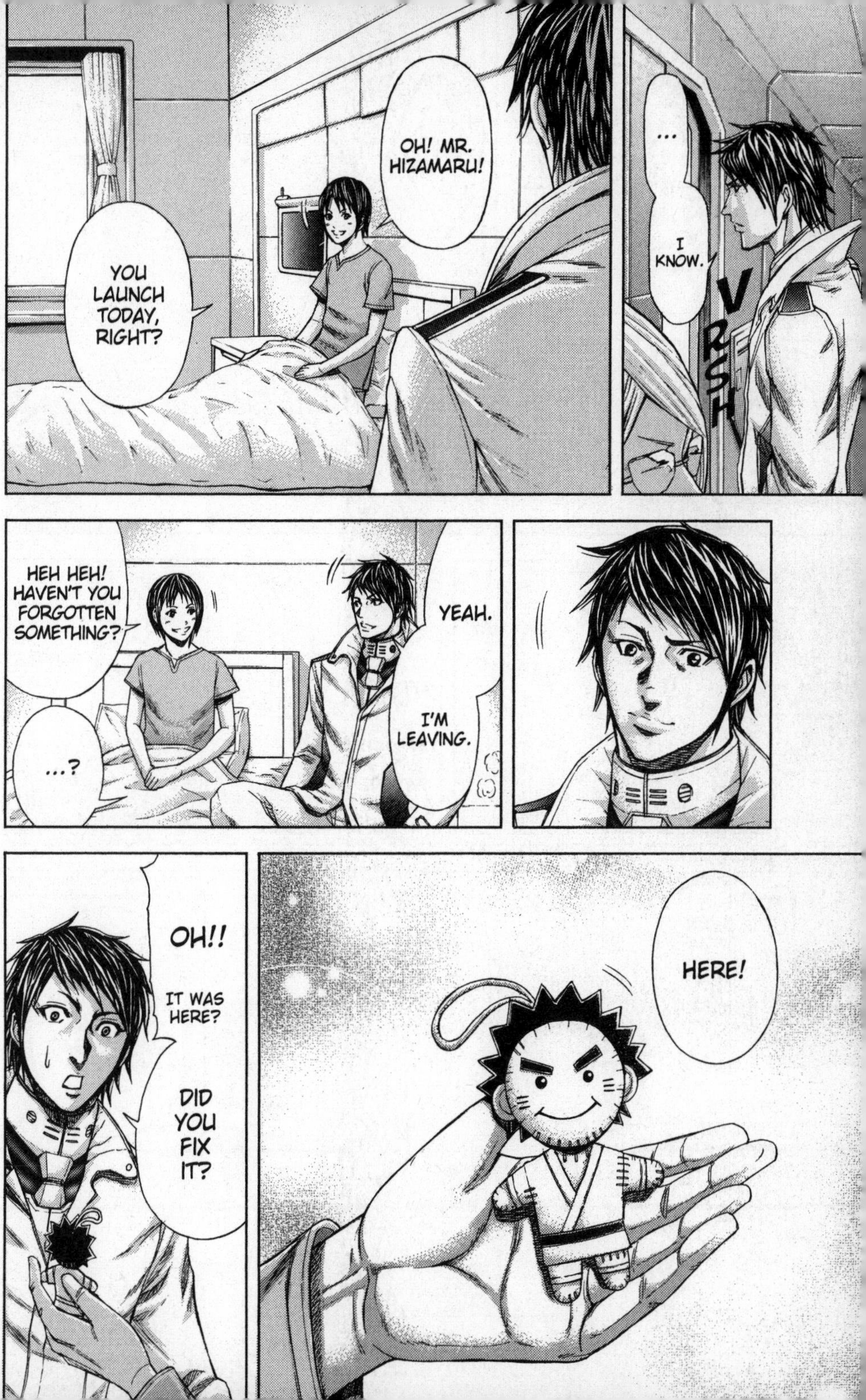
...
I KNOW.
VRSH
OH! MR. HIZAMARU!
YOU LAUNCH TODAY, RIGHT?
YEAH.
I'M LEAVING.
HEH HEH! HAVEN'T YOU FORGOTTEN SOMETHING?
...?
HERE!
OH!!
IT WAS HERE?
DID YOU FIX IT?

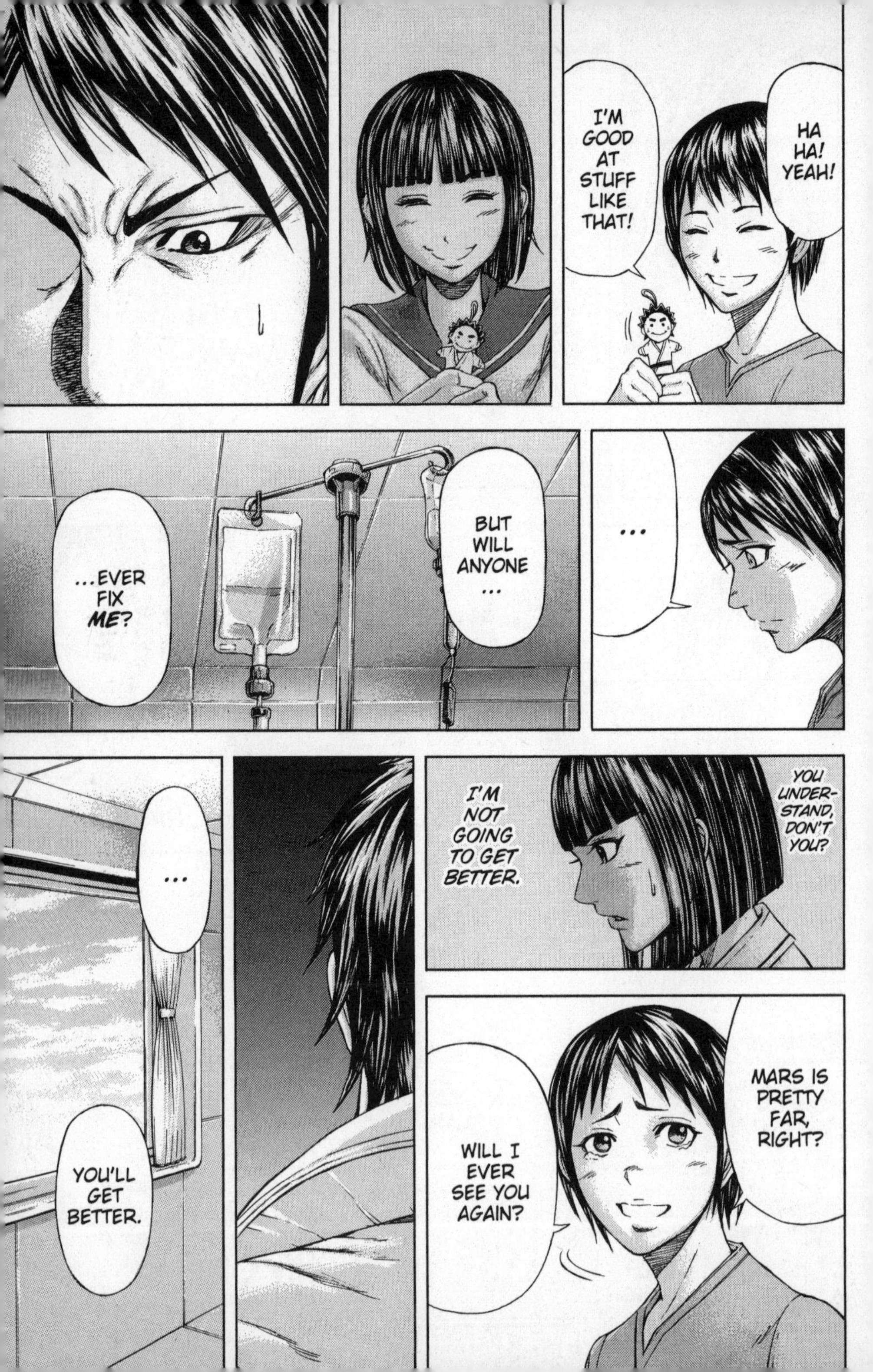
HA HA! YEAH!
I'M GOOD AT STUFF LIKE THAT!
...
BUT WILL ANYONE ...
...EVER FIX *ME*?
YOU UNDERSTAND, DON'T YOU?
I'M NOT GOING TO GET BETTER.
MARS IS PRETTY FAR, RIGHT?
WILL I EVER SEE YOU AGAIN?
...
YOU'LL GET BETTER.

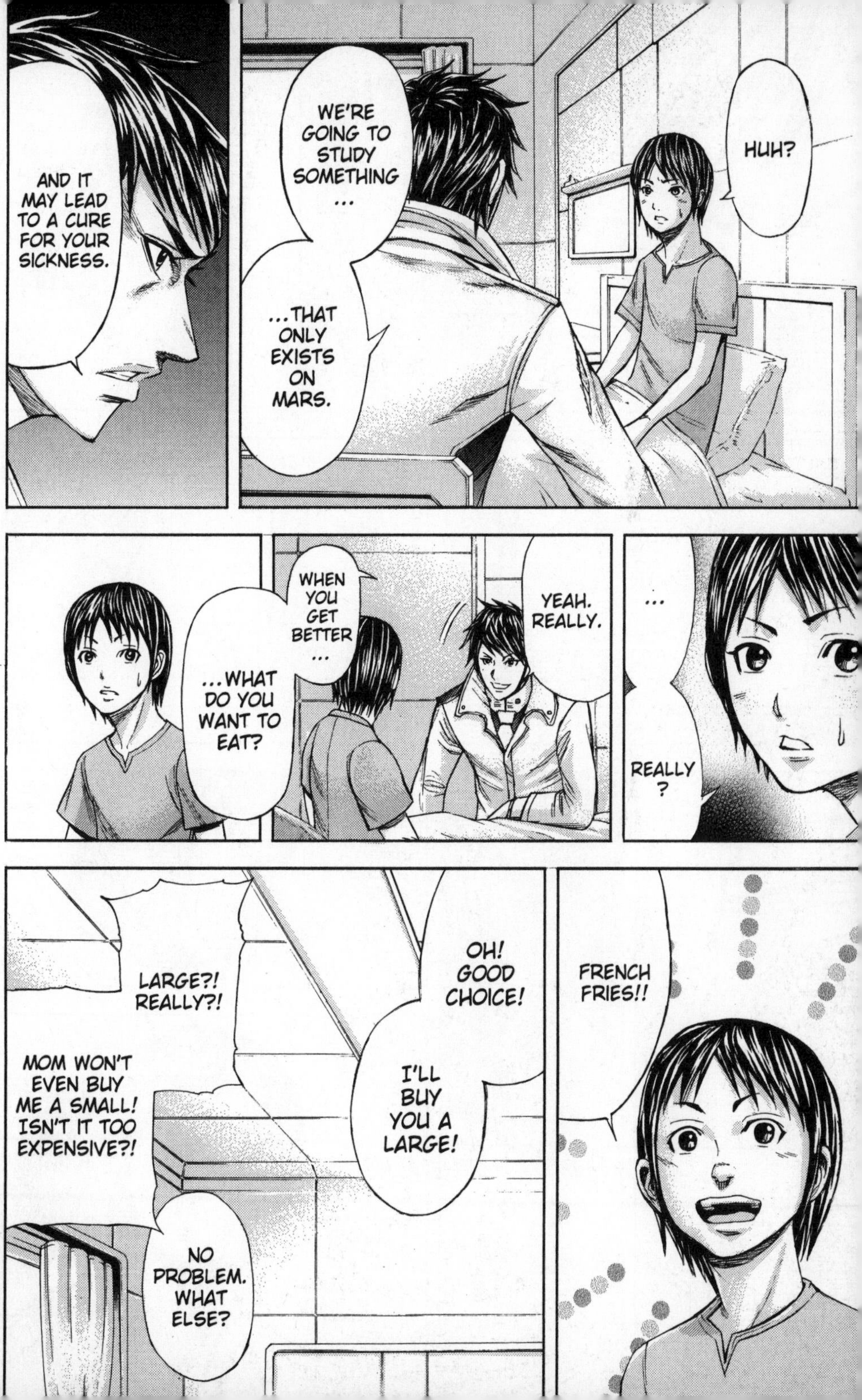
HUH?
WE'RE GOING TO STUDY SOMETHING...
...THAT ONLY EXISTS ON MARS.
AND IT MAY LEAD TO A CURE FOR YOUR SICKNESS.
...
REALLY?
YEAH. REALLY.
WHEN YOU GET BETTER...
...WHAT DO YOU WANT TO EAT?
FRENCH FRIES!!
OH! GOOD CHOICE!
I'LL BUY YOU A LARGE!
LARGE?! REALLY?!
MOM WON'T EVEN BUY ME A SMALL! ISN'T IT TOO EXPENSIVE?!
NO PROBLEM. WHAT ELSE?

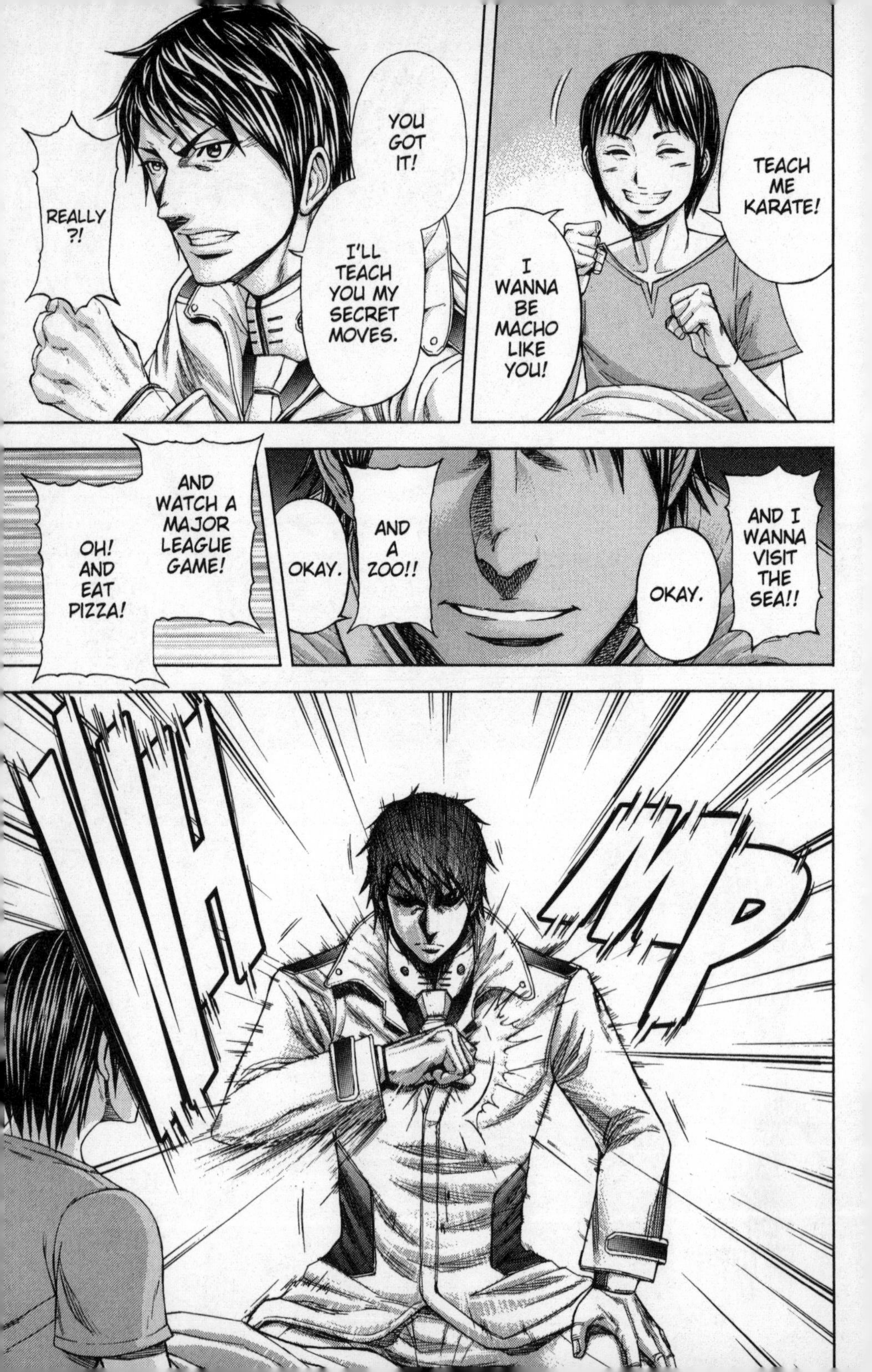
TEACH ME KARATE!
I WANNA BE MACHO LIKE YOU!
YOU GOT IT!
I'LL TEACH YOU MY SECRET MOVES.
REALLY ?!
AND I WANNA VISIT THE SEA!!
OKAY.
AND A ZOO!!
OKAY.
AND WATCH A MAJOR LEAGUE GAME!
OH! AND EAT PIZZA!
WH
MP

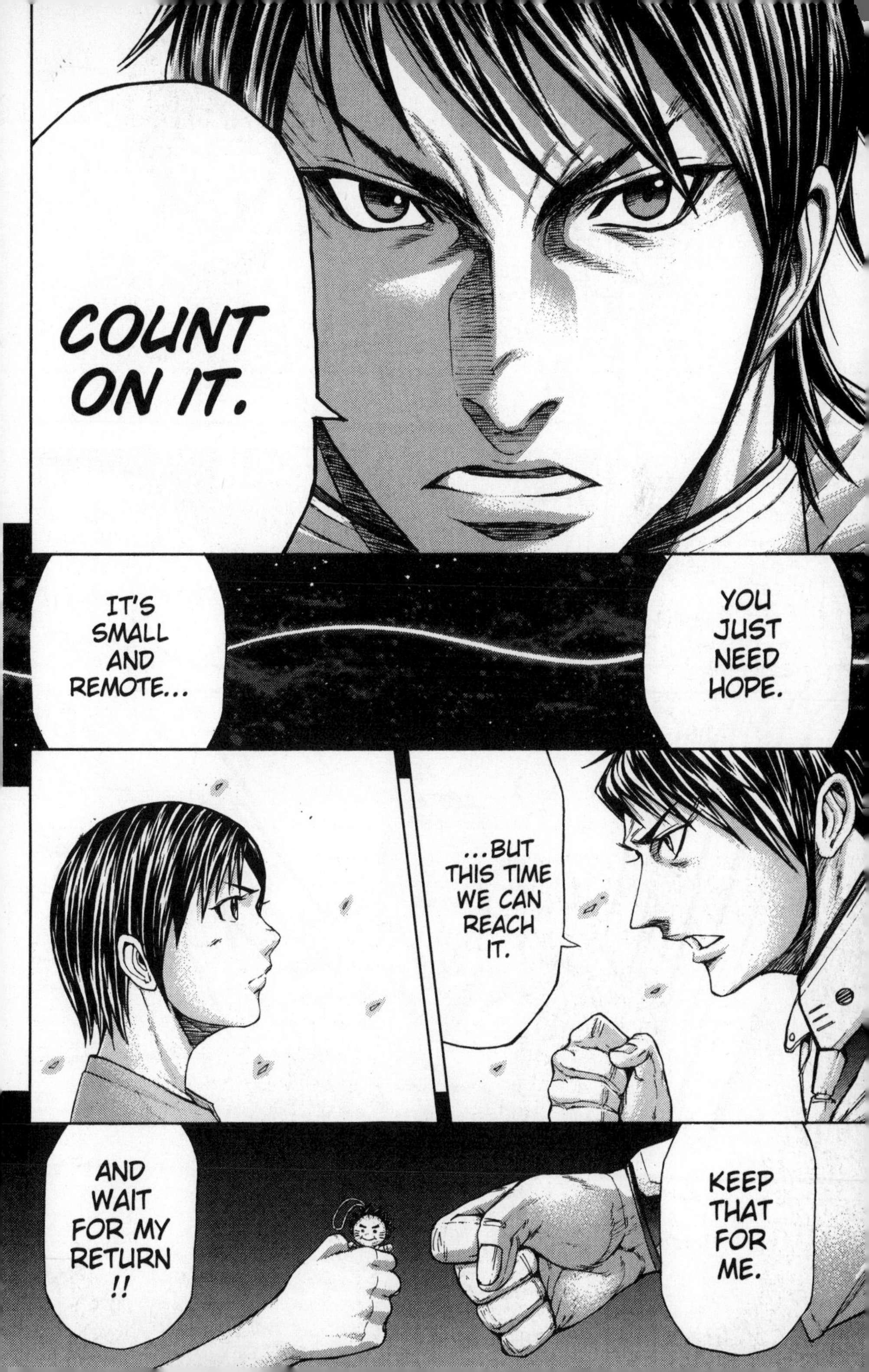
COUNT ON IT.
YOU JUST NEED HOPE.
IT'S SMALL AND REMOTE...
...BUT THIS TIME WE CAN REACH IT.
KEEP THAT FOR ME.
AND WAIT FOR MY RETURN!!

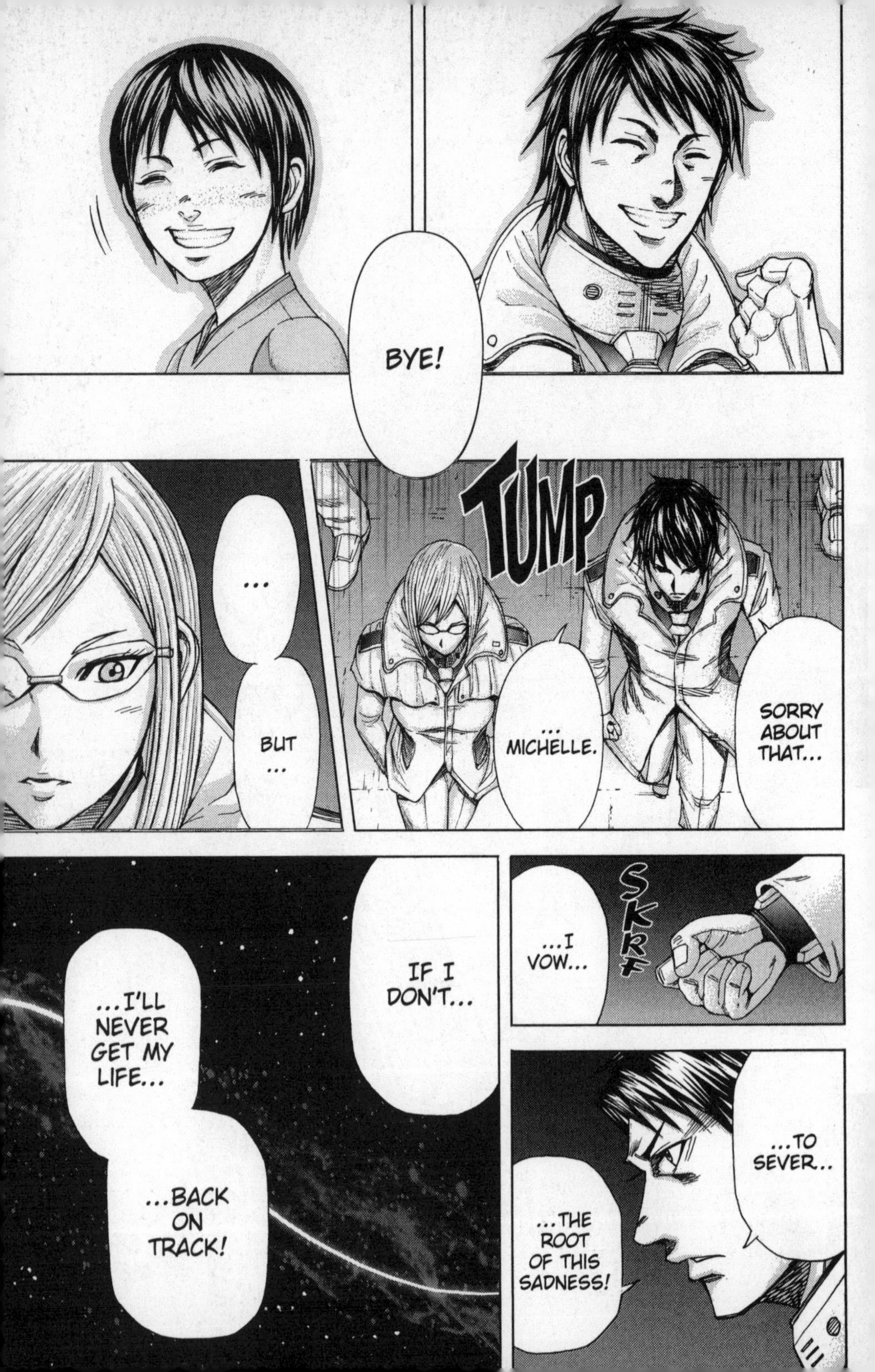
BYE!
TUMP
SORRY ABOUT THAT...
...MICHELLE.
...
BUT ...
SKRF
...I VOW...
...TO SEVER...
...THE ROOT OF THIS SADNESS!
IF I DON'T...
...I'LL NEVER GET MY LIFE...
...BACK ON TRACK!

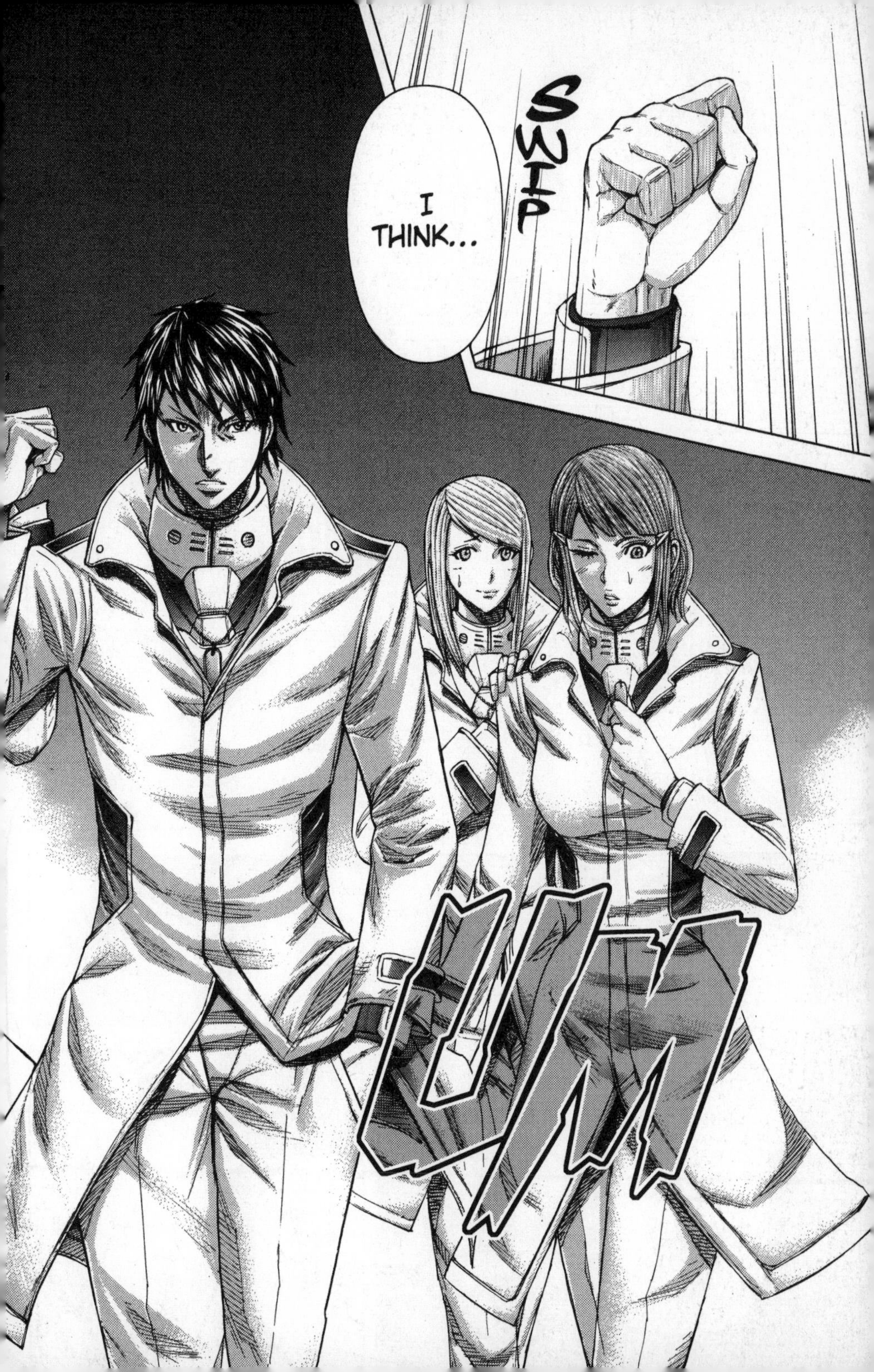
SWIP
I THINK...
UM

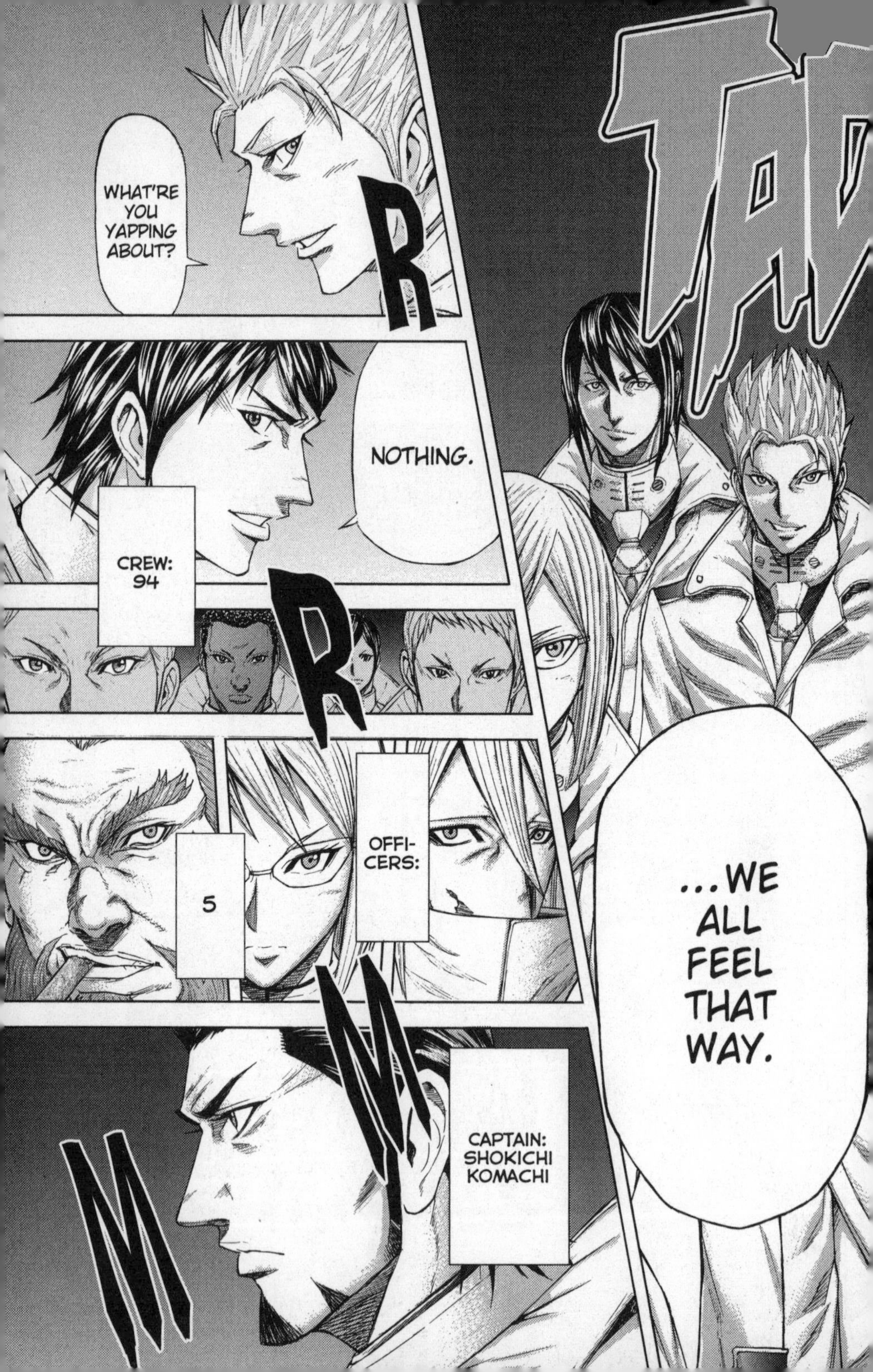
TA
...WE ALL FEEL THAT WAY.
WHAT'RE YOU YAPPING ABOUT?
R
NOTHING.
CREW: 94
R
OFFI-CERS:
5
M
M
CAPTAIN: SHOKICHI KOMACHI

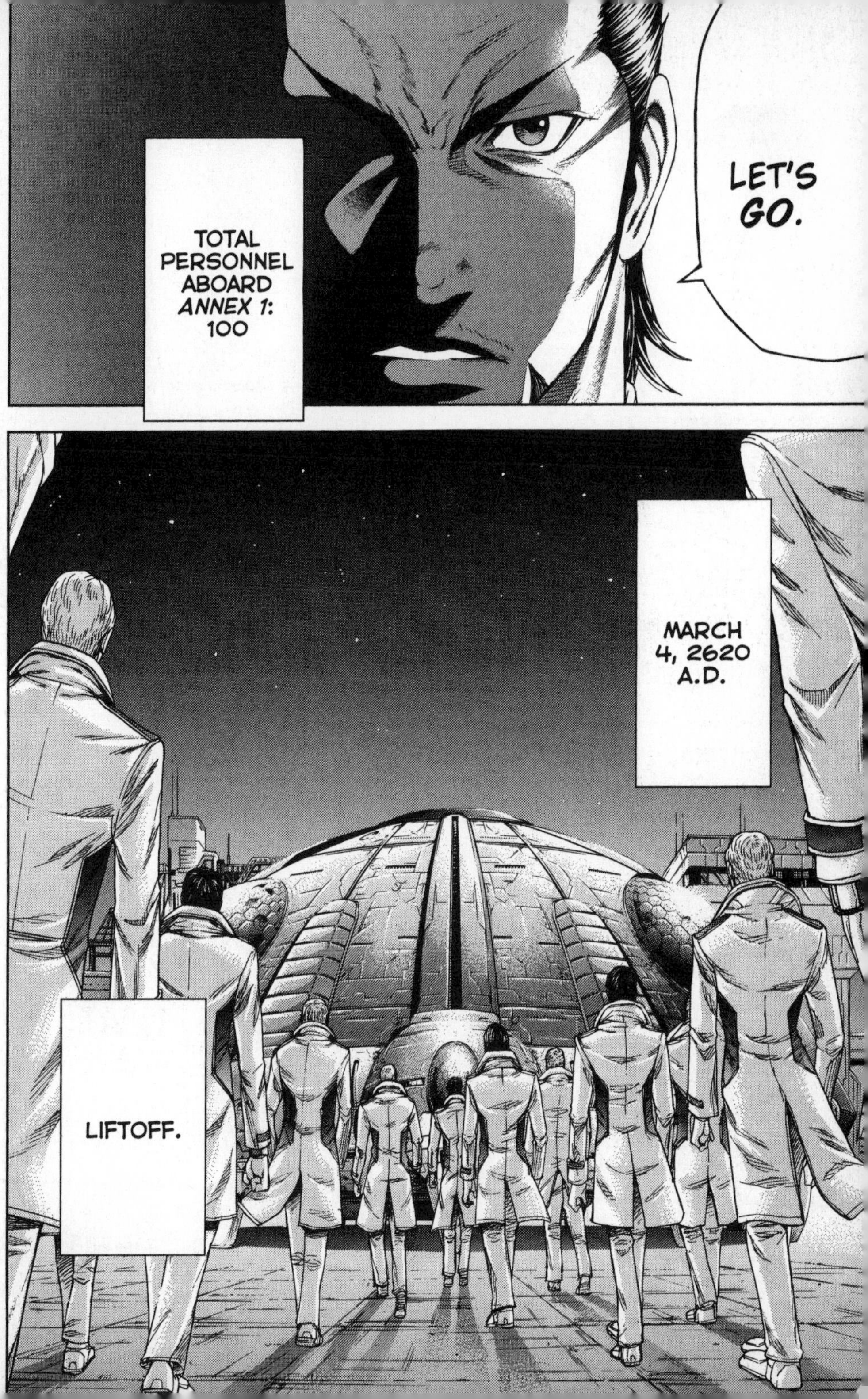
LET'S GO.
TOTAL PERSONNEL ABOARD *ANNEX 1:* 100
MARCH 4, 2620 A.D.
LIFTOFF.

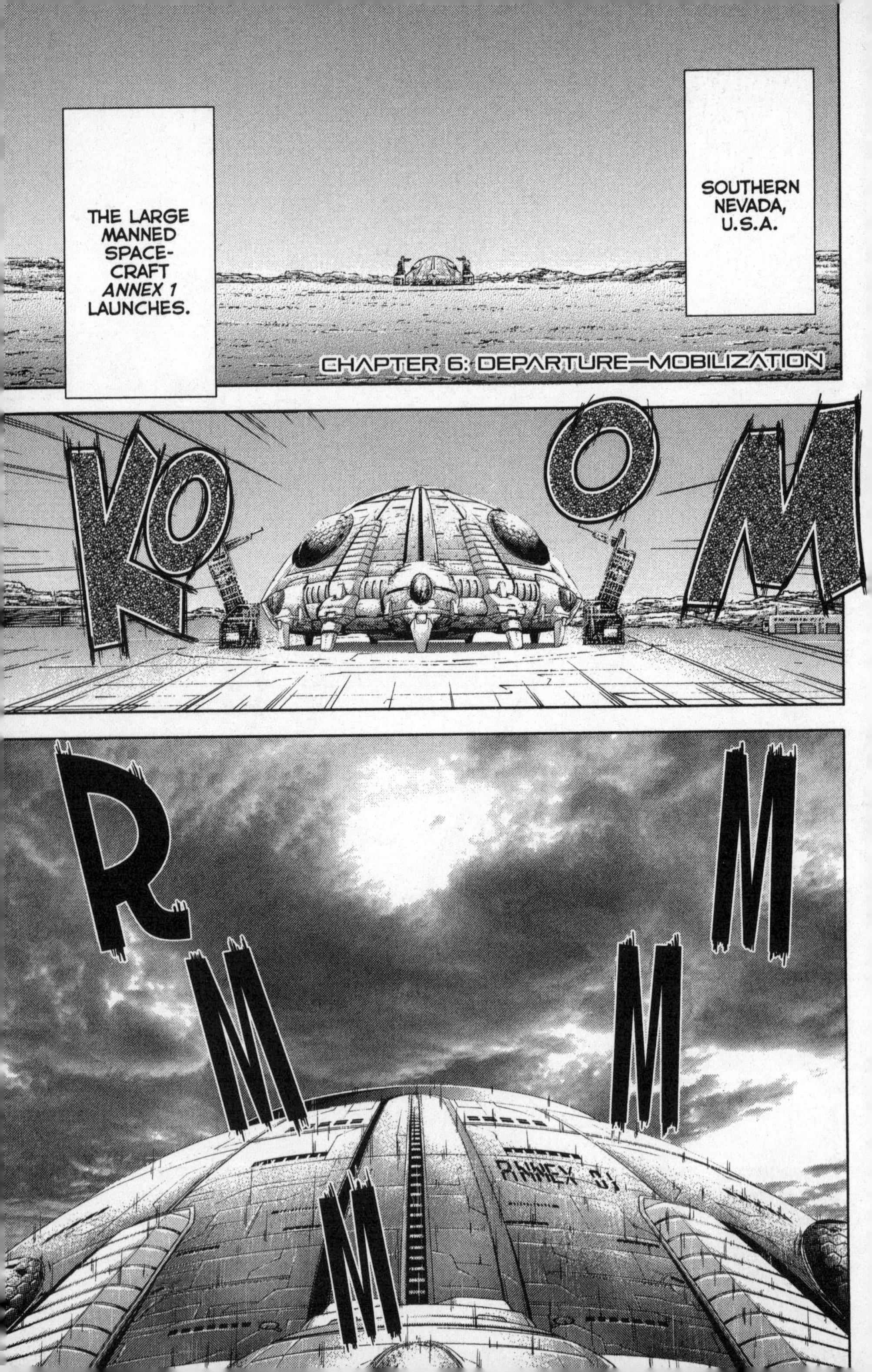
SOUTHERN NEVADA, U.S.A.
THE LARGE MANNED SPACE-CRAFT *ANNEX 1* LAUNCHES.
CHAPTER 6: DEPARTURE—MOBILIZATION
KOOM
RMMMM

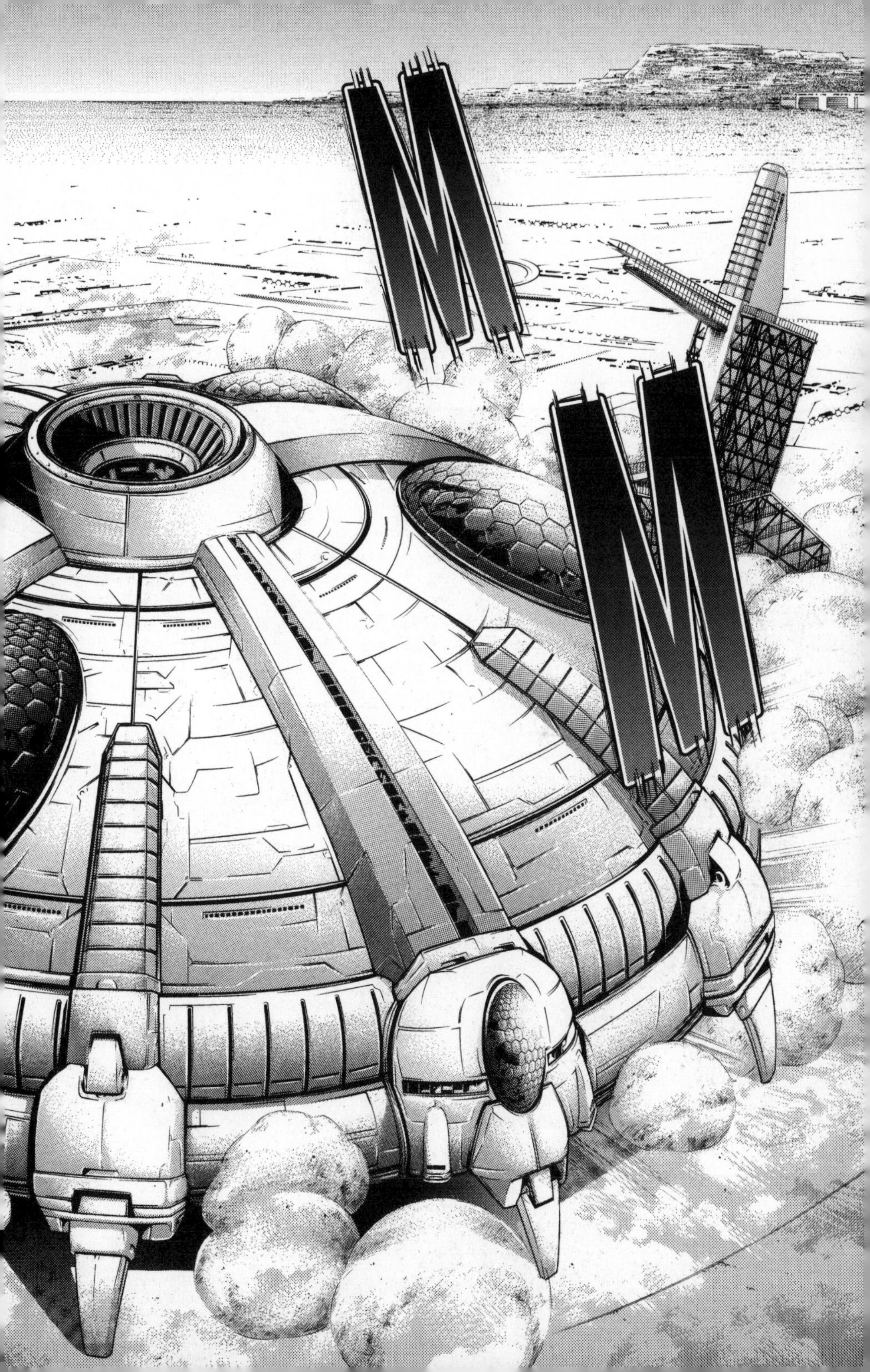

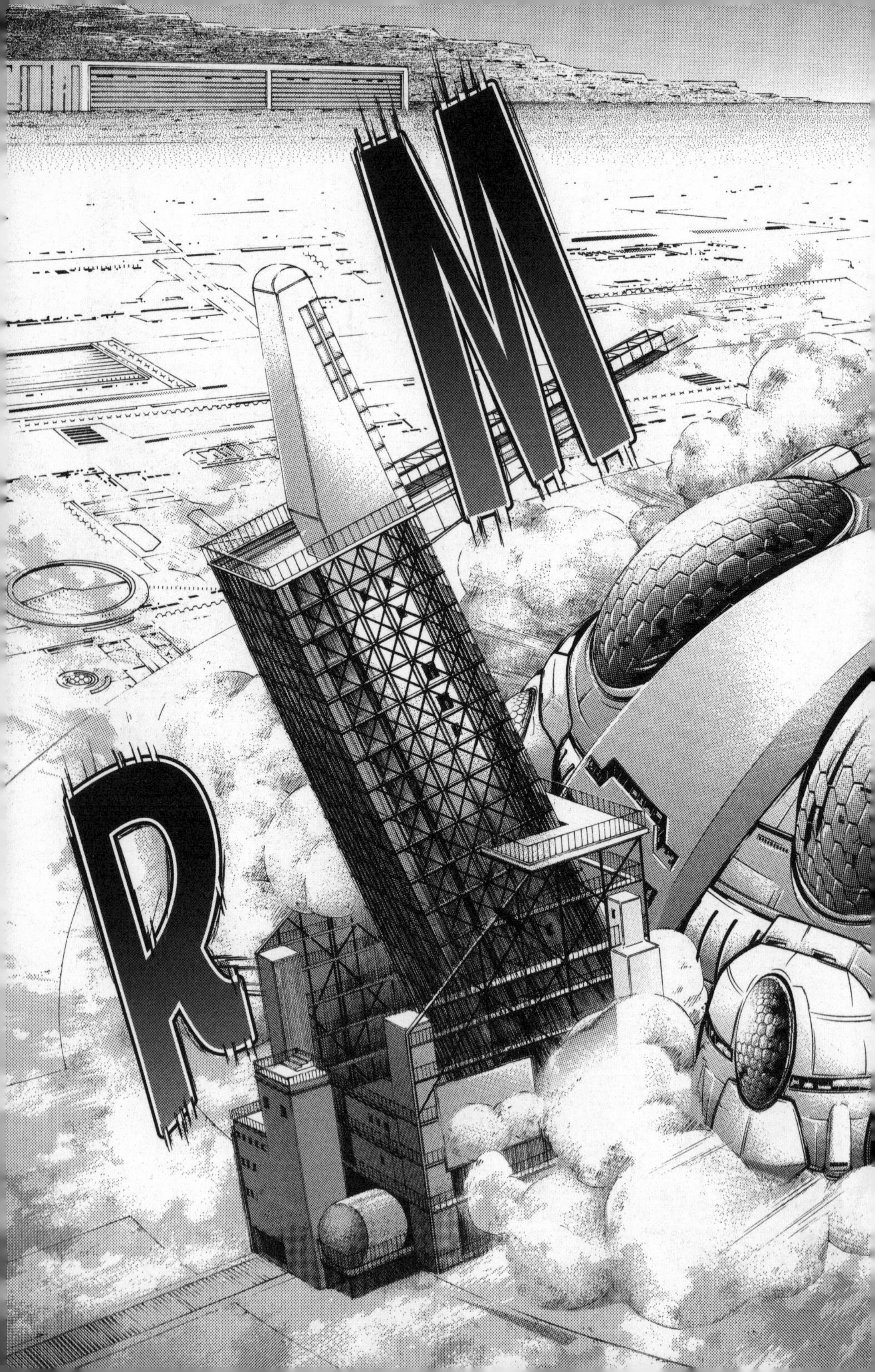
RM

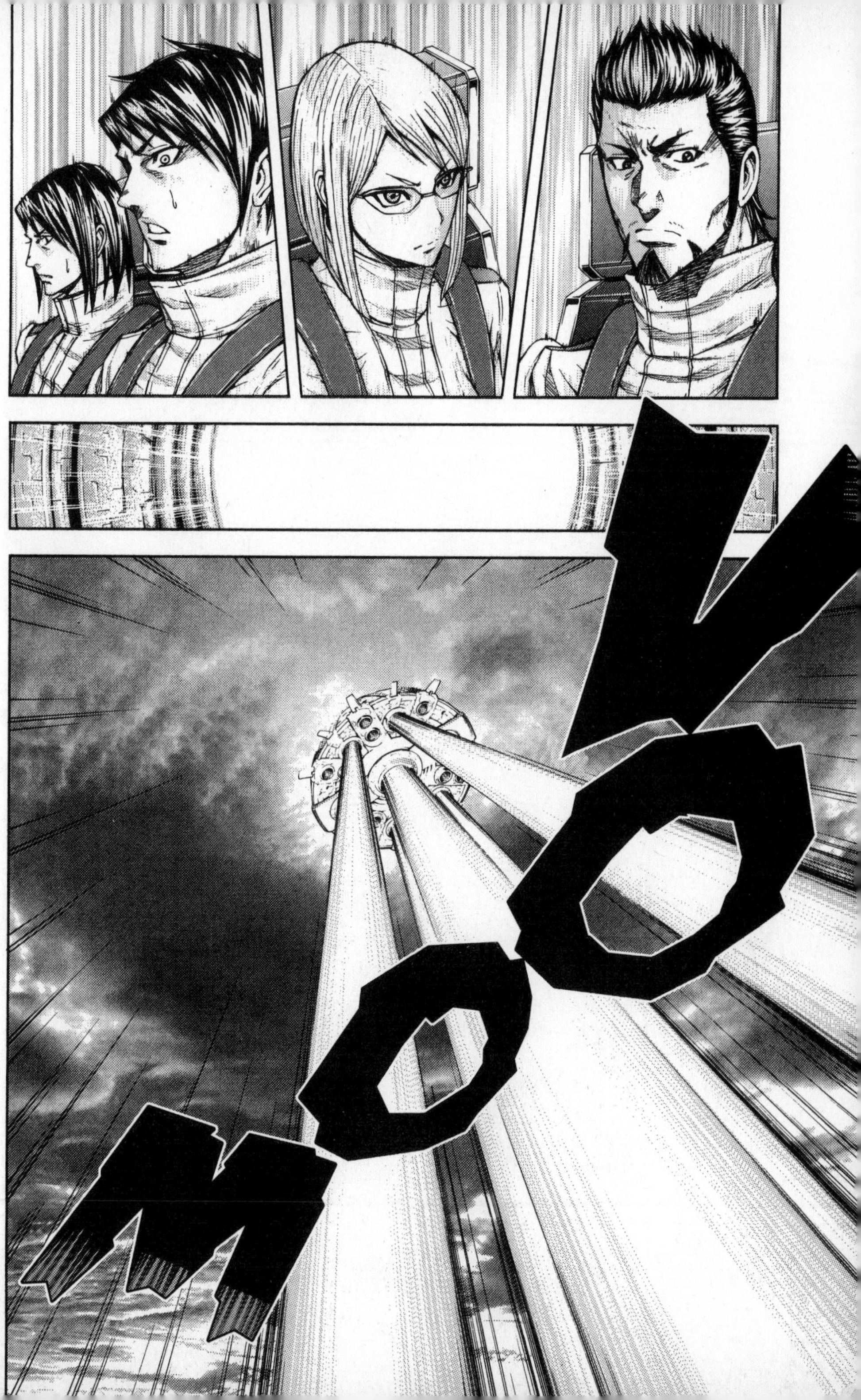
WOOM

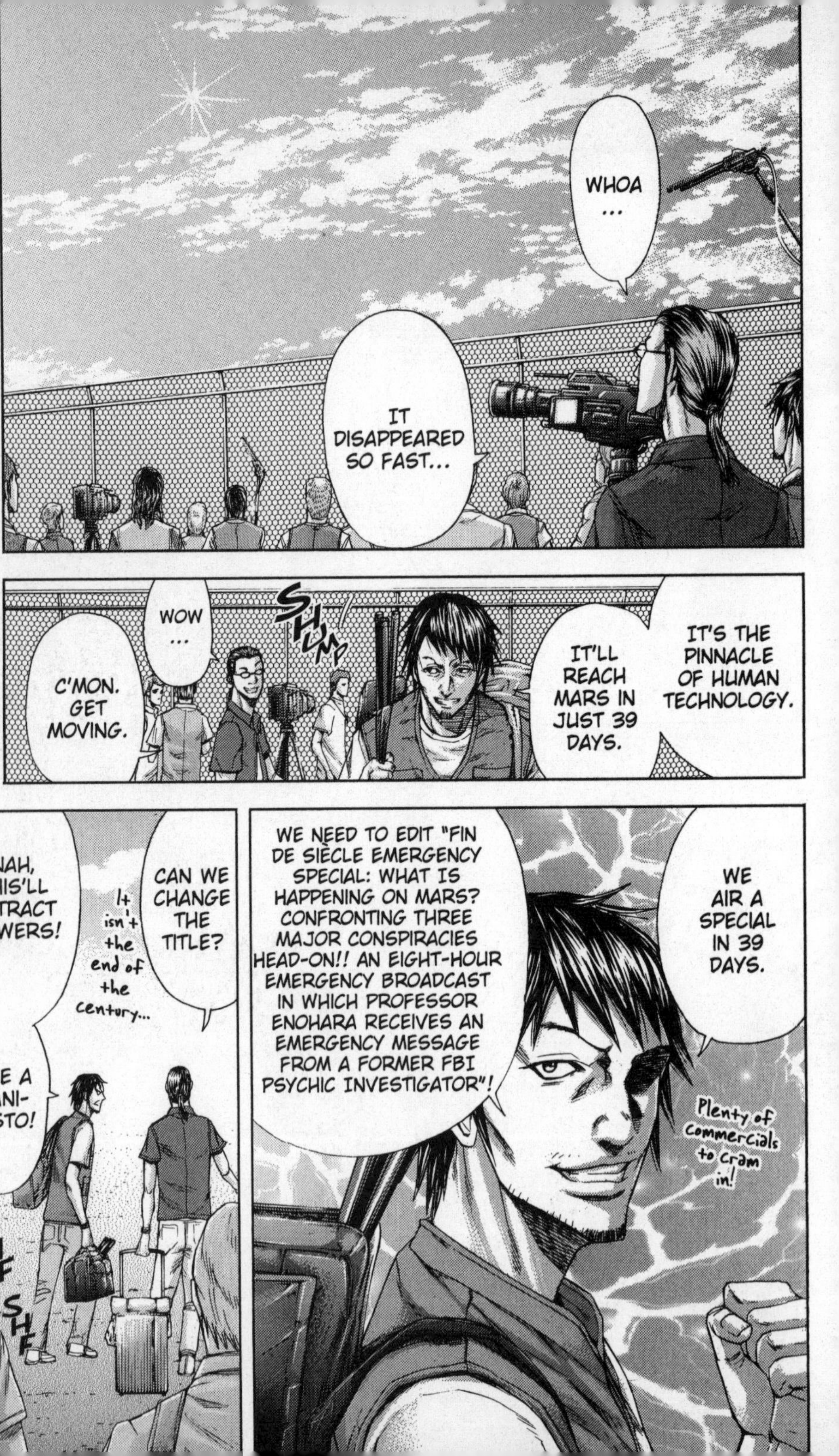
WHOA ...
IT DISAPPEARED SO FAST...
IT'S THE PINNACLE OF HUMAN TECHNOLOGY.
IT'LL REACH MARS IN JUST 39 DAYS.
SHUMP
WOW ...
C'MON. GET MOVING.
WE AIR A SPECIAL IN 39 DAYS.
WE NEED TO EDIT "FIN DE SIÈCLE EMERGENCY SPECIAL: WHAT IS HAPPENING ON MARS? CONFRONTING THREE MAJOR CONSPIRACIES HEAD-ON!! AN EIGHT-HOUR EMERGENCY BROADCAST IN WHICH PROFESSOR ENOHARA RECEIVES AN EMERGENCY MESSAGE FROM A FORMER FBI PSYCHIC INVESTIGATOR"!
Plenty of commercials to cram in!
CAN WE CHANGE THE TITLE?
It isn't the end of the century...
NAH, THIS'LL ATTRACT VIEWERS!
LIKE A MANI-FESTO!
SHF
SHF

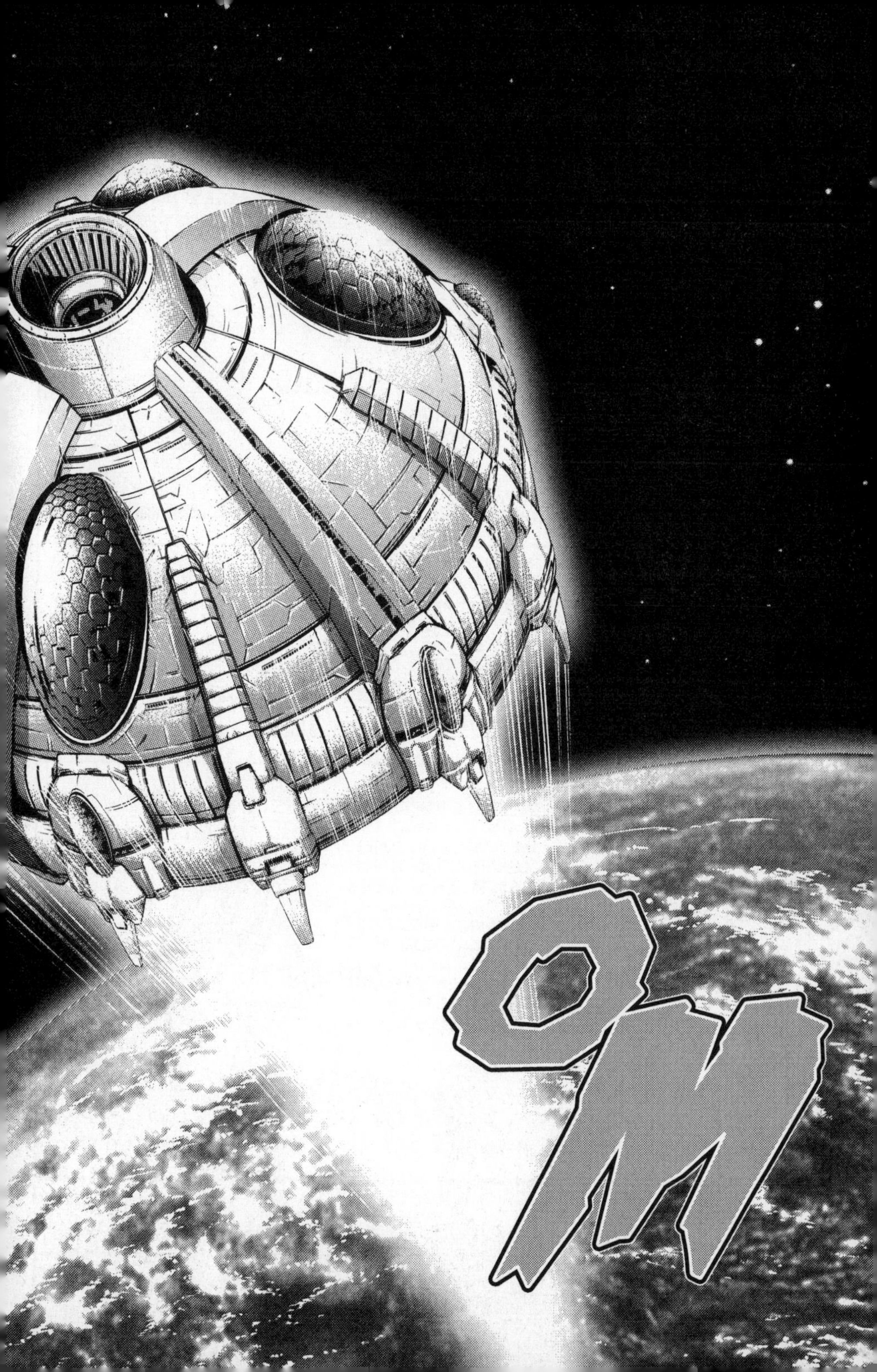

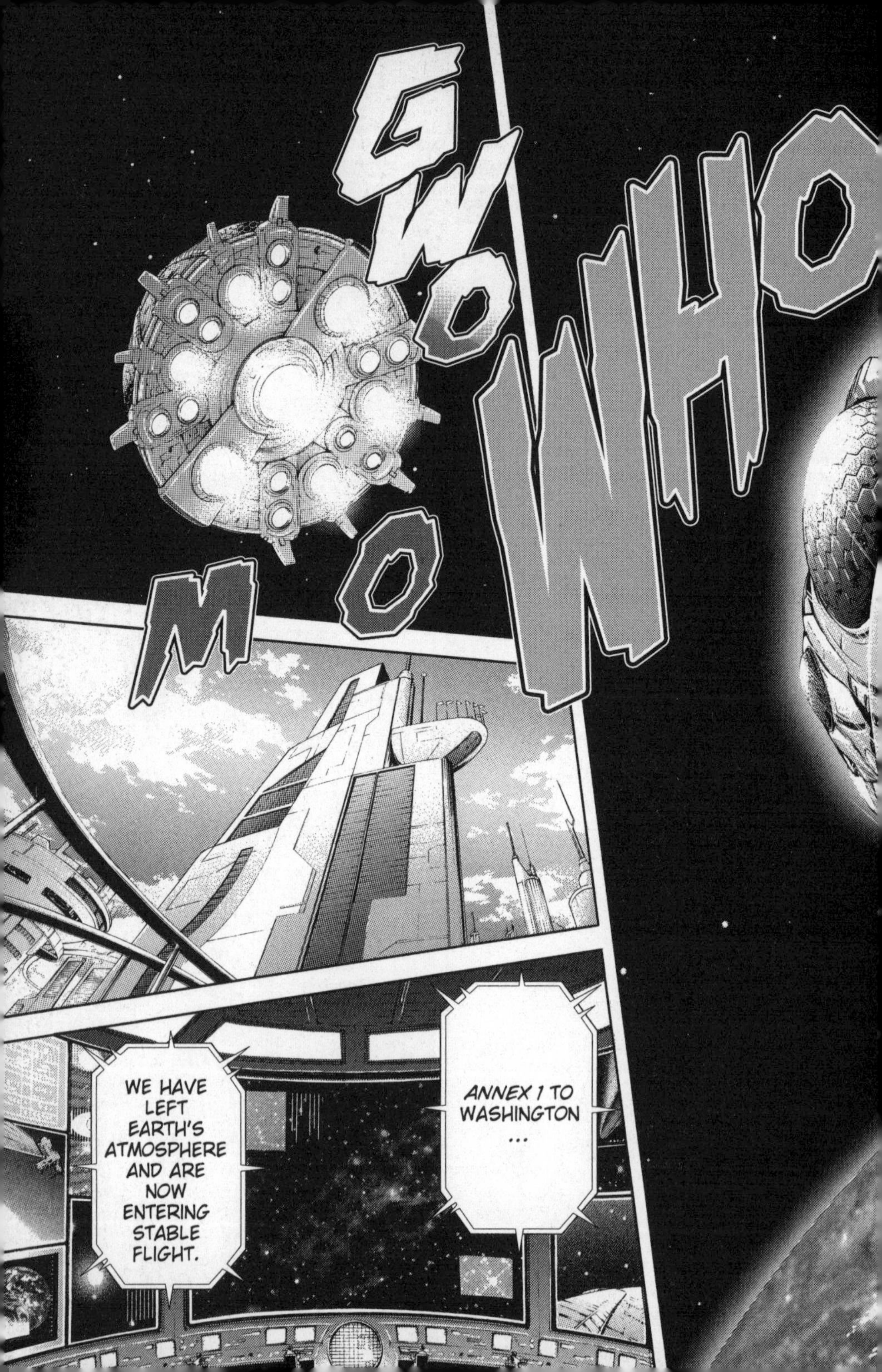
WHO
GWOOM
ANNEX 1 TO WASHINGTON ...
WE HAVE LEFT EARTH'S ATMOSPHERE AND ARE NOW ENTERING STABLE FLIGHT.

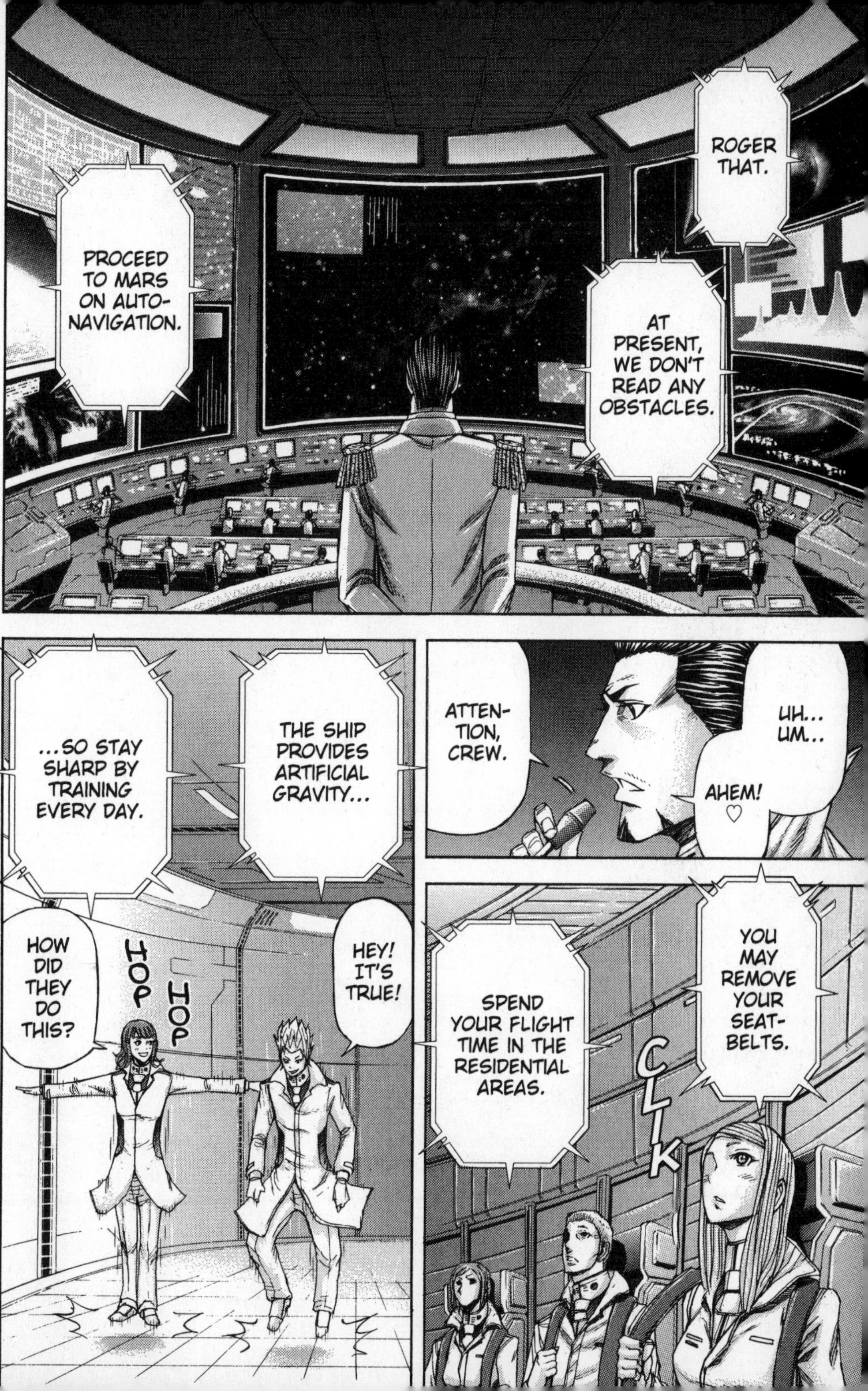
ROGER THAT.
AT PRESENT, WE DON'T READ ANY OBSTACLES.
PROCEED TO MARS ON AUTO-NAVIGATION.
UH... UM...
AHEM! ♡
ATTEN-TION, CREW.
THE SHIP PROVIDES ARTIFICIAL GRAVITY...
...SO STAY SHARP BY TRAINING EVERY DAY.
YOU MAY REMOVE YOUR SEAT-BELTS.
CLIK
SPEND YOUR FLIGHT TIME IN THE RESIDENTIAL AREAS.
HEY! IT'S TRUE!
HOP HOP
HOW DID THEY DO THIS?

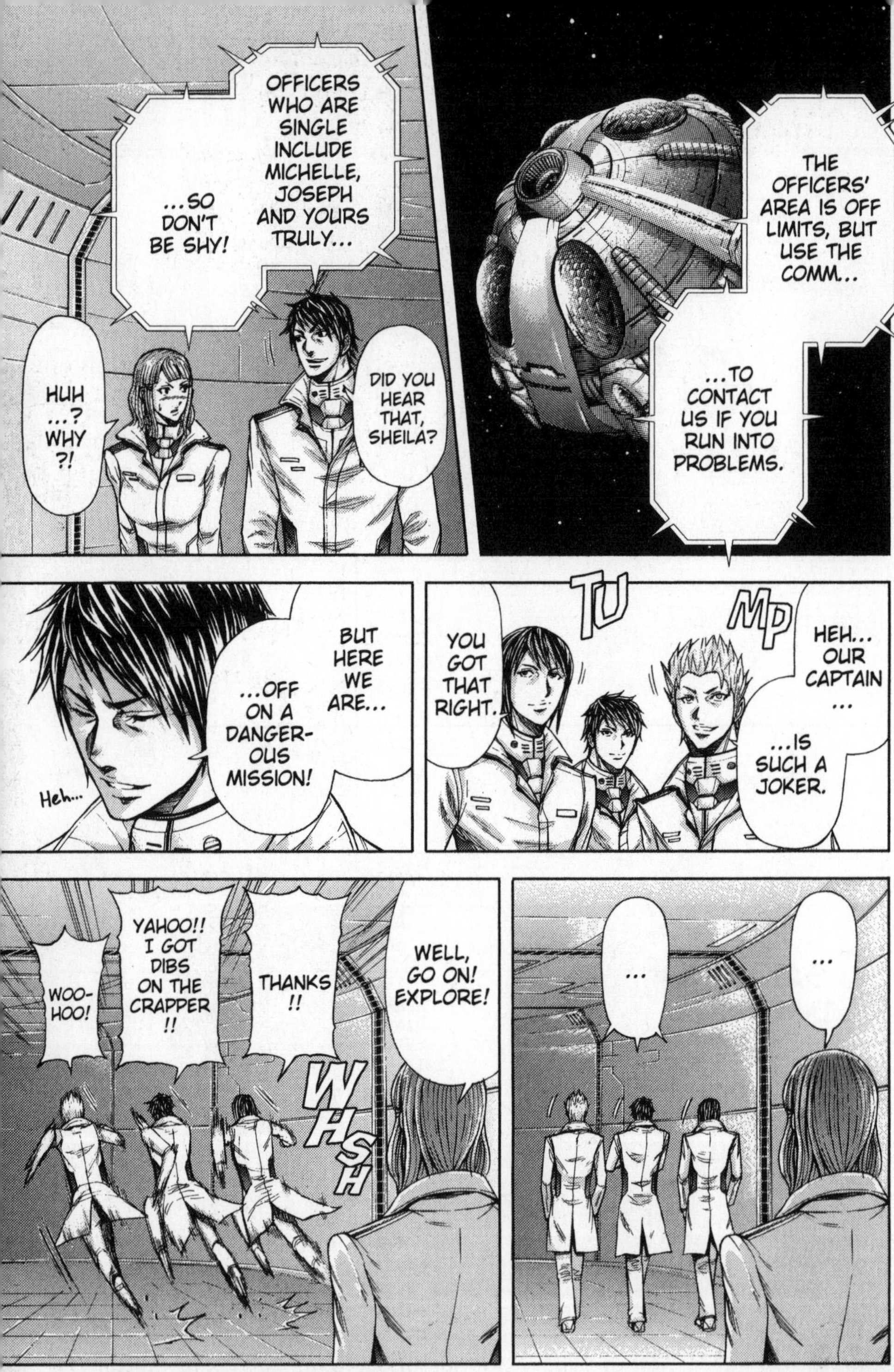
THE OFFICERS' AREA IS OFF LIMITS, BUT USE THE COMM...
...TO CONTACT US IF YOU RUN INTO PROBLEMS.
OFFICERS WHO ARE SINGLE INCLUDE MICHELLE, JOSEPH AND YOURS TRULY...
...SO DON'T BE SHY!
DID YOU HEAR THAT, SHEILA?
HUH...? WHY?!
HEH... OUR CAPTAIN...
...IS SUCH A JOKER.
YOU GOT THAT RIGHT.
TU
MP
BUT HERE WE ARE...
...OFF ON A DANGER-OUS MISSION!
Heh...
...
...
WELL, GO ON! EXPLORE!
THANKS!!
YAHOO!! I GOT DIBS ON THE CRAPPER!!
WOO-HOO!
WHSH

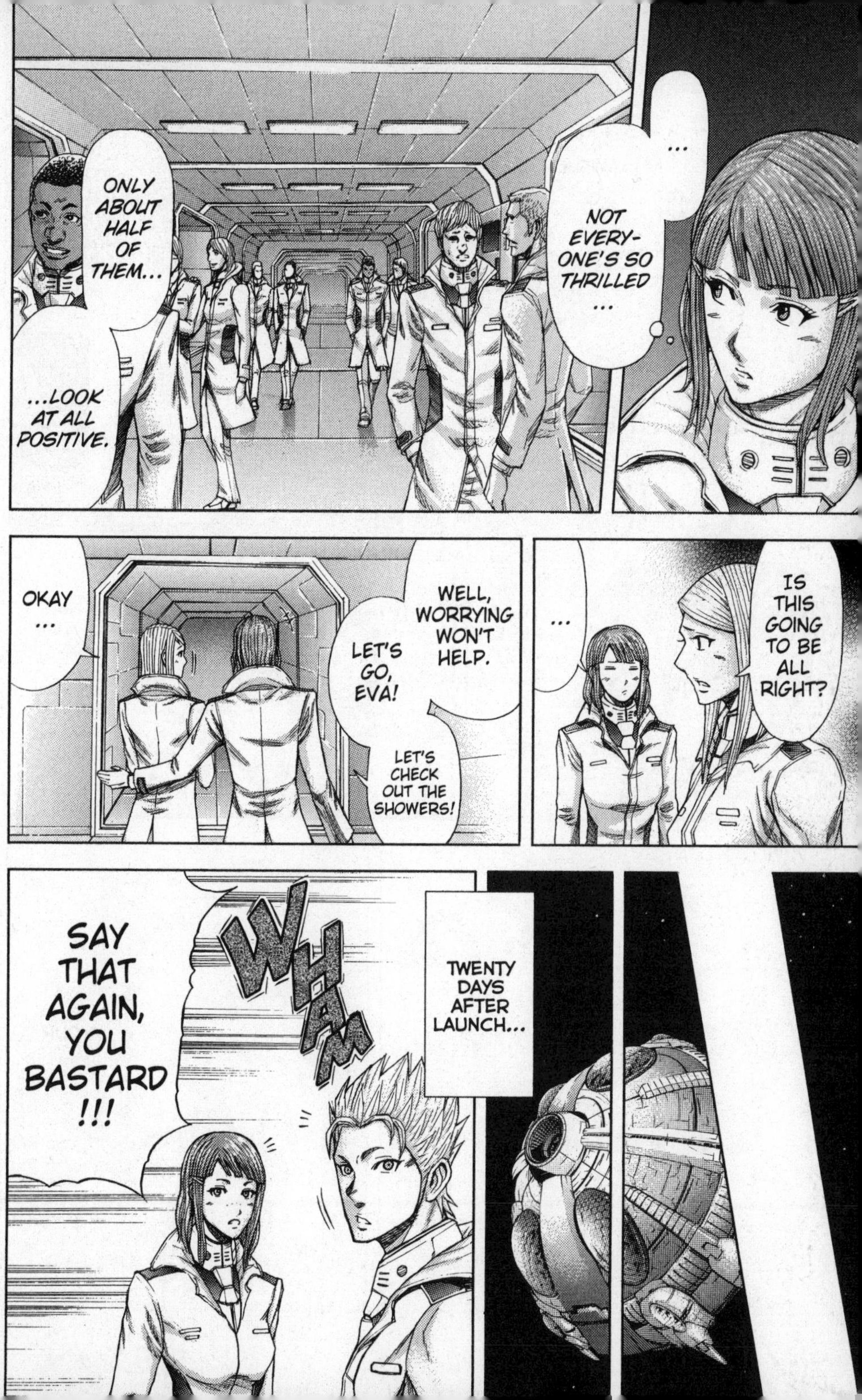
...
NOT EVERY-ONE'S SO THRILLED ...
ONLY ABOUT HALF OF THEM...
...LOOK AT ALL POSITIVE.
IS THIS GOING TO BE ALL RIGHT?
...
WELL, WORRYING WON'T HELP.
LET'S GO, EVA!
LET'S CHECK OUT THE SHOWERS!
OKAY ...
TWENTY DAYS AFTER LAUNCH...
WHAM
SAY THAT AGAIN, YOU BASTARD !!!

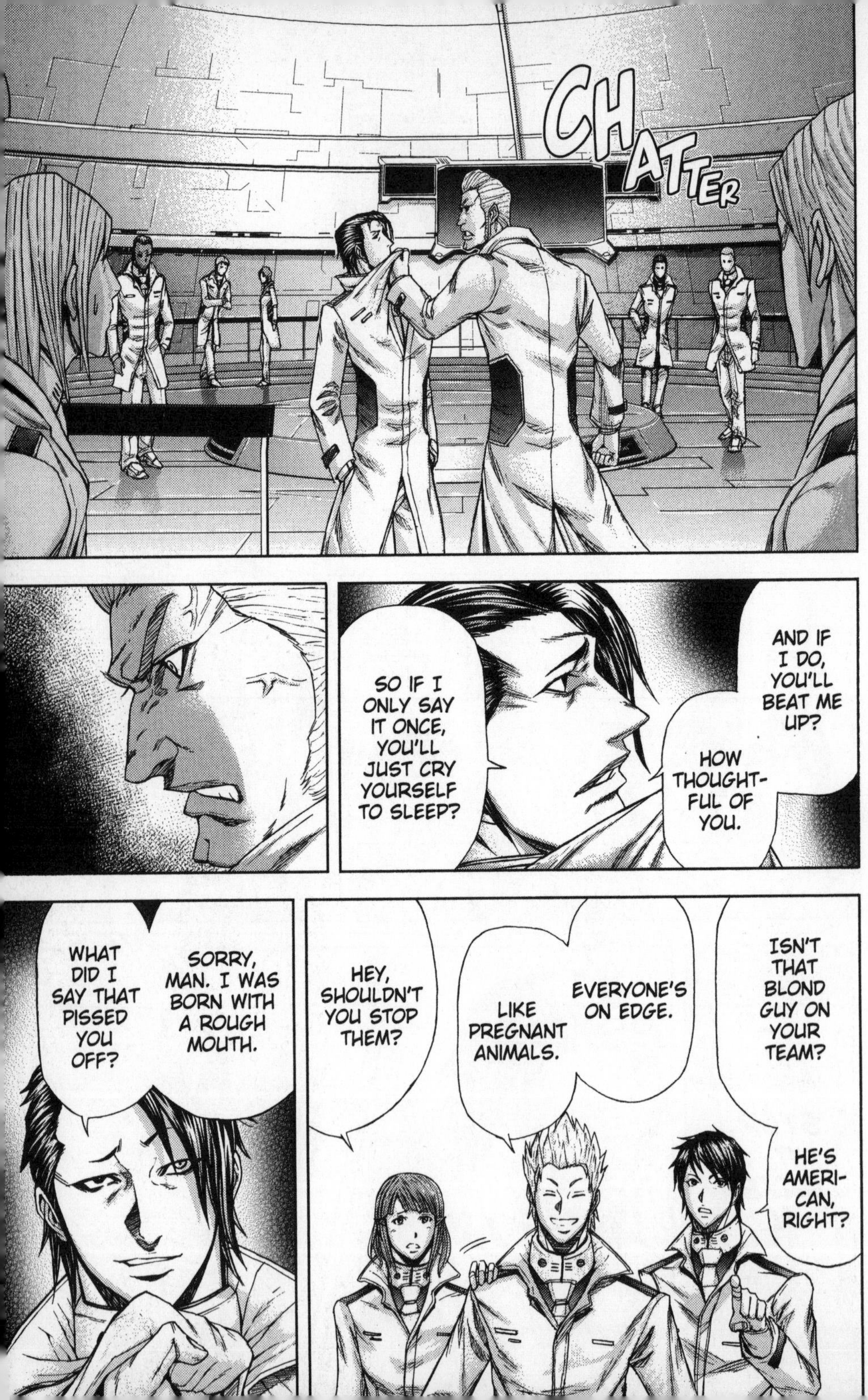
CHATTER
AND IF I DO, YOU'LL BEAT ME UP?
HOW THOUGHT-FUL OF YOU.
SO IF I ONLY SAY IT ONCE, YOU'LL JUST CRY YOURSELF TO SLEEP?
ISN'T THAT BLOND GUY ON YOUR TEAM?
EVERYONE'S ON EDGE.
LIKE PREGNANT ANIMALS.
HEY, SHOULDN'T YOU STOP THEM?
HE'S AMERI-CAN, RIGHT?
SORRY, MAN. I WAS BORN WITH A ROUGH MOUTH.
WHAT DID I SAY THAT PISSED YOU OFF?

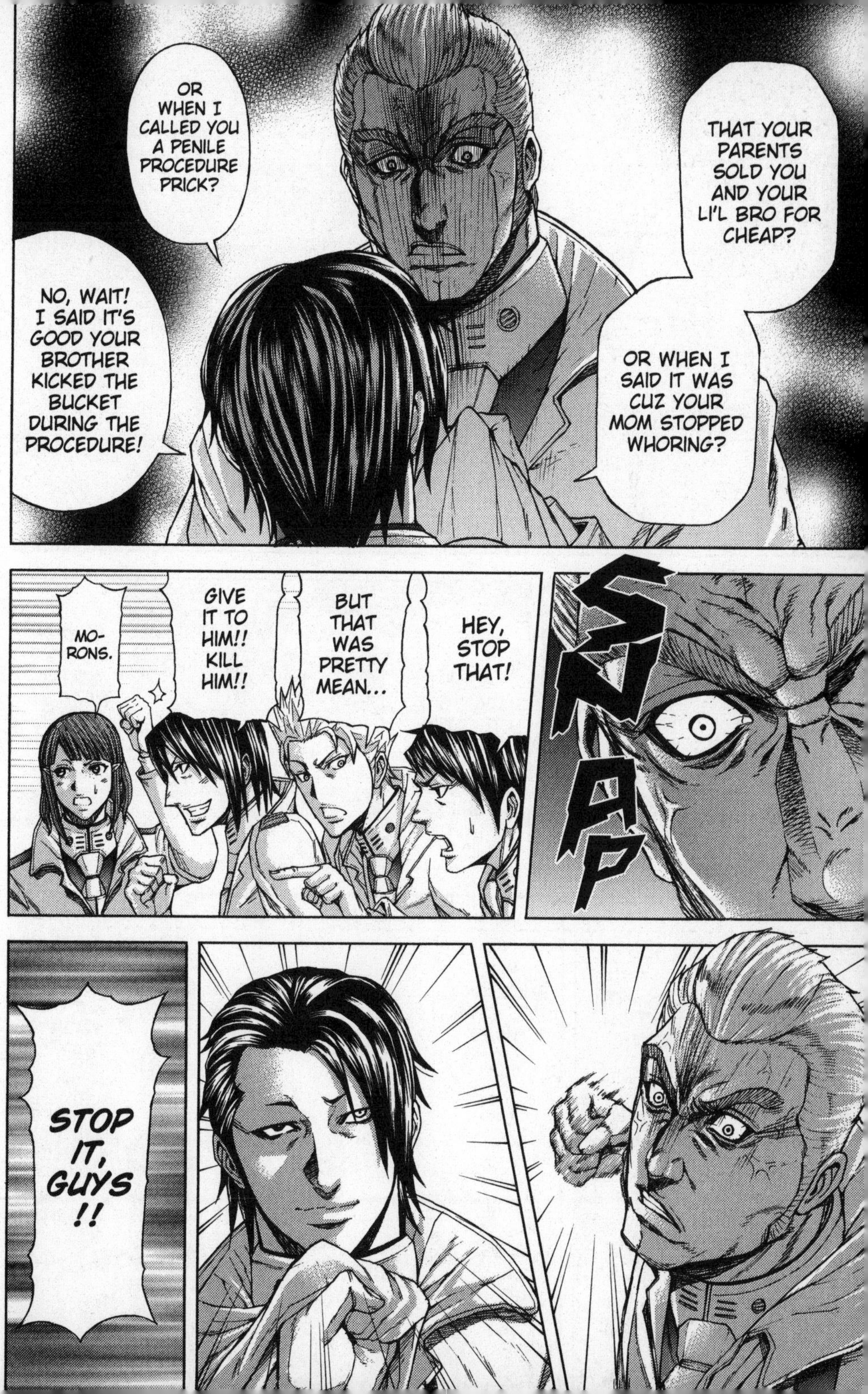
THAT YOUR PARENTS SOLD YOU AND YOUR LI'L BRO FOR CHEAP?
OR WHEN I CALLED YOU A PENILE PROCEDURE PRICK?
OR WHEN I SAID IT WAS CUZ YOUR MOM STOPPED WHORING?
NO, WAIT! I SAID IT'S GOOD YOUR BROTHER KICKED THE BUCKET DURING THE PROCEDURE!
SNAP
HEY, STOP THAT!
BUT THAT WAS PRETTY MEAN...
GIVE IT TO HIM!! KILL HIM!!
MO-RONS.
STOP IT, GUYS!!

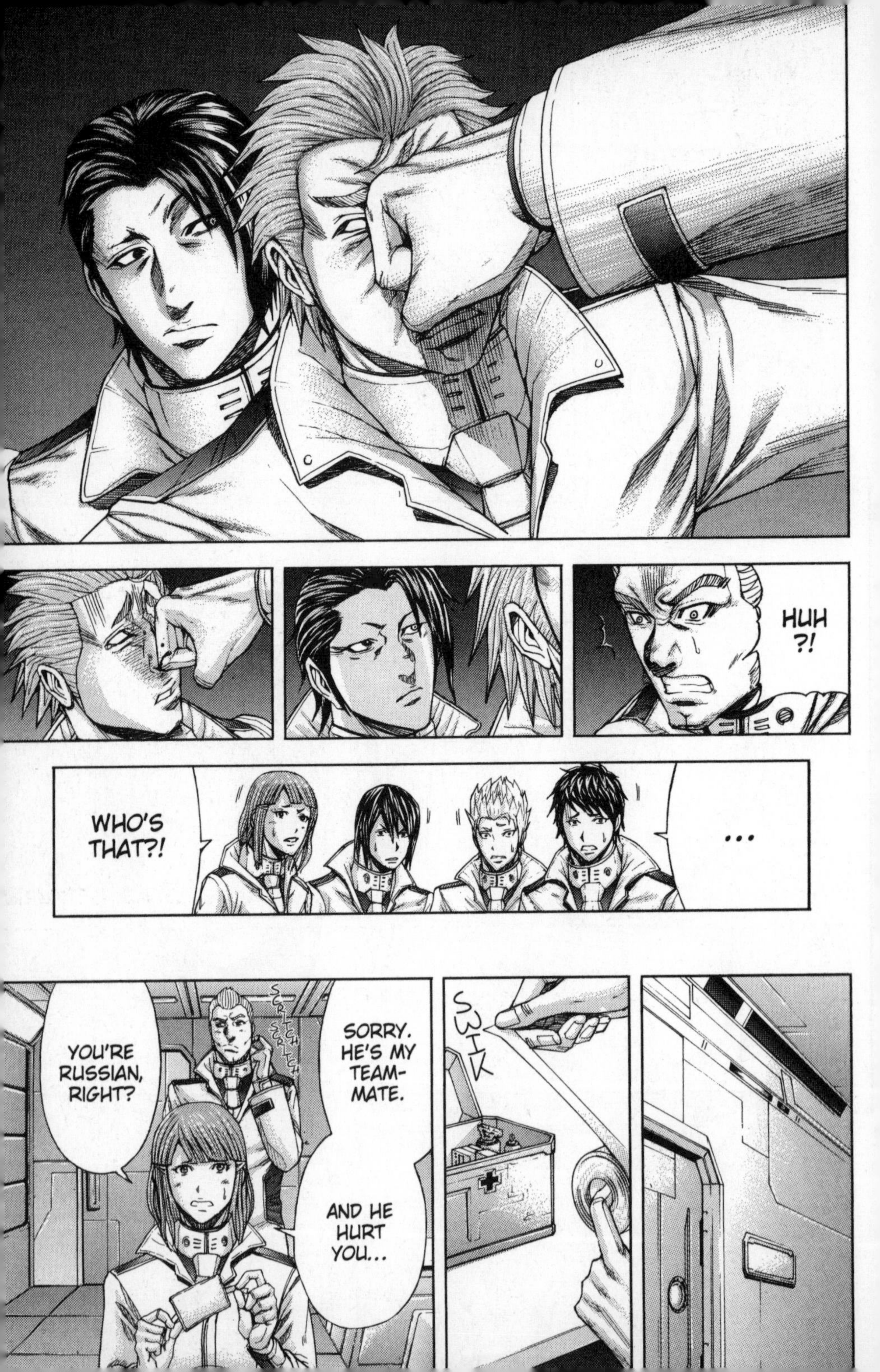
HUH ?!
...
WHO'S THAT?!
SWIK
SORRY. HE'S MY TEAM-MATE.
SCRITCH SCRITCH
YOU'RE RUSSIAN, RIGHT?
AND HE HURT YOU...

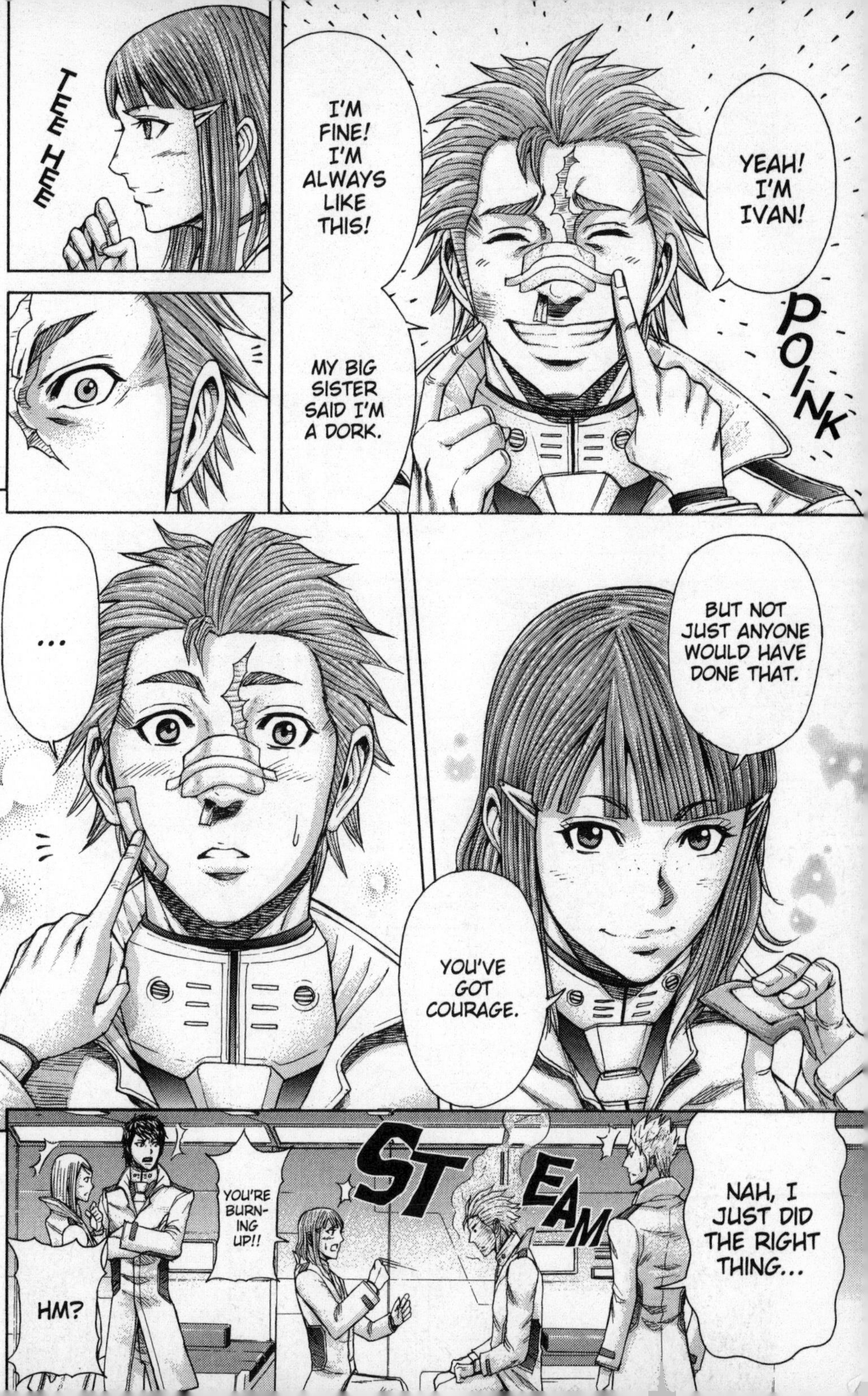
YEAH! I'M IVAN!
POINK
I'M FINE! I'M ALWAYS LIKE THIS!
MY BIG SISTER SAID I'M A DORK.
TEE HEE
BUT NOT JUST ANYONE WOULD HAVE DONE THAT.
YOU'VE GOT COURAGE.
...
NAH, I JUST DID THE RIGHT THING...
STEAM
YOU'RE BURN-ING UP!!
HM?

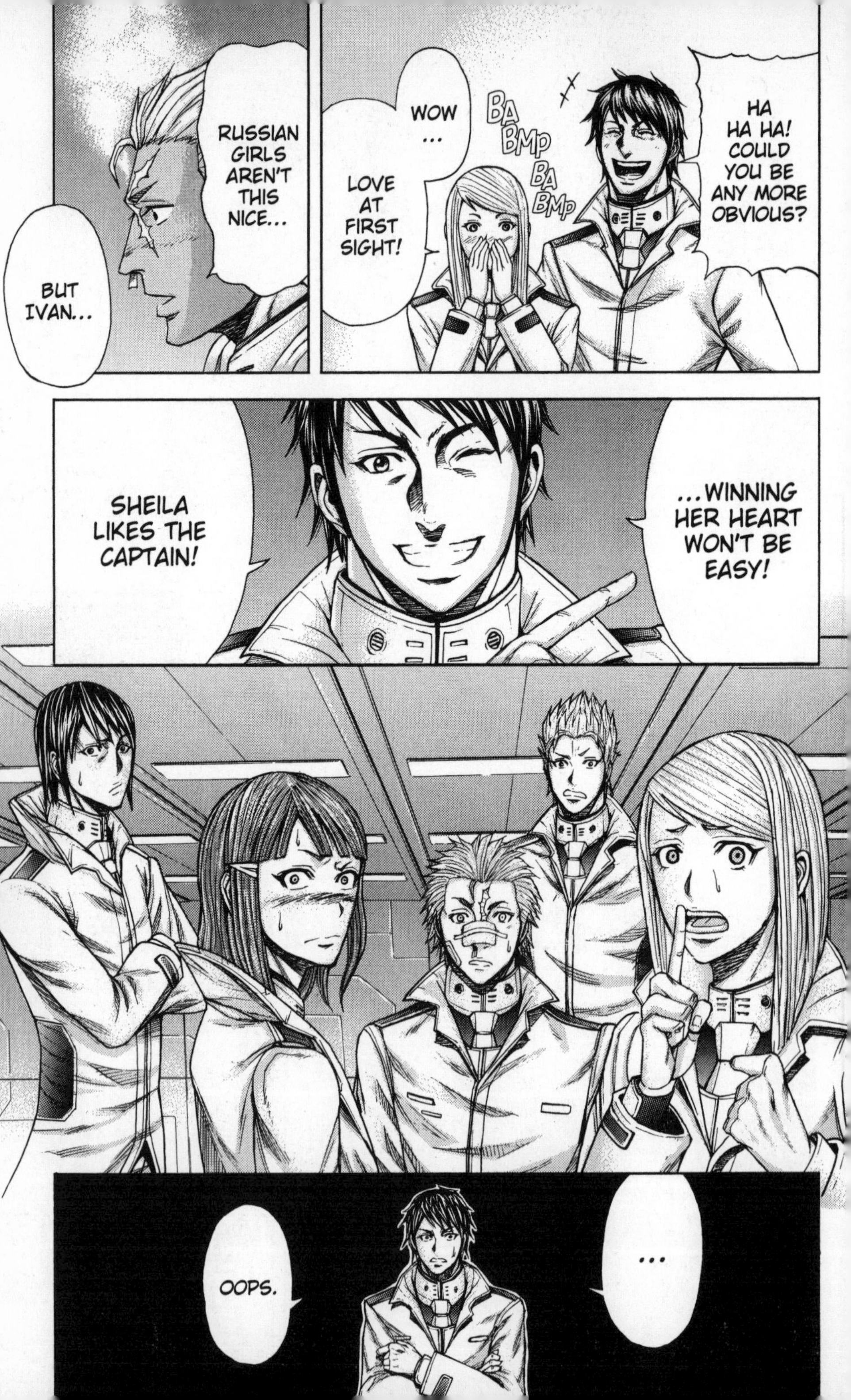
HA HA HA! COULD YOU BE ANY MORE OBVIOUS?
BA BMP BA BMP
WOW ...
LOVE AT FIRST SIGHT!
RUSSIAN GIRLS AREN'T THIS NICE...
BUT IVAN...
...WINNING HER HEART WON'T BE EASY!
SHEILA LIKES THE CAPTAIN!
...
OOPS.

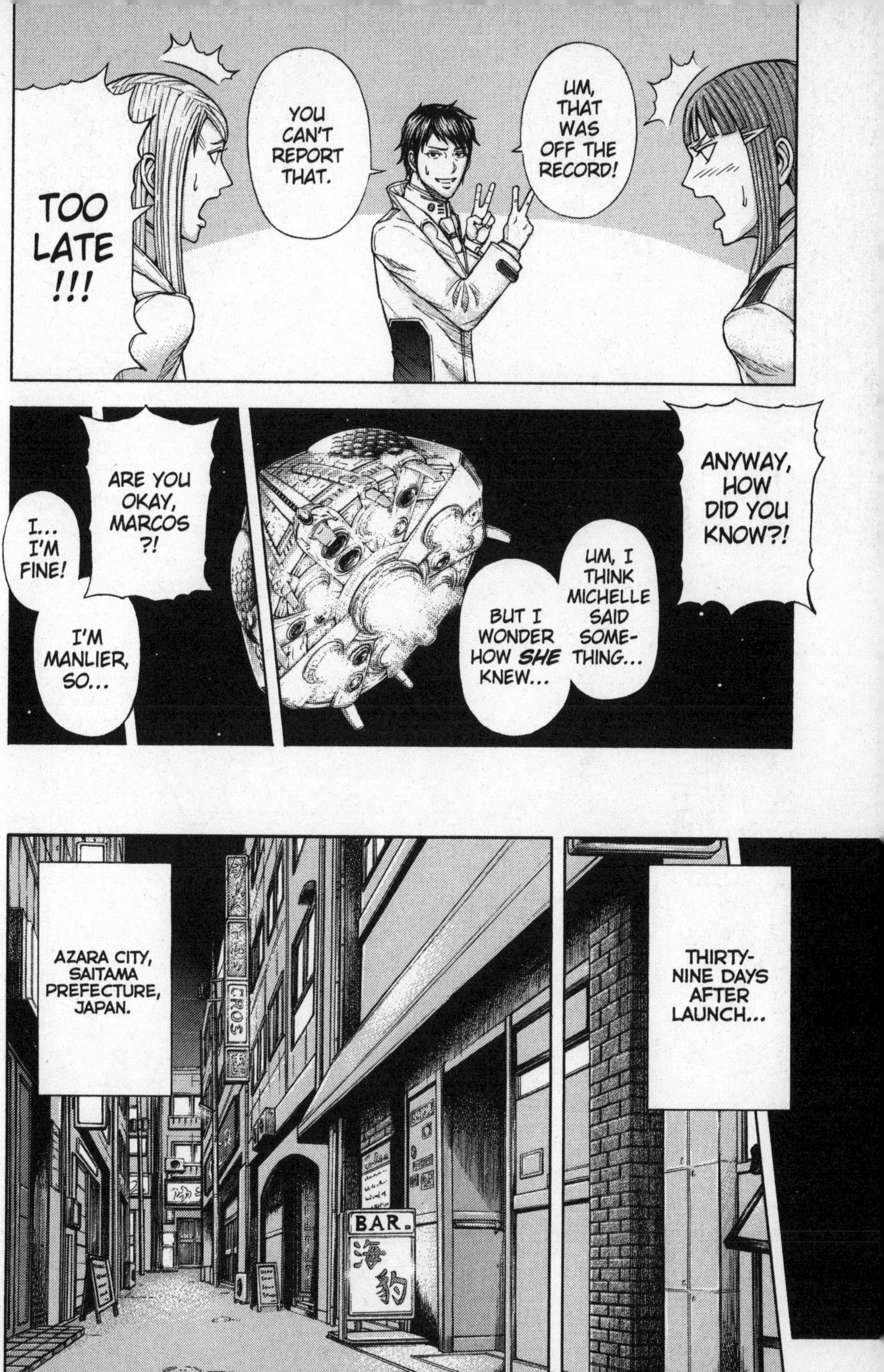
UM, THAT WAS OFF THE RECORD!
YOU CAN'T REPORT THAT.
TOO LATE!!!
ANYWAY, HOW DID YOU KNOW?!
UM, I THINK MICHELLE SAID SOME-THING...
BUT I WONDER HOW *SHE* KNEW...
ARE YOU OKAY, MARCOS?!
I... I'M FINE!
I'M MANLIER, SO...
THIRTY-NINE DAYS AFTER LAUNCH...
AZARA CITY, SAITAMA PREFECTURE, JAPAN.
CROS
BAR.
海豹

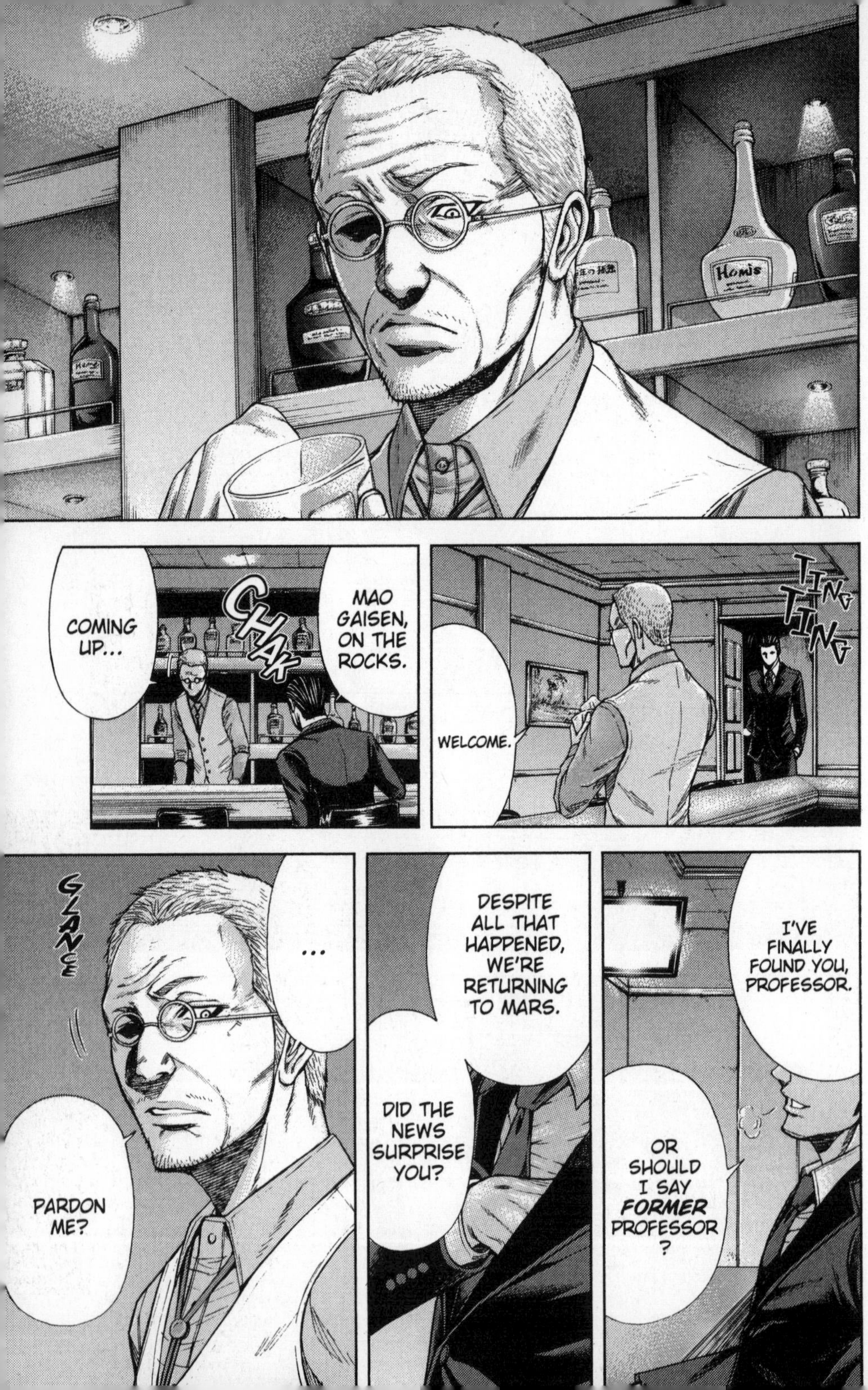
Homis
TING TING
WELCOME.
MAO GAISEN, ON THE ROCKS.
CHAK
COMING UP...
I'VE FINALLY FOUND YOU, PROFESSOR.
OR SHOULD I SAY *FORMER* PROFESSOR?
DESPITE ALL THAT HAPPENED, WE'RE RETURNING TO MARS.
DID THE NEWS SURPRISE YOU?
...
GLANCE
PARDON ME?

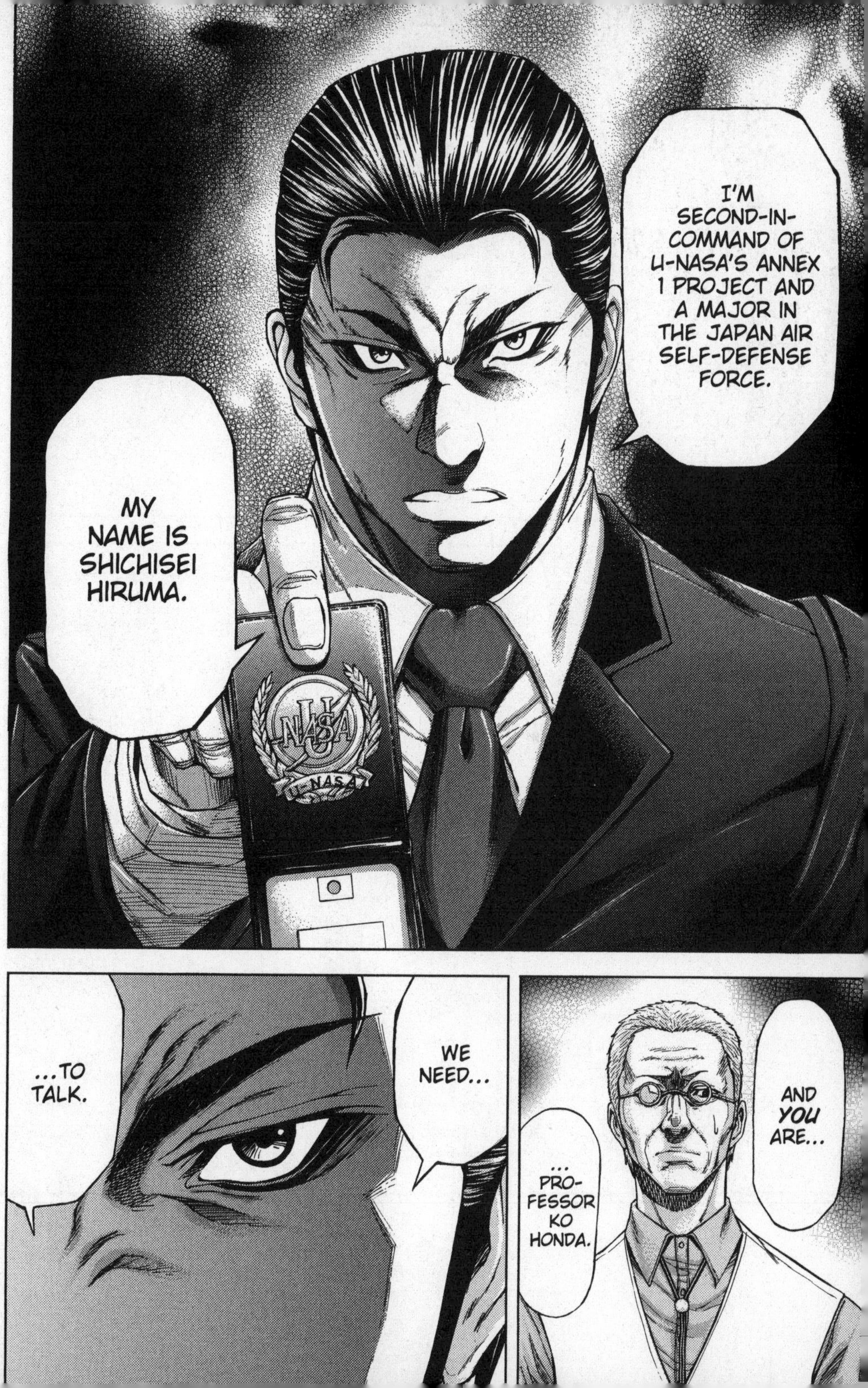
I'M SECOND-IN-COMMAND OF U-NASA'S ANNEX 1 PROJECT AND A MAJOR IN THE JAPAN AIR SELF-DEFENSE FORCE.
MY NAME IS SHICHISEI HIRUMA.
U-NASA
AND *YOU* ARE...
...PROFESSOR KO HONDA.
WE NEED...
...TO TALK.

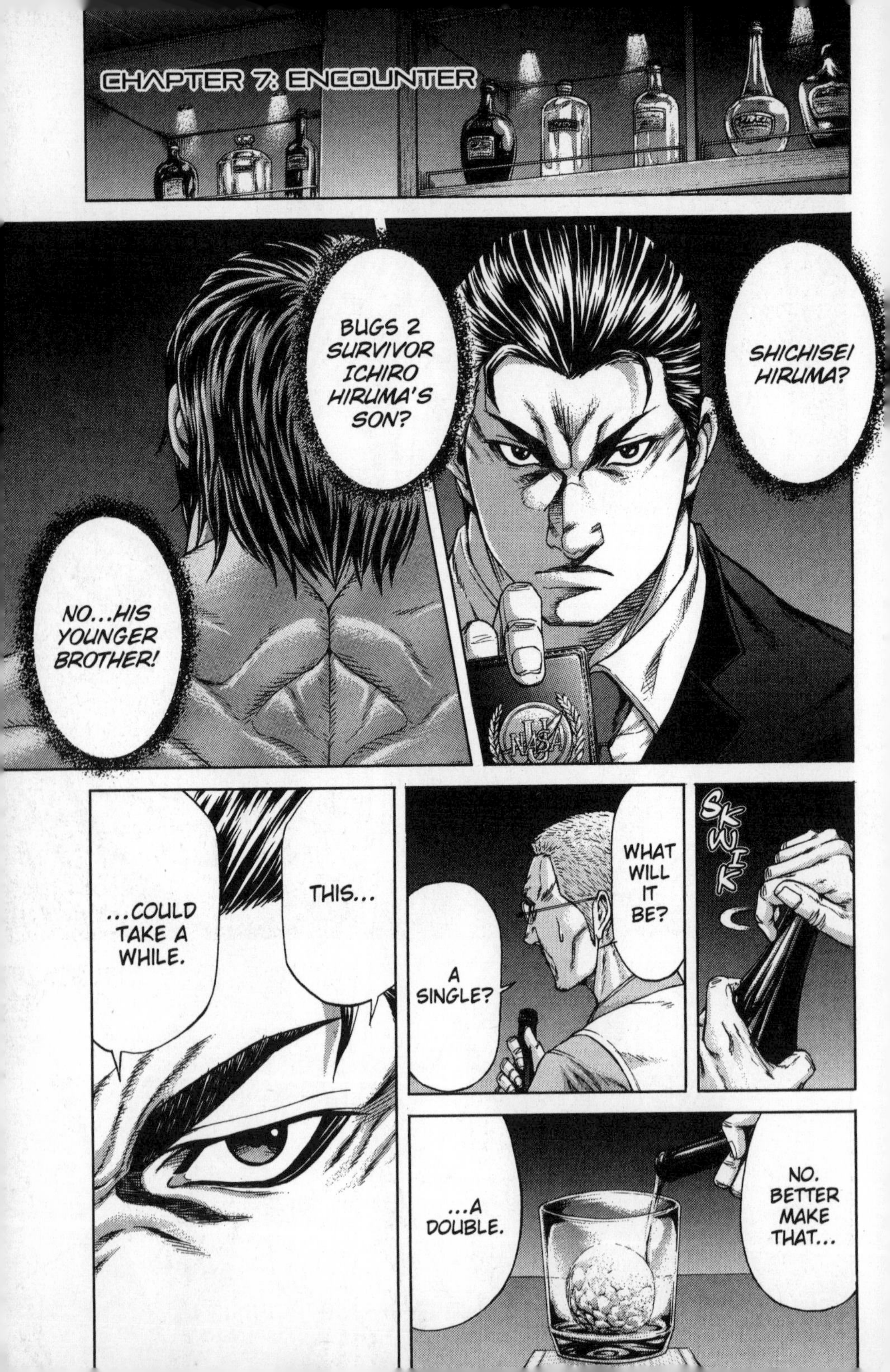
CHAPTER 7: ENCOUNTER
SHICHISEI HIRUMA?
BUGS 2 SURVIVOR ICHIRO HIRUMA'S SON?
NO...HIS YOUNGER BROTHER!
SKWIK
WHAT WILL IT BE?
A SINGLE?
NO. BETTER MAKE THAT...
...A DOUBLE.
THIS...
...COULD TAKE A WHILE.

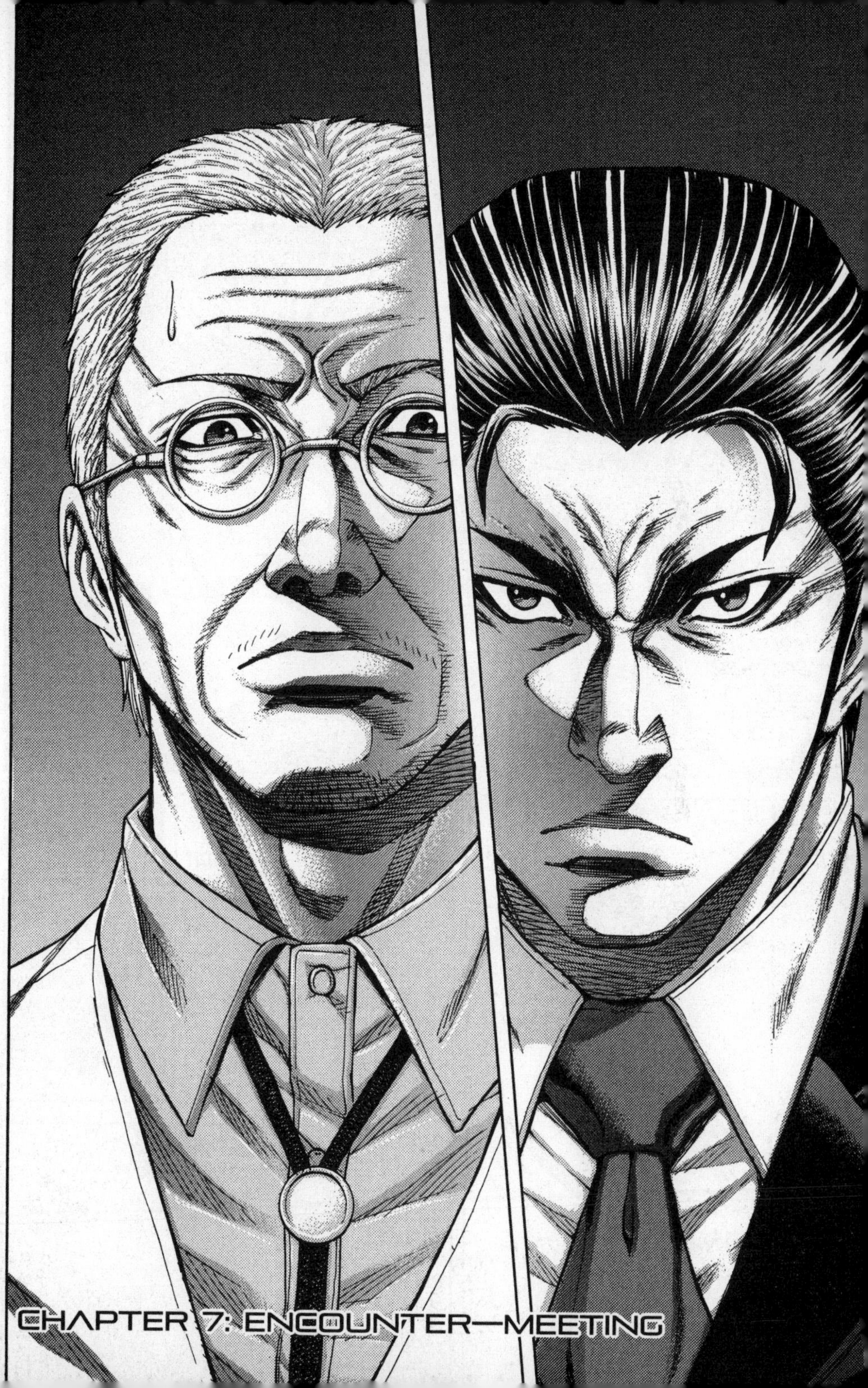
CHAPTER 7: ENCOUNTER—MEETING

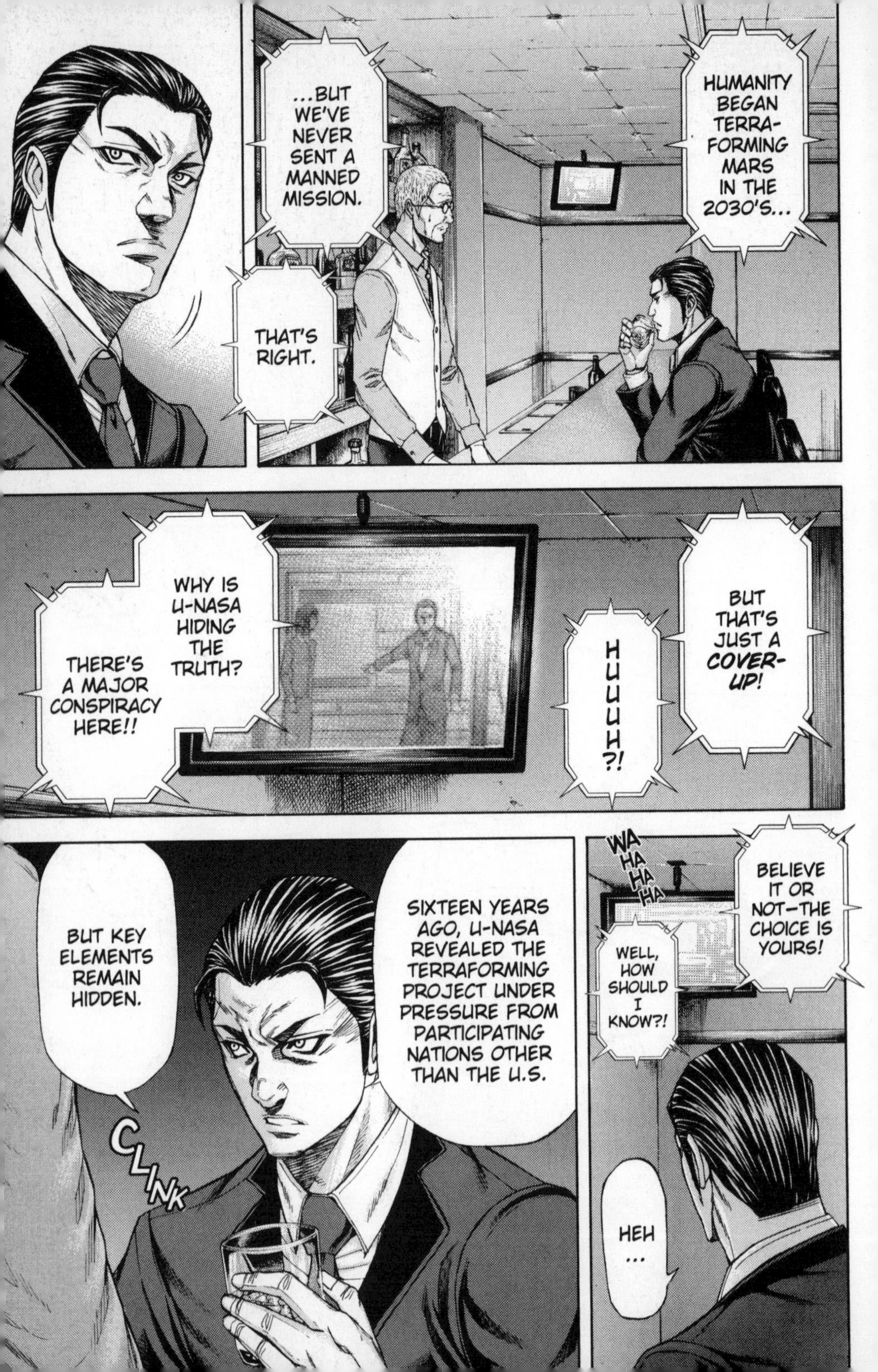
HUMANITY BEGAN TERRA-FORMING MARS IN THE 2030'S...
...BUT WE'VE NEVER SENT A MANNED MISSION.
THAT'S RIGHT.
BUT THAT'S JUST A COVER-UP!
HUUUH?!
WHY IS U-NASA HIDING THE TRUTH?
THERE'S A MAJOR CONSPIRACY HERE!!
BELIEVE IT OR NOT—THE CHOICE IS YOURS!
WA HA HA HA
WELL, HOW SHOULD I KNOW?!
HEH ...
SIXTEEN YEARS AGO, U-NASA REVEALED THE TERRAFORMING PROJECT UNDER PRESSURE FROM PARTICIPATING NATIONS OTHER THAN THE U.S.
BUT KEY ELEMENTS REMAIN HIDDEN.
CLINK

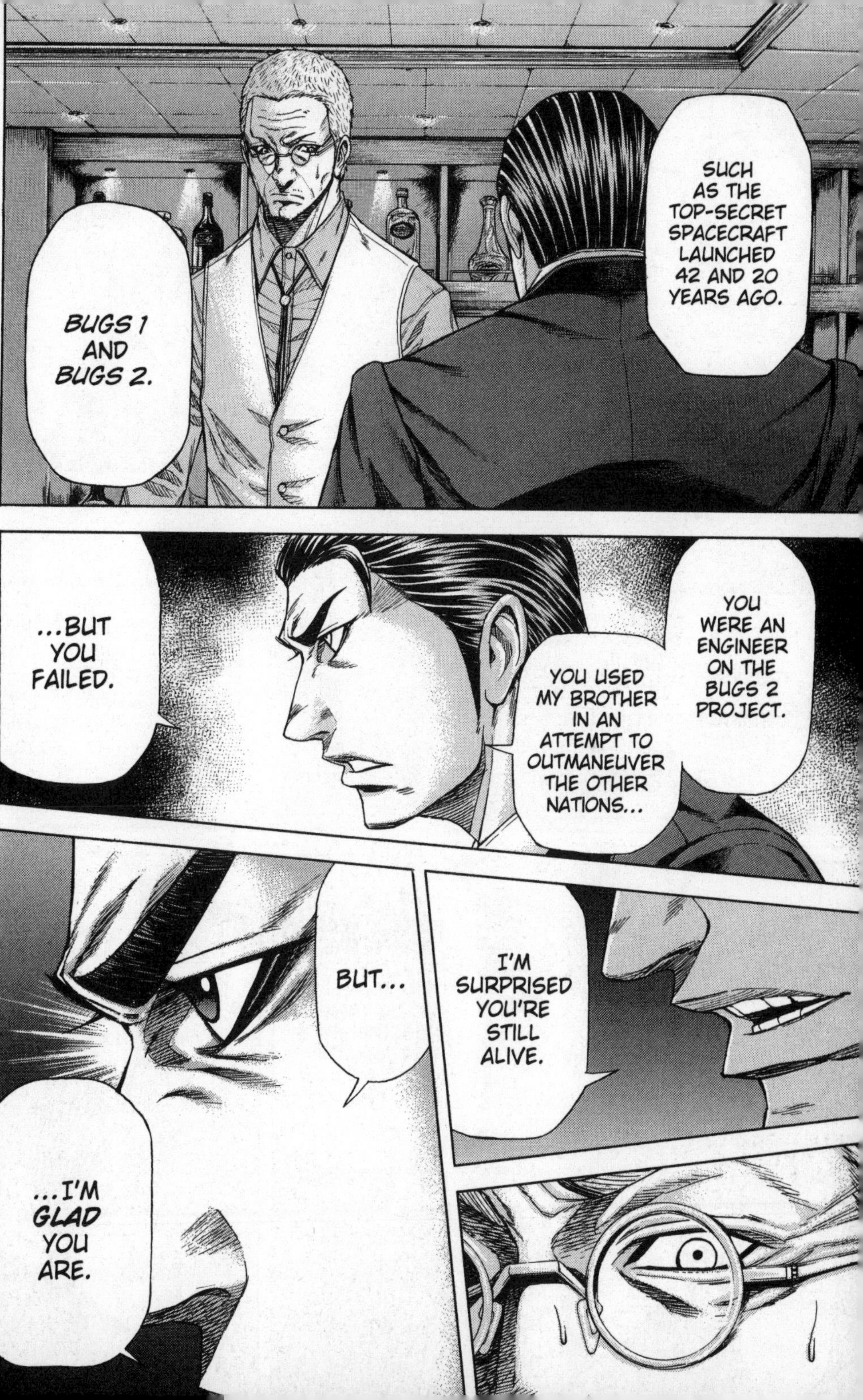
SUCH AS THE TOP-SECRET SPACECRAFT LAUNCHED 42 AND 20 YEARS AGO.
BUGS 1 AND BUGS 2.
YOU WERE AN ENGINEER ON THE BUGS 2 PROJECT.
YOU USED MY BROTHER IN AN ATTEMPT TO OUTMANEUVER THE OTHER NATIONS...
...BUT YOU FAILED.
I'M SURPRISED YOU'RE STILL ALIVE.
BUT...
...I'M *GLAD* YOU ARE.

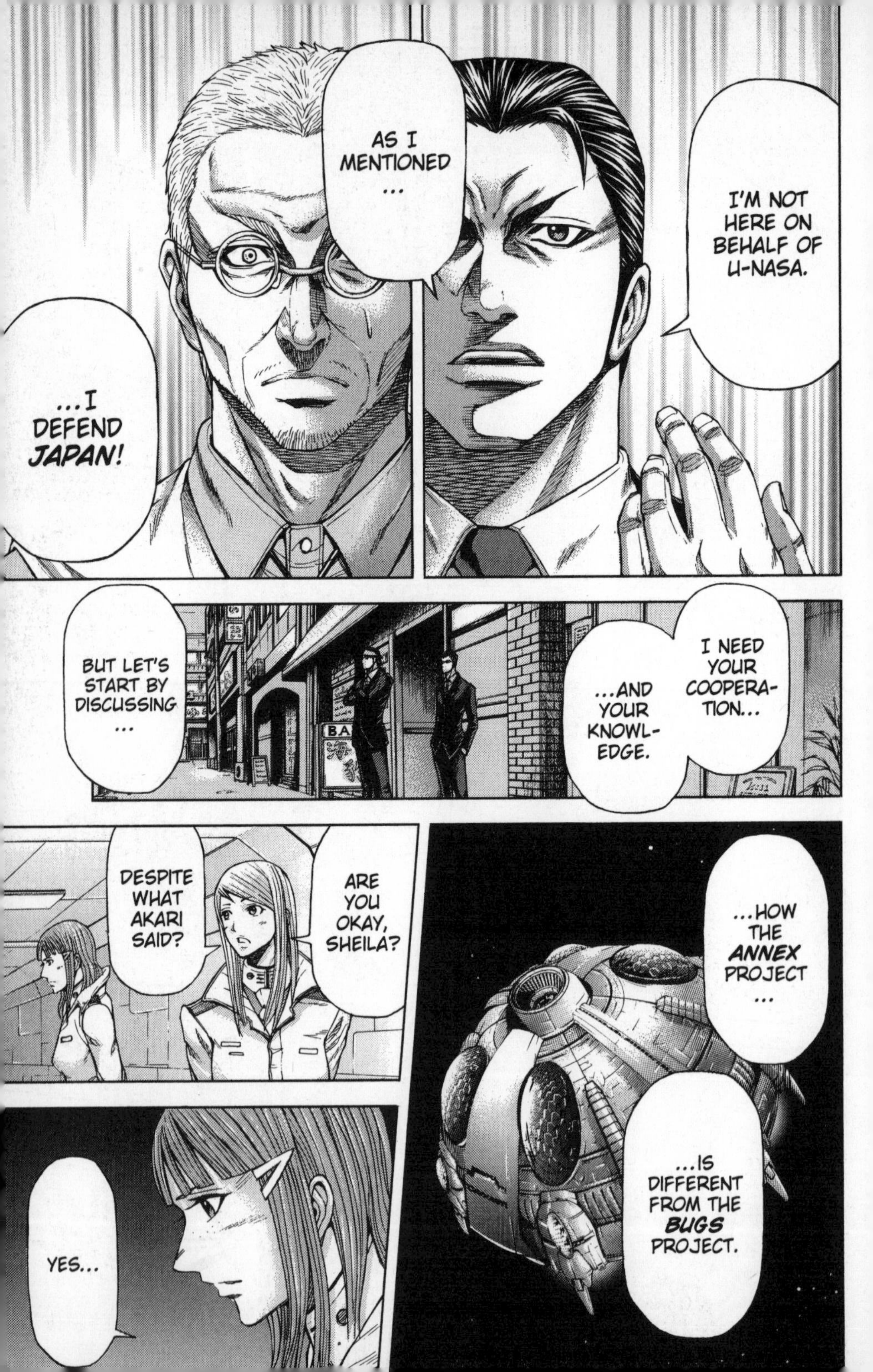
AS I MENTIONED ...
I'M NOT HERE ON BEHALF OF U-NASA.
...I DEFEND *JAPAN!*
I NEED YOUR COOPERATION...
...AND YOUR KNOWLEDGE.
BUT LET'S START BY DISCUSSING ...
...HOW THE *ANNEX* PROJECT ...
...IS DIFFERENT FROM THE *BUGS* PROJECT.
ARE YOU OKAY, SHEILA?
DESPITE WHAT AKARI SAID?
YES...

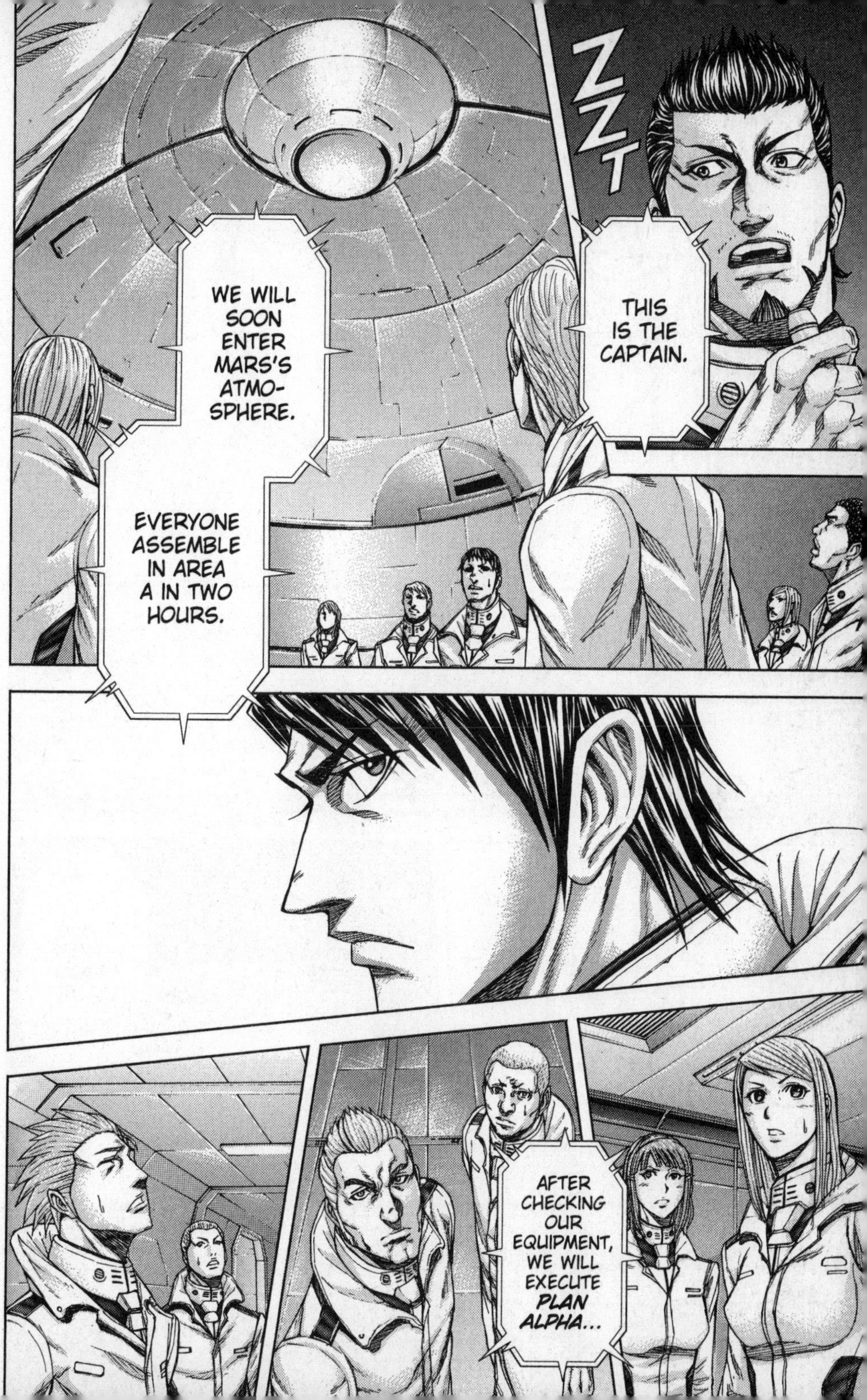
ZZZT
THIS IS THE CAPTAIN.
WE WILL SOON ENTER MARS'S ATMO-SPHERE.
EVERYONE ASSEMBLE IN AREA A IN TWO HOURS.
AFTER CHECKING OUR EQUIPMENT, WE WILL EXECUTE *PLAN ALPHA*...

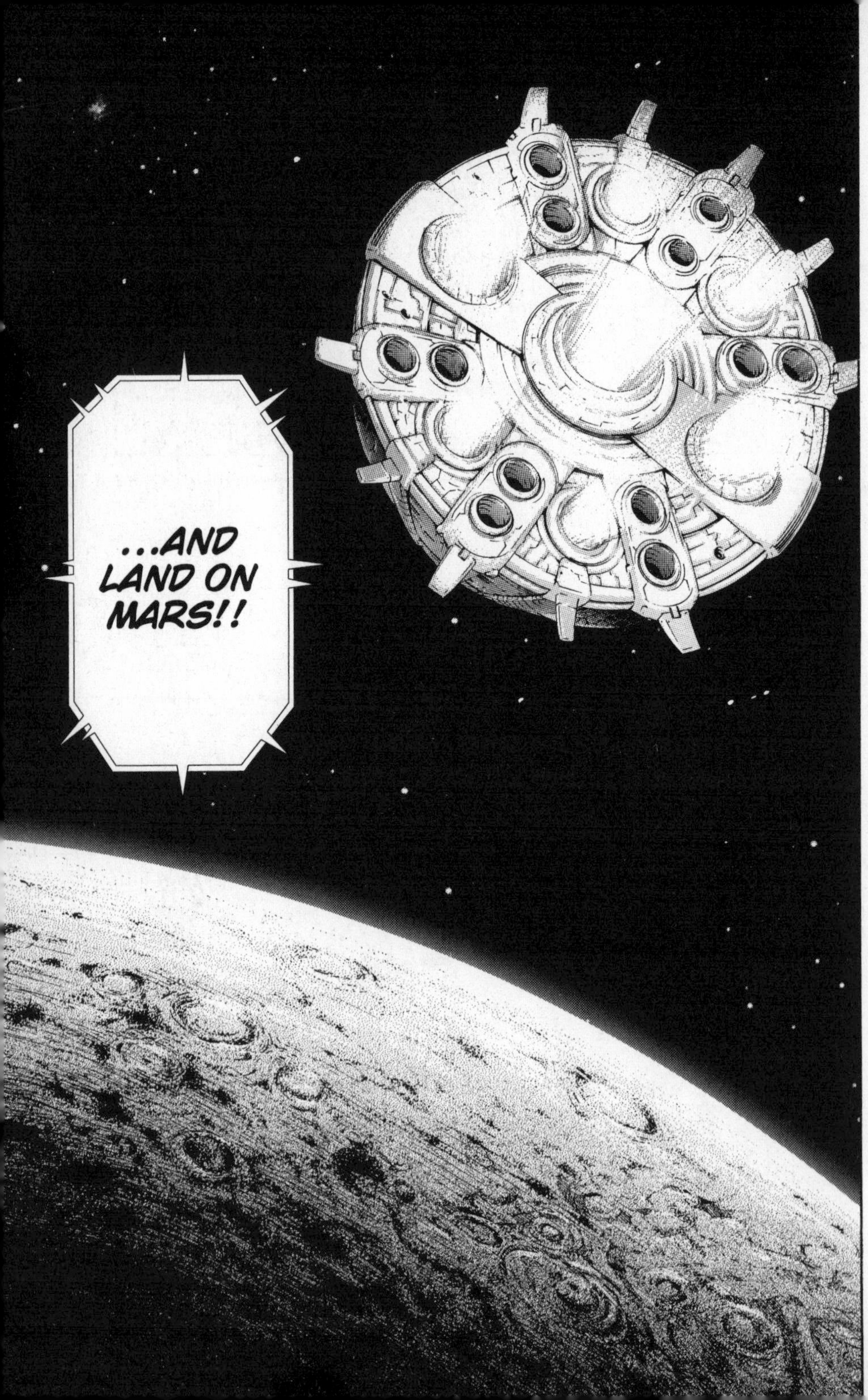
...AND LAND ON MARS!!

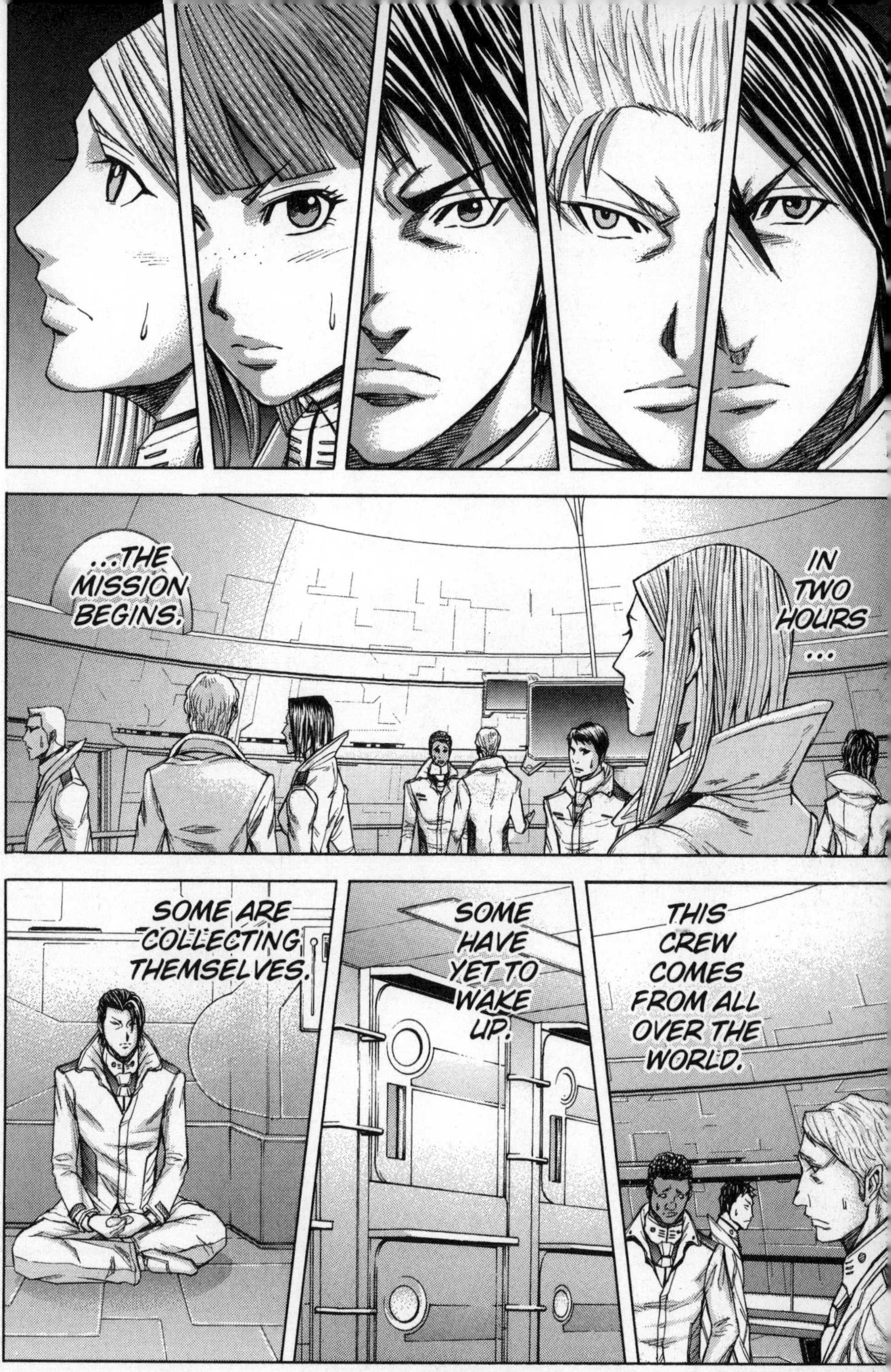
IN TWO HOURS...
...THE MISSION BEGINS.
THIS CREW COMES FROM ALL OVER THE WORLD.
SOME HAVE YET TO WAKE UP.
SOME ARE COLLECTING THEMSELVES.

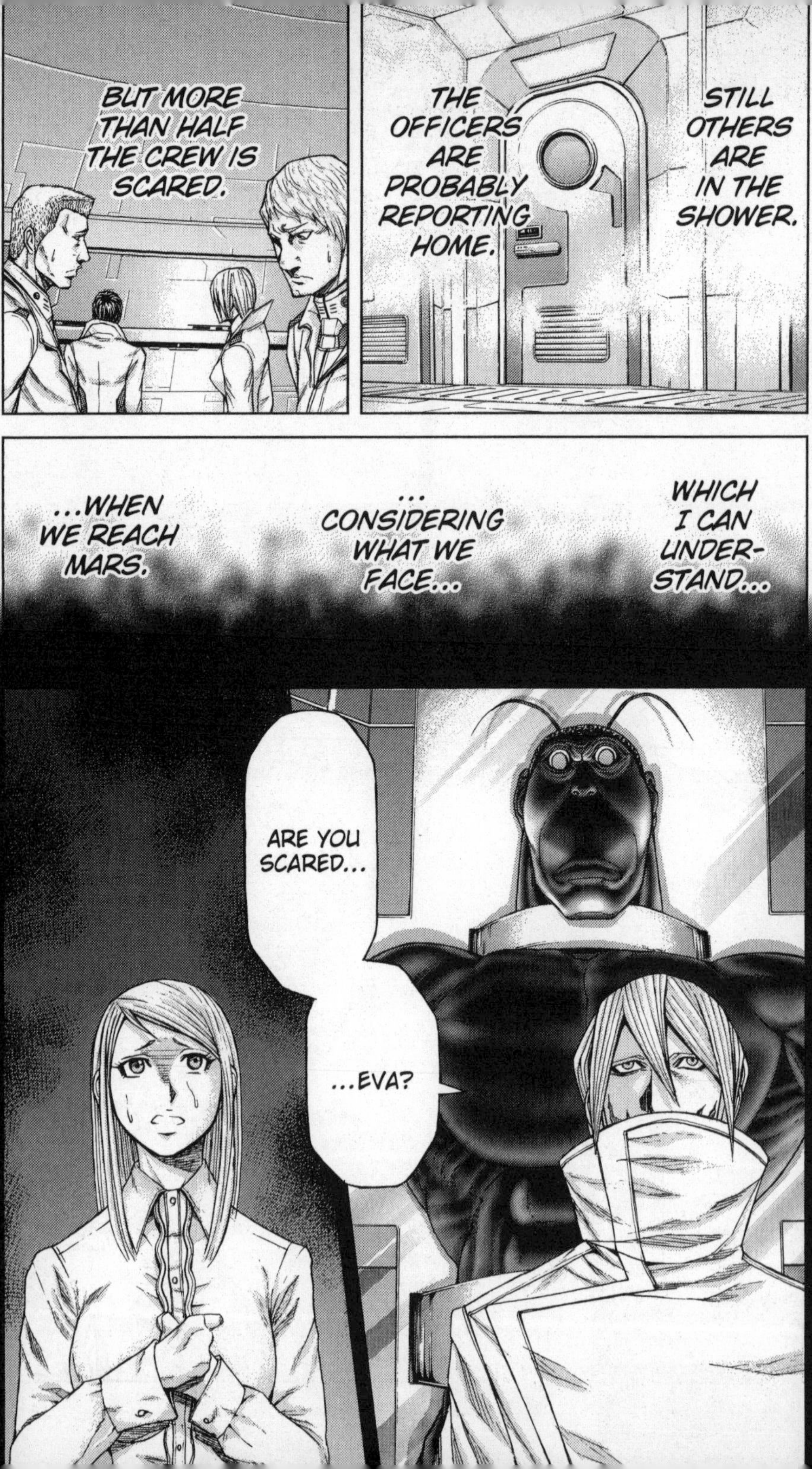
STILL OTHERS ARE IN THE SHOWER.
THE OFFICERS ARE PROBABLY REPORTING HOME.
BUT MORE THAN HALF THE CREW IS SCARED.
WHICH I CAN UNDER-STAND...
...CONSIDERING WHAT WE FACE...
...WHEN WE REACH MARS.
ARE YOU SCARED...
...EVA?

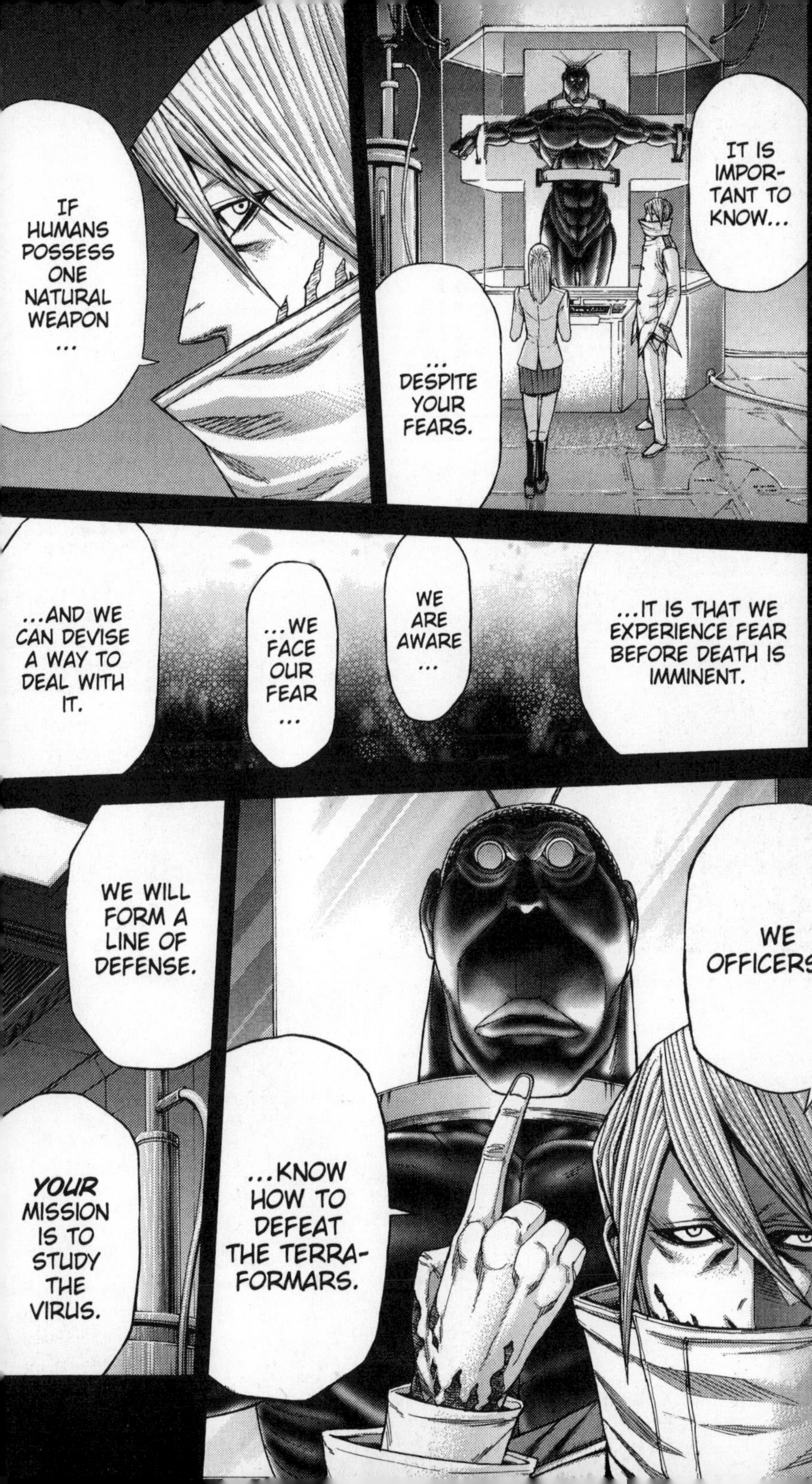
IT IS IMPORTANT TO KNOW...
...DESPITE YOUR FEARS.
IF HUMANS POSSESS ONE NATURAL WEAPON...
...IT IS THAT WE EXPERIENCE FEAR BEFORE DEATH IS IMMINENT.
WE ARE AWARE...
...WE FACE OUR FEAR...
...AND WE CAN DEVISE A WAY TO DEAL WITH IT.
WE OFFICERS...
...KNOW HOW TO DEFEAT THE TERRA-FORMARS.
WE WILL FORM A LINE OF DEFENSE.
YOUR MISSION IS TO STUDY THE VIRUS.

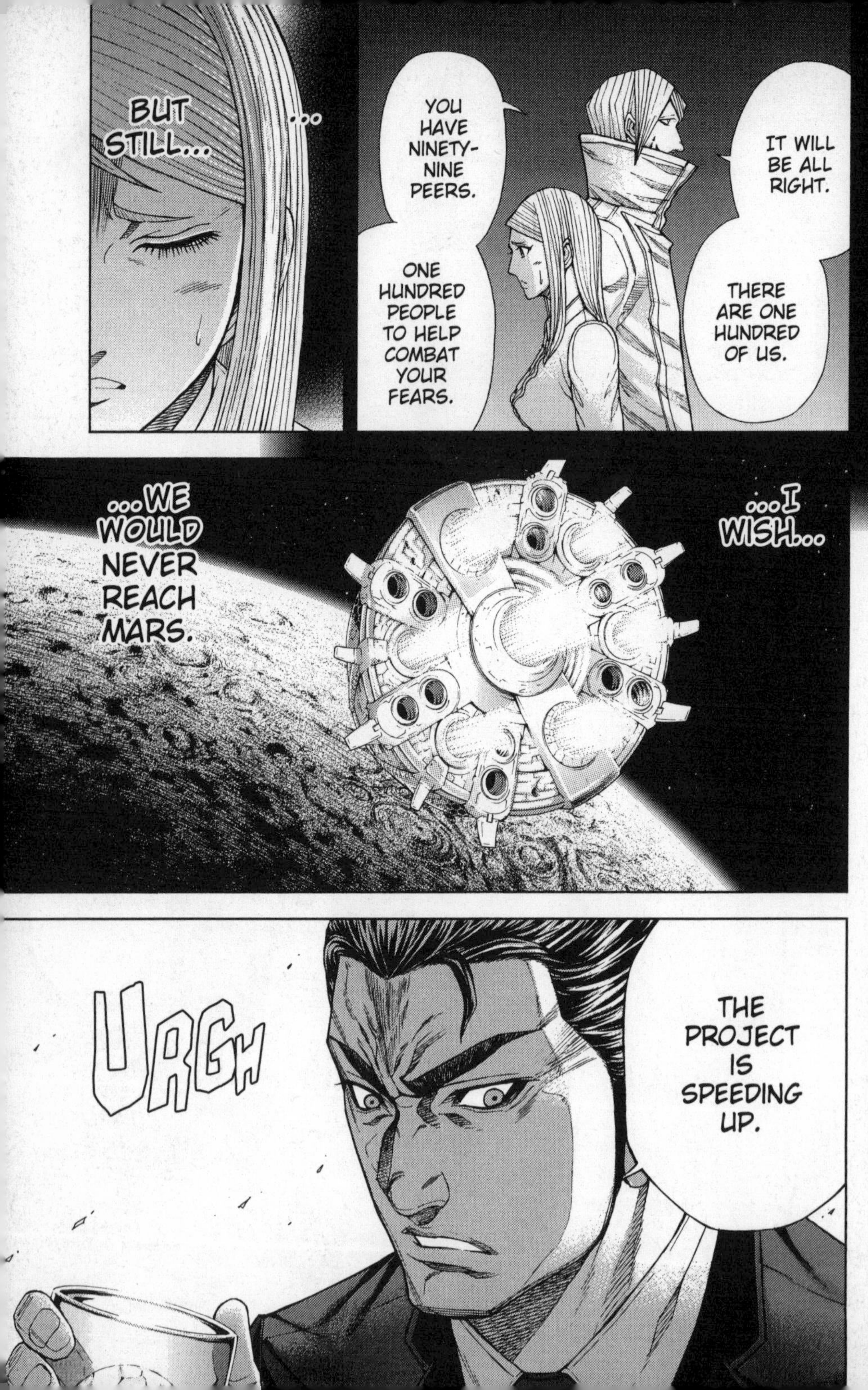
IT WILL BE ALL RIGHT.
THERE ARE ONE HUNDRED OF US.
YOU HAVE NINETY-NINE PEERS.
ONE HUNDRED PEOPLE TO HELP COMBAT YOUR FEARS.
...
BUT STILL...
...I WISH...
...WE WOULD NEVER REACH MARS.
THE PROJECT IS SPEEDING UP.
URGH

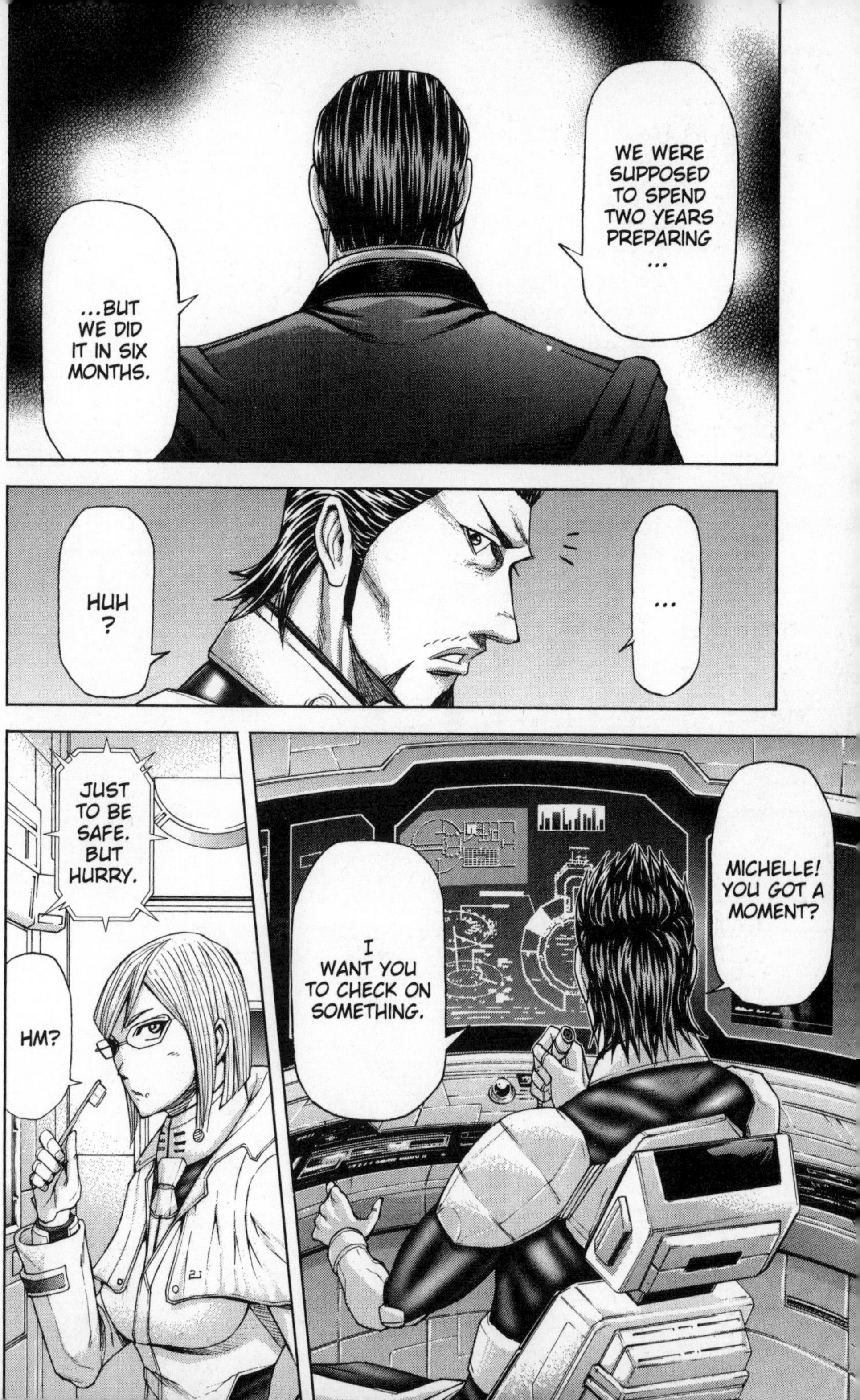
WE WERE SUPPOSED TO SPEND TWO YEARS PREPARING ...
...BUT WE DID IT IN SIX MONTHS.
...
HUH?
MICHELLE! YOU GOT A MOMENT?
I WANT YOU TO CHECK ON SOMETHING.
JUST TO BE SAFE. BUT HURRY.
HM?

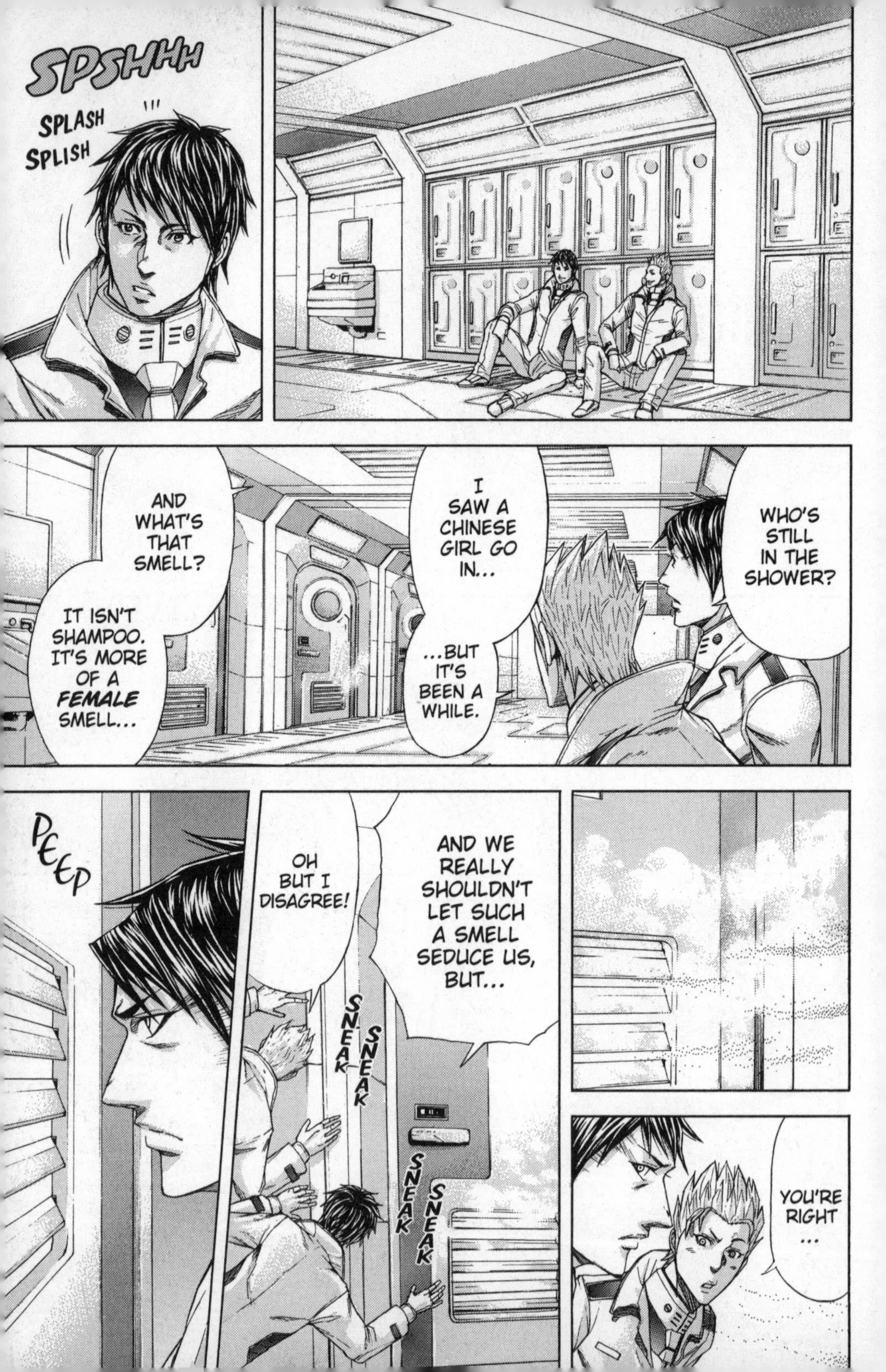
SPSHHH
SPLASH
SPLISH
WHO'S STILL IN THE SHOWER?
I SAW A CHINESE GIRL GO IN...
...BUT IT'S BEEN A WHILE.
AND WHAT'S THAT SMELL?
IT ISN'T SHAMPOO. IT'S MORE OF A *FEMALE* SMELL...
YOU'RE RIGHT...
AND WE REALLY SHOULDN'T LET SUCH A SMELL SEDUCE US, BUT...
OH BUT I DISAGREE!
SNEAK SNEAK
SNEAK SNEAK
PEEP

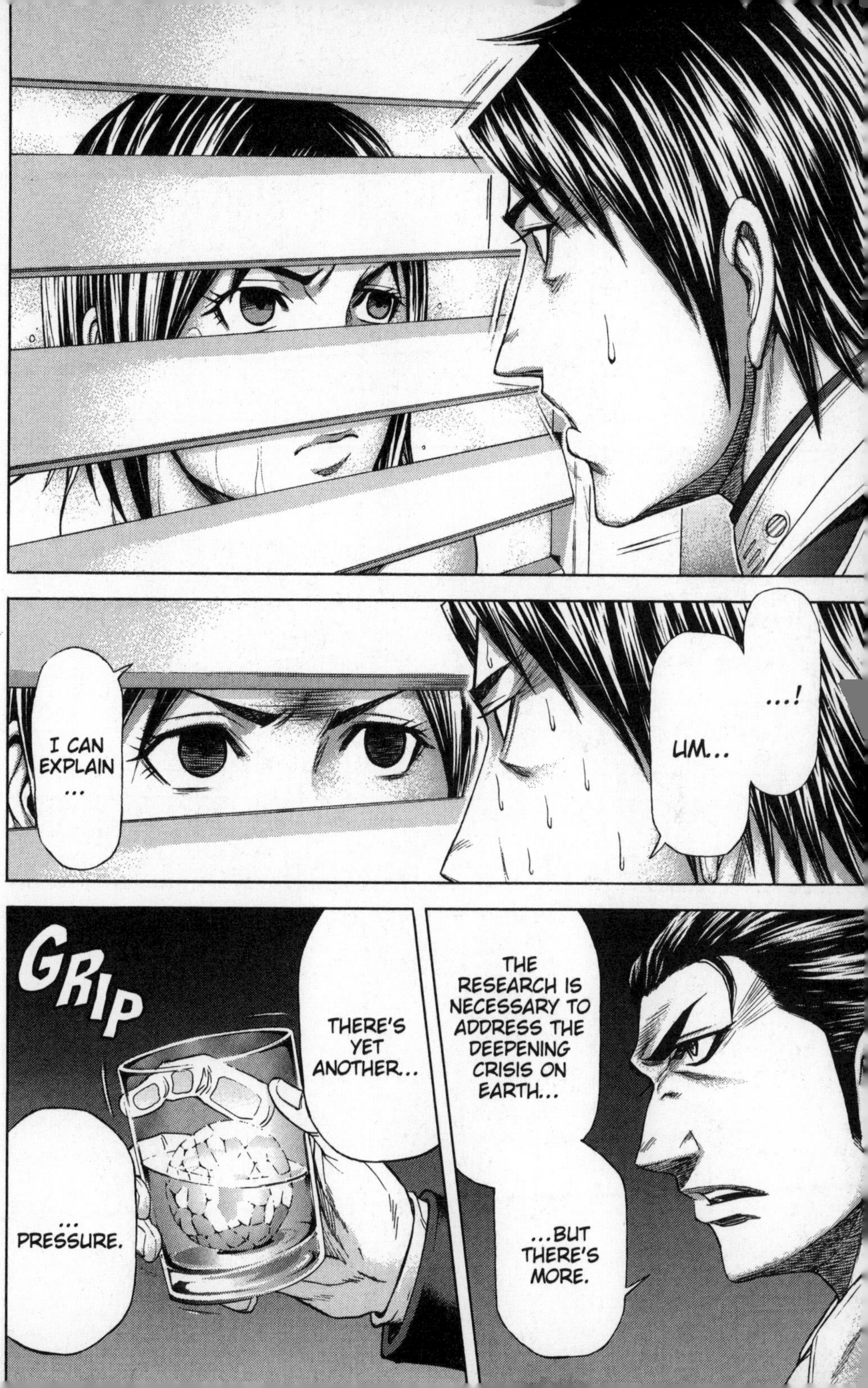
...!
UM...
I CAN EXPLAIN ...
THE RESEARCH IS NECESSARY TO ADDRESS THE DEEPENING CRISIS ON EARTH...
...BUT THERE'S MORE.
GRIP
THERE'S YET ANOTHER...
... PRESSURE.

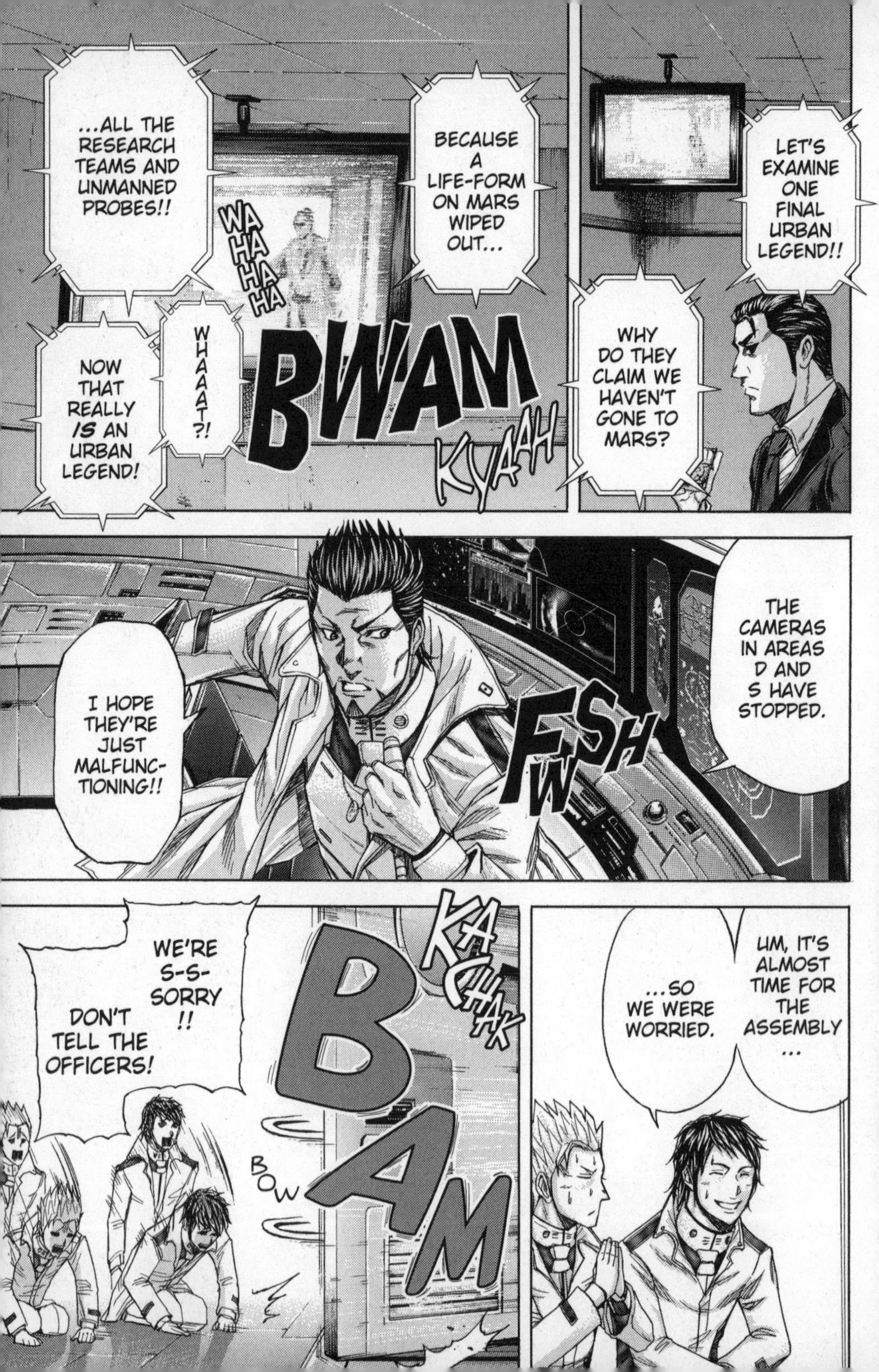
LET'S EXAMINE ONE FINAL URBAN LEGEND!!
WHY DO THEY CLAIM WE HAVEN'T GONE TO MARS?
BECAUSE A LIFE-FORM ON MARS WIPED OUT...
...ALL THE RESEARCH TEAMS AND UNMANNED PROBES!!
WA HA HA HA HA
BWAM
KYAAH
WHAAAAT?!
NOW THAT REALLY *IS* AN URBAN LEGEND!
THE CAMERAS IN AREAS D AND S HAVE STOPPED.
FWSH
I HOPE THEY'RE JUST MALFUNCTIONING!!
UM, IT'S ALMOST TIME FOR THE ASSEMBLY...
...SO WE WERE WORRIED.
KACHAK
BAM
BOW
WE'RE S-S-SORRY!!
DON'T TELL THE OFFICERS!

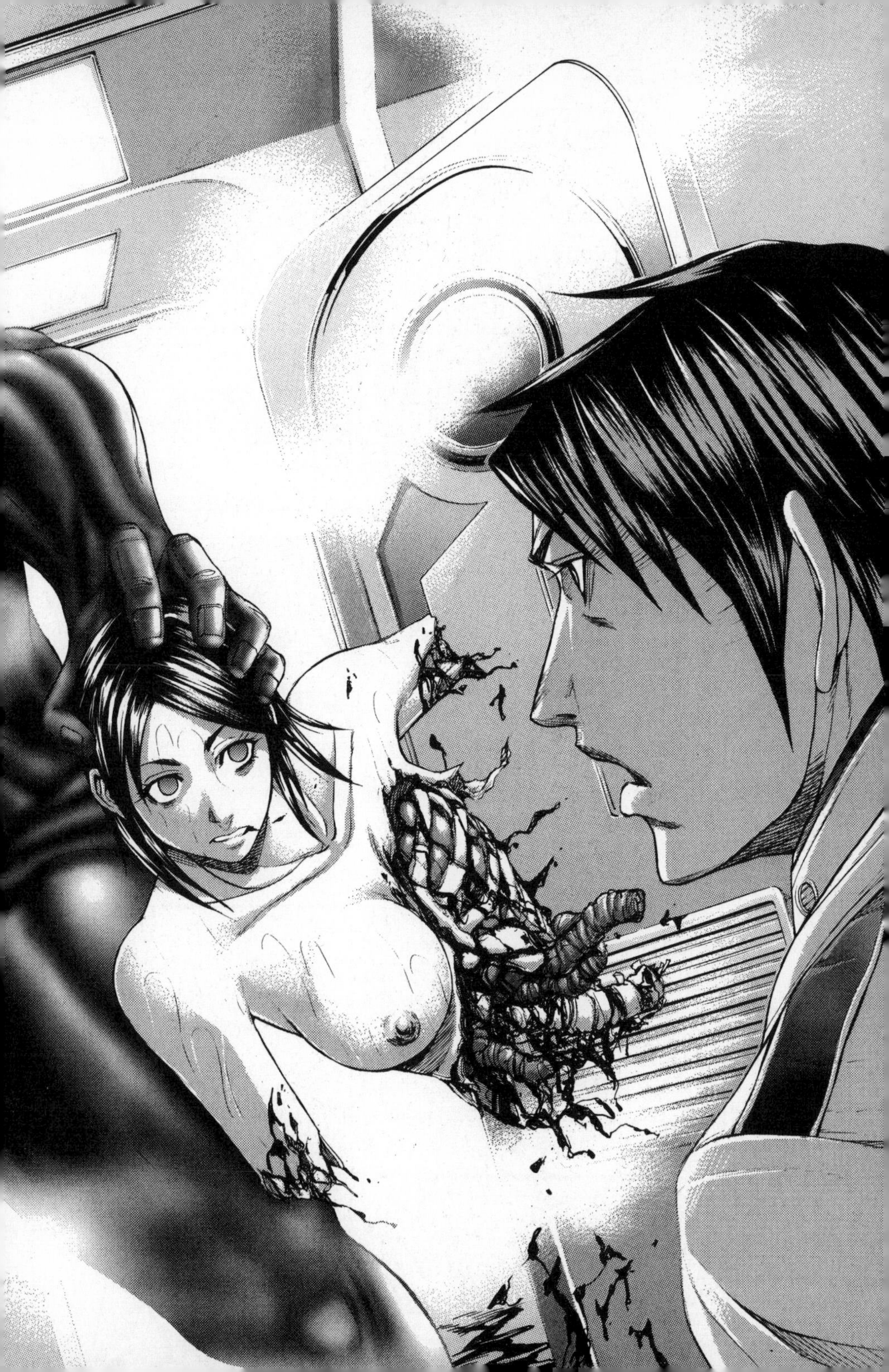

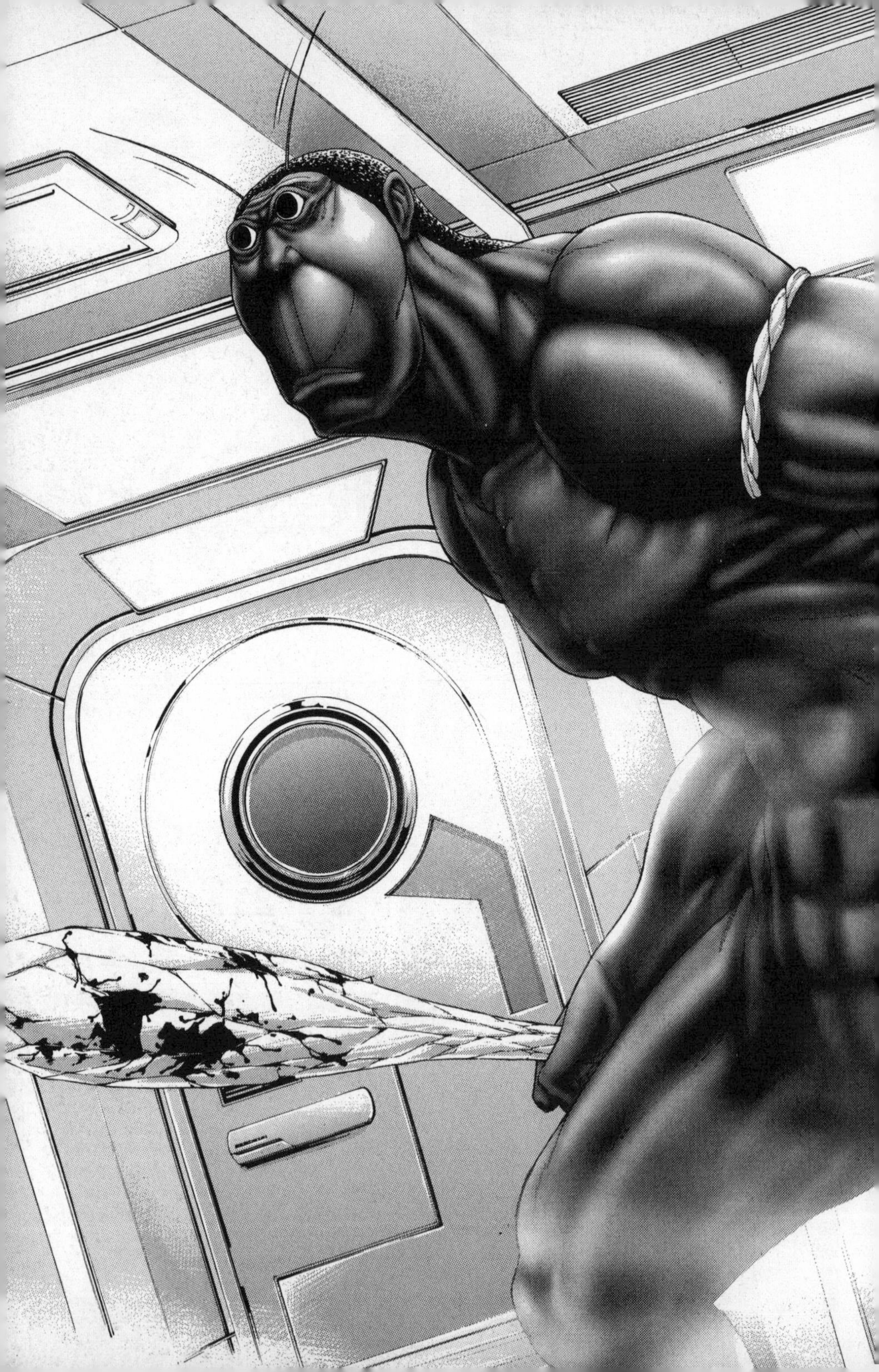

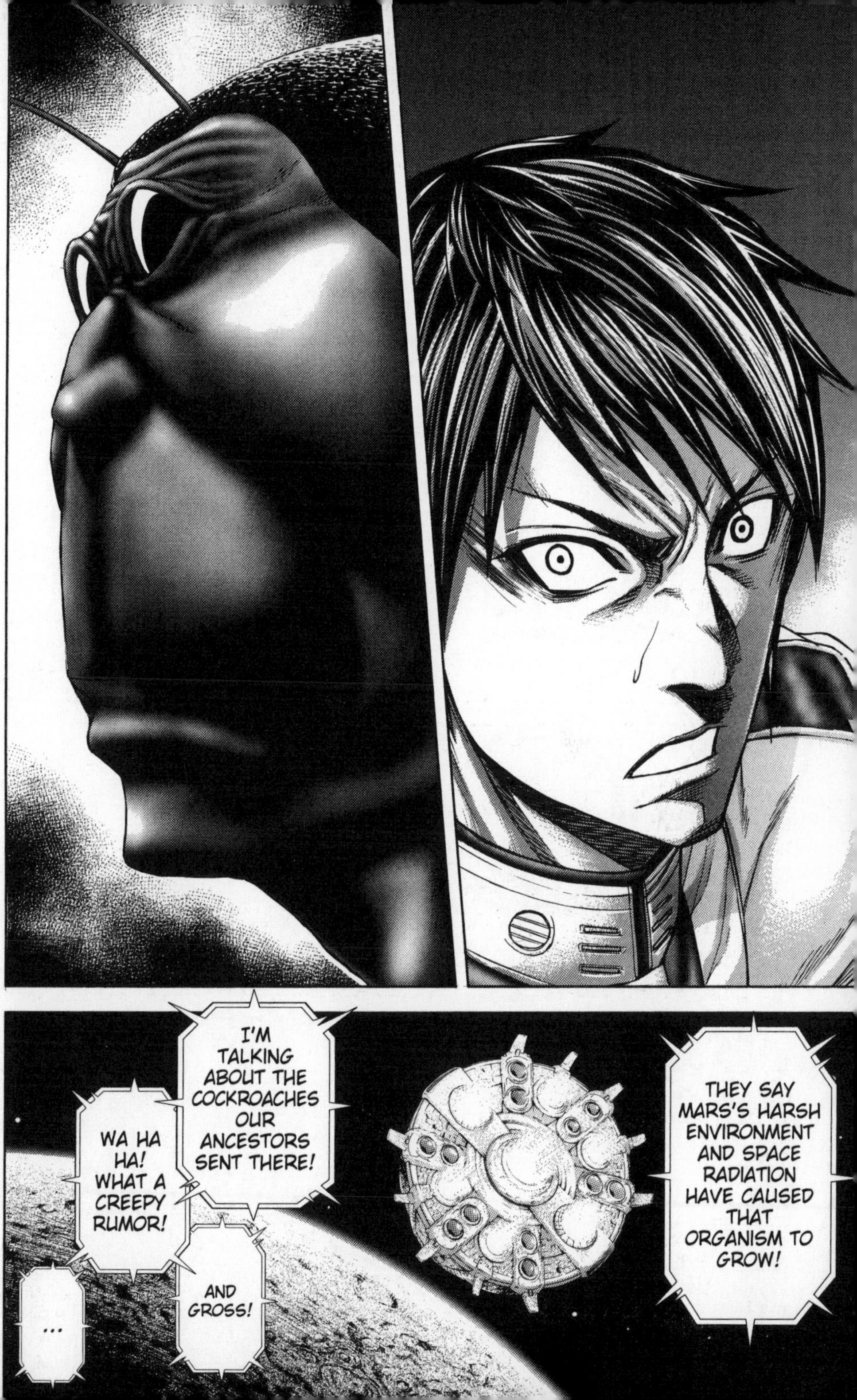
THEY SAY MARS'S HARSH ENVIRONMENT AND SPACE RADIATION HAVE CAUSED THAT ORGANISM TO GROW!
I'M TALKING ABOUT THE COCKROACHES OUR ANCESTORS SENT THERE!
WA HA HA! WHAT A CREEPY RUMOR!
AND GROSS!
...

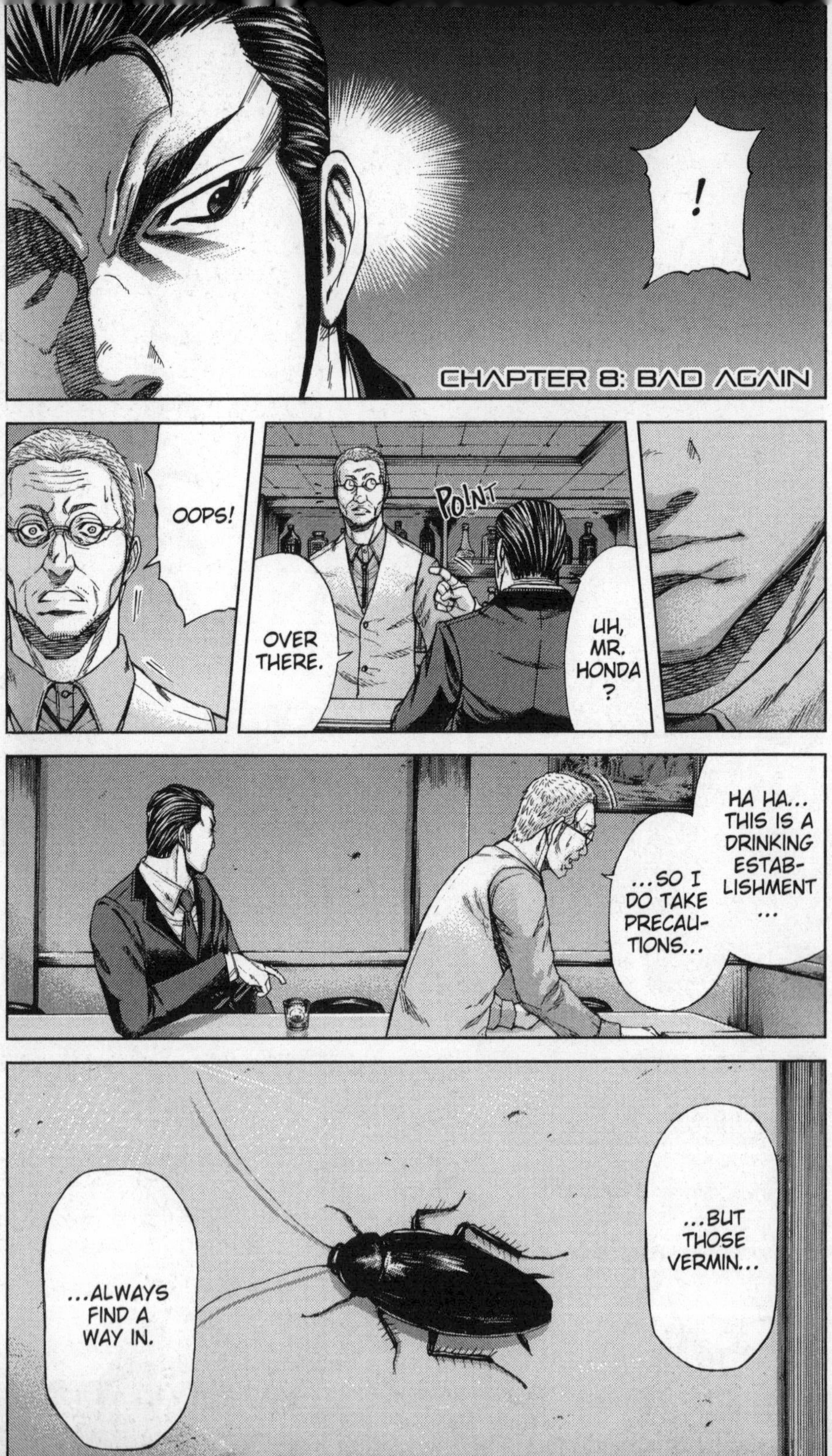
!
CHAPTER 8: BAD AGAIN
UH, MR. HONDA?
POINT
OVER THERE.
OOPS!
HA HA... THIS IS A DRINKING ESTABLISHMENT...
...SO I DO TAKE PRECAUTIONS...
...BUT THOSE VERMIN...
...ALWAYS FIND A WAY IN.

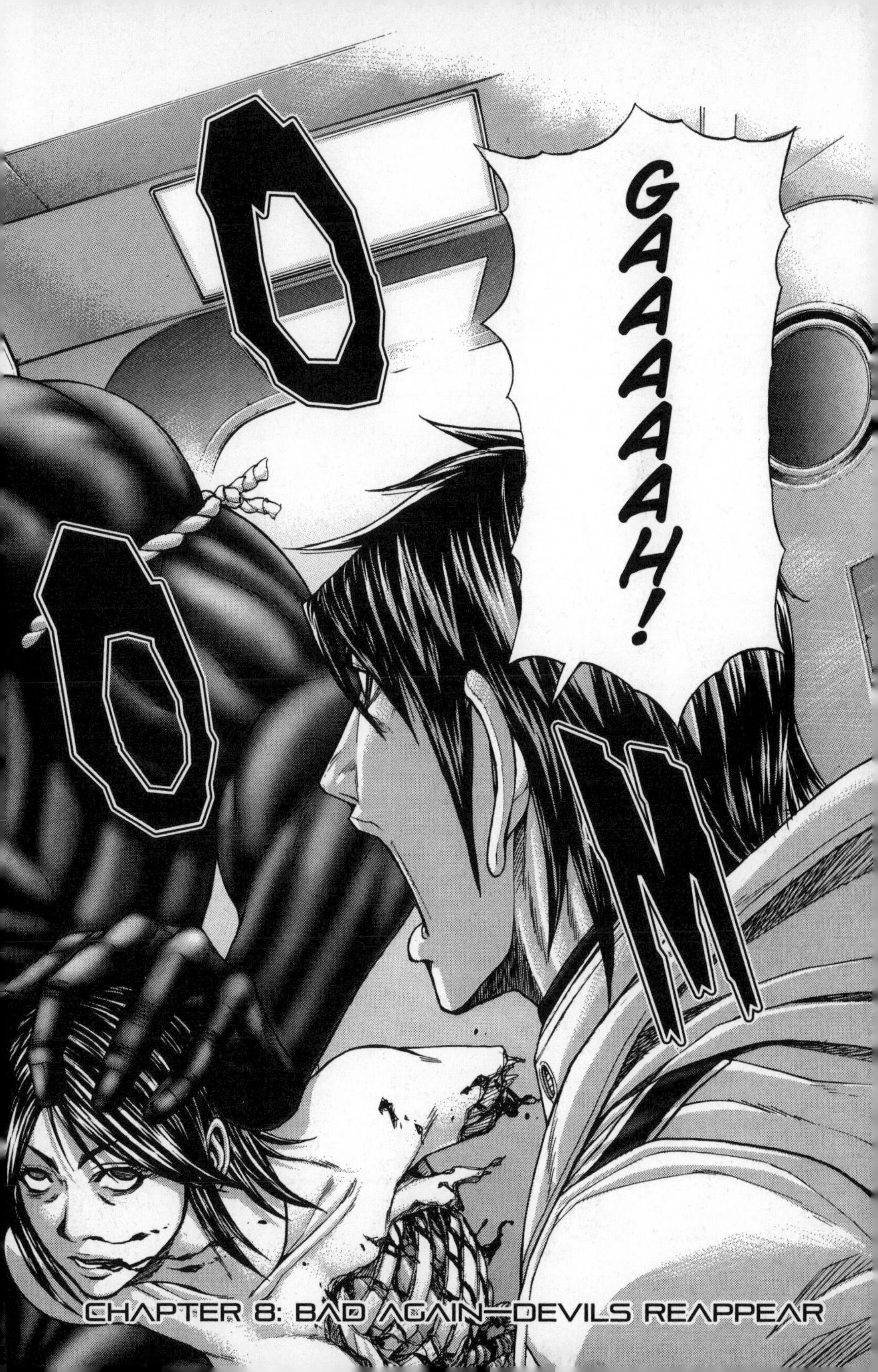
GAAAAAH!
CHAPTER 8: BAD AGAIN—DEVILS REAPPEAR

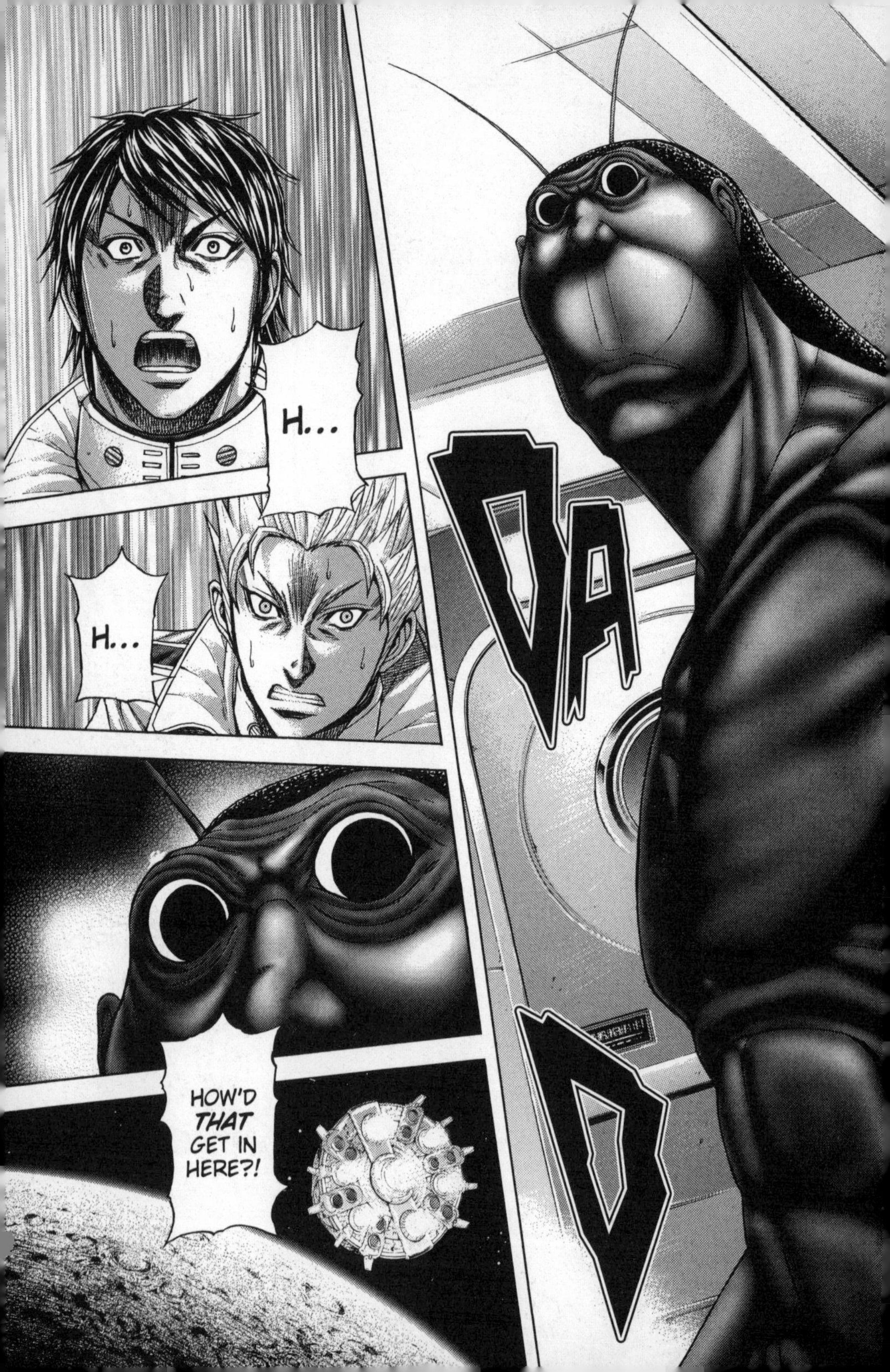
DA
D
H...
H...
HOW'D *THAT* GET IN HERE?!

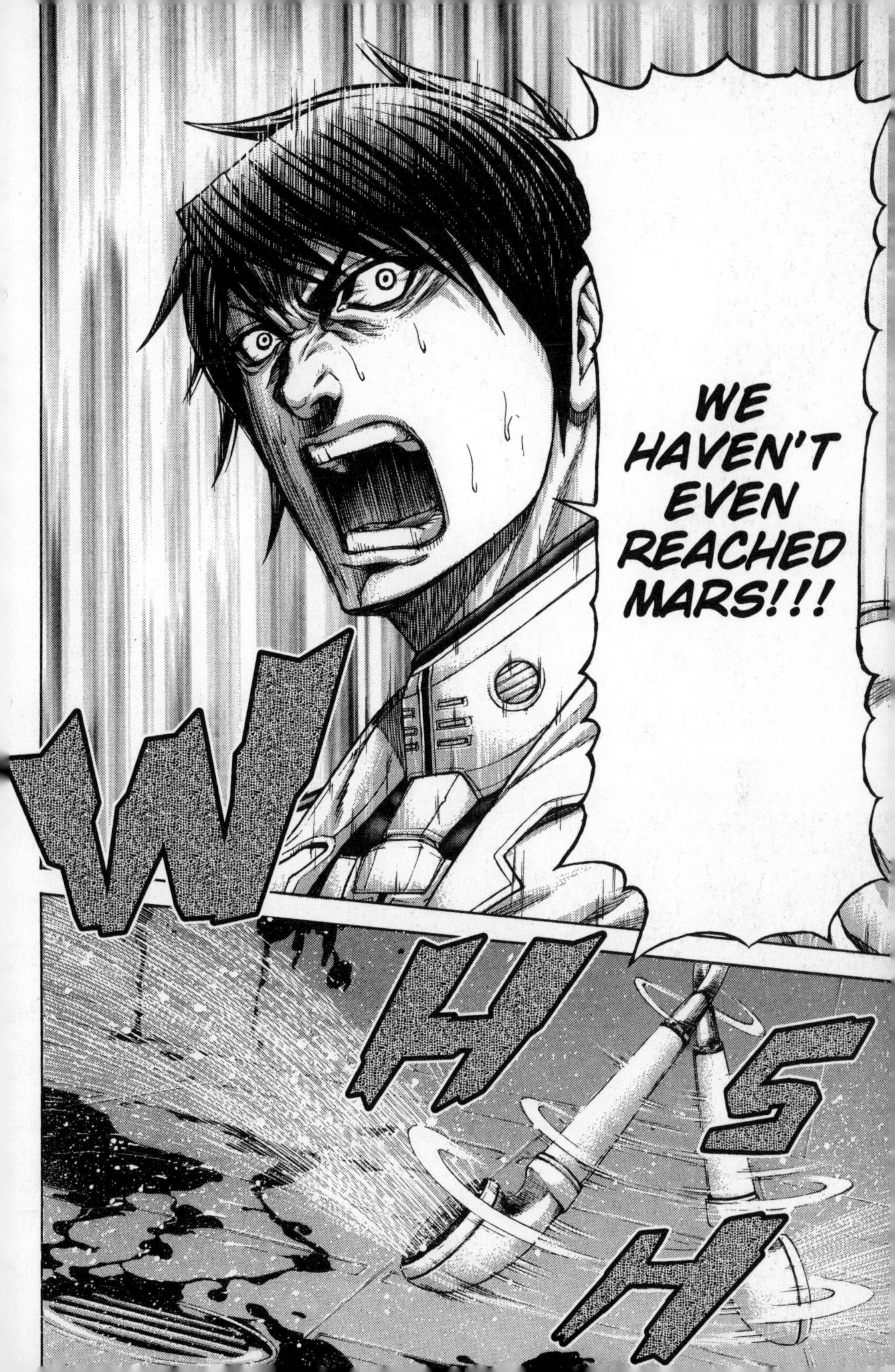
WE HAVEN'T EVEN REACHED MARS!!!
WHHSH

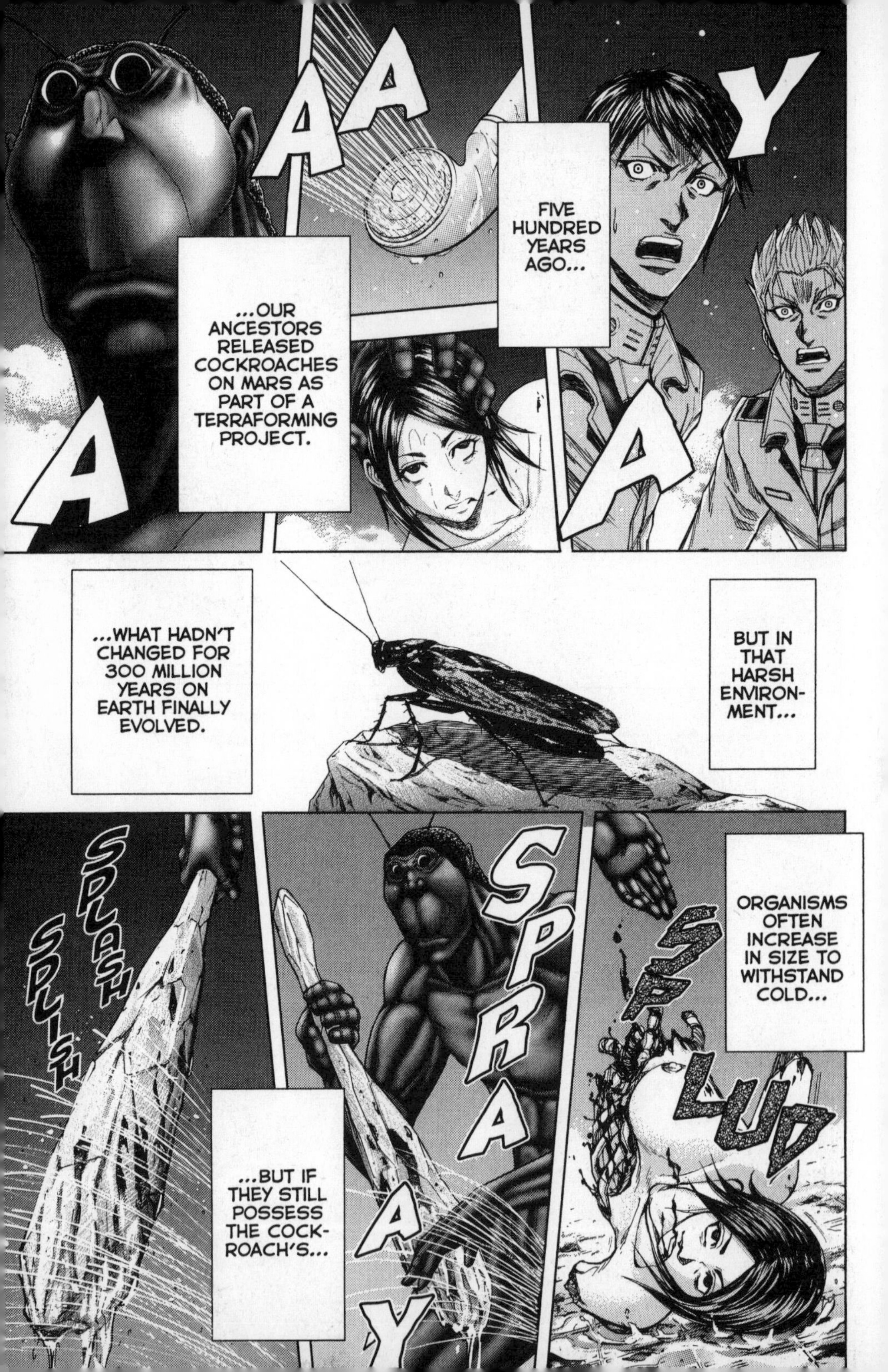
FIVE HUNDRED YEARS AGO...
...OUR ANCESTORS RELEASED COCKROACHES ON MARS AS PART OF A TERRAFORMING PROJECT.
AAAAY
BUT IN THAT HARSH ENVIRONMENT...
...WHAT HADN'T CHANGED FOR 300 MILLION YEARS ON EARTH FINALLY EVOLVED.
ORGANISMS OFTEN INCREASE IN SIZE TO WITHSTAND COLD...
SPLUD
SPRAAY
...BUT IF THEY STILL POSSESS THE COCKROACH'S...
SPLASH
SPLISH

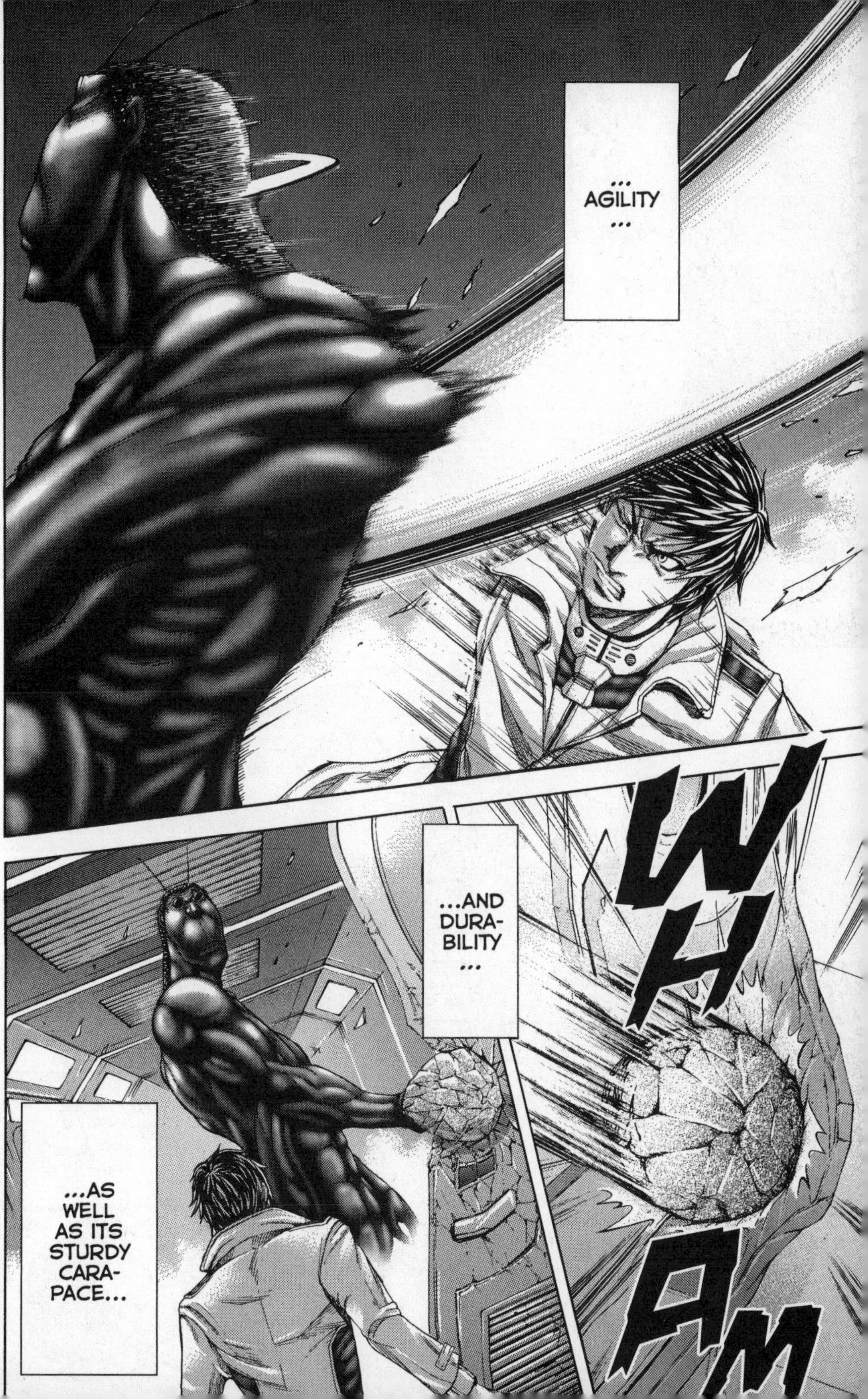
...AGILITY...
WH
AM
...AND DURA-BILITY...
...AS WELL AS ITS STURDY CARA-PACE...

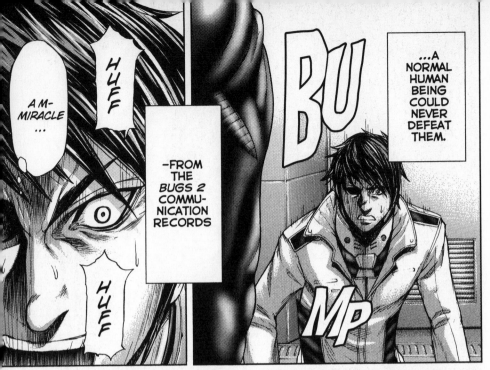

...A NORMAL HUMAN BEING COULD NEVER DEFEAT THEM.
BU
MP
-FROM THE *BUGS 2* COMMUNICATION RECORDS
HUFF
A M-MIRACLE...
HUFF
IT'S A MIRACLE HE DODGED IT!
JUST AS A COCKROACH ALWAYS EVADES THE FIRST SWAT...
THE DIFFERENCE IN COMBAT STRENGTH...
...IS INCOMPARABLE.
MARCOS...

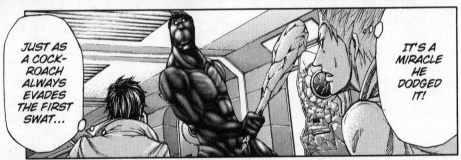

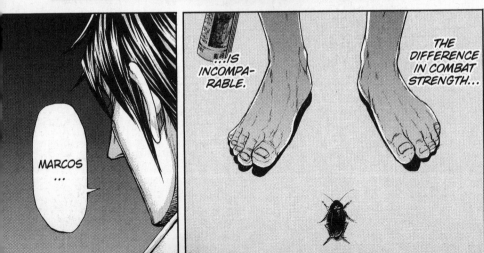

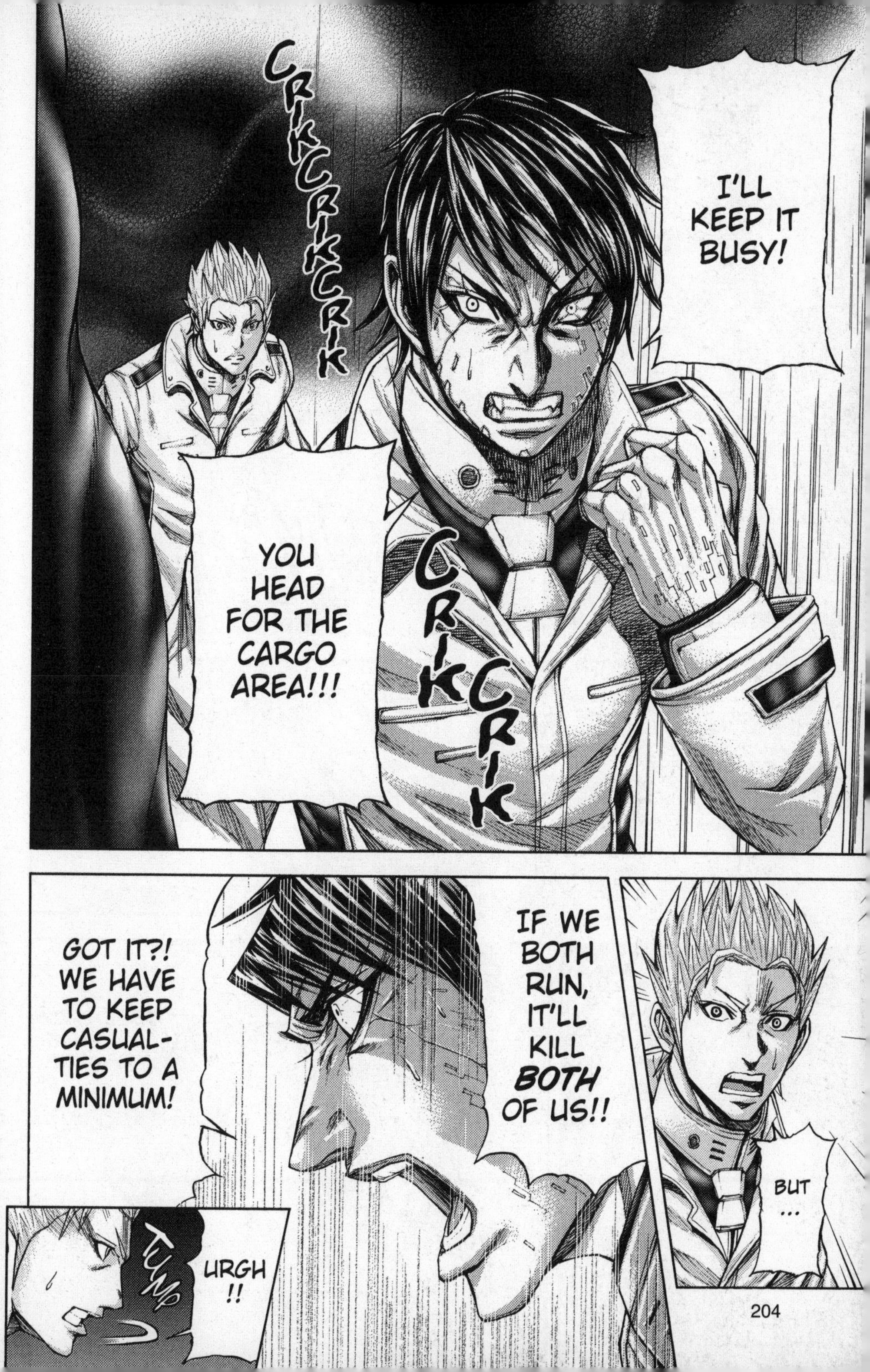
I'LL KEEP IT BUSY!
CRIKCRIKCRIK
YOU HEAD FOR THE CARGO AREA!!!
CRIK CRIK
BUT ...
IF WE BOTH RUN, IT'LL KILL *BOTH* OF US!!
GOT IT?! WE HAVE TO KEEP CASUAL-TIES TO A MINIMUM!
TUMP
URGH !!

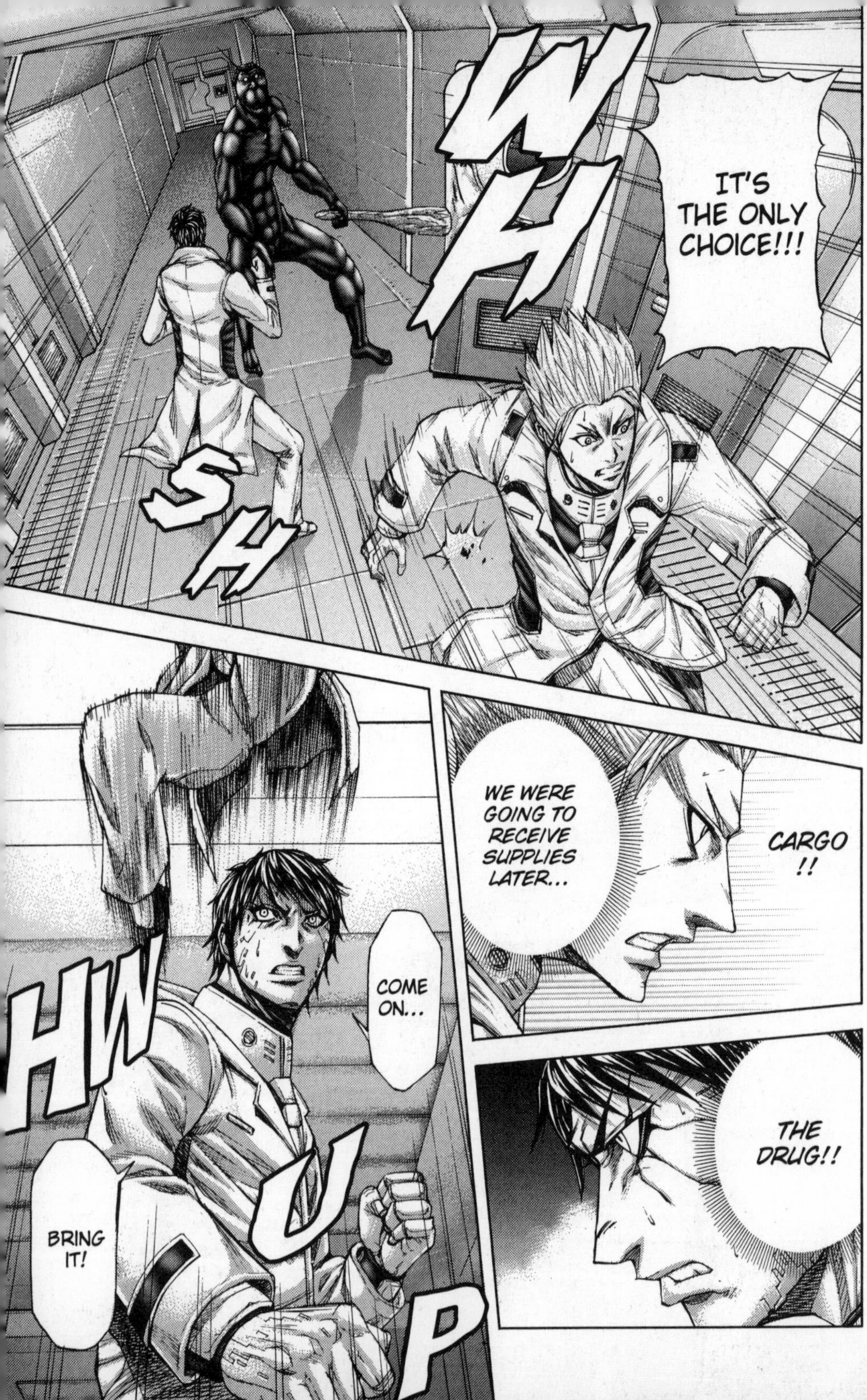
IT'S THE ONLY CHOICE!!!
WH
SH
CARGO !!
WE WERE GOING TO RECEIVE SUPPLIES LATER...
THE DRUG!!
COME ON...
BRING IT!
HWUP

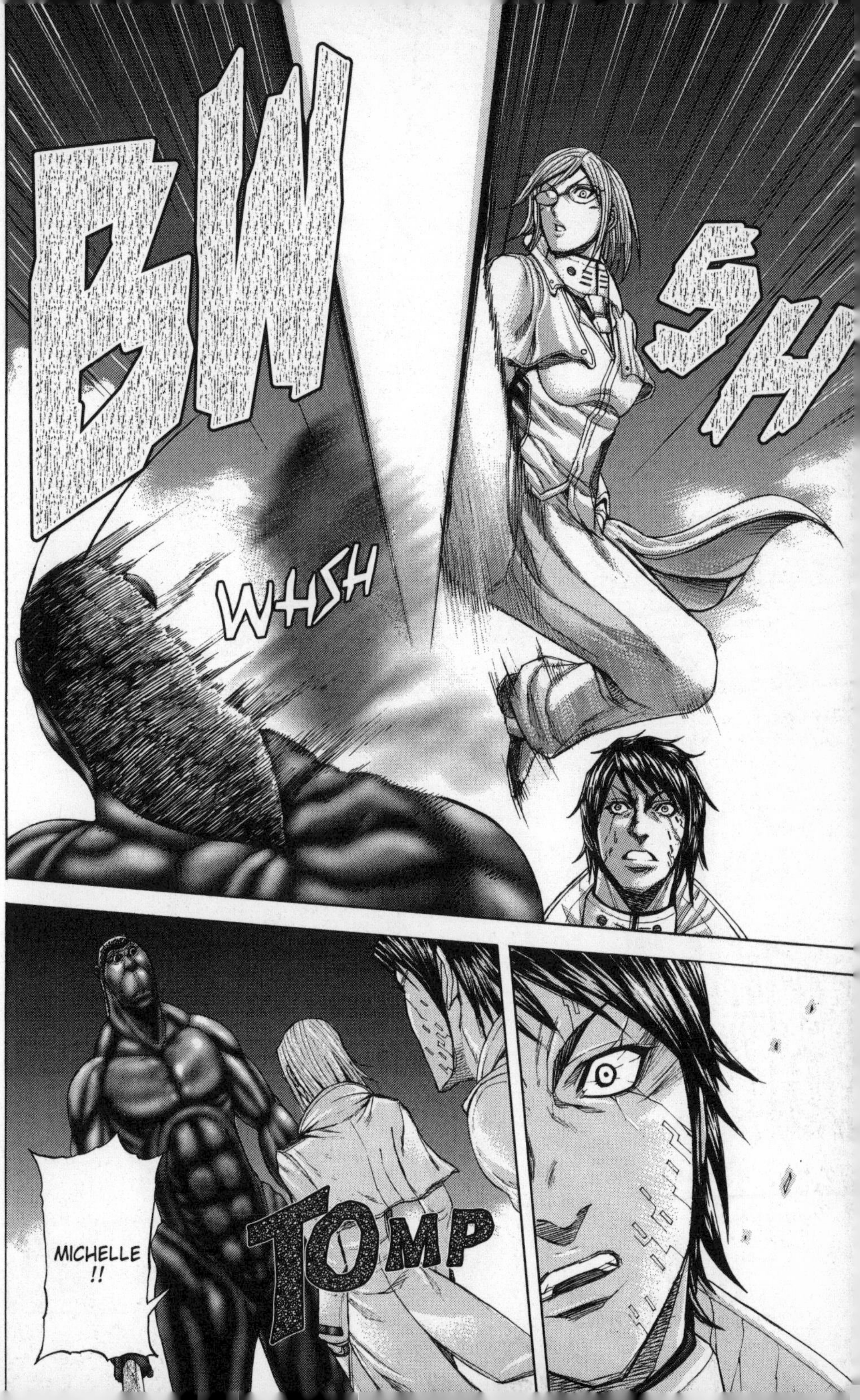
BW
SH
WHSH
TOMP
MICHELLE !!

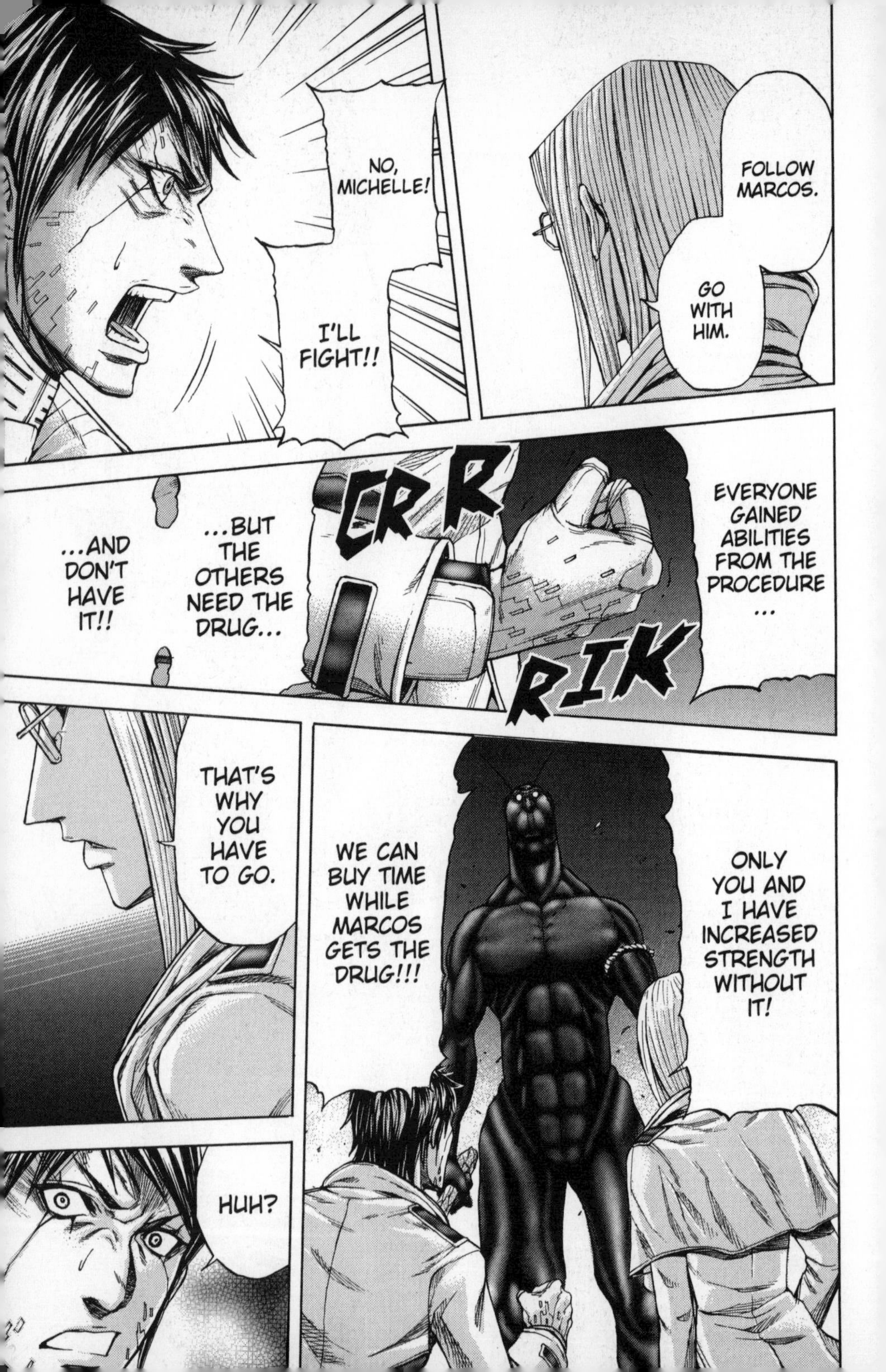
FOLLOW MARCOS.
GO WITH HIM.
NO, MICHELLE!
I'LL FIGHT!!
EVERYONE GAINED ABILITIES FROM THE PROCEDURE...
CRRRIK
...BUT THE OTHERS NEED THE DRUG...
...AND DON'T HAVE IT!!
ONLY YOU AND I HAVE INCREASED STRENGTH WITHOUT IT!
WE CAN BUY TIME WHILE MARCOS GETS THE DRUG!!!
THAT'S WHY YOU HAVE TO GO.
HUH?

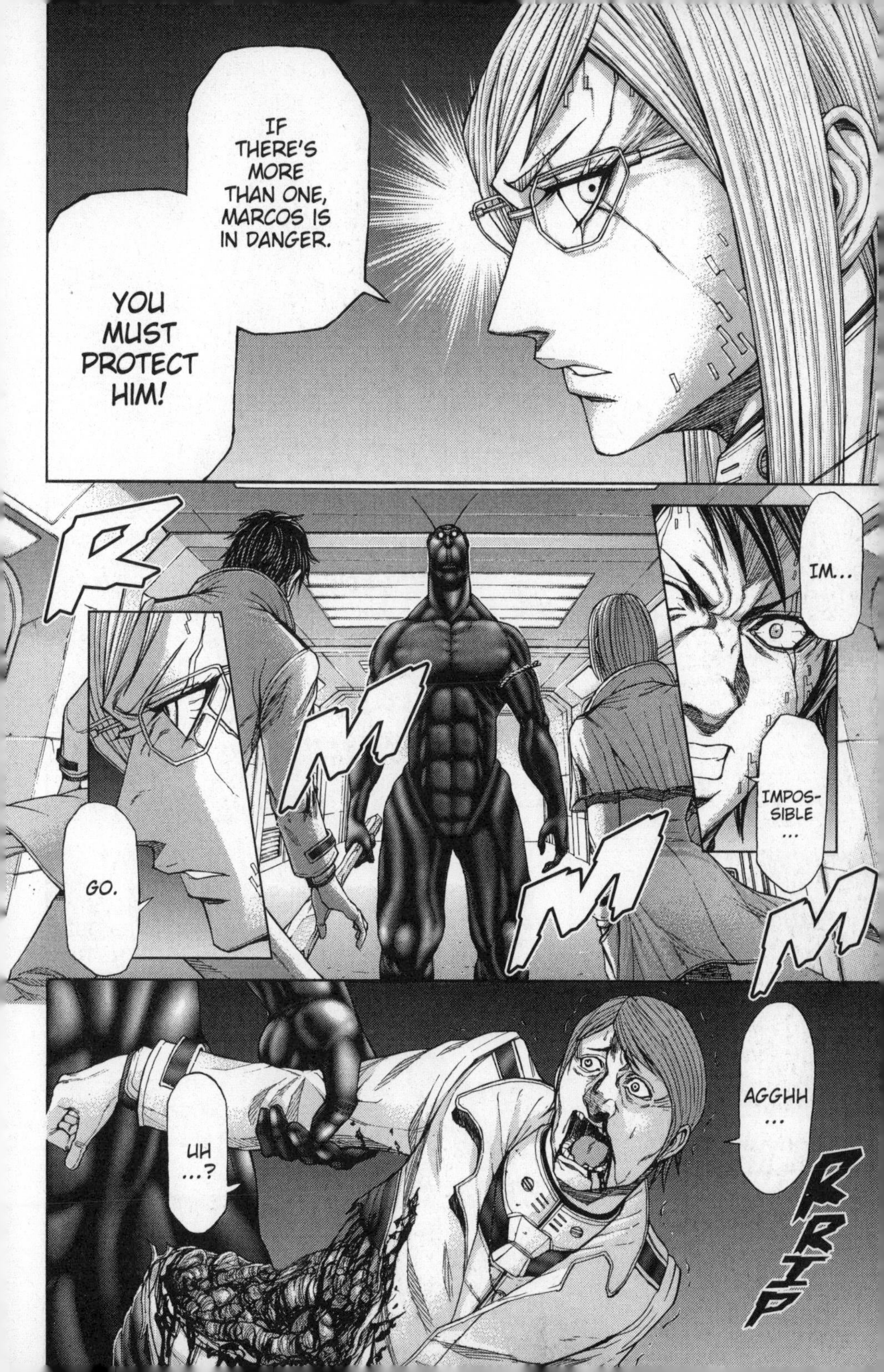
IF THERE'S MORE THAN ONE, MARCOS IS IN DANGER.
YOU MUST PROTECT HIM!
IM...
IMPOS-SIBLE ...
RMMM
GO.
AGGHH ...
UH ...?
RRIP

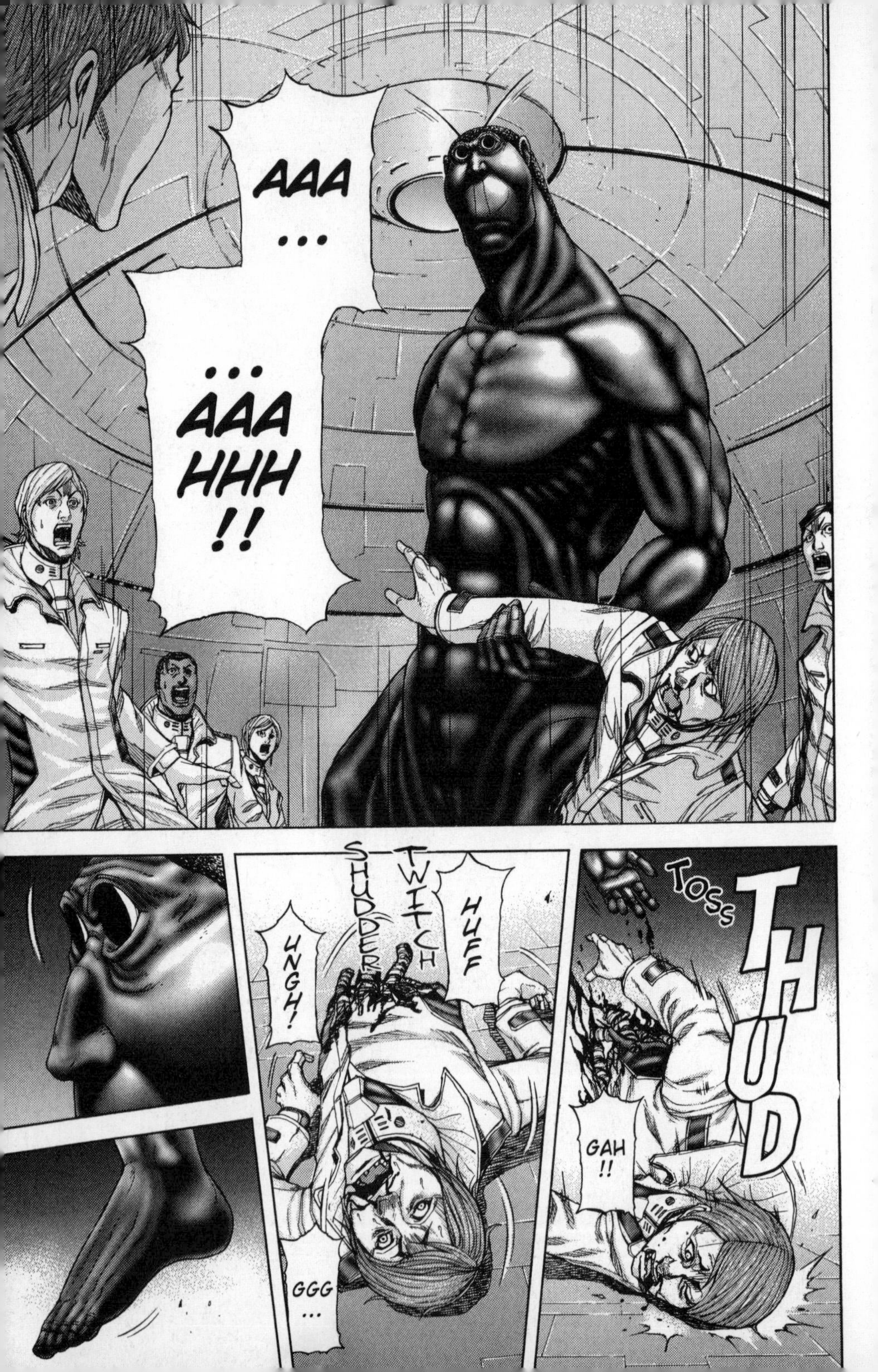
AAA ... ...AAA HHH!!
TOSS
THUD
GAH!!
HUFF
TWITCH
SHUDDER
UNGH!
GGG...

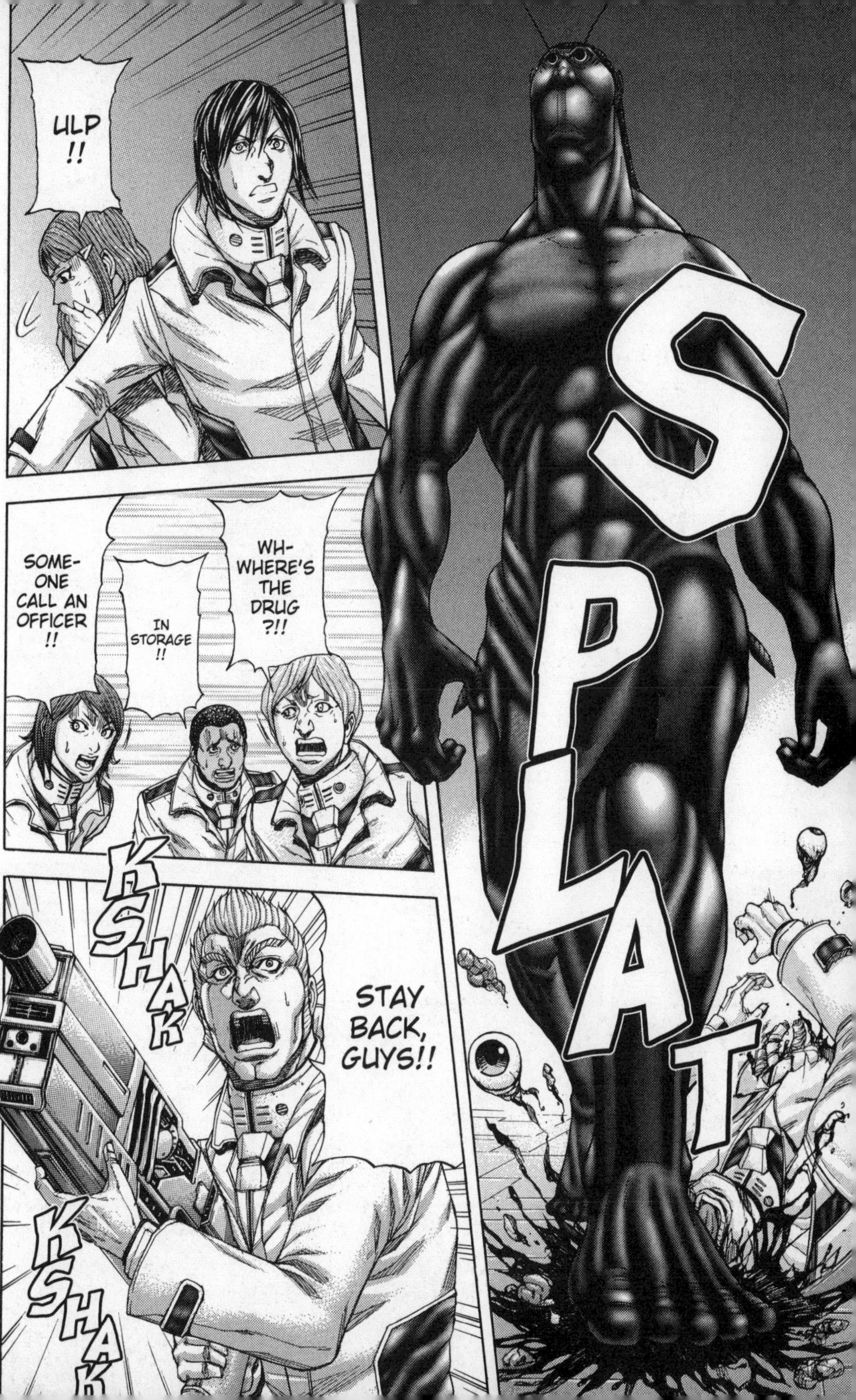
SPLAT
ULP!!
WH- WHERE'S THE DRUG?!!
IN STORAGE!!
SOME-ONE CALL AN OFFICER!!
STAY BACK, GUYS!!
KSHAK
KSHAK

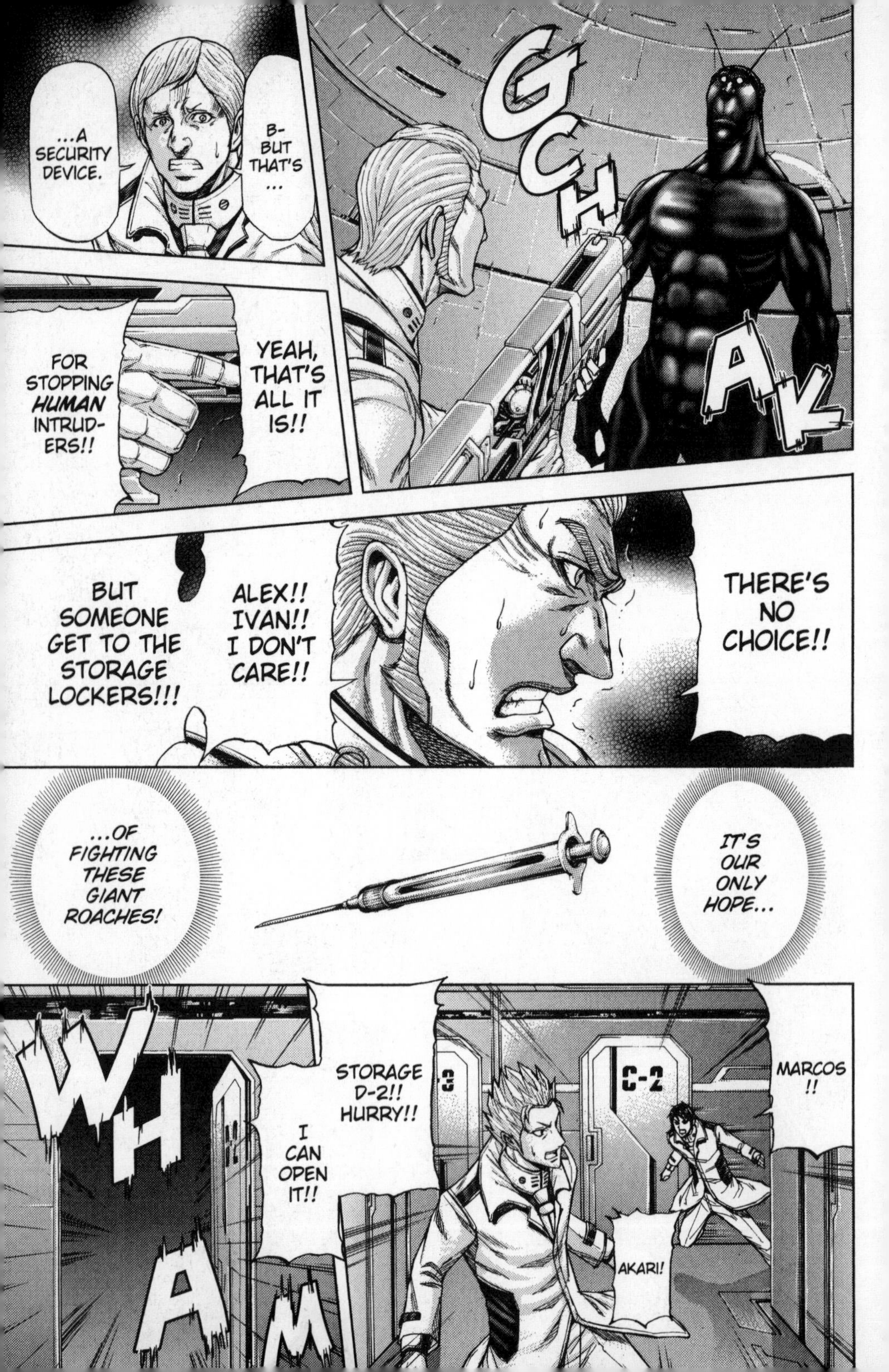
GCHAK
B-BUT THAT'S...
...A SECURITY DEVICE.
YEAH, THAT'S ALL IT IS!!
FOR STOPPING *HUMAN* INTRUDERS!!
THERE'S NO CHOICE!!
ALEX!! IVAN!! I DON'T CARE!!
BUT SOMEONE GET TO THE STORAGE LOCKERS!!!
IT'S OUR ONLY HOPE...
...OF FIGHTING THESE GIANT ROACHES!
MARCOS!!
C-2
AKARI!
STORAGE D-2!! HURRY!!
I CAN OPEN IT!!
WHAM

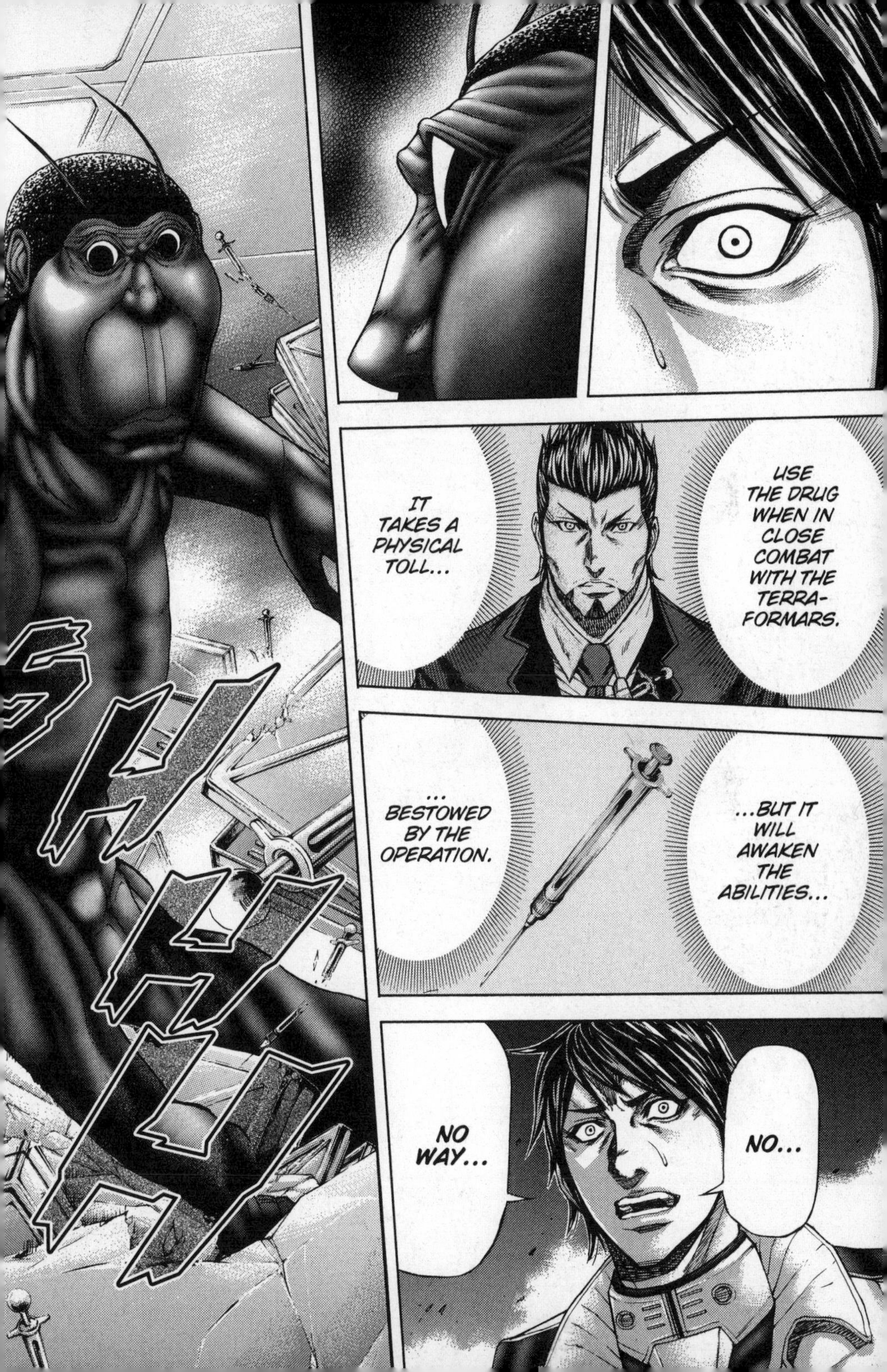
USE THE DRUG WHEN IN CLOSE COMBAT WITH THE TERRA-FORMARS.
IT TAKES A PHYSICAL TOLL...
...BUT IT WILL AWAKEN THE ABILITIES...
...BESTOWED BY THE OPERATION.
NO...
NO WAY...

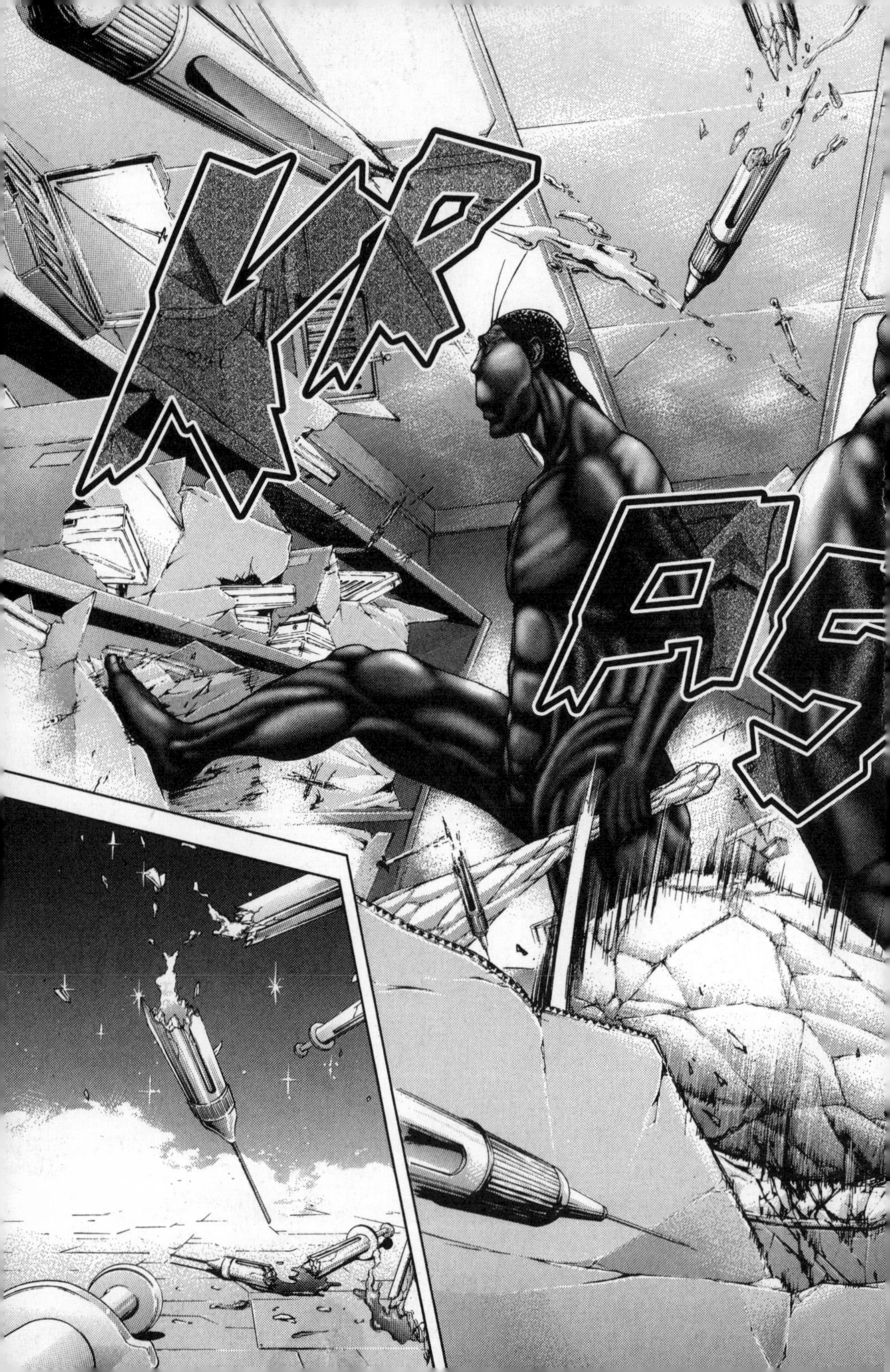

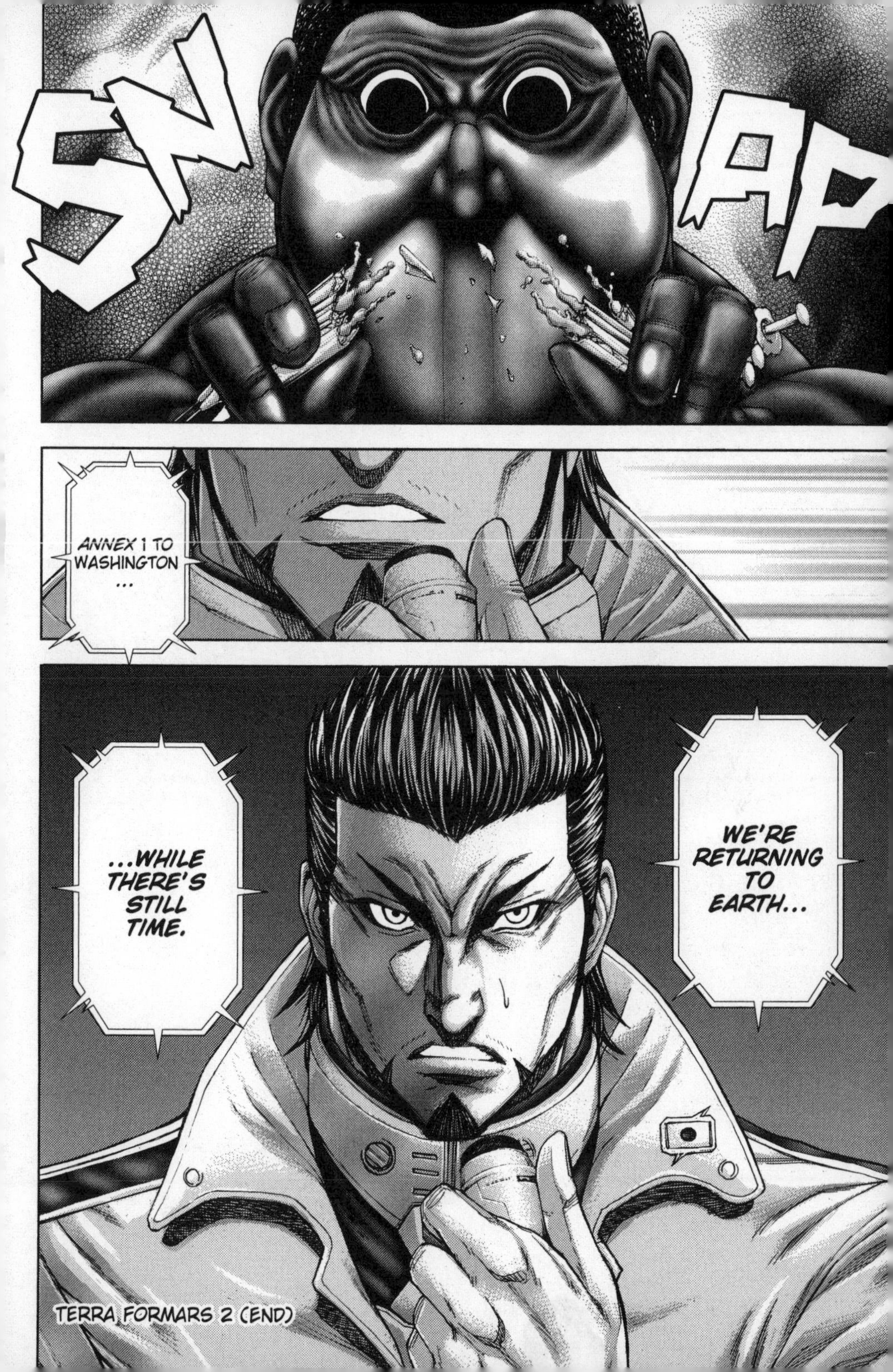
SNAP
ANNEX 1 TO WASHINGTON ...
WE'RE RETURNING TO EARTH...
...WHILE THERE'S STILL TIME.
TERRA FORMARS 2 (END)